AN EVALUATION OF THE VEDĀNTIC CRITIQUE OF BUDDHISM

AN EVALUATION OF THE VEDĀNTIC CRITIQUE OF BUDDHISM

GREGORY J. DARLING

MOTILAL BANARSIDASS PUBLISHING HOUSE · SINCE 1903

MOTILAL BANARSIDASS
PUBLISHING HOUSE • DELHI
Email: naraina@mlbd.in • Website: www.mlbd.in
@mlbdofficial
+91 89 2999 9000

*2nd Reprint: Delhi, **2024***
Reprint: Delhi, 2007
First Edition: Delhi, 1987

ISBN: 978-93-5903-153-8 (Hardcover)
ISBN: 978-93-5903-193-4 (Paperback)

Printed & Published by
Rajendra P Jain *for*
Motilal Banarsidass Publishing House
A-44, Naraina Industrial Area, Phase I,
New Delhi–110 028 (INDIA)
Email: naraina@mlbd.in Website: www.mlbd.in
Tel.: (+91-11)4751 1592
Delhi Showroom:
4637/20, F 2, Hari Sadan, First Floor, Ansari Road, Daryaganj
Delhi–110 002 (Opp. Fire Station) ***Tel.***: (+91-11)4559 7999
Bengaluru Showroom:
1st Floor, 1/2 Rathnavilas Road, Basvanagudi, Next to Pai Vista
Convention Hall, South End Circle Bengaluru - 560004 (India)

To My Mother

MRS JUSTINE DARLING

PREFACE

This book represents an attempt to compare the critique of Buddhism as set forth in the interpretations of Śaṅkara, Rāmānuja and Madhva to the *Brahma-sūtra* II.2.18-32, with the positions actually elaborated by the Buddhists in their own texts. It is also an attempt to compare the conflicting interpretations of the three commentators. In order to provide a background for the study of these *sūtras*, however, it is necessary to explore the following topics : A) The Text; B) The Three Vedāntins; C) Arguments Among the Buddhist Realists—Sarvāstivādins and Sautrāntikas; D) Vijñānavādins and the Logicians; E) The Mādhyamikas; F) The Later Logicians; G) Śaṅkara's "crypto"-Buddhism.

ACKNOWLEDGEMENT

I wish to express my gratitude to Professor Alex Wayman, Professor of Sanskrit at Columbia University, for his kind, patient, and generous assistance to me in the preparation of this work. He has been a constant source of insight to me during the course of this study of the Vedāntic critique of Buddhism. I also wish to thank Professor James A. Martin, Professor of Religion at Columbia University, for being a constant source of inspiration and encouragement to me during my years at Columbia University, and the Metropolitan Museum of Art who have very kindly permitted me to use the photograph of a seated stone statue of Brahmā, South India, 10th-11th century, on the jacket.

CONTENTS

Preface vii

Acknowledgements ix

Part I : INTRODUCTORY BACKGROUND

A. THE TEXT 3

B. THE THREE VEDĀNTINS 9

C. THE BUDDHIST REALISTS 15
1. Causation 19
   (a) Dependent Origination and the Aggregates 19
   (b) Causeless Destruction (*ākasmika vināśa*) 26
2. Momentariness 28
3. The Unconstructed (*asaṃskṛta*) *Dharmas* 36
   (a) The Cessations (*nirodha*) 36
   (b) Space (*ākāśa*) 44

D. VIJÑĀNAVĀDA AND THE LOGICIANS 47
1. Knowledge (*jñāna*) and the Knowable (*jñeya*) 49
2. The "Self" of the Vijñānavādins 50
3. The Dream and Waking States 51
4. Habit-Energies (*vāsanā*) 53
5. The Ideation-Store (*ālaya-vijñāna*) 56
6. Separation of Authorities (*pramāṇa-vyavasthā*) 58
7. Memory (*smṛti*) 59
8. The Three Factors 60
9. Causality of the *Saṃskāras* 61
10. Introspective Perception (*svasaṃvedana-pratyakṣa*) 63

E. THE MĀDHYAMIKAS 67

F. THE LATER LOGICIANS 73
   (a) The Atom (*aṇu*) 75
   (b) Ratnakīrti on Momentariness 78

(c) Causation 82

(d) Destruction (*vināśa*) and Disruption (*pradhvaṃsa*) 85

(e) Remembrance (*smṛti*) and Recognition (*pratyabhijñā*) 90

G. ŚAṄKARA'S "CRYPTO"-BUDDHISM 95

1. The "crypto"-Buddhism of Gauḍapāda 99
2. Śaṅkara's Association with the Gauḍapāda School 105
   (a) Śaṅkara's Relationship with the Gauḍapāda School 105
   (b) The Authorship of the *Gauḍapāda-kārikā-bhāṣya* 109
3. The Characterization of Śaṅkara as "crypto"-Buddhist 118
4. The Two Truths 123
   (a) The Two Truths in Relation to Gauḍapāda 123
   (b) The Two Truths in Relation to Śaṅkara 125
5. Nescience (*Avidyā*) 132
6. Name-and-formation (*nāma-rūpa*) in Śaṅkara's Thought 145

Part II : A STUDY OF THREE COMMENTARIES TO *BRAHMA-SŪTRA* II.2.18-32

A. *Introduction* 159

B. *Brahma-sūtra* II.2.18 : "*samudāya ubhayahetuke 'pi tadaprāptiḥ*" 165

1. Śaṅkara's Interpretation 167
2. Rāmānuja's Interpretation 172
3. Madhva's Interpretation 176

C. *Brahma-sūtra* II.2.19 : "*itaretara-pratyayatvād iti cen notpattimātra-nimittatvāt*" 181

1. Śaṅkara's Interpretation 183

2. Rāmānuja's Interpretation 187
3. Madhva's Interpretation 190

D. *Brahma-sūtra* II.2.20 :
"*uttarotpāde ca pūrvanirodhāt*" 197
1. Śaṅkara's Interpretation 199
2. Rāmānuja's Interpretation 204
3. Madhva's Interpretation 206

E. *Brahma-sūtra* II.2.21 :
"*asati pratijñoparodho yaugapadyam anyathā*" 211
1. Śaṅkara's Interpretation 213
2. Rāmānuja's Interpretation 214
3. Madhva's Interpretation 215

F. *Brahma-sūtra* II.2.22 :
"*pratisaṃkhyā 'pratisaṃkhyā-nirodhāprāptir avicchedāt*" 219
1. Śaṅkara's Interpretation 221
2. Rāmānuja's Interpretation 223
3. Madhva's Interpretation 226

G. *Brahma-sūtra* II.2.23 :
"*ubhayathā ca doṣāt*" 233
1. Śaṅkara's Interpretation 235
2. Rāmānuja's Interpretation 236
3. Madhva's Interpretation 238

H. *Brahma-sūtra* II.2.24 :
"*ākāśe cāviśeṣāt*" 243
1. Śaṅkara's Interpretation 245
2. Rāmānuja's Interpretation 248
3. Madhva's Interpretation 250

I. *Brahma-sūtra* II.2.25:
"*anusmṛteśca*" 257
1. Śaṅkara's Interpretation 259
2. Rāmānuja's Interpretation 264
3. Madhva's Interpretation 271

J. *Brahma-sūtra* II.2.26 :
"*nāsato 'dṛṣṭatvāt*" 279
1. Śaṅkara's Interpretation 281
2. Rāmānuja's Interpretation 284
3. Madhva's Interpretation 288

K. *Brahma-sūtra* II.2.27 :
"*udāsīnānām api caivaṃ siddhiḥ*" 293
1. Śaṅkara's Interpretation 295
2. Rāmānuja's Interpretation 295
3. Madhva's Interpretation 297

L. *Brahma-sūtra* II.2.28 :
"*nābhāva upalabdheḥ*" 303
1. Śaṅkara's Interpretation 305
2. Rāmānuja's Interpretation 320
3. Madhva's Interpretation 323

M. *Brahma-sūtra* II.2.29 :
"*vaidharmyāc ca na svapnādivat*" 329
1. Śaṅkara's Interpretation 331
2. Rāmānuja's Interpretation 333
3. Madhva's Interpretation 335

N. *Brahma-sūtra* II.2.30 :
"*na bhāvo 'nupalabdheḥ*" 339
1. Śaṅkara's Interpretation 341
2. Rāmānuja's Interpretation 343
3. Madhva's Interpretation 345

O. *Brahma-sūtra* II.2.31 :
"*kṣaṇikatvāc ca*" 353
1. Śaṅkara's Interpretation 355
2. Madhva's Interpretation 359

P. *Brahma-sūtra* II.2.32 : "*sarvathānupapatteśca*" 361
1. Śaṅkara's Interpretation 363
2. Rāmānuja's Interpretation 364
3. Madhva's Interpretation 368

Conclusion 369

Bibliography 383

Index 389

PART I

INTRODUCTORY BACKGROUND

A. THE TEXT

The central text of this study is the *Brahma-sūtra*, a collection of *sūtras* in four sections, or *adhyāyas*, which comprise a *mīmāṃsā*, or investigation, into the nature of the Brahman as revealed in the Vedic texts. The Mīmāṃsā texts are of two sorts: the Pūrva-mīmāṃsā (investigation of the earlier) by Jaimini which is concerned with Vedic ritual, and the Uttara-mīmāṃsā (investigation of the later) which is also termed *Brahma-mīmāṃsā* or *Śārīraka-mīmāṃsā* (investigation of the embodied one) and which is concerned with the nature of the Brahman. the *Brahma-sūtra* as Uttara-mīmāṃsā is an attempt to systematize the teachings of the Upaniṣads. The *Brahma-sūtra* is also called the *Vedānta-sūtra* or *Śārīraka-sūtra*. The term "Vedānta" signifies that the text is concerned with the embodied one (*śārīraka*) or individual and his essential nature as Brahman. According to Govindānanda in the *Ratnaprabhā*, a commentary on this text, as Radhakrishnan points out, the text is called *Śārīraka* in that it is concerned with the Brahman-hood of the individual soul (*śārīrako jīvas tasya brahmatvavicāro mīmāṃsā*).[1] According to Thibaut, the Mīmāṃsā scriptures were composed in order to summarize, systematize, and haromnize the various teachings of the Vedas.

> The task of taking a comprehensive view of the contents of the Vedic writings as a whole, of systematising what they present in an unsystematised form, of showing the mutual co-ordination or subordination of single passages and sections, and of reconciling contradictions—which, according to the view of the orthodox commentators, can be apparent only—is allotted to a separate *śāstra* or body of doctrine which is termed Mīmāṃsā, i.e. the investigation or inquiry *kat'exochen*, viz. the enquiry into the connected meaning of the sacred texts.[2]

---

1. Radhakrishnan, Sarvepalli, *The Brahma Sūtra*, translation and introduction, (London : George Allen & Unwin, Ltd., 1960), p. 22.
2. Thibaut, George, *The Vedānta-sūtras*, Part I, Volume XXXIV of

According to Thibaut, the Pūrva-mīmāṃsā is concerned with *karma-kāṇḍa*, or the section of the Vedas relating to sacrificial action, and the Uttara-mīmāṃsā is concerned with *jñāna-kāṇḍa*, or the section of the Vedas (including the Āraṇyakas and the Upaniṣads) relating to knowledge.[3] The reputed author of the *Pūrva-mīmāṃsā-sūtra* is Jaimini; the reputed author of the *Brahma-sūtra* is Bādarāyaṇa. It is assumed, as Radhakrishnan explains, that since the Uttara-mīmāṃsā is concerned with the later portions of the Vedic texts (i.e. the Upaniṣads and Āraṇyakas), they were composed at a later period.[4] But there are cross-references to Jaimini and Bādarāyaṇa in both the *Pūrva-mīmāṃsā-sūtra* and the *Brahma-sūtra*, as Radhakrishnan himself notes.[5] There are references to Jaimini in three places in the *Brahma-sūtra* : I.2.28, 31, and I.3.31. It is difficult to say for certain whether the *Pūrva-mīmāṃsā-sūtra* and the *Kalpa-sūtras* were composed previous to the *Brahma-sūtras* of the Uttara-mīmāṃsā class. According to Radhakrishnan, the *Brahma-sūtra* was composed about the second century B. C. by an author named Bādarāyaṇa.[6] There had been other teachers who had tried to interpret the teachings of the Upaniṣads, such as Auḍulomi, Kāśakṛtsna, Jaimini. Bādarāyaṇa, according to Radhakrishnan, cites the earlier teachers and takes into account their efforts of interpretation.[7] That Jaimini is cited, however, indicates that it may not be possible to draw a clear and distinct division between the Pūrva-mīmāṃsā and the Uttara-mīmāṃsā, in that a teacher supposedly concerned exclusively with ritual is mentioned in a text supposedly concerned exclusively with knowledge (*jñāna*). Mayeda holds that although the *Brahma-sūtra* is attributed to Bādarāyaṇa, it cannot be considered a work composed by a single author, that it represents about 700 years of thought, and that it did not take final form until around 400-450

Sacred Books of the East, translation of Bādarāyaṇa's *Vedānta-sūtra* with Śaṅkara's commentary, (New York : Dover Publications, Inc., 1962, reprint), p. ix.

3. Ibid., p. x.
4. Radhakrishnan, Sarvepalli, *The Brahma Sūtra*, p. 22.
5. Ibid., p. 22.
6. Ibid., p. 22.
7. Ibid., p. 22.

A.D.[8] According to Ingalls, the *Brahma-sūtra* could not have been composed later than the time of Christ.[9] Ingalls rejects the argument which he attributes to Jacobi that the *Brahma-sūtra* must have been composed five centuries later than the time of Christ because of *Brahma-sūtra* II.2.28-32—*sūtras* which seem to be directed against later Buddhist schools.[10] Mayeda notes that Śaṅkara does not clearly say that the author of the *Brahma-sūtra* is Bādarāyaṇa, but he does mention Bādarāyaṇa when he introduces the last *sūtra*.

—ityata uttaraṃ bhagavānbādarāyaṇa ācāryaḥ paṭhati[11]

hence Bhagavān Bādarāyaṇa Ācārya interprets the last (*sūtra*)

From this evidence, Mayeda concludes that Śaṅkara regarded Bādarāyaṇa to be the author of the *Brahma-sūtra*.[12] Mayeda remarks that the identification of Veda-vyāsa with Bādarāyaṇa begins with Vācaspati-miśra (*maṅgalācaraṇa* of his *Bhāmatī*).[13]

The *sūtras* of the *Brahma-sūtra* are arranged into four sections or *adhyāyas*, each of which is divided into *pādas* or chapters. These chapters are further sub-divided into *adhikaraṇas* or groups. The number of *sūtras* in each *adhikaraṇa* or group depends on the arrangement by topic of the different commentators. The commentary presents first the *prima facie* view (*pūrva-pakṣa*), and secondly, the reply (*siddhānta*). According to the Pūrva-mīmāṃsā, as Radhakrishnan explains, every group or *adhikaraṇa* has five factors : 1) *viṣaya* (subject-matter); 2) *viśaya* (doubt or uncertainty); 3) *pūrva-pakṣa* (*prima facie* view); 4) *siddhānta* (reply or established conclusion); 5) *saṃgati*

---

8. Mayeda, Sengaku, *A Thousand Teachings*, translation with Introduction and Notes of the *Upadeśasāhasrī* of Śaṅkara, (Tokyo : University of Tokyo Press, 1979), p. 12.

9. Ingalls, Daniel H.H., "Śaṁkara's Arguments Against the Buddhists," *Philosophy East and West*, Volume III, Number 4, (January 1954), p. 299.

10. Ibid., p. 299.

11. Balasubrahmanyam, T.K., *The Works of Śrī Śaṅkarāchārya*, Volume III, *Brahmasūtra Bhāshya*, (Śrīrangam, India : Sri Vani Vilas Press). commentary to *Brahma-sūtra* IV.4.21, p. 861.

12. Mayeda, Sengaku, *Thousand Teachings*, p. 14.

13. Ibid., p. 14.

(connection between different groups). If the group (*adhikaraṇa*) contains more than one *sūtra*, the first *sutra* is regarded as primary (*mukhya*) and the others as secondary (*guṇa*).[14] The first section (*adhyāya*) is concerned with *samanvaya* (harmony), and attempts to harmonize seemingly conflicting scriptural passages. The second section is concerned with *avirodha* (refutation), and attempts to refute opposing schools such as the Buddhist ones. The third section is concerned with *sādhana* (means), and attempts to describe the fruits of knowledge in terms of *mokṣa* (release) or heavenly rewards. The readings of the various *sūtras* may vary from commentator to commentator. Sometimes one *sūtra* is read as two or two as one. Sometimes the last word of a *sūtra* is treated as the beginning of the next *sūtra*. Sometimes *sūtras* that are regarded as representative of the *prima facie* view (*pūrvapakṣa*) by one commentator are regarded by another as the established conclusion (*siddhānta*). Thus Śaṅkara in his commentary to *Brahma-sūtra* IV.3.14, which is concerned with the soul's going to the Brahman-with-attributes (*saguṇa-Brahman*) remarks that for some, this represents the established conclusion, but for him they represent the *prima facie* view.

> kecitpunaḥ pūrvāṇi pūrvapakṣasūtrāṇi bhavanti uttarāṇi siddhāntasūtrāṇi—ityetāṃ vyavasthāmanurudhyamānāḥ paraviṣayā eva gatiśrutīḥ pratiṣṭhāpayanti; tad anupapannaṃ, gantavyatvānupapatter— brahmaṇaḥ.[15]

Others again, adhering to the principle that the former are *sūtras* relating to the *prima facie* view, and that the later ones are *sūtras* related to the *siddhānta* view, maintain that the scriptural texts pertaining to going are of the higher domain (Brahman). This is not adequate because of objection to the requirement of going in connection with the Brahman.

---

14. Radhakrishnan, Sarvepalli, *The Brahma Sūtra*, p. 24.
15. Balasubrahmanyam, T.K., *The Works of Śrī Śaṅkarāchārya*, Volume III, commentary to *Brahma-sūtra* IV.3.14, p. 833.

B. THE THREE VEDĀNTINS

In this study, the commentaries of three Vedāntic figures—Śaṅkara (788-820 A.D.), Rāmānuja (1017-1127 A.D.), and Madhva (1197-1276 A.D.)[1]—to those aphorisms of the *Brahma-sūtra* concerned with the refutation of Buddhism will be compared. Although this study will concentrate on these particular aphorisms, a brief review will be undertaken at this point of the systems advocated by these figures : Śaṅkara's unqualified non-dualism (*nirviśeṣādvaita*), Rāmānuja's qualified non-dualism (*viśiṣṭādvaita*), and Madhva's dualism (*dvaita*).

Śaṅkara's system is that of unqualified non-dualism (*nirviśeṣā-dvaita*). In the background of Śaṅkara's system lies the Upaniṣadic refrain, "*tat tvam asi*" (That thou art), uttered nine times by the Upaniṣadic sage Uddālaka Āruṇi to his son, Śvetaketu as set forth in the *Chāndogya Upaniṣad* (VI.8-16). There also is the Upaniṣadic refrain, "*ahaṃ brahmāsmi*" (I am Brahman), set forth in the *Bṛhadāraṇyaka Upaniṣad* (I.4.10). For Śaṅkara, both these "great sentences" (*mahāvākya*) indicated the identity of the Self (Ātman) and Brahman. Referring to the *mahāvākya* "*tat tvam asi,*" Śaṅkara claims that the oneness of the Ātman and the Brahman is taught.

jñānaikārthaparatvāttaṃ vākyamekaṃ tato viduḥ/
ekatvaṃ hyātmano jñeyaṃ vākyārthapratipattitaḥ/[2]

Hence, as a consequence of the one meaning, the knowledge (*jñāna*), there is this one sentence, according to the wise :

The oneness of the Self is to be known, from the apprehension (*pratipatti*) of the meaning.

According to Śaṅkara in the *Upadeśasāhasrī*, the attainment of the Self (*ātmalābha*) is the highest aim. Furthermore, it is an

1. Das Gupta, Surendranath, *History of Indian Philosophy*, (Cambridge, England : University Press, 1963, reprint). (All dates, unless otherwise mentioned, are taken from Dasgupta's *History of Indian Philosophy*.)

2. Balasubrahmanyam, T.K., *The Works of Śrī Śaṅkarāchārya*, Volume 14, *Upadeśasāhasrī*, (Srirangam, India : Sri Vani Vilas Press), *Upadeśasāhasrī* I.17.9, p. 201.

attainment which is already attained in itself and cannot be attained from another (*anyataḥ*). Śaṅkara seems to be saying that there is nothing to attain but the Self which is in a sense already attained, and that there is no other from whom the attainment of the Self can be given. The notion that the attainment is dependent upon another (*anyāpekṣa*) is an appearance (*samudbhava*) by reason of the view (*dṛṣṭi*) of another. Such a view is nescience (*avidyā*); the elimination of such a view is liberation.

ātmārtho 'pi yo lābhaḥ sukhāyeṣṭo viparyayaḥ/
ātmalābhaḥ paraḥ prokto nityatvādbrahmavedibhiḥ//5/
svayaṃ labdhasvabhāvatvāllābhastasya na cānyataḥ
anyāpekṣastu yo lābhaḥ so 'nyaddṛṣṭisamudbhavaḥ//6//
anyaddṛṣṭistvavidyā syāttannāśo mokṣa ucyate/
jñānenaiva tu so 'pi syādvirodhatvānna karmaṇā//7//[3]

(5) For that attainment (*lābha*) which is desired (*iṣṭa*) for the sake of happiness, even for the sake of the Self (*ātmārtha*) is contrary (*viparyaya*). The attainment of the Self is declared by the knowers of the Brahman (*brahmavedin*) to be the supreme because it is eternal.

(6) Because it is nature (*svabhāvatva*) attained by its Self, there is no attainment of it by another. That attainment which is dependent upon another is an appearance by reason of the view of another.

(7) It is said that nescience is the view of another, that its destruction (*nāśa*) is liberation (*mokṣa*). That is so by means of knowledge, because it (knowledge) is the opposite; there is no liberation by means of action (*karman*).

The unqualifiedness, therefore, consists in that there is no other apart from the Self (Ātman) to be attained or by which one is to attain.

Rāmānuja's approach is that of qualified non-dualism (*Viśiṣṭādvaita*). According to Rāmānuja, the relationship of the conscious (*cetana*) and unconscious (*acetana*) to the Lord or highest person (*paramapuruṣa*) is as body (*śarīra*) and soul (Ātman), as is stated in Rāmānuja's interpretation of *Brahma-sūtra* II.1.3.

3. Ibid., Volume 14, *Upadeśasāhasrī* I.17.5-7, p. 200.

> ataḥ sarvaṃ paramapuruṣeṇa sarvātmanā svārthe niyāmyaṃ dhāryam taccheṣataikasvarūpamiti sarvaṃ cetanācetanaṃ tasya śarīram/[4]
>
> Hence in reference to the fact that in their own sense they all have the one nature (*ekasvarūpa*) of secondariness (*śeṣatā*) to that to be supported (*dhārya*) and controlled (*niyāmya*) according to its own significance by the Self of all (*sarvātman*), by the highest person, the conscious and the unconscious are its body.

Rāmānuja in this respect approves of the view of Kāśakṛtsna, for whom identity (*tādātmya*) is established through the relationship of soul and body.

> evamātmaśarīrabhāvena tādātmyopapādane parasya brahmaṇo 'pahatapāpmatvasarvajñatvādigocarāḥ, jīvasyāviduṣaśśocato brahmopāsanānmokṣavādinyaḥ, jagatsṛṣṭipralayābhidhāyinyaḥ, jagato brahmatādātmyopadeśaparāśca sarvāḥ śrutayaḥ samyagupapāditā bhavantīti kāśakṛtsnīyameva mataṃ sūtrakāraḥ svīkṛtavān/[5]
>
> The author of the *sūtra* (*sūtrakāra*) has accepted the opinion of Kāśakṛtsna—that in the case of establishing the identity through the relationship of soul and body, all the Śrutis, which have as their scope (*gocara*) the omniscience (*sarvajñatva*) and freedom from sin (*apahatapāpmatva*) of the highest Brahman, which proclaim liberation by means of the contemplation (*upāsana*) on Brahman for the unwise (*aviduṣaḥ*) and grieving individual soul (*Jīva*), which designate the creation (*sṛṣṭi*), and destruction (*pralaya*) of the world (*jagat*), which have as their object (*para*) the teaching of the identity of the Brahman with the world, are correctly presented.

Madhva's approach is that of dualism (*Dvaita*). In the *Mahābhārata-tātparya-nirṇaya*, Madhva teaches dualism (*Dvaita*) with a five-fold difference (*pañca-bheda*).

---

4. Viraraghavacharya, Sri Uttamur T., *Brahmasūtra-Śrībhāshya*, Volumes I and II, (Madras, India : Sreevathsa Press, 1963), commentary to *Brahma-sūtra* II.1.3, p. 459.

5. Ibid., commentary to *Brahma-sūtra* I.4.22, p. 424.

jagat-pravāhaḥ satyo 'yam pañca-bhedasamanvitaḥ
jīveśayor bhidā caiva jīva-bhedaḥ parasparaṃ
jaḍeśayor jaḍānāṃ ca jaḍa-jīva-bhedā tathā
pañca-bhedā ime nityāḥ sarvāvasthāsu nityaśaḥ
muktānām ca na hīyante tāratamyaṃ ca sarvadā.[6]

The world-flux (*jagat-pravāha*) is real, and is accompanied by a five-fold difference (*pañca-bheda*);

the distinction of individual soul (*Jīva*) and Lord and the difference of individual souls among themselves

the difference of matter (*jaḍa*) and Lord, (the differences in) matter (*jaḍa*),

the difference of matter and individual souls. Thereupon, this five-fold difference, eternally constant in every situation is not left behind even by the liberated ones (*mukta*). There is the difference (*tāratamya*) always.

6. Radhakrishnan, Sarvepalli, *The Brahma Sūtra*, (*Mahābhārata-tātparyanirṇaya* I.69-71), p. 64, footnoate 3.

C. THE BUDDHIST REALISTS : THE SARVĀSTIVĀDINS AND SAUTRĀNTIKAS

In their attempted refutation of the Buddhists, the Vedāntins often failed to distinguish between two schools of Buddhists, the Sarvāstivādins and the Sautrāntikas. In this section, an attempt will be made to discern the respective positions of the two schools in connection with the following topics : 1) Causation; 2) Momentariness; 3) The Unconstructed (*asaṃskṛta*) *dharmas*. In opposition to the Vibhajjavādins (advocates of distinction) the Sarvāstivādins held that "all exists" (*sarvam asti*). The doctrine, "all exists", refers to the Sarvāstivāda notion that all the times exist, as is set forth in the *Abhidharmakośa*.

avaśyaṃ ca kilaitatsarvāstivādena satā'bhyupagantavyam/ yasmāt
tadastivādāt sarvāstivāda iṣṭaḥ
ye hi sarvamastīti vadanti atītamanāgataṃ pratyutpannaṃ ca te sarvāstivādāḥ/[1]

Necessarily, by the Sarvāstivādins indeed it is to be maintained that this is existing, since (it is said :)
Because of the existence of that (*tadastivāda*), they are declared Sarvāstivādins.
Those who say that all exists—past, present, and future—are Sarvāstivādins.

The Sarvāstivādins, according to de La Vallée Poussin, possessed their own *Vinaya* and scriptures, and were advocates of the *Abhidharma* texts, in which they included the seven books of the *Abhidharma*, the Scriptures (*śāstra*) and the Discussions (*prakaraṇa*), the *Jñānaprasthāna* and its six feet (*pāda*), *Dharmaskandha* etc.[2] There were some, according to de La Vallée Poussin, who adhered to these works alone, although in the first century

1. Pradhan, Professor P., *Abhidharmakośabhāṣyam of Vasubandhu*, (Patna, India : K. P. Jayaswal Research Institute, 1975), (*Abhidharmkośa* V.25), p. 296.

2. Poussin, Louis de La Vallée, *L'Abhidharmakośa de Vasubandhu*, Tome I, Volume XVI, Mélanges Chinoises et Bouddhiques, translation with notes, (Brussels : Institut Belge des hautes études Chinoises, 1971, reprint), p. ix-x.

A.D., around the time of the Council of Kaniṣka, there was written a commentary to the *Jñānaprasthāna* known as the *Vibhāṣā*. Those who advocated the *Vibhāṣā* as well as the works advocated by the other Sarvāstivādins were called Vaibhāṣikas.[3] It is to be noted, however, according to de La Vallée Poussin, that both the Sarvāstivādins and the Vaibhāṣikas believed that the *Abhidharmas* present the word of the Buddha. But there were also those who believed that the three baskets (*piṭaka*) of the Buddha's word are contained in the *sūtras* alone. These latter were called Sautrāntika in that they rejected the authority of the *Abhidharma* and advocated the authority of the *Sūtras* alone. It is to be observed, however, notes de La Vallée Poussin, that although the Sautrāntikas rejected a few of the positions of the *Vibhāṣā* and advanced a more novel theory of the Buddhas, they nevertheless accepted much in the Vaibhāṣika system.[4]

> Mais on ne doit pas se méprendre sur leur attitude. Quoique formellement opposés à quelques-unes des thèses dé la *Vibhāṣā* et des Vaibhāṣikas, quoique de leur côté, ils aient une spéculation et peut-être une bouddhologie assez modernistes, ils ne combattent pas systematique leurs adversaires, qui furent, sans doute, leurs devanciers. Ils admettent, du système des Vaibhāṣikas, tout ce qu'ils n'ont pas une raison formelle de nier.[5]

Whereas the Sarvāstivādins held that all the times are real, the Sautrāntikas denied this notion on the basis of the argument that if the times (*kāla*) are real, then the eternality (*śāśvatatva*) of all *dharmas* is admitted, in contradiction to Buddhist teachings concerning impermanence (*anityatā*). In opposition to the Sarvāstivāda position that a *dharma* has a nature (*svabhāva*) to be distinguished from its characteristics (*lakṣaṇa*) the Sautrāntika argued that if a *dharma* is existent (*sat*) by its own nature, then it cannot be explained how it is born or destroyed, and that therefore the three times are in no way established. In any case, the positions of these two schools will be clarified in the following sub-sections.

3. Ibid., Tome I, p. x.
4. Ibid., Tome I, p. xi.
5. Ibid., p. xi.

1. CAUSATION

a. Dependent Origination and the Aggregates

There was a tendency among the Vedāntins to treat the Buddhist notion of dependent origination as a theory of the origin of being. Thus Śaṅkara in his interpretation of the *sūtra* "*itare-tara-pratyayatvād iti cen notpattimātranimittatvāt*" (*Brahma-sūtra* II.2.19), charges the Sarvāstivādins with attempting to account for the origin of the aggregates through a series of causes (*nidāna*) considered altogether as efficient cause (*nimitta*). It is important to ask, however, whether the Buddhists, and in particular the Sarvāstivādins, regarded the series of causes involved in dependent origination as the efficient cause of the aggregates. The significance of the teaching of dependent origination, according to Nalinaksha Dutt, lies not in the fact that it supposedly engenders the aggregates, but in the fact that it explains the this-conditioned (*idappaccayatā*) nature of things.

> This formula explains the fixed, unchangeable, and this-conditioned (*idappaccayatā*) nature of things; hence it is a key to the eternal truth.[1]

Dutt has noted that many ancient and modern commentators have a tendency to consider *pratītyasamutpāda* to be Buddha's theory of the origin of a being and that some have tried to draw parallels between the links of the formula and Sāṅkhya terminology. Dutt indicates, however, that Buddhaghosa, an ancient commentator, was aware of this tendency and responded to it by declaring that *avijjā*, the first link in the chain of dependent origination, must not be regarded as similar to the "*pakati*" (*prakṛti*) of the "*pakativādins*" (Sāṅkhya) because *avijjā* (*avidyā*) or nescience, has causes.

> Buddhaghosa has, however, pointed out that *avijjā*, the first link of the chain, must not be regarded as similar to *pakati* (*prakṛti*) of the *Pakativādins* (Sāṅkhya) because *avijjā* is neither

1. Dutt, Nalinaksha, *Aspects of Mahāyāna Buddhism*, (London : Luzac and Company, 1930), p. 208.

uncaused (*akāraṇa*) nor is it the primary cause (*mūlakāraṇa*) of the world. It owes its origin to *āsavas* (impurities).[2]

For Buddhaghosa, *avijjā*, or nescience, is itself an outgrowth of the *āsavas* (*āsrava*), or fluxes (or as Warren translates, depravities). *Avijjā* is only declared to be the starting point of the series of causes (*nidāna*) when the Buddha is discoursing upon the round of rebirths.

> But why is ignorance put at the beginning ? Is it because ignorance, like the *natura naturans* of the Sāṅkhya philosophers, is the causeless primary cause of the world ? It is not causeless. For in the quotation, "On the arising of the depravities depends the arising of ignorance," the cause of ignorance is declared. But there is an occasion when ignorance may be said to be a primary cause. What is that occasion? When it is made the starting point of discourse concerning the round of rebirth.[3]

In the *Visuddhi Magga*, Buddhaghosa remarks that the series could have begun as well with *bhavataṇhā*, or the craving for becoming.[4] Thus Dutt notes that dependent origination is not meant to be an explanation of the origin of the world but rather an illustration of the "this-conditioned nature" (*idappaccayatā*) of things.[5] It can be seen that the doctrine of dependent origination illustrates not so much the genesis of the *dharmas* composing the aggregates, but their interdependence. The Pali Text Society Pali-English Dictionary explains the term "*idappaccayatā*" as follows: "having its foundation on this, that is to say, causally connected, by way of a cause."[6] Buddhaghosa explains it in terms of conditionality.

> From the standpoint of the condition (*hetu*) or group of

---

2. Ibid., p. 208.
3. Warren, Henry Clarke, *Buddhism in Translations*, (New York : Athenaeum, 1963, reprint), translation of *Visuddhi Magga* XVII, p. 171.
4. Ibid., *Visuddhi Magga* XVII, p. 171.
5. Dutt, Nalinaksha, *Aspects of Mahāyāna Buddhism*, p. 209.
6. Kalupahana, David J., *Causality : The Central Philosophy of Buddhism*, (Honolulu : University Press of Hawaii), p. 54.

conditions (*hetusamūha*) that gives rise to such states as decay and death, as stated, there is said to be conditionality.[7]

The Buddhist teaching of dependent origination was often misinterpreted by the Vedāntins, as is revealed in their critique of the absence of a conscious aggregating agent in Sarvāstivāda doctrine. Śaṅkara, for instance, in his interpretation of the *sūtra* "*ubhayahetuke 'pi tadaprāptiḥ*" (*Brahma-sūtra* II.2.18) criticizes the Sarvāstivāda notion of the atom on the basis of the absence of a conscious agent who could bring about the aggregation. He neglects, however, the Sarvāstivāda notion of dependent origination, according to which a constructed thing is accomplished by means of conditions having assembled together.

> saṃskṛtatvaṃ pratītyasamutpannatvam iti paryāyāvetau; sametya sambhūya pratyayaiḥ kṛtaṃ saṃskṛtaṃ; taṃ taṃ pratyayaṃ pratītya samutpannaṃ, pratītyasamutpannam iti[8]
>
> The state of being constructed is the state of being dependently originated—these are the regular recurrences; by means of conditions having assembled together, the constructed thing is accomplished; having depended on this and that condition, it is originated—thus it is dependently originated.

Stcherbatsky explains the passage as follows :

> This concerted life of the elements (*saṃskṛtatva*) is but another name for the laws of causation—the combined origination (*samutpāda*) of some elements with regard (*pratītya*) to other elements.[9]

Furthermore, in his interpretation of the *sūtra*, "*itaretarapratyayatvād iti cen notpattimātranimittatvāt*" (*Brahma-sūtra* II.2.19), Śaṅkara raises the question whether the causes (*nidāna*), links in the chain of dependent origination, constitute the efficient

---

7. Ibid., p. 54.

8. Shastri, Swami Dwarikadasa, *Abhidharmakośam* with an auto-commentary of Vasubandhu and *Sphuṭārtha* commentary of Yaśomitra, Bauddha Bharati Series-5, Part I, (Varanasi : Bauddha Bharati, 1970), (*Abhidharmakośa* III. 45), p. 258.

9. Stcherbatsky, Th., *The Central Conception of Buddhism* (Delhi, India : Indological Book House, 1970, reprint), p. 24.

cause of the aggregates. This question, however, is related to a question discussed in the *Abhidharmokśa*: the relationship between dependent origination (*pratītyasamutpāda*) and the dependently originated (*pratītyasamutpanna*). The discussion in the *Abhidharmakośa* is initiated by a passage in the *Sūtras* (identified by de La Vallée Poussin as *Saṃyutta Nikāya* II. 25),[10] where the Buddha declares dependent origination and the *dharmas* dependently originated.

> uktaṃ bhagavatā pratītyasamutpādaṃ vo bhikṣavo deśayiṣyāmi pratītyasamutpannāśca dharmā...[11]

> It is said by the Lord, "*Bhikṣus*, I teach dependent origination and the dependently originated *dharmas*..."

According to the Sarvāstivādins, as set forth in the *Abhidharmakośa*, dependent origination constitutes the cause (*hetu*) and the dependently originated constitutes the effect. Every cause (*nidāna*) is simultaneously effect (in that it is dependent upon other causes) and cause (in that other effects depend upon it). No cause ((*nidāna*) or limb (*aṅga*) is a cause by the same relationship with which it is an effect.

> *heturatra samutpādaḥ samutpannaṃ phalaṃ matam*/ hetubhūtamaṅgaṃ pratītyasamutpādaḥ samutpadyate 'smāditi kṛtvā phalabhūtamaṅgaṃ pratītyasamutpannam/ evaṃ sarvāṇyaṅgānyubhayathā sidhyanti/ hetuphalabhāvāt/ na caivaṃ satyavyavasthā bhavantyapekṣābhedāt/ yadapekṣya pratītyasamutpādo na tadevāpekṣya pratīyasmutpannaṃ hetuphalavat pitṛputravacca/[12]

> *In this case, that origination* (*samutpāda*) *is the cause, and that the originated* (*samutpannam*) *is the effect, is the doctrine.* Dependent origination, the limb which composes the cause, is born; from it, there is the dependently originated, the limb which composes the effect. All the limbs are manifested as both, because of the state of being cause and effect. If it were

10. Poussin, Louis de La Vallée, *L'Abhidharmakośa de Vasubandhu*, Tome I, p. 72, footnote 4.

11. Pradhan, Professor P., *Abhidharmakośam of Vasubandhu*, *Abhidharmakośa* III. 27, p. 136.

12. Ibid., *Abhidharmakośa* III. 28, p. 136.

not so (that all the limbs are both cause and effect), then there would be confusion, because of the difference of dependence. With regard to that which is dependent origination, there is not the dependently originated; as father and son, so cause and effect.

The *Abhidharmakośa* states that according to Sthavirapūrṇāśa, dependent origination cannot be the dependently originated in four cases: first, *dharmas* of the future (*anāgata*); secondly, the last (*carama*) *dharmas* of an *Arhat*; thirdly, *dharmas* past (*atīta*) and present (*pratyutpanna*); fourthly, unconstructed *dharmas*.

sthavirapūrṇāśaḥ kilāha syāt pratītyasamutpādo na pratītyasamutpannā dharmā iti/ catuṣkoṭikaḥ/ (24a.8A.IV) prathamā koṭiranāgatā dharmāḥ/ dvitīyā 'rhataścaramāḥ/ tṛtīyā tadanye 'tītapratyutpannā dharmāḥ/ caturthyasaṃskṛtā dharmā iti/[13]

Sthavirapūrṇāśa indeed has said that dependent origination would not be the dependently originated *dharmas*. There are four alternatives. The first alternative consists of *dharmas* not yet arrived. The second consists of the last ones of an *Arhat*. The third consists of *dharmas* past and present. The fourth consists of unconstructed *dharmas*.

The Sautrāntikas criticize the position of the Sarvāstivādins on the basis that by declaring the limbs of dependent origination to be composed of the personal aggregates (*skandha*), the Sarvāstivādins are contradicting the *sūtra* which declares nescience (*avidyā*) to be ignorance relative to the past. Then the Sautrāntikas, according to the *Abhidharmakośa*, argue that if nescience is composed of the personal aggregates, as the Sarvāstivādins postulate in connection with the situational (*āvasthika*) type of dependent origination, then the Sarvāstivāda position, that the five personal aggregates remain to the *Arhat* in whom nescience has disappeared, is contradicted. If nescience has disappeared, how is it possible to explain the presence in the *Arhat* of the two personal aggregates of perception (*vijñāna*) and motivation (*saṃskāra*), which are supposedly dependent upon the presence of nescience? The Sautrāntikas argue that the various limbs of dependent

13. Ibid., *Abhidharmakośa* III. 28, p. 136.

origination can only be called limbs if the presence or absence of other limbs depends upon them.

> yadyapi ca tāsvavasthāsu pañca skandhā vidyante yasya tu bhāvābhāvayoryasya bhāvābhāvaniyamaḥ tadevāṅgaṃ vyavasthāpayitum/ satyapi ca pañcaskandhake 'rhataḥ saṃskārā na bhavanti pañcaskandhahetukāḥ/ kiṃ tarhi/ avidyāhetukā eva/ tathā puṇyāpuṇyāneñjyopagaṃ vijñānaṃ tṛṣṇādayaśceti/yathānirdeśameva sūtrārthaḥ/ yadapyuktam "heturatra samutpādaḥ samutpannaṃ phalaṃ yāvaccatuṣkoṭika" iti/[14]

> If five personal aggregates exist in this state, that which is the principle of presence or absence for the presence or absence of another is the member to prove (logically) tenable. Although in connection with the *Arhat*, there are the five personal aggregates, motivations are not caused by the five personal aggregates. How then? They (the motivations) are caused by nescience. Hence perceptions approaching the meritorious, and non-meritorious craving, etc. do not exist (for the *Arhat*). Thus is this teaching the meaning of the *sūtra*? It is said: "Here dependent origination is the cause, the dependently originated is the fruit, insofar as the four causes are concerned."

It appears, therefore, that according to the Sarvāstivādins, dependent origination assumes the existence of the five personal aggregates; for nescience is considered by them to be constituted of the five personal aggregates. The Sarvāstivādins do not seem to hold that dependent origination is the cause (*nimitta*) of the personal aggregates. The Sautrāntikas argue that the Sarvāstivāda position that nescience is composed of the five personal aggregates leads to contradiction, for it does not explain the presence of perception (*vijñāna*) and motivation (*saṃskāra*) among the limbs of dependent origination.

The Buddhist explanation of dependent origination in terms of the formula "When this is, that is" (*asmin satīdaṃ bhavati*), and the formula "From the birth of this that is born" (*asyotpādād idam utpadyate*) has also been misrepresented or neglected by the Vedāntins. In the *Abhidharmakośa*, it is asked why the

14. Ibid., *Abhidharmakośa* III. 28, p. 137.

Buddha explains dependent origination in terms of these two fomulas. The Buddha replies that he declares these explanations for several reasons: first, in order to emphasize that the motivations are dependent upon nescience; secondly, in order to reveal the succession (*paramparā*) of members (*aṅga*); thirdly, in order to reveal the succession of birth. The Buddha here notes that a thing can proceed from its condition (*pratyaya*) either immediately or gradually after an interval. It is to be noted, however, that in neither case is a thing considered to be simultaneous with its condition.

> kimarthaṃ punarbhagavān paryāyadvayamāha "asmin satīdaṃ bhavati asyotpādādidamutpadyate" iti/ avadhāraṇārthaṃ/ yathā 'nyatrāha "avidyāyām satyāṃ saṃskārā bhavanti nānyatrāvidyāyāḥ saṃskārā" iti/ aṅgaparamparāṃ vā darśayitum/ asminnaṅge satīdaṃ bhavati asya punaraṅgasyotpādādidamutpadyata iti/ janmaparamparāṃ vā/ pūrvānte sati madhyānto bhavati madhyāntasyotpādādaparānta utpadyata iti/ sākṣāt pāramparyeṇa pratyayabhāvaṃ darśayati/ kadāciddhi samanantaramavidyāyāḥ saṃskārā bhavanti kadācit pāramparyeṇeti/[15]
>
> For what reason did the Lord declare two alternatives (*paryāyadvaya*): "Given this, that is; from the birth of this, that is born"? For the sake of emphasis (*avadhāraṇa*). He declares otherwise: "When there is nescience, there are the motivations; from nescience are the motivations and not otherwise." (He so declares) in order to reveal the succession of members: "When there is this member, that is; from the birth of this member again that is born." (He so declares in order to reveal the) succession of birth: "When there is the former portion, there is the middle portion; from the birth of the middle portion the later portion is born. He reveals the relationship of condition immediately and gradually. For sometimes the motivations are immediately preceded by nescience and sometimes after an interval.

It is to be observed that Śaṅkara in his interpretation of the *sūtra* "*itaretara-pratyayatvād iti cen notpattimātranimittatvāt*"

15. Ibid., *Abhidharmakośa* III. 28, p. 138-139.

(*Brahma-sūtra* II.2.19) attempts to refute the Sarvāstivādins for supposedly holding the position that causes (*nidāna*) involved in dependent origination are the efficient cause (*nimitta*) of the aggregates. It is evident, however, that the Sarvāstivādins interpret dependent origination in terms of the principle "when this is, that is," (*asmin sati, idaṃ bhavati*). Furthermore, in his interpretation of the *sūtra* "*ubhayathā ca doṣāt*" (*Brahma-sūtra* II.2.23), Madhva and his school attempt to refute the Buddhist principle, "When this is, that is" by arguing that this principle signifies the simultaneity of cause and effect and that thereby an endless series of effects is created. As is noted above, however, the principle is set forth in order to reveal the succession of birth and of members. Furthermore, a thing is declared to proceed from its condition either immediately or gradually after an interval, but in no case simultaneously.

b. Causeless Destruction (*ākasmika vināśa*)

The Sautrāntika position of causeless destruction (*ākasmika vināśa*) was misinterpreted by the Vedāntins. Causeless destruction in the *Abhidharmakośa* is proved in order to establish the principle of momentariness. Vasubandhu argues with a hypothetical member of the Vātsīputrīya school, which supposedly denies the thesis of causeless destruction, as de La Vallée Poussin notes.[16] Vasubandhu first argues that destruction, since it is an absence, cannot be the effect of a cause and that only an entity can be an effect.

> syādetadeva yadi sarvasya kṣaṇikatvaṃ sidhyet/ siddhamevaitat viddhi/ kutaḥ/ saṃskṛtasyāvaśyaṃ/ *vyayāt*//2// ākasmiko hi bhāvānāṃ vināśaḥ/ kiṃ kāraṇaṃ/ kāryasya hi kāraṇaṃ bhavati/ vināśaścābhāvaḥ/ yaścābhāvastasya kiṃ kartavyam/ so 'sāvākasmiko vināśo yadi bhāvasyotpannamātrasya na syāt paścādapi na syādbhāvasya tulyatvāt/[17]

---

16. Poussin, Louis de La Vallée, *L'Abhidharmakośa de Vasubandhu*, Tome III, Volume XVI, *Melánges Chinoises et Bouddhiques*, translation with notes, (Brussels : Institut Belge des hautes études Chinoises, 1971, reprint), pp. 5-6.

17. Pradhan, Professor, *The Abhidharmakośam of Vasubandhu*, *Abhidharmakośa* IV. 2-3, p. 193.

If this (their immediate destruction) should be, then the momentariness of all would be established. This is established as the rule. How? Necessarily, in connection with the constructed thing, *because of disappearance*, the destruction of entities is causeless. What is the reason? For a cause is in connection with an effect. Destruction is an absence. In connection with that which is absence, is there anything to be done? That very destruction is causeless if it is not in connection with an arisen entity only, or afterwards if it is not on account of similarity to an entity.

2. MOMENTARINESS

One of the issues that arise in Śaṅkara's critique of the Buddhist realists (*bāhyārthavādins*) in his interpretation of the *sūtra* "*uttarotpāde ca pūrva-nirodhāt*" (*Brahma-sūtra* II.2.20), is the problem of reconciling causal continuity with the doctrine of momentariness. The problem consists in that if the cause disappears before the effect comes to existence, then there is no continuity between the so-called effect and cause, and that if the cause continues to exist at the time of the production of the effect, then the doctrine of momentariness is contradicted. It is necessary, therefore, to study the actual positions of the Sarvāstivādins and Sautrāntikas in connection with momentariness in order to discover how this problem is treated, either explicitly or implicitly. It may be noted, at the beginning, that the Sarvāstivādins distinguished between the nature of a constructed *dharma* (*dharma-svabhāva*) and the characteristics of a constructed *dharma* (*dharma-lakṣaṇa*), whereas the Sautrāntikas had recourse to the notion of the series (*pravāha*). According to Stcherbatsky, the Sarvāstivādins met the difficulty of accounting for causal continuity by distinguishing between the element in itself (*dharma-svabhāva*) and the element in its manifestation (*dharma-lakṣaṇa*).

> The Sarvāstivādins met the objection by pointing to the difference between an element in itself, its real nature (*svabhāva*) and its efficiency-moment, its function, or manifestation (*kāritva-lakṣaṇa*).[1]

The element in itself (*dharma-svabhāva*) for the Sarvāstivādins, according to Stcherbatsky, represents a potentiality which exists forever.

> As stated above, the Sarvāstivādins maintain that all elements exist on two different planes, the real essence of the element (*dharma-svabhāva*) and its momentary manifestation (*dharma-lakṣaṇa*). The first exists always in past, present, and future.

1. Stcherbatsky, Th., *The Central Conception of Buddhism*, p. 34.

It is not eternal (*nitya*) because eternality means absence of change, but it represents the potential appearances of the element into phenomenal existence, and its past appearances as well. This potentiality is existing for ever (*sarvadā asti*).[2]

According to the Sarvāstivāda position as it is represented in the *Abhidharmakośa*, the characteristics (*lakṣaṇa*) of constructed (*saṃskṛta*) *dharmas* are four: birth (*jāti*), duration (*sthiti*), decay (*jarā*), and impermanence (*anityatā*).

lakṣaṇāni punarjātirjarā sthitiranityatā//45//

etāni hi saṃskṛtasya catvāri lakṣaṇāni/ yatraitāni bhavanti sa dharmaḥ saṃskṛto lakṣyate/viparyayādasaṃskṛtaḥ/ tatra jātistaṃ dharmaṃ janayati sthitiḥ sthāpayati jarā jarayati anityatā vināśayati/[3]

The characteristics are birth (*jāti*), *decay* (*jarā*), *duration* (*sthiti*), *cessation* (*anityatā*).

These four are the characteristics (*lakṣaṇa*) in the case of the constructed. That *dharma* is the constructed. On the opposite polarity (*viparyaya*) there is the unconstructed. In that case, birth gives birth to the *dharma*, duration maintains, decay wears it out, cessation destroys it.

It is to be noted that Śaṅkara, in his interpretation of the *sūtra* "*uttarotpāde ca pūrva-nirodhāt*" (*Brahma-sūtra* II.2.20), examines three alternatives supposedly held by the Sarvāstivādins for explaining the origination and cessation of a thing: that origination and cessation constitute a thing's own form (*svarūpa*), or another state of it (*avasthāntara*), or an altogether different thing (*vastvantara*). The difficulty with this representation, however, is that the Sarvāstivādins regard birth (*jāti*), duration (*sthiti*), decay (*jarā*), and impermanence (*anityatā*) to be only characteristics (*lakṣaṇa*) of the *dharma* to be distinguished from the nature (*svabhāva*) of the *dharma*.

The four characteristics postulated by the Sarvāstivādins are denied by the Sautrāntikas, who adhere to the notion of the

2. Ibid., p. 35.
3. Pradhan, Professor P., *Abhidharmakośam of Vasubandhu, Abhidharmakośa* II. 45-46, p. 75.

series (*pravāha*). They deny that the four characteristics exist because of the continuing entity (*dravya*), and that there is any authority (*pramāṇa*) which warrants such a position.

> tadetadākāśaṃ pāṭhyata iti sautrāntikāḥ/ na hyete jātyādayo dharmā dravyataḥ saṃvidyante yathā 'bhivyajyante/ kim kāraṇaṃ/ pramāṇābhāvāt/ nahyeṣāṃ dravyato 'stitvekiṃcidapi pramāṇamasti pratyakṣamanumānamāptāgamo vā yathā rūpādīnāṃ dharmāṇāmiti/[4]
>
> "So space has been thereby revealed?" asked the Sautrāntikas. These, pertaining to the set beginning with birth, are not known as *dharmas*, in accordance with the continuing entity (*dravya*) in such a way that they are manifested. What is the reason? The absence of authority (*pramāṇa*). For in connection with the case of the existence of these in accordance with the material flow, there is no authority whatsoever—perception, inference, or inherited scripture—as is also the case with the *dharmas* beginning with formation (*rūpa*).

The Sarvāstivādin objects that according to the *sūtras* the birth, etc. of the constructed are objects of perception.

> yattarhi sūtra uktaṃ "saṃskṛtasyotpādo 'pi prajñāyate vyayo 'pi sthityanyathātvamapī" ti/[5]
>
> In this case, it is said in the *sūtra*, "The very birth of a constructed thing is recognized as well as the disintegration of it, and the very evolution of that abiding."

To this objection, the Sautrāntika replies that fools imagine the series (*pravāha*) of *saṃskāras* to be possessed of a self. The Sautrāntika notes that the *sūtra* referring to the three characteristics of the constructed is intended to illuminate the constructed existence (*saṃskṛtatva*) and dependent origination (*pratītyasamutpannatā*) of the series. Furthermore, the Sautrāntika argues that the characteristics are in connection with the series, not with a particular moment (*kṣaṇa*) of the series, for the birth, etc. of an individual moment cannot be discerned.

> granthajño devānāṃ priyo natvarthajñaḥ/ arthaśca pratiśaraṇa-

4. Ibid., *Abhidharmakośa* II. 46, p. 76.
5. Ibid., *Abhidharmakośa* II. 46, p. 76.

muktaṃ *bhagavatā*/ kaḥ punarasyārthaḥ/ avidyāndhā hi bālāḥ saṃskārapravāhamātmata ātmīyataścādhimuktā abhiṣvajante/ yasya mithyādhimokṣasya vyāvarttanārthaṃ bhagavāṃstasya saṃskārapravāhasya saṃskṛtatvaṃ pratītyasamutpannatāṃ dyotayitukāma idamāha "trīṇimāni saṃskṛtasya saṃskṛtalakṣaṇāni"/ na tu kṣaṇasya/ nahi kṣaṇasyotpādādayaḥ prajñāyante/ nacāprajñāyamānā ete lakṣaṇaṃ bhavitumarhante/[6]

Knowing the scriptures, you are attached to them, but you do not know their meaning. The significance (*artha*) is explained in a frank manner by the Lord. What is the significance of that again? Blinded by nescience, the childish ones (*bālā*) inclined towards a series of *saṃskāras* possessed of Self, pertaining to Self, are attached. To the one who was inclined towards falsity, the Lord (*Bhagavat*) desirous of illuminating (*dyotayitukāma*) the dependently originated and the constructed existence of the flow of *saṃskāras* declared: "The three characteristics of a constructed thing are in connection with the constructed." It is not in connection with the moment, for the births, etc. of the moment are not recognized (*prajñāyante*). These, not being recognized are not able to be characteristics.

Having averred that the characteristics enunciated by the Sarvāstivādins do not exist by reason of the continuing entity, and having noted that the three characteristics mentioned in the *sūtras* apply to the series rather than to the moment, the Sautrāntikas proceed to redefine the four characteristics in terms of the series. Birth (*jāti*) is the beginning of the series. Disappearance (*vyaya*) is the cessation (*cheda*) of the series. Duration (*sthiti*) is defined as the series itself. The evolution of that abiding (*sthityanyathātva*) is the distinction (*viśiṣṭatā*) of successive states (*pūrvāpara*).

jātirā[illegible] pravāhasya vyayaśchedaḥ sthitistu saḥ/
sthityanyathātvaṃ tasyaiva pūrvāparaviśiṣṭatā//
jātirapūrvo bhāvaḥ sthitiḥ prabandho vyayastaducchedaḥ/
sthityanyathātvamiṣṭam prabandhapūrvāparaviśeṣa" iti//
kṣaṇikasya hi dharmasya vinā sthityā vyayo bhavet/

6. Ibid., *Abhidharmakośa* II. 46, pp. 76-77.

na ca vyetyeta tenāsya vṛthā tatparikalpanā//[7]

Birth is the beginning of the series (*pravāha*), the disappearance (*vyaya*) is the cessation (*cheda*), the duration (*sthiti*) is that (the series).

The evolution (*sthityanyathātva*) of that abiding is the distinction (*viśiṣṭatā*) of successive states (*pūrvāpara*).

Birth is a subsequent state, the series (*prabandha*) is the duration, the disappearance is the cutting off (of the series).

The evolution of that abiding is declared to be the distinction of successive parts of the series.

Without the duration of the momentary *dharma* would there be disappearance?

No, it perishes; therefore, the determination of that (i.e. duration) is in vain.

The *Sphuṭārtha* commentary emphasizes that duration is the series itself and that the *dharma* perishes in the midst of its duration.

etamevārthaṃ ślokadvayena saṃgṛhṇannāha *jātirādiḥ pravāhasyeti* sarvaṃ/*sthitistu sa* iti/ sa eva pravāhaḥ sthitiḥ/ tasyaiveti/ tasyaiva pravāhasya/

taducheda iti/ prabandhocchedaḥ/ kṣaṇikasya hi dharmasyeti ślokaḥ/ kṣaṇiko hi dharmaḥ, sthitimantareṇa vinaśyedityarthaḥ sthitirastīti manyase cet? sa ca dharmo vyetyeva satyāmapi sthitau, vinaśyatyeva kṣaṇikatvāt/ vināśahetvabhāvāt/ tasmād vṛthā tatparikalpanā/ niṣprayojanā sthitiparikalpanetyarthaḥ/[8]

He explains the acquisition of the significance by two *ślokas*. The statement, "Birth is the beginning of the series," is sufficient unto itself. "The duration is that": "that" refers to the series (*pravāha*) and is duration (*sthiti*). "Of that" refers to the series (*pravāha*).

The "cutting off of that" refers to the cutting off of the series.

---

7. Ibid., *Abhidharmakośa* II. 46, p. 77.
8. Shastri, Swami Dwarikadasa, *Abhidharmakośaṃ*, Volume I, *Sphuṭārtha* commentary to *Abhidharmakośa* II. 46, p. 259.

Then there is the *śloka* beginning with the words, "For, of a momentary (*kṣaṇika*) *dharma*." For a *dharma* is momentary. The meaning of the passage is that a *dharma* disintegrates in the midst of duration. What if you think there is duration? That very *dharma* perishes when there is duration; it disintegrates on account of momentariness, on account of the existence of the cause of destruction. Therefore it is said, "The determination of that." By this phrase is meant the vain determination that there is duration.

On the assumption that a characteristic does not represent an internal continuing entity (*dravyāntara*) the characteristics are applied to every moment (*pratikṣaṇam*) in terms of the series.

pratikṣaṇaṃ cāpi saṃskṛtasyaitāni lakṣaṇāni (3b.4B1.VI) yujyante vinā 'pi dravyāntarakalpanayā/kathamiti/pratikṣaṇamabhūtvābhāva utpādaḥ/ bhūtvā 'bhāvo vyayaḥ/ pūrvasya pūrvasyottarakṣaṇānubandhaḥ sthitiḥ/ tasyāvisadṛśatvaṃ sthityanyathātvamiti/[9]

Every moment these characteristics of a constructed thing are enjoined without the assumption (*kalpanā*) of an internal continuing entity (*dravyāntara*). How? Birth (*utpāda*) is the existence (*bhāva*) subsequent to non-existing (*abhūtvā*) every moment. Disappearance (*vyaya*) is the absence (*abhāva*) subsequent to existing (*bhūtvā*). The continuation (*anubandha*) of successive moments is the duration. The dissimilarity (*visadṛśatva*) of that is the evolution of the abiding (*sthityanyathātva*).

Dissimilarity (*visadṛśatva*) in the series is explained on the basis of time (*kāla*), as in the example of a thunderbolt, the force of which never varies over time.

yadā tarhi sadṛśā utpadyante/ na te nirviśeṣā bhavanti/ kathamidaṃ jñāyate/ kṣiptākṣiptabalidurbalakṣiptasya vajrādeścirāśutarapātakālabhedāttanmahābhūtānāṃ pariṇāmaviśeṣasiddheḥ/[10]

---

9. Pradhan, Professor P., *Abhidharmakośam of Vasubandhu, Abhidharmakośa* II. 46, p. 77.

10. Ibid., *Abhidharmakośa* II. 46, p. 7.

At that time, when similar things (*sadṛśa*) are born, these are not dissimilar (*nirviśeṣa*). How is this known?
Because of the evidence of special properties of modification (*pariṇāmaviśeṣa*), in connection with the great elements on account of the difference of time (*kāla*) of the fall (*pāta*) of the thunderbolt whether slowly or more quickly, thrown weakly or strongly, thrown or not thrown.

In this way, the Sautrāntikas have emphasized the series in their explanation of the characteristics of constructed things. The danger of contradiction posed by momentariness to causal continuity is avoided, for, according to Yaśomitra in the *Sphuṭārtha*, the subsequent moment of the series is the duration of the antecedent, so that in a sense the antecedent moment abides when there is the subsequent moment. In this way, the moments following one another are connected in a sense and the notion of causal continuity is upheld.

uttarottarakṣaṇānubandhaḥ sthitiriti/ pūrvasya kṣaṇasyottaraḥ kṣaṇaḥ pratinidhibhūtaḥ, sādṛśyāt/ ataḥ sa pūrvaḥ kṣaṇo 'dyāpyavatiṣṭhata iveti kṛtvottaraḥ kṣaṇaḥ sthitirucyate/[11]
The uninterrupted succession of moments following one another is duration. The later moment is the substitute of the former moment, because of similarity.

Therefore, that former moment abides as it were; the later moment, having accomplished, is its duration.

It may be noted here that Rāmānuja, in his interpretation of the *sūtra* "*samudāya ubhayahetuke 'pi tadaprāptiḥ*" (*Brahma-sūtra* II.2.17), attempts to refute the Sautrāntika notion of the series, flow, or stream through the argument that the series would be composed of parts, each of which is momentary or perishing; hence, according to Rāmānuja, the notion of the series like the notion of the aggregate is contradicted by the doctrine of momentariness. Rāmānuja, however, ignores the Sautrāntika doctrine, as set forth in the *Abhidharmakośa*, that the duration of the series is the series itself and that thus the series cannot easily be broken into parts.

---

11. Shastri, Swami Dwarikadasa, *Abhidharmakośam*, Volume I, *Sphuṭārtha* commentary to *Abhidharmakośa* II. 46, p. 77.

The Buddhist teachings of existence subsequent to non-existing (*abhūtvā bhāva*) and of absence subsequent to existing (*bhūtvā abhāva*) was misrepresented by the Vedāntins. Rāmānuja in his interpretation of the *sūtra* "*ubhayathā ca doṣāt*" (*Brahma-sūtra* II.2.22), attributes to the Buddhists the positions of origination from emptiness or passing into emptiness. Rāmānuja may be referring to the Sautrāntika teaching of birth as subsequent to non-existing (*abhūtvā bhāva utpāda*) and of absence subsequent to existing (*bhūtvā abhāva*). But to say that existence is subsequent to non-existing and *vjce versa* is not to say that the existence arises out of non-existence or that existence passes into non-existence. Otherwise, the Sautrāntika teaching could have been expressed "*abhāvād-bhāva*" (entity from absence) or "*bhāvād abhāva*" (absence from entity). Śaṅkara in his interpretation of the *sūtra* "*nāsato 'dṛṣṭatvāt*" (*Brahma-sūtra* II.2.26) also accuses the Buddhists of maintaining that entity springs from absence (*abhāvād-bhāva*). If Śaṅkara is referring to the Sautrāntika teaching of birth as the existence subsequent to non-existing (*abhūtvā bhāva utpāda*), he is also inaccurately representing their position.

3. THE UNCONSTRUCTED (*ASAMSKṚTA*) *DHARMAS*

a. The Cessations (*nirodha*)

Although both Śaṅkara and Rāmānuja in their interpretations of the *sūtra* "*pratisaṃkhyā 'pratisaṃkhyā nirodhāprāptir avicchedāt*" attribute to the Sarvāstivādins the position that the cessations (*nirodha*) involve absolute destruction (*niranvaya vināśa*), it is not the case according to the *Abhidharmakośa* that either the cessation-with-understanding or the cessation-without-understanding signifies for the Sarvāstivādins the annihilation of *dharmas*. The cessation-with-understanding (*pratisaṃkhyā-nirodha*) refers to the non-attainment of contact with *dharmas* whose fluxes are increasing (*sāsrava dharma*). The cessation-without-understanding refers to the obstruction of the origination of *dharmas* when they are not arising. According to the *Abhidharmakośa*, the cessation-with-understanding for the Sarvāstivādins is a "disjunction" from *dharmas* whose fluxes are increasing and is obtained by way of insight.

> pratisaṃkhyānirodho yo visaṃyogaḥ yaḥ sāsravairdharmair-visaṃyogaḥ sa pratisaṃkhyānirodhaḥ/ duḥkhādīnāmāryasatyānāṃ pratisaṃkhyānāṃ pratisaṃkhyā prajñāviśeṣastena prāpyo nirodhaḥ/[1]
>
> That which is disjunction is cessation-with-understanding. That disjunction from *dharmas* whose fluxes are increasing is the cessation-with-understanding. The understanding relates to the understanding of the Noble Truths beginning with pain; the understanding is a type of insight. By way of (understanding) cessation is to be attained.

According to the Sarvāstivādins, as explained in the *Abhidharmakośa*, the cessation-without-understanding (*apratisaṃkhyā-nirodha*) consists in the prevention of the birth of *dharmas* when they are not arising (*anutpatti dharma*), not by way of the under-

---

1. Pradhan, Professor P., *Abhidharmakośam of Vasubandhu, Abhidharmakośa* I. 5, p. 3.

standing (*pratisaṃkhyā*), but because of the insufficiency of the originating causes.

> *utpādātyantavighno 'nyo nirodho 'pratisaṃkhyayā//6//*
>
> anāgatānāṃ dharmāṇāmutpādasyātyanta vighnabhūto visaṃyogād yo 'nyo nirodhaḥ so 'pratisaṃkhyānirodhaḥ/ nahyasau pratisaṃkhyayā labhyate kiṃ tarhi/ pratyayavaikalyāt/[2]
>
> *There is another cessation which is a perpetual obstacle to origination, and (it is) not by means of understanding.*
>
> That cessation which is different from disjunction (*visaṃyoga*), and which is a perpetual obstacle to the origination of future *dharmas*; it is the cessation without understanding. It is not attained by understanding. How then? It is caused from the insufficiency of conditions.

It is evident, therefore, that according to the Sarvāstivādins, the interruption (*viccheda*) of the series in cessation-with-understanding signifies disjunction from *dharmas* whose fluxes are increasing, and that according to the Sarvāstivādins the cessation-without-understanding signifies the prevention of *dharmas* when they are not arising. In any case, neither type of cessation for the Sarvāstivādins according to the *Abhidharmakośa*, involves the absolute destruction of *dharmas*.

There is a difference, however, between the positions of the Sarvāstivādins and the Sautrāntikas in connection with the cessation-with-understanding and the cessation-without-understanding. According to the Sarvāstivādins, these are continuing entities (*dravya*), as the *Abhidharmakośa* indicates.

> tasmādanyathā tatsvabhāvo vaktavyaḥ/ āryaireva tatsvabhāvaḥ pratyātmavedyaḥ etāvattu śakyate vaktuṃ nityaṃ kuśalam cāsti dravyāntaraṃ/ tadvisaṃyogaścocyate pratisaṃkhyānirodhaśceti/[3]
>
> In a manner different from this, the nature of that (*dharma*) is to be discussed. Just by the *Āryas*, the nature of that (*dharma*) is to be known as an eternal, good, internal continuing entity.

2. Ibid., *Abhidharmakośa* I. 6, p. 4.
3. Ibid., *Abhidharmakośa* II. 55, p. 92.

That (*dharma*) is the disjunction said to be the cessation with understanding.

For the Sautrāntikas, however, according to the *Abhidharmakośa*, the three unconstructed *dharmas* (*ākāśa*, *prati-saṃkhyā-nirodha*, *apratisaṃkhyā-nirodha*) are non-continuing entities (*adravya*).

> sarvamevāsaṃskṛtamadravyamiti sautrāntikāḥ/ nahi tadrūpa-vedanādivat bhāvāntaramasti/[4]
>
> The Sautrāntikas say that every unconstructed *dharma* is a non-continuing entity (*adravya*), for that (*dharma*) is not an internal (*antara*) entity like the set beginning with formation, feeling.

For the Sautrāntikas, the cessation-with-understanding is synonymous with the destruction of the traces (*anuśaya*) due to the force of *prajñā* (insight).

> kiṃ tarhi? spraṣṭavyābhāvamātramākāśam/ tadyathā hyandhakāre pratighātamavindanta ākāśamityāhuḥ/ utpannānuśayajanmanirodhaḥ pratisaṃkhyābalenānyasyānutpādaḥ pratisaṃkhyāniro (47b.5B1.IV) dhaḥ/[5]
>
> How then? Space has for its measure the absence of the tangible.
>
> For example, not finding a solid thing in the dark, they say that this (*tad*) is space. Where there is the cessation of the traces and birth, when there is non-origination of another thing by the force of understanding (*pratisaṃkhyā*), there is the cessation-with-understanding.

The cessation-without-understanding for the Sautrāntika is synonymous with the non-origination of certain *dharmas* solely by reason of the absence of the causes that engender such *dharmas*.

> vinaiva pratisaṃkhyayā pratyayavaikalyādanutpādo yaḥ so 'pratisaṃkhyānirodhaḥ/ tadyathā nikāyasabhāgaśeṣasyāntarāmaraṇe/[6]

---

4. Ibid., *Abhidharmakośa* II. 55, p. 92.
5. Ibid., *Abhidharmakośa* II. 55, p. 92.
6. Ibid., *Abhidharmakośa* II. 55, p. 92.

> That which is the non-origination (*anutpāda*) without understanding due to the insufficiency of conditions (*pratyaya*) is the cessation-without-understanding, as in the case, for example, of death in the middle of the remainder of the ordinary span of life.

For the Sautrāntika, *Nirvāṇa* is like the disappearing flame, as is cited in the *Abhidharmakośa*.

> ayam ca dṛṣṭānta evam sūpanīto bhavati "pradyotasyeva nirvāṇam vimokṣastasya cetasaḥ" iti/ yathā pradyotasya nirvāṇamabhāva evaṃ bhagavato 'pi cetaso vimokṣa iti/[7]

> This example is thus adduced. "The liberation of the mind is like the extinction of a flame" is explained. As the extinction and absence of a flame the liberation of the mind (*cetas*) of the Lord is described.

The Sautrāntika teaching in connection with the basis (*āśraya*) seems to have been neglected by the Vedāntins. It is to be noted that Śaṅkara argues in his interpretation of the *sūtra* "*itaretara-pratyayatvād iti cen notpattimātranimittatvāt*" (*Brahma-sūtra* II.2.19), that if aggregates are born from other aggregates in an endless series (*saṃtati*), then in effect liberation would be desired by one but attained by another. The Sautrāntika position as set forth in the *Sphuṭārtha*, however, is that the basis subsists only as long as the defilement (*kleśa*) exists and then vanishes. It is not the case for the Sautrāntikas that "another" attains liberation; rather, it is the case that the basis vanishes. It is also to be observed that the Sautrāntika outlook towards the basis is different from Rāmānuja's treatment of the basis. Rāmānuja argues in his interpretation of the *sūtra* "*itaretara-pratyayatvād iti cen notpattimātranimittatvāt*" (*Brahma-sūtra* II.2.18) that the motivations require a basis for their continuance and that a basis which is momentary and perishing cannot support the motivations. According to the *Abhidharmakośa*, however, the basis subsists only as long as the defilements subsist. When the defilements disappear by the capacity engendered through the path of the cultivation of vision, the basis too disappears.

---

7. Ibid., *Abhidharmakośa* II. 55, p. 94.

The Sautrāntikas do not speak in terms of reach (*prāpti*), but rather in terms of the special property (*viśeṣa*) of the basis. When the capacity to produce defilements that are to be eliminated (*praheya*) by the paths of vision and cultivation is no more, the basis vanishes. When the basis no longer forms a seed, it is called one which has eliminated the defilements (*prahīṇakleśa*). If the seed is merely damaged, the basis can be said to be that which has not eliminated the defilements by the worldly path because of the possibility of reversion. The good *dharmas* are said to be of two types—those possessed (*bhāvin*) of effort, and those not possessed of effort.

> āśrayaviśeṣādetatsidhyati/ āśrayo hi sa aryāṇāṃ darśanabhāvanāmārgasāmarthyāttathā parāvṛto bhavati yathā na punastatpraheyāṇāṃ kleśānāṃ prarohasamartho bhavati/ ato 'gni dagdhavrīhivadabījībhūte āśraye kleśānāṃ prahīṇakleśa ityucyate/ upahatabījabhāve vā laukikena mārgeṇa viparyayādaprahīṇakleśaḥ/ yaścāprahīṇastena samanvāgato yaḥ prahīṇastenāsamanvāgata iti prajñapyate/ kuśalā api dharmā dviprakārā ayatnabhāvino yatnabhāvinaśca ye ta ucyante utpattipratilambhikaḥ prāyogikāś ceti/[8]

> That is accomplished because of the special property of the basis. As surely as the germinating capacity in connection with the defilements that are to be eliminated is no more, so truly the basis has vanished according to the noble tones, because of the capacity (engendered) by way of the path of cultivation and vision. Hence, when the basis does not form a seed like rice burnt over a fire, it is called, in relation to the defilements, one which has eliminated the defilements. But in the situation of a (merely) damaged seed, on the other hand, it is called one which has not eliminated the defilements (only) according to the worldly path, because of reversion. That in this way, the one which has eliminated defilement (*prahīṇakleśa*) is not attended (*asamanvāgata*) by this, that the one which has not eliminated defilement is attended by this, is designated. The good *dharmas* are of two types—possessed of effort, not possessed of effort; these are said to be those attained by birth, those attained by effort.

8. Ibid., *Abhidharmakośa* II. 36, p. 63.

In any case, it seems that for the Sautrāntikas, the path is useful towards the destruction of the defilements represented as seed, and hence towards the disappearance of the basis. Within this framework constructed by the Sautrāntikas, the path has a necessary transformative function.

Related to the above considerations is the question of the relationship of the Buddhist path to the unconstructed *dharmas*. It is questionable whether the unconstructed *dharmas* can be causes or effects. In particular, can the unconstructed *dharmas* be an effect of the path? For the Sarvāstivādins, according to the *Abhidharmakośa*, the unconstructed has neither cause nor effect because one cannot attribute to it any of the six causes (*hetu*) or any of the five effects (*phala*).

nāsaṃskṛtasya te//55//

kiṃ kāraṇaṃ/ ṣaḍvidhahetvasambhavāt pañcavidhaphalāsambhavācca/[9]

These (cause and effect) are not connected with the unconstructed.

What is the reason? The reason is the impossibility of the six types of causes and the five types of effects.

To the question why the unconstructed cannot have the efficient cause (*kāraṇa-hetu*) as cause, it is answered that the efficient cause is a cause in the sense of being non-obstacle to that which takes birth—but the unconstructed does not take birth.

kasmāt mārgo visaṃyogasya kāraṇaheturneṣyate/yasmāt sa utpādāvighnabhāvena vyavasthāpito na cāsaṃskṛtamutpattimat/[10]

Why is not the path considered to be the efficient cause (*kāraṇa-hetu*) of the disjunction? It is not so considered because it (the efficient cause) has been established through being a non-obstacle (*avighna*) to birth, and the unconstructed does not take birth.

Yet according to the *Abhidharmakośa*, the unconstructed is an effect in the sense that it is an effect of the path.

9. Ibid., *Abhidharmakośa* II. 55, p. 92.
10. Ibid., *Abhidharmakośa* II. 55, p. 91.

kasyedānīm tatphalam kathaṃ vā mārgasya phalam/tadbalena prāpteḥ/[11]

Now of what is that (disjunction) the effect? And how is that (disjunction) the effect? It (the disjunction) is the effect of the path, because of its reach by the strength of the path.

The *Abhidharmakośa* is careful to explain, however, the Sarvāstivāda position that it is not the disjunction (*visaṃyoga*) which is obtained, but the *dharma* of reach (*prāpti*).

anyathā hyasya prāptau sāmarthyamanyathā visaṃyoge/ kathamasya prāptau sāmarthyam/utpādanāt/katham visaṃyoge/ prāpaṇāt/ tasmānna tāvadasya mārgaḥ kathaṃcidapi hetuḥ/phalam cāsya visaṃyogaḥ/[12]

On the one hand, (the path) is efficacious in connection with the reach of that (the fruit of disjunction, the *visaṃyogaphala*), and on the other hand, it (the path) is efficacious in connection with the disjunction. How is it (the path) efficacious in connection with reach?

Bacause of the birth (of reach). How is the path efficacious in connection with the disjunction? Because of the attainment (of the effect of disjunction by way of the *prāpti*). Therefore, the path is certainly not the cause of that (the disjunction) in any way whatsoever but the disjunction (*visaṃyoga*) is the effect of that (the reach).

The unconstructed is a cause in the sense that the three unconstructed *dharmas* are efficient causes: they do not hinder the birth of other *dharmas*. Yet it has no effect since it is outside time.

athāsatyadhipatiphale kathamasaṃskṛtam kāraṇahetuḥ/utpattyanāvaraṇabhāvena kāraṇahetuḥ/ na cāsya phalamastyadhvavinirmuktasya phalapratigrahaṇadānāsamarthatvāt/[13]

Now since there is no effect by way of dominance, how is an unconstructed thing an efficient cause? It is an efficient cause through the situation of being a non-hindrance to arising.

---

11. Ibid., *Abhidharmakośa* II. 55, p. 92.
12. Ibid., *Abhidharmakośa* II. 55, p. 92.
13. Ibid., *Abhidharmakośa* II. 55, p. 91.

> Moreover, there is no effect for that which is freed from the times (*adhva*), because of the incapacity of giving or receiving an effect.

It is to be noted that Śaṅkara in his interpretation of the *sūtra* "*ubhayathā ca doṣāt*" (*Brahma-sūtra* II.2.23) attempts to refute the Sautrāntika notion of causeless destruction, or "*nirhetuka-vināśa*" for Śaṅkara, by arguing that if the two kinds of cessation occur without cause, then the Buddhist path is useless, and that if the two kinds of cessation are the result of perfect knowledge, then the doctrine of momentariness by which *dharmas* appear and disappear of themselves is abandoned. According to the Sautrāntika doctrine of causeless destruction (*ākasmika vināśa*), however, the destruction synonymous with momentariness is causeless because it is an absence and because only an entity can possess a cause. The Sautrāntikas also held, however, that the defilements are eliminated (*prahīṇa*) by the paths of cultivation (*bhāvanā*) and vision (*darśana*). The Sautrāntikas define the cessation-with-understanding to be the cessation of the traces and birth and birth already arisen (*utpannānuśaya-janmanirodha*). It is not clear, however, whether they regard the paths to be causes (*hetu*) of the cessation of the traces. It may also be observed that Rāmānuja in his interpretation of the *sūtra* "*udāsīnānām api caivam siddhiḥ*" (*Brahma-sūtra* II.2.26) attempts to refute the Buddhist concept of momentariness by arguing that if there were momentary destruction (*kṣaṇapradhvaṃsa*), there would be production from a non-existent (*asadutpatti*) and hence nothing whatsoever would be achieved by effort : in other words, the Buddhist path would be useless. For the Sarvāstivādins, however, although the cessation-with-understanding does not have the path as its cause, yet it is an effect of the path through the medium of the *dharma* of reach (*prāpti*). In this way, the path is declared to be meaningful by the Sarvāstivādins, for whom the reach of the disjunction which is the cessation-with-understanding is not to be attained by the indifferent. Likewise, the cessation-with-understanding for the Sautrāntikas represents the cessation of the traces and is not subject to destruction. Furthermore, the Sautrāntikas explain the continuation or elimination of the defilements by reference to the basis which vanishes when the defilements are eliminated through the paths of vision and cultivation.

b. Space (*ākāśa*)

The Buddhist teachings in connection with space (*ākāśa*) were often misconstrued by the Vedāntins. In his interpretation of the *sūtra* "*ākāśe cāviśeṣāt*" (*Brahma-sūtra* II.2.24), Śaṅkara attributes to the Buddhist realists the position that space is the mere absence of hindrance (*āvaraṇābhāvamātra*). According to the *Abhidharmakośa*, however, the Sautrāntikas define space as that having for its measure (*mātra*) the absence of the tangible (*spraṣṭavyābhāvamātramākāśam*), and the Sarvāstivādins defined it as that which has the nature of non-hindrance (*anāvaraṇasvabhāvamātramākāśam*). Furthermore, the "*abhāvamātra*" of the Sautrāntika definition refers to the fact that according to the Sautrāntikas, space is that which has the characteristics of being insubstantial and of having absence for its measure. It has been noted that for the Sautrāntikas, according to the *Abhidharmakośa*, the unconstructed *dharmas* are non-continuing entities (*adravya*). Space for the Sautrāntika is defined as that having for its measure (*mātra*) the absence of the tangible.

> kim tarhi/spraṣṭavyābhāvamātramākāśam/tadyathā hyandhakāre pratighātamavindanta ākāśamityāhuḥ/[14]

> How then? Space is that having for its measure the absence of the tangible. In such a manner as follows, not finding an obstacle (*pratighāta*) in the dark, they say that this (*tad*) is space.

The Sarvāstivādins distinguish between two kinds of space : as an unconstructed *dharma*, and the space-element (*ākāśadhātu*) which is included within the sense-base of the visible (*rūpāyatana*). Space as an unconstructed *dharma* has for its nature (*svabhāva*) non-hindrance (*anāvaraṇa*). The *Abhidharma* explains space (*ākāśa*) as that which has the nature of non-hindrance in which there is the movement of formations.

tatrākāśamanāvṛtiḥ//5//

---

14. Ibid., *Abhidharmakośa* II. 5, p. 3.

anāvaraṇasvabhāvamākāśaṃ yatra rūpasya gatiḥ[15]
There space is non-hindrance||5||

Space has the nature of non-hindrance in which there is the movement of formations.

In his interpretation of the *sūtra "ākāśe cāviśeṣāt"* (*Brahma-sūtra* II.2.23), Rāmānuja also mistakenly represents the Buddhist realists' conception of space as "mere absence." Madhva and his school, in their interpretations of this *sūtra*, attempt to demonstrate that whatever is existent is non-momentary and that space is an example of their thesis. The difficulty with this argument is that it is not clear whether the Buddhist would agree with Madhva and his school that space is existent (*sat*) in the same sense that a jar is existent. For both the Sautrāntikas and Sarvāstivādins space is an unconstructed *dharma* to be distinguished from constructed *dharmas*.

15. Ibid., *Abhidharmakośa* II. 55, p. 92.

D. VIJÑĀNAVĀDA AND THE LOGICIANS

1. Knowledge (*jñāna*) and the Knowable (*jñeya*)

There is a tendency to equate Vijñānavāda with an idealism that denies an object external to the mind. It should be noted that although Śaṅkara and Rāmānuja, in their interpretations of the *sūtra* "*nābhāva upalabdheḥ*," attribute to the Vijñānavādins the position that the knowable (*jñeya*) is not different from knowledge (*jñāna*), the Vijñānavādins do not deny that there is an object external to the mind. Jñānagarbha's commentary on the Maitreya chapter of the *Saṃdhinirmocanasūtra*, for instance, as discussed by Wayman in his article "Yogācāra and the Buddhist Logicians," gives the illustration of the stream of water seen differently by animals, hungry ghosts, human beings, and gods, but does not deny that there is an external object, albeit badly reported.[1] Furthermore, Dignāga in the *Ālambana-parīkṣā* speaks of atoms as the cause of sensory representation although they do not appear therein.

(1) Although atoms are the cause of the sensory representation, they do not appear therein, so its sense object (*viṣaya*) is not the atoms, like a sense organ (has objects).[2]

That the knowable (*jñeya*) is not different from knowledge (*jñāna*) is true for Dignāga only in the sense that the inner form of the knowable (*antar-jñeya-rūpa*) is the object-entity (*artha*).

yad antar-jñeya-rūpaṃ tu bahirvad avabhāsate so'rthaḥ[3]

6. The form of the inner knowable, which appears as though it were external, is the object.[4]

---

1. Wayman, Alex, "Yogācāra and the Buddhist Logicians," *The Journal of the International Association of Buddhist Studies*, Volume II, Number 1, 1979.

2. Wayman, Alex, "Yogācāra and the Buddhist Logicians," p. 60.

3. Hattori, Masaaki, *Dignāga on Perception*, translation of *Pratyakṣa-pariccheda* of Dignāga's *Pramāṇa-samuccaya* from the Sanskrit and Tibetan versions, Harvard Oriental Series, Volume 47, (Cambridge, Massachusetts: Harvard University Press, 1968), p. 102, footnote 1.61.

4. Wayman, Alex, "Yogācāra and the Buddhist Logicians," p. 69.

Wayman notes that Dignāga has a kind of nominalism here in that he distinguishes between atoms and the form of atoms. The former is the cause of sensory representation, not an aggregation of "form" of atoms.[5] Furthermore, in connection with the principle of simultaneous ascertainment (*sahopalambha-niyama*), there is the following verse of Dharmakīrti.

> Sahopalambha-niyamād abhedo nīla-tad-dhiyoḥ /
> Bhedaś ca bhrānti-vijñānair dṛśyetendau ivādvaye[6] //

Ingalls translates as follows :

> Blue and the cognition of blue are not different entities, for the one invariably occurs with the other. One should recognize their difference as due to the false cognition, like (the double moon seen by an astygmatic) in the moon, which is single.[7]

It is to be questioned, however, whether this verse of Dharmakīrti represents a denial of the external object, or merely a statement to the effect that perception (*pratyakṣa*) is in touch with absolute reality (*paramārtha-sat*), for there is doubt whether the term "*dhī*" refers to perception (*pratyakṣa*) or inference (*anumāna*).

2. The "Self" of the Vijñānavādins

The momentariness of the Yogācāra *vijñāna* is compared to the permanence of the Vedāntic *Ātman* by Vedāntins like Śaṅkara in his interpretation of the *sūtra* "*nābhāva upalabdheḥ*" (*Brahma-sūtra* II.2.28). Such a comparison, however, only raises the question whether or not the Vijñānavādins are suggesting a different expression for the "Self," an expression which emphasizes its dynamic, changing nature. This question has been discussed by Alex Wayman in his review of *The Yogācāra Idealism* where he notes the association of *karma* (action) and *citta* (thought, from the root *cit*-, to think) and the use of the

5. Ibid., p. 69.

6. Ingalls, Daniel H.H., "Śaṃkara's Arguments Against the Buddhists," *Philosophy East and West*, Volume III, No. 4, (January 1954), p. 300.

7. Ibid., p. 70.

expression *citta-saṃtati* (stream of thoughts) for the transmigrating entity. Alex Wayman is noting that for later Buddhism, the transmigratory self is conceived in terms of a stream of thoughts.

Later Buddhism used the expression *citta-saṃtāna* or "*citta-saṃtati*" (both : "stream of thoughts") for the transmigrating entity. Thus, the words "*karma*" and "*citta*" are doctrinally equivalent to indicate the transmigrating entity.[8]

3. The Dream and Waking States

According to the Vedāntins, the Vijñānavādins declare the waking state and the dream state to be similar in order to deny the external object. In his interpretation of the *sūtra* "*vaidharmyāc ca na svapnādivat,*" (*Brahma-sūtra* II.2.29), Śaṅkara attributes to the Vijñānavādins the position that the waking state and the dream state are alike and that therefore the external object is to be denied. Perception, at least of the mental sort (*manovijñāna*), however, is being compared in the *Viṃśatikā* to the dream-state in that both occur at some remove from their objects, not because as Śaṅkara claims, the *Viṃśatikā* is denying that there is an object external to the mind. The analogy of the dream is employed in the *Viṃśatikā* only to emphasize the temporal gap that exists between sensory perception and mental perception which is subsequent to the former as is remembrance. Furthermore, Rāmānuja in his interpretation of the same *sūtra*, attributes to the Vijñānavādins the position that since the waking-state and the dream-state are alike, all cognitions (*jñāna*) are void (*śūnya*). According to the *Viṃśatikā*, however, the idea (*buddhi*) of direct perception (*pratyakṣa*) is compared to a dream because there is the defining activity of the mental perception (*mano-vijñāna*) and the cessation (*niruddhatva*) of the eye-perception, so that consequently the object-entity is not seen.

Whether the Vijñānavādins, however, are postulating the similarity of the waking-state and the dream-state in order to deny the external object is a question to be examined. In stanza

8. Wayman, Alex, review of *The Yogācāra Idealism* by A.K. Chatterjee, *Philosophy East and West*, Volume XV, Number I, (January, 1965), p. 69.

15 of the *Viṃśatikā*, the question of the similarity of the waking-state and the dream-state arises.

> pratyakṣabuddhiḥ svapnādau yathā sa ca yadā tadā/
> na so 'rtho dṛśyate tasya pratyakṣatvaṃ kathaṃ matam//16//[9]

> The idea of direct perception (*pratyakṣa*) is as a dream, etc. When it (direct perception) is there, then the object-entity is not seen. How can it be thought that there is the direct perception of it?

The point here is that on account of momentariness, mental perception does not operate at the same time as sensory perception but a moment afterwards. It may then be questioned how there can be mental perception when sensory perception has vanished. In other words, does mental perception have the same object as sensory perception? Such reflection may have led Dignāga and the Buddhist logicians to declare the separation of the two authorities (*pramāṇa*)—perception (*pratyakṣa*) and inference (*anumāna*). The external object is not being denied here, but rather only the external object of which our representation is a faithful copy is being denied. What Vasubandhu is explaining in the *Viṃśatikā* reminds one of Dignāga's verse in the *Ālambana-parīkṣā* to the effect that the mind contributes the form of the object.

> yad antar-jñeya-rūpaṃ tu bahirvad avabhāsate so 'rthaḥ[10]

> 6. The form of the inner knowable, which appears as though it were external, is the object.[11]

It may be claimed that the difference between the dream-state and the waking-state can be compared to the difference between perception (*upalabdhi*) and remembrance (*smṛti*). According to the *Viṃśatikā*, perception itself involves the representation of an object, not presentation. Both mental perception and remembrance occur subsequent to the fading out of sensory perception.

---

9. Lévi, Sylvain, *Vijñaptimātratāsiddhi*, Bibliotheque de L'École des Hautes Études, 145th Fascicule, (Paris : Librairie Ancienne Honore Champion, 1925), *Viṃśatikā* 16, pp. 8-9.

10. Hattori, Masaaki, *Dignāga on Perception*, p. 102, footnote 1.61.

11. Wayman, Alex, "Yogācāra and the Buddhist Logicians," p. 60.

uktaṃ yathā tadābhāso vijñaptiḥ smaraṇaṃ tataḥ/[12]

It has been said that the representation (*vijñapti*) is an appearance of that; hence, (there is) memory.

Perception, at least of the mental sort, is being compared in the *Viṃśatikā* to the dream-state in that both occur at some remove from their objects, not because the *Viṃśatikā* is denying that there is an object external to the mind. The analogy of the dream is employed in the *Viṃśatikā* only to emphasize the temporal gap that exists between sensory perception and mental perception which is subsequent to the former no less than remembrance. Although the waking-state and the dream-state are being compared, however they are not considered as equivalent.

4. Habit-Energies (*vāsanā*)

Śaṅkara in his interpretation of the *sūtra* "*na bhāvo'nupalabdheḥ*" (*Brahma-sūtra* II.2.30) attributes to the Vijñānavādins the position that knowledge can be explained on the basis of habit-energies, without any reference to external object-entities. His attribution, however, may be based on mistaken notions of the habit-energies and ideation-store held by the Early Vijñānavādins.

The concept of habit-energy (*vāsanā*) is closely allied with the concept of the ideation-store (*ālaya-vijñāna*) which is not necessarily hospitable to idealism. According to de La Vallée Poussin, both the fact that images develop within the *ālaya-vijñāna* which are archetypes and which are ulterior objects of sense-perception, and the fact that one can explain the difference between the perception of a single moon and the perception of a double moon, are hardly compatible with idealism.[13] Furthermore, it is to be observed that the notions of the ideation-store and habit-energy are primarily associated with the notions of action (*karma*) and effect (*phala*). The *ālaya-vijñāna* is even defined in the *Mahāyāna-*

12. Lévi, Sylvain, *Vijñaptimātratāsiddhi*, *Viṃśatikā* 17, p. 9.

13. Poussin, Louis de La Vallée, "Note sur *L'Ālayavijñāna*," introduction to the translation of *Mahāyāna-saṃgraha* by Etienne Lamotte. Volume III, 1934-1935, *Melanges Chinoises et Bouddhiques*, (Brussels : l'Institut Belge des Hautes Etudes Chinoises), p. 163.

saṃgraha of Asaṅga, as translated by Étienne Lamotte, in terms of the doctrine of retribution (*vipāka*). The ideation-store is the perception of the ripened karma of all the "seeds."

> En somme (*samāsatas*), la nature propre (*svabhāva*) de la connaissance-receptacle est d'être une connaissance de retribution munie de tous les germes (*sarvabījakavipāka-vijñāna*). Elle saisit (*saṃgṛhṇāti*) toutes les existences (tse t'i = *ātmabhāva*; tib lus) du triple monde (*traidhātuka*) et toutes les destinées (*gati*).[14]

The concept *vāsanā*, propensity or habit-energy, is also very much concerned with action (*karma*) and retribution (*vipāka*). Its purport is not to deny the external object, but to explicate the law of *karma* and *vipāka*. The definition of *vāsanā* given in the *Mahāyāna-saṃgraha* reminds one of de La Vallée Poussin's summation that the *ālaya-vijñāna* seems to resemble a quasi-substance which renders it incompatible with an idealism that denies the external object. According to the *Mahāyāna-saṃgraha*, *vāsanā* (translated by Wayman as habit-energy and by de La Vallée Poussin as "impregnation") represents the generative cause of things by virtue of their simultaneous birth and destruction.

> Qu'est ce que l'impregnation (*vāsanā*) ? Quelle est la chose designée (*abhidheya*) par cette expression (*abhidhāna*) ?
> Ce qui, en vertu (i, 9 et 6 = brten nas = *niśritya*, *pratītya*) de naissance et destruction simultanées (*sahotpādanirodha*) aux choses (*dharma*), forme la cause génératrice (*janmahetu*) de ces memes choses : voilà ce qu'on entend par imprégnation.[15]

The generative cause (*janmahetu*) which is the habit-energy or "impregnation" (*vāsanā*) is explained through examples. It is compared to the succession of originating and disappearing sesame seeds which carry on the fragrance of the flower.

> Ainsi, dans les grains de sésame (*tila*) où il y a le parfum d'une fleur (*puṣpabhāvanā*), les grains naissent et perissent en même

14. Lamotte, Étienne, "*L'Ālayavijñāna* (Le Receptacle) dans le *Mahāyāna-saṃgraha*." *Melanges Chinoises et Bouddhiques*. (Brussels : l' Institut Belge des Hautes Études Chinoises). Volume III, 1934-1935, p. 226.

15. Ibid., p. 226.

> temps que la fleur, et les grains naissent (*utpadyante*) comme étant la cause (*hetulakṣaṇa*) qui reproduit l'odeur (*gandha*) de la fleur.[16]

The "impregnation" or habit-energy of desire originates and disappears simultaneously with the desire, and the idea is that which gives birth to desire.

> Ainsi encore, chez ceux qui se livrent aux désirs mauvais (*rāgādicarita*), l'imprégnation du désir, etc. (*rāgādivāsanā*), nâit et périt en meme temps que le désir, etc. et leur pensée (*citta*) nâit comme étant la cause qui engendre ce (désir).[17]

The "impregnation" or habit-energy of hearing the instruction originates and disappears simultaneously with reflection upon the teaching, and the thought (*citta*), which is the cause of hearing the instruction at a later time, is born. One who is possessed by this habit-energy or "impregnation" is called "possessor of the law."

> Ainsi enfin, chez les savants (*bahuśruta*), l'imprégnation d'enseignement (*bahuśrutavāsanā*) nâit et périt en même temps de l'acte de reflexion sur l'enseignement (*śrutamanasikāra*), et leur pensée nâit comme étant la cause de la production de l'enseignement. L'homme qui est saisi (*parigṛhīta*) par cette impregnation (d'enseignement) est appelé un "saisisseur de la loi" (*dharmagrāhaka*). On appliquera le meme raisonnement a la connaissance-réceptacle.[18]

In the Chinese versions of the *Mahāyāna-saṃgraha* the "impregnation" or habit-energy is described in terms of the perfumed (*vāsya*) and the perfuming agent (*vāsaka*). The *vāsanā* is the perfumed which originates and disappears simultaneously with the perfuming agent (*vāsaka*), and its perfume (*bhāvanā*) is that which gives birth to an effect (*phaladharma*) capable of acting as a perfuming agent in its turn.

> "Ce qui, en vertu (litt. *niśritya*) de naissance et destruction

16. Ibid., p. 226.
17. Ibid., p. 226.
18. Ibid., p. 226.

> simultanées aux choses, forme la cause de la naissance de ces mêmes choses" : ce parfumé-ci (*vāsya*) nâit et périt en mëme temps que parfumant-la (*vāsaka*). A cause de ce (parfumant)-là ce (parfumé)-ci possede, en conformité (avec le parfumant), un parfum (*bhāvanā*) capable d'engendrer un fruit (*phala-dharma*) d'un genre special qui, (à son tour), est capable de parfumer.[19]

It can be seen, therefore, that the notions of ideation-store (*ālaya-vijñāna*) and habit-energy of "impregnation" (*vāsanā*) are not intended by the Vijñanavādins to replace the external object. Rather, these notions are intended by the Vijñānavādins to explicate the processes of action and retribution.

5. The Ideation-Store (*ālaya-vijñāna*)

The Vijñānavāda notion of the ideation-store (*ālaya-vijñāna*) which is associated with the "imagination of unreality" (*abhūta-parikalpa*) was misinterpreted by the Vedāntins. It is to be noted that Śaṅkara in his interpretation of the *sūtra* "*kṣaṇikatvācca*" (*Brahma-sūtra* II.2.31) attempts to refute the Vijñānavāda notion of the ideation-store by arguing that if the ideation-store is momentary then it is subject to the arguments he has earlier brought forth against momentariness, and if it is permanent (*sthira*) there is abandonment of the principle of momentariness. It is to be observed, however, that the coexistence of the two, the principle of voidness (*śūnyatā*) and the principle of "the imagination of unreality" (*abhūtaparikalpa*) as revealed in the *Madhyānta-vibhaṅga*, attests that for the Vijñānavādins the principles of the eternal absolute and the changing phenomenal were not mutually exclusive. Wayman has noted in his review article on Chatterjee's *The Yogācāra Idealism*, however, that in the *Viṃśatikā*, Vasubandhu stresses ideation-only (*vijñapti-mātra*) because he is discussing the "imagination of unreality" (*abhūta-parikalpa*) of the *Madhyānta-vibhaṅga*.

> Of course, there is good reason for thinking, "The Yogacāra holds that consciousness is the sole reality." This is an interpretation of Vasubandhu's intent in his two little treatises—

19. Ibid., p. 227.

> Twenty Stanzas (On Ideation Only) and Thirty Stanzas (On Ideation Only). In the former work, Vasubandhu stresses ideation-only (*vijñaptimātra*) because he is setting forth the process of world illusion created by the *Madhyānta-vibhaṅga's* "imagination of unreality."[20]

According to Wayman, the Buddhist Yogācāra text called the *Madhyānta-vibhaṅga* sets up a rival system to the Sāṅkhya by replacing *puruṣa* with the *abhūtaparikalpa* (imagination of unreality) and *prakṛti* with *śūnyatā* (voidness). Wayman also explains that Vijñānavāda, particularly in the *Madhyānta-vibhaṅga,* conceives reality in terms of a dualistic cosmology which rivals that of Sāṅkhya.

> The Buddhist Yogācāra text called *Madhyānta-vibhaṅga* sets up a rival theory to that of the Sāṅkhya for showing the evolution and resolution of the worlds, but in common with other Indian schools has the influential Sāṅkhya system before it as a guide. Thus, the Buddhist text replaces the Sāṅkhya *puruṣa* with the "imagination of unreality" (*abhūtaparikalpa*) and replaces *prakṛti* with voidness (*śūnyatā*). In this Buddhist system, both the "imagination of unreality" and "voidness" are real, co-exist, and are yet distinct.[21]

According to Wayman, the "imagination of unreality" (*abhūtaparikalpa*) represents the material cause. The dynamic aspect of reality is embodied in the "imagination of unreality" which "covers" the pure *dharmadhātu* with transient *dharmas.* The "imagination of unreality" represents the covering process; thus it possesses *saṃvṛtisatya.*

> The reality of the "imagination of unreality" is *saṃvṛtisatya,* literally : the actual fact of the covering process. Thus, the "imagination of unreality" covers the pure *dharmadhātu* with transient *dharmas* (*saṃskṛta-dharmas*), which arise and pass away with "dependency characteristic" (*paratantra-lakṣaṇa*), while it covers itself with corruptions (*kleśa*) having the "imaginary characteristic" (*parikalpitalakṣaṇa*).[22]

---

20. Wayman, Alex, review of *The Yogācāra Idealism,* p. 68.
21. Ibid., p. 66.
22. Ibid., p. 70.

6. Separation of Authorities (*pramāṇa-vyavasthā*)

The Logicians' position that the two authorities of perception and inference are separate seems to have been misconstrued by the Vedāntins. It is to be noted that Madhva and his school, in their interpretations of the *sūtra* "*anusmṛteśca*" (*Brahma-sūtra* II.2.25), attempt to refute the Buddhist's supposed assertion that recognition insofar as it affirms the oneness of things, as in the case of the flames of the burning lamp, is to be branded as illusory. Madhva argues that even the perception of differences (*viśeṣadarśana*) in the burning lamp is to be regarded as illusory. Dignāga, however, has defined perception to be free of conceptualization (*pratyakṣam kalpanāpoḍham*); in consequence, judgements concerning the oneness or non-oneness of the fire properly belong to the realm of inference (*anumāna*) in Dignāga's system. Jayatīrtha of Madhva's school, in his interpretation of this *sūtra* in the *Nyāya-sudhā*, argues that it is the nature of perception only to reveal a given thing as existing in the present, not in the past or future, and that thus there can be no objection to the notion of a stable (*sthāyin*) object-entity. For Dignāga, however, the attribution of existence to a thing that will be or that has been or that is "before the eyes" (*pratyakṣa*) would represent a process of inference (*anumāna*), not perception (*pratyakṣa*). Furthermore, Madhva, in his interpretation of the *sūtra* "*kṣaṇikatvācca*" (*Brahma-sūtra* II.2.31) attempts to refute the supposed Buddhist identification of the momentary cognition (*jñāna*) and the stable (*sthāyin*) object-entity. Such an attribution, however, ignores the fact that Dignāga had distinguished between the inherent character (*svalakṣaṇa*) and the generalizing character (*sāmānya-lakṣaṇa*).

In connection with the object-entity, it must be recalled that it has been defined by Dignāga as the inner form of the knowable (*antar-jñeya-rūpa*) as distinguished from atoms (*aṇu*) which are the cause of sensory representation (*viṣaya*) and do not appear therein. According to Dignāga, as reported by the *Nyāya-vārttika-tātparyaṭīkā*, the inherent character (*svalakṣaṇa*) is concerned with absolute reality.

svalakṣaṇaṃ hi pratyakṣa-gocaraḥ, tadeva paramārthasat[23]

23. Tripathi, Chhote Lal, *The Problem of Knowledge in Yogācāra Bud-*

For this inherent character is within the range of perception; that is absolute reality (*paramārthasat*).

In contrast, Dignāga relates the contradictions pertaining to the notion of the generalizing character (*sāmānya-lakṣaṇa*) in the *Pramāṇa-samuccaya.*

anyatra vartamānasya tato 'nyasthānajanmani.
Tasmād acalaḥ sthānād vṛttirityatiyuktatā.
Yatrāsau vartate bhāvas tena sambadhyate na tu.
Taddeśinaṃ ca vyāpnoti kimapyetan mahādbhutam.[24]

When there is birth in one place of a thing existing in another place, therefore there is procession from a place in reference to an unmoving (*acala*) thing. Where it exists an entity is not bound by it. It pervades the place of it. Is not this wonderful?

7. Memory (*smṛti*)

Whereas the phenomena of memory (*smṛti*) and remembrance (*anusmṛti*) are adduced by Śaṅkara in his interpretation of the *sūtra* "*anusmṛteśca*" (*Brahma-sūtra* II.2.25) to be evidence of the perceiving subject (*upalabdhṛ*), they are for Dignāga and the Buddhist logicians evidence only for the existence of introspection (*svasaṃvedana*) and self-intuition (*sva-saṃvitti*). The reason is that memory (*smṛti*) is never of something which has not been experienced before (*avibhāvita*).

Hc-1. (That cognition has two forms follows)[25]
smṛter uttarakālaṃ ca[26]
k.11c. "later also from (the fact of) recollection" (in k. 11c) refers back to "cognition has two forms" (in k. 11ab). Some time after (we have perceived a certain object), there occurs (to our mind) the recollection of our cognition as well as the recollection of the object. So it stands that cognition is of two forms. Self-cognition is also (thus) established. Why ?[27]

---

dhism, (Varanasi : Bharat-Bharati, 1972), (*Nyāya-vārttika-tātparya-ṭīkā*, p. 12, lines 17-19), p. 158, footnote 8.

24. Ibid., (*pramāṇa-samuccaya*, chapter 5), p. 273, footnote 149.

25. Hattori, Masaaki, *Dignāga on Perception* (quoted from *Tattva saṃgraha* 2011), p. 101, footnote 1.60

26. Ibid., p. 30.

27. Ibid., p. 30.

na hy asau avibhāvite[28]
k. 11d. because it (viz. recollection) is never of that which has not been previously experienced. It is unheard of to have a recollection of something without having experienced (it before). For instance, the recollection of a thing of color, etc. (does not arise unless the thing of color or the like has been experienced.)[29]

8. The Three Factors

That the Buddhist concept of self-intuition (*svasaṃvitti*) is related to the non-separation of the three factors—the subject (*grāhaka*), the object (*grāhya*), and self-intuition (*sva-saṃvitti*)—was misinterpreted by the Vedāntins. In his interpretation of the *sūtra* "*nābhāva upalabdheḥ*" (*Brahma-sūtra* II.2.28), Śaṅkara attempts to refute the Buddhist notion of self-intuition by characterizing it as the notion that the perception experiences itself (*svayam anubhūyate*). Moreover, Jayatīrtha of Madhva's school, in his interpretation of the *sūtra* "*na bhāvo 'nupalabdheḥ*" (*Brahma-sūtra* II.2.30) in the *Tattvaprakāśikā*, argues that knowledge (*jñāna*) does not "shine forth" (*prakāśate*) in that knowledge cannot be an object to itself. But Jayatīrtha's and Śaṅkara's arguments falsely assume the separation of object, subject, and self-intuition.

According to Dignāga in the *Pramāṇa-samuccaya*, only when the subject, the object, and self-intuition are seen as separate, the notion of self-intuition of perception becomes inconceivable. In the *Pramāṇa-samuccaya*, it is specifically stated that the three factors are not separate from one another.

yad-ābhāsaṃ prameyaṃ tat pramāṇa-phalate punaḥ /
grāhakākāra-saṃvittitrayaṃ nātaḥ pṛthakkṛtam[30] //

Whatever is the appearance, that is the sanctionable; the authority and authority-as-result are the form of the apprehender and the intuition; the three are not separate.

---

28. Ibid., (from *Pramāṇa-vārttika-bhāṣya* 425.20, 426.18), p. 110, footnote 1.75.

29. Ibid., p. 30.

30. Hattori, Masaaki, *Dignāga on Perception*, (quoted from *Nyāya-mañjarī* of Jayanta Bhaṭṭa), p. 107, footnote 1.67.

Dharmakīrti also treats of the distinction between authority (*pramāṇa*), the sanctionable (*prameya*), and authority-as-result (*pramāṇa-phala*), and sets forth the mistaken three-fold division of the indivisible *vijñāna* in the following verse of the *Pramāṇa-vārttika*.

avibhāgo 'pi buddhy-ātmā viparyāsita-darśanaiḥ /
grāhya-grāhaka-saṃvitti-bhedavān iva lakṣyate[31] //

The nature of intelligence (which is) distinct, appears to those of distorted vision (*viparyāsita-darśana*) as though possessed of the difference of intuition, apprehender, and apprehended.

It is evident, therefore, that according to Dignāga and Dharmakīrti the three-fold division of perception into subject, object, and self-intuition is mistaken and that they are in reality not separate.

9. Causality of the *Saṃskāras*

There is another question to be reviewed in this study of the Vijñānavādins: their position on the causality of *saṃskāras*. Both Śaṅkara and Rāmānuja, in their interpretations of the *sūtra* "*uttarotpāde ca pūrvanirodhāt*," for instance, attribute to the Vijñānavādins the position that the existence of the antecedent moment constitutes the causality of the antecedent moment. Such a position is not found in the texts of the Vijñānavādins. According to the *Paramārtha-gāthā* and commentary, it is the origin (*bhūti*) of momentary things that is their activity, and that origin is looked upon as agent or doer (*kāraka*) or as the activity (*kriyā*) depending on one's standpoint. That is to say, from the standpoint of cause, it is doer, from the standpoint of effect it is activity. The question motivating the articulation of this position is, How is one to explain the activity of momentary things which lack the requisite stability for activity? The verse from the *Paramārtha-gāthā* proceeds as follows, as edited and translated by Alex Wayman.

5. kṣaṇikāḥ sarvasaṃskārā (MS: sarvasaṃskārāḥ) asthitānāṃ kutaḥ kriyā/
bhūtir yeṣāṃ kriyāsau ca kārakaḥ saiva cocyate//

31. Ibid., p. 107, footnote 1.67.

All the *saṃskāras* are momentary; whence the activity of unstable things?
Their origin is that activity, and that (origin) is called the doer.[32]

According to Asaṅga in his auto-commentary to this verse, the origin of momentary *saṃskāras* is their activity and that origin is looked upon as doer if examined from the standpoint of cause (*hetu*), and as activity if examined from the standpoint of effect (*kārya*).

dharmāḥ sarve 'pi niśceṣṭā ity uktaṃ/ na tūktaṃ katham niśceṣṭā (MS: nityeṣṭā) iti/ ata āha/ kṣaṇikāḥ sarvasaṃskārā (MS: sarva-saṃskārāḥ) asthitānāṃ kutaḥ kriyeti/ atha ced vartate kriyety uktam/ tat katham asatyāṃ kriyāyāṃ kriyā vartate iti āha/ bhūtir yeṣāṃ kriyāsau ca kārakas saiva cocyate/ phalatvāt kriyā hetutvāt kārakaḥ/ tam punar bhūtir yāyatanebhyo vijñānotpattyā sūcayati/ tadutpattyā ca/ cakṣurādīnāṃ nāntareṇa tatsiddheḥ/[33]

It was stated, "Although all the *dharmas* are inactive," but it was not stated how they are inactive. Hence he says (5a-b): "All the *saṃskāras* are momentary; whence the activity of unstable things?" It was stated, "yet activity evolves." Then, in the light that activity is unreal, how does activity evolve? He says (5c-d): "Their origin is that activity, and that (origin) is called the doer." From the standpoint of effect, it is activity; from the standpoint of cause, it is the doer. Further more, that origin he indicates by the production of perception (*vijñāna*) at the sense bases (*āyatana*) and by the production of that through accomplishing it in a manner not apart from the eye, and so on.[34]

It is to be observed here that according to Asaṅga perception only requires a sense-base, and that the sense-object is not needed. As though mindful of the argument of Śāntarakṣita and Kamala-

32. Wayman, Alex, *Analysis of the Śrāvakabhūmi Manuscript*, University of California Publications in Classical Philology, Volume 17, (Berkeley : University of California Press, 1961), *Paramārthagāthā* 5, p. 168.

33. Ibid., *Paramārthagāthā*, p. 175.

34. Ibid., p. 180.

śīla that a cause possesses no activity apart from its being, Śaṅkara argues in his interpretation of the *sūtra "uttarotpāde ca pūrva-nirodhāt"* (*Brahma-sūtra* II.2.20) that if the existence (*bhāva*) of the cause should be its activity (*vyāpāra*), then the effect would be imbued with the nature (*svabhāva*) of the cause. Consequently, Śaṅkara argues, the cause lasts for more than one moment and the principle of momentariness is abandoned. Śaṅkara does not take into account, however, Asaṅga's position that it is the origin which is the activity of *saṃskāras*. Cause and effect are standpoints for Asaṅga. It is also to be noted that Jayatīrtha of Madhva's school, in his interpretation of the *sūtra "pratisaṃkhyā 'pratisaṃkhyā-nirodhaprāptir avicchedāt"* (*Brahma-sūtra* II.2.22) in the *Tattva-prakāśikā*, in connection with the destruction-without-series (*nissaṃtānanāśa*), argues that as the cause must be there at the time of the origination of the effect, and as the same moment will be the cessation of the effect, the cause as existing at the moment of the cessation of the effect would be producing another effect, and so on endlessly. Jayatīrtha ignores the fact that for Asaṅga, the question does not arise whether the doer would consume its activity or exert further activity to produce an effect, for the origin is the activity and the activity is the doer. Cause and effect, again, are only standpoints from which the origin is to be considered.

10. Introspective Perception (*svasaṃvedana-pratyakṣa*)

The issues involved in the concept of introspective perception (*svasaṃvedana-pratyakṣa*) were often misinterpreted by the Vedāntins. These issues were discussed by Alex Wayman in his discussion of the *sākāra-nirākāra* controversy in the article "Reflections on the Study of Buddhist Logic." He discusses Tsoṅ-kha-pa's "Guided Tour," where the term *ākāra* is used in the context of an explanation of the introspective type of perception (*svasaṃvedana-pratyakṣa*). He explains that in the "Guided Tour," among the ways of taking something as an object (*viṣaya*), there is the *pratibhāsa-viṣaya* (object recognized by its appearance), which is then accepted as an object to be grasped (*grāhya-viṣaya*) of two kinds—the extroverted type of perception (*parasaṃvedana-pratyakṣa*), and the introverted type of perception (*svasaṃvedana-pratyakṣa*). Wayman translates a passage of the "Guided

Tour" which discusses the imagery (*ākāra*) as a resemblance of the feature (*dharma*) when the external entity is fastened upon as a given thing.

> When one fastens upon the external entity as a given thing, there is the imagery (*ākāra*) resembling a feature (*dharma*); for example, when one resorts to the organ of mind, there are the five, form, etc.[35]

According to Tsoṅ-kha-pa, the resemblance involved in imagery relates to a feature. Rāmānuja in his interpretation of the *sūtra* "*nāsato 'dṛṣṭatvāt*" (*Brahma-sūtra* II.2.25) attributes to the Sautrāntikas the position that the imagery (*ākāra*) of an object-entity is imparted to the cognition, and rejects their supposed position by arguing that the attributes (*dharma*) of a factual base (*dharmin*) cannot be transferred to another object-entity. There is no question, however, of the "passing over" (*kramaṇa*) of the features of the object-entity which is the factual base, because it is introspective perception which grasps the imagery as a reflection of an external feature without discursive thought. In the "Guided Tour," according to Wayman, there is given a description of the introspective type of perception in terms of imagery, examples of which are the blue (visual) and the mental phrase "Sound is impermanent."

> The characteristic of the introspective direct perception is the imagery which grasps (*grahaṇa*) only on the inner side of the mind.[36]

Wayman has explained that the *nirākāra-sākāra* controversy was basically an argument between the followers of the "store-consciousness" (*ālayavijñāna*) theory on the one hand, and the espousers (i.e. Dignāga, Dharmakīrti) of the "introspective perception" on the other hand. It seems that the *ākāra* involves a reflection of an external feature.

> Thus the theory of introspection's grasping the *ākāra* (imagery) as a reflection of an external feature (*dharma*) and as a *prat-*

35. Wayman, Alex, "Reflections on the Study of Buddhist Logic," *Indologica Taurinensia*, Turin, Volume V, (1977), p. 303.
36. Ibid.

yakṣa doing so without discursive thought (*kalpanā*) and without delusion (*bhrānti*)—so the Buddhist logicians claimed—implies that such grasping and experiencing is always new and for the first time. Asaṅga and his Yogācāra followers deny such an *ākāra* along with the introspection said to grasp it, because they believe the grasping and experiencing is not new, rather it is by dint of the old seeds of the "store consciousness" (*ālayavijñāna*), and it is not without delusion.[37]

37. Ibid., p. 304.

E. THE MĀDHYAMIKAS

The "middle view" of the Mādhyamikas (adherents of the middle view) was misconstrued by Śaṅkara, Rāmānuja, and Madhva as nihilism (Śūnyavāda in a derogatory sense); their doctrines were dismissed by Rāmānuja, for instance, as "*tuccha-tva*" (emptiness). That the Mādhyamikas did not adopt the position of nihilism is amply affirmed by their texts. The term "Mādhyamika" itself indicates that the followers of this school were adherents of the middle view, which avoids the extremes of existence and non-existence. In the introduction to his book, *Calming the Mind and Discerning the Real*, Wayman discusses Tsoṅ-kha-pa's criticism of the realist (*vastu-sat-padārtha-vādin*) for over-pervasion (*ati-vyāpti*) by reason of adherence to the extremes of existence and non-existence. Wayman notes that the realist opponents of the Mādhyamikas—the Sarvāstivādins, for instance—criticized such Mādhyamika statements as "The natures (*dharma*) arise void of self-existence (*svabhāva*)"[1] as nihilism. That the Mādhyamikas are guilty of nihilism is denied by no less a figure than Candrakīrti, whose denial has been cited by Tsoṅ-kha-pa and translated by Alex Wayman. First there is Nāgārjuna's statement in the *Yuktiṣaṣṭikā* which is to be commented upon by Candrakīrti.

> What arises in dependence is not born; That is proclaimed by the supreme knower of reality.[2]

Candrakīrti comments as follows :

> The realist opponent says : If (as you say) whatever thing arises in dependence is not even born, then why does (the Mādhyamika) say it is not born ? But if (you Mādhyamika) have a reason for saying (this thing) is not born, then you should not say "arises in dependence." Therefore, because of

1. Wayman, Alex, *Calming the Mind and Discerning the Real*, (A translation in part of Tsoṅ-kha-pa's Lam rim chen mo), (New York : Columbia University Press, 1979), p. 66.

2. Ibid., p. 66.

mutual inconsistency, (what you have said) is not valid. (The Mādhyamika replies with compassionate interjection:)

> Alas ! Because you are without ears or heart you have thrown a challenge that is severe on us ! When we say that anything arising in dependence, in the manner of a reflected image, does not arise by reason of self-existence—at that time where is the possibility of disputing (us) ! [3]

Wayman explains this passage as follows :

> So when in this Mādhyamika literature one frequently finds such statements as "The natures (*dharma*) arise void of self-existence (*svabhāva*)," the opponents declare this to be a nihilistic position (thus willing to attribute a "position" or "view" to the Mādhyamika), asserting that the Mādhyamika denies self-existence (*svabhāva*) or denies the natures (*dharma*).[4]

The nihilistic position for the Mādhyamikas represents an extreme that results from the assumption that entities either possess or do not possess self-existence (*svabhāva*) and from neglect of the middle view expressed in the saying "What arises in dependence is not born." According to Wayman, the fault of the realists (including both the eternalists and nihilists) is clearly stated by Nāgārjuna in his *Madhyamaka-kārikā* (XXIV.16).

> svabhāvādyadi bhāvānāṃ sadbhāvamanupaśyasi/ ahetupratyayān bhāvāṃstvamevaṃ sati paśyasi/
>
> If you look upon the occurrence of entities as being from self-existence, then you regard the entities as without causes or conditions.[5]

The over-pervasion (*ati-vyāpti*) of the realists is explained by Wayman as follows :

> Otherwise stated : the realist has not distinguished the mean (i.e., the shoot without self-existence, that has arisen from causes and conditions) from an extreme (i.e., absence of the shoot, or presence of the shoot by own-nature). Therefore, the

3. Ibid., p. 66.
4. Ibid., p. 66.
5. Ibid., p. 62.

realist over-pervades with a reason of "presence" (*bhāva*) or "absence" (*abhāva*).[6]

The appeal to authority (*pramāṇa*) on the part of Buddhist schools and non-Buddhist schools as proof of the empirical world (*sarvapramāṇasiddha lokavyavahāra*) is undermined by Nāgārjuna's rejection of direct sense-perception as set forth in the *Mūlamadhyamakakārikā* (III.2).

svamātmānaṃ darśanaṃ hi tattameva na paśyati/
na paśyati yadātmānaṃ kathaṃ drakṣyati tatparān//[7]

Vision does not see itself as itself. Now, if it does not see what is itself, how will it see what is another?[8]

Furthermore, despite Śaṅkara's assertion to the contrary in his interpretation of the *sūtra* "*kṣaṇikatvāc ca*" (*Brahma-sūtra* II.2.31), it need not be elaborated that the Mādhyamikas had discovered "another truth" (*anyatattva*), as evident in Nāgārjuna's definition of "*tattva*" in the *Mūlamadhyamakakārikā* (XVIII.9).

aparapratyayaṃ śāntaṃ prapañcairaprapañcitaṃ/
nirvikalpam ananarthametattattvasya lakṣaṇam//[9]

Not having another for a condition, quiescent (*śānta*), not manifested (*prapañcita*) by manifestations (*prapañca*), free from differences (*nirvikalpa*), not meaningless (*ananartha*)—these are the characteristics of reality (*tattva*).

6. Ibid., p. 62.

7. Inada, Kenneth, *Nāgārjuna*, (Tokyo : Hokuseido Press, 1970) *Mūlamadhyamakakārika* III. 2, p. 31.

8. Wayman, Alex, *Calming the Mind and Discerning the Real*, p. 62.

9. Inada, Kenneth, *Nāgārjuna, Mūlamadhyamakakārikā* XVIII. 9, p. 115.

F. THE LATER LOGICIANS

In this section, the critical positions taken by Śāntarakṣita in the *Tattva-saṃgraha*, by Kamalaśīla in the *Tattva-saṃgraha-pañjikā*, and by Ratnakīrti in the *Kṣaṇa-bhaṅga-siddhi* towards the doctrines of the atom, causation, and momentariness will be discussed. According to Das Gupta, the work of Śāntarakṣita with Kamalaśīla's *Pañjikā* in the eighth century A.D. was a remarkable instance of the adoption by Buddhist writers of critical and dialectical ways of discussion.

It has also been pointed out that not only Nāgārjuna and Candrakīrti, but many other Buddhist writers, had taken to critical and dialectical ways of discussion. The criticism of the different schools of Indian thought, as contained in Śāntarakṣita's *Tattva-saṃgraha* with Kamalaśīla's commentary *Pañjikā*, is a remarkable instance of this. Śāntarakṣita lived in the first half of the eighth century A.D., and Kamalaśīla was probably his junior contemporary.[1]

(a) The Atom (*aṇu*)

Śāntarakṣita and Kamalaśīla were critical of the notions of whole (*avayavin*) and part (*avayava*) and of the atom (*aṇu*). It is argued by Vedāntins such as Madhva in his interpretation of the *sūtra* "*itaretarapratyayatvād iti cen notpattimātra-nimittatvāt*" (*Brahma-sūtra* II.2.19) that there must be an admission on the part of the Buddhists of "real organized wholes over and above the fleeting atoms of which they are supposed to be constituted."[2] In the case of later Buddhists such as Śāntarakṣita and Kamalaśīla, however, not only is there a denial of the notion of the whole (*avayavin*) but also of the notion of the part (*avayava*). According to Śāntarakṣita and Kamalaśīla, even atoms are looked upon as merely assumed (*kalpita*) by the world, comparable to a poor man's being addressed as "Lord."

1. Dasgupta, Surendranath, *History of Indian Philosophy*, Volume I, p. 171.

2. Sharma, B.N.K., *The Brahmasūtras and Their Principal Commentaries*, Volume II, (Bombay : Bharatiya Vidya Bhavan, 1974), p. 52.

avijñātārthatattvastu piṇḍamekaṃ ca manyate/
lokastatkalpitāpekṣaḥ paramāṇurihocyate//603//
tatkalpitāpekṣa iti/ tasminkalpite sūtre apekṣā yasyeti vigrahaḥ//603//parihārāntaramāha—nimittetyādi/[3]

One not having understood the real nature of things thinks that there is one mass.
Dependent on that which is assumed by the world, the atom is here said to be.
The statement,
"Dependent on that which is assumed, etc." is in reference to that thread (*sūtra*) which is assumed—such is the analysis.
Another refutation is given : The efficient cause, etc.

nimittanirapekṣā vā saṃjñeyaṃ, tādṛśi sthitā/
saṅketānvayinī yadvannirvitte 'pīśvaraśrutiḥ//(604)
tādṛśīti/anaṃśe 'pratighe/yathā daridre'pīśvaraśrutiḥ saṅketavaśādaiśvaryākhyaṃ nimittamantareṇaiva pravartate, tadvadīyamapyaṇuśrutirityadoṣaḥ//604//[4]

In reference to the nameable (*saṃjñeya*) there is non-dependence (*nirapekṣā*) upon an efficient cause situated in such a one.
That non-dependence is associated with convention, just as the appellation "Lord" is heard in the case of one destitute.
In such a one, that is to say, the impartite the impenetrable just as in reference to the designation of a poor man as "Lord," the name "Lord" from the strength of convention is applied without an efficient cause, so in reference to the designation of this atom there is no fault.

Then Śāntarakṣita and Kamalaśīla explain that the notion of whole composed of parts is unintelligible on the basis that what is multiple (e.g. straw, huts) is not accompanied by or permeated by one continuing entity (*dravya*), and on the basis that what is unitary (e.g. the *paramāṇu*, the atom) is based on one continuing entity. They also mention the reduction *ad absurdum* of the one

3. Krishnamacharya, Embar, *Tattvasaṃgraha of Śāntarakṣita* (and commentary of Kamalaśīla), (Baroda : Central Library, 1926) Gaekwad's Oriental Series 30, Volume I, *Tattvasaṃgraha* fn, 603, p. 201.

4. Ibid., *Tattvasaṃgraha*, fn, 604, p. 201.

supposed part (*avayava*), which cannot be accompanied by or permeated by one continuing entity, because a part cannot be one without being a whole—in which case it is multiple. In this way, Śāntarakṣita and Kamalaśīla conclude that there is no possibility of the occurrence of the whole in the parts.

evaṃ tāvatsāmānyenaivāvayavairārabdhamanārabdhaṃ vā sthūlamekaṃ dravyaṃ na yujyate iti pratipāditam/idānīṃ yenāvayavī prārabdha iṣyate, tasya viśeṣeṇa dūṣaṇamāha—eketyādi/
ekāvayavyanugatā naiva tantukarādayaḥ/
anekatvādyathāsiddhāḥ kaṭakuṭyakuṭādayaḥ//605//
yadi vābhimataṃ dravyaṃ nānekāvayavāśritam/
ekatvādaṇuvadvṛtterayuktirbādhikā pramā//606//
prayogaḥ—yadanekaṃ na tadekadravyānugataṃ, yathā kaṭakuṭyādayo bahavo naikadravyānugatāḥ, aneke cāmī tantukarādaya iti vyāpakaviruddhopalabdheḥ/ athavā—yadekaṃ tadekadravyāśritaṃ yathaikaḥ paramāṇuḥ ekaṃ cāvayavisaṃjñitaṃ dravyamiti vyāpakaviruddhopalabdhiprasaṅgaḥ/prasaṅgasādhanaṃ caitat/prayogadvaye 'pi viparyaye bādhakaṃ pramāṇamāha—vṛtterayuktirbādhikā prameti/avayaveṣu yā 'vayavino vṛttistasyā ayogaḥ pramāṇairaghaṭanaṃ tadatra bādhakaṃ pramāṇaṃ//605//606//[5]

That certainly thus in a general way one gross continuing entity, undertaken (*ārabdha*) or not undertaken by means of parts, is not enjoined, is established. Now, in connection with that by which the whole is said to be commenced, the particular vitiating thing is explained in the next verse.

Threads, the hands, etc. are not accompanied by one whole because of multiplicity like the well-known straw, hut, jar.

If the intended continuing entity is not based on many parts because of oneness like the atom the impossibility of its occurrence is the refuting measure.

The explanation is as follows. That which is many is not accompanied by one continuing entity as straw, huts, etc. which are many are not accompanied by one continuing entity, because of the perception of the contradicted reason in that hands, threads, etc. are many. Moreover, that which is one is based on one continuing entity, as one atom; in reference to

5. Ibid., *Tattvasaṃgraha*, vv 605-606, p. 201.

the continuing entity, designated as one part there is the occurrence of the ascertainment of the contradicted reason. This is the *reductio ad absurdum* (*prasaṅgasādhana*). It explains the authority refuting (*bādhaka*) the opposite (*viparyaya*) of the two (arguments) for their support: "the impossibility of the occurrence is a refuting authority." In connection with the occurrence of the whole in the parts, there is the impossibility of the establishment (*aghaṭana*) by the authorities. This is the refuting authority in this case.

(b) Ratnakīrti on Momentariness

It is well to examine the argument of the momentariness of existents on the basis of efficiency as it is presented in a Buddhist source, Ratnakīrti's *Kṣaṇabhaṅga-siddhi*. This work is being cited because according to Surendranath Dasgupta, Hindu writers after Ratnakīrti refer to his work in connection with the doctrine of efficiency (*arthakriyākāritva*).

> Whenever Hindu writers after Ratnakīrti refer to the Buddhist doctrine of *arthakriyākāritva* they usually refer to this doctrine in Ratnakīrti's sense.[6]

It should be noted that according to Ratnakīrti, as explained by Dasgupta, the term *arthakriyākāritva* signifies efficiency, and is the characteristic definition of existence (*sattva*).

> But with Ratnakīrtti (950 A.D.) the word *arthakriyākāritva* has an entirely different sense. It means with him efficiency of producing any action or event, and as such it is regarded as the characteristic definition of existence (*sattva*). Thus he says in his *Kṣaṇabhaṅgasiddhi*, pp.20,21, that though in different definitions of existence or being, he will open his argument with the universally accepted definition of existence as *arthakriyākāritva* (efficiency of causing any action of event).[7]

According to Ratnakīrti, existence (*sattva*) is equivalent to efficiency (*arthakriyākāritva*). In his *Kṣaṇabhaṅgasiddhi Vyatirekātmikā*, Ratnakīrti argues by means of the pervasion (*vyāpti*)

---

6. Dasgupta, Surendranatha, *A History of Indian Philosophy*, Volume I, p. 163, fn 3.

7. Ibid., p. 163, fn 3.

composed of difference (*vyatireka*) that whatever exists is momentary in that whatever is existent or efficient can be shown to be momentary. First, he claims however that the argument of pervasion based on difference refers to the affirmative argument (*anvaya-vyāpti*).

(77·4) vyatirekātmikā vyāptir ākṣiptānvayarūpiṇī vaidharmyavati dṛṣṭānte sattva-hetor ihocyate.
(77·6) yat sat tat kṣaṇikaṃ yathā ghaṭaḥ. santaścāmī vivādāspadībhūtāḥ padārthā iti svabhāva-hetuḥ.

(77·8) na tāvad asyāsiddhiḥ sambhavati yathāyogaṃ pratyakṣānumānapramāṇapratīte dharmiṇi sattvaśabdenābhipretasyārthakriyākāritvalakṣaṇasya sādhanasya pramāṇasamadhigatatvāt.[8]

The pervasion composed of difference has as its formation the indicated affirmative argument. If there is a divergent example of something having being as reason, it is said to be included here.

That which is existent (*sat*) is momentary, as a pot. In reference to these object-entities which are existing and are the subjects of dispute there is the reason of nature (*svabhāva-hetu*).
Certainly, no inconclusiveness is possible in connection with this, because of obtaining the authority of the reason having the characteristic of efficiency signified by the word "existence" when there is a factual base known by the authorities of perception and inference.

But Ratnakīrti goes on to say that there is an authority refuting the contention that whatever is existent is non-momentary in that existence is not seen to pervade non-momentariness. He argues that efficiency implies succession and non-succession (*kramākrama*), and that since a non-momentary thing is neither successive nor non-successive, it is not efficient (*arthakriyākārin*) and therefore non-existent.

8. McDermott, A.C. Senape, *An Eleventh Century Buddhist Logic of 'Exists'*, (translation of Ratnakīrti's *Kṣaṇabhaṅgasiddhiḥ Vyatirekātmikā*), (Dordrecht, Holland : D. Reidel Publishing Company, 1969), p. 14.

(77.10) naca viruddhānaikāntikate vyāpakānupalambhātmanā viparyaye bādhakapramāṇena vyāpteḥ prasādhanāt.
(77.11) yasya kramākramau na vidyete na tasyārthakriyāsāmarthyaṃ. yathā śaśaviṣāṇasya. na vidyete cākṣaṇikasya kramākramāviti vyāpakānupalambhaḥ.[9]

There is no uncertainty or contradiction because of the accomplishment of the pervasion by means of the authority which is composed of the non-perception of the pervader and which is assailant to the opposite case. Wherever succession and non-succession (*kramākrama*) do not exist, there is no efficiency, as the horns of a hare. In reference to the succession and non-succession of a non-momentary thing, there is non-perception of the pervader.

Ratnakīrti goes on to demonstrate that it is impossible for succession or non-succession to exist in a non-momentary thing. First, he argues that since permanence implies identity of past and future moments and since succession or non-succession requires difference of two moments, succession or non-succession are not possible in the case of a non-momentary thing. Secondly, he argues that if two moments are identical, and if the first moment has already brought about an imminent effect, there can be no room for another succession if another effect is produced.

(77.12) na tāvadayamasiddho hetuḥ. akṣaṇike dharmiṇi kramākramasadbhāvāyogāt, tathāhi prāptāparakālayorekatve nityatvaṃ. tasya kramākramayoge kṣaṇadvayepyavaśyaṃ bhedaḥ. bhedābhedayośca parasparavirodhāt kuto 'kṣaṇike kramākramasambhavaḥ. kṣaṇadvaye 'pi bhede kramākramayogaḥ. abhede hi prathama eva kṣaṇe śaktatvād. bhāvino 'pi kāryasya karaṇaprasaṅge kathaṃ kāryāntarakāraṇe kramāntarāvakāśaḥ. na cākṣaṇikasyākrameṇaiva sakalasvakāryaṃ kṛtvā svāsthyam. kṣaṇāntare 'pi śaktatvāt punastatkāryakaraṇaprasaṅgāt.[10]

Certainly this reason is not inconclusive, because of the impossibility of the true existence of succession and non-succession in the case of a non-momentary factual base.
For, there is eternity (*nityatva*) in the unity of the attained

9. Ibid., p. 14.
10. Ibid., p. 14.

and future times. In the case of the possibility of succession and non-succession of it (the non-momentary thing), there is necessarily the difference of two moments. Because of the mutual opposition of difference and non-difference, how is there the possibility of succession and non-succession in a non-momentary thing? When there is the difference of two moments, there is the possibility of succession and non-succession, because of the potency in the first moment in the case of non-difference. When there is the occurrence of a cause for the imminent (*bhāvin*) effect, how is there room for another succession in the case of the cause of another effect? It is not good that there is in connection with a non-momentary thing its own entire effect (*sakalasvakārya*) by means of the non-succession, because of the occurrence of cause and effect repeatedly on account of potency in other moments.

Ratnakirti then notes that since a non-momentary factual base is characterized by the absence of succession and non-succession, it is non-efficient and therefore non-existent.

(77.18) tasmādakṣaṇikamiti pūrvāparakālayorabhedaḥ kramākramayoga iti pūrvāparakālayorbhedaḥ. anayośca parasparaparihārasthitilakṣaṇo virodhaḥ.
(77.20) tadayamakṣaṇike dharmiṇi kramākramābhāvalakṣaṇo hetur nāsiddho vaktavyaḥ. kramākramayogitvākṣaṇikatvayorvirodhādeva.[11]

Therefore, in reference to a non-momentary thing, there is the non-difference of the earlier and later times. In reference to the possibility of succession and non-succession, there is the difference of earlier and later times. Between these two (difference and non-difference) there is opposition characterized by the abiding of mutual removal by arguments (*parihāra*).
Thus in the case of a non-momentary factual base the reason characterized by the absence of succession and non-succession is said to be inconclusive because of the opposition of non-momentariness and the existence of conjunction with succession and non-succession.

11. Ibid., p. 1 4.

c. Causation

Śantarakṣita's explanation of the relationship of cause and effect in terms of moments was also misconstrued by the Vedāntins. Madhva and his school, in their interpretation of the *sūtra* "*ubhayathā ca doṣāt*" (*Brahma-sūtra* II.2.23) attempt to refute the Buddhist principle, "When this is, that is" (*asmin satīdam bhavati*), which they interpret as the simultaneity of cause and effect. Madhva and his school argue that if cause and effect are simultaneous, then there is an endless series of effects. They ignore the fact, however, that according to Śāntarakṣita and Kamalaśīla, the effect is born in the second moment from a cause which is yet capable (*śakta*) and undestroyed (*anaṣṭa*), and that thereby the dangers of simultaneity of cause and effect on the one hand and of disconnectedness of cause and effect on the other hand are avoided. Śāntarakṣita and Kamalaśīla explain that the effect is born in the second moment and is yet undestroyed. In this way, the possible objection that an effect cannot be born of a cause which has ceased to exist is avoided.

tasmādanaṣṭāttaddhetoḥ prathamakṣaṇabhāvinaḥ /
kāryamutpadyate śaktāddvitīyakṣaṇa eva tu//512//
vinaṣṭāttu bhavetkāryaṃ tṛtīyādikṣaṇe yadi/
vipākahetoḥ pradhvastādyathā kāryaṃ ca vakṣyate//513//
yaugapadyaprasaṅgo 'pi prathame yadi tadbhavet/
sahabhūhetuvattacca na yuktyā yujyate punaḥ//514//
vinaṣṭavikalpastvanabhyupagamādevāyuktaḥ/ tathāhi—yadi tṛtīyādiṣu kṣaṇeṣu kāryaṃ bhavatītyabhyupetaṃ bhavet, yathā vaibhāṣikairaṅgīkṛtameko 'tītaḥ prayacchatīti/ tadā vinaṣṭātkāraṇātkāryotpādo 'ṅgīkṛtaḥ syāt/ na cāyaṃ pakṣo 'smākam/ ayuktyupetatvāt/yaugapadyaprasaṅgo 'pi kadācidbhavet, yadi prathama eva kṣaṇe kāryamiṣyate/ yathā taireva vaibhāṣikaiḥ sahabhūrheturiṣyate/taccaitadayuktam//[12]

Therefore, the effect is born in the second moment from the capable, undestroyed cause of that, existent (*bhāvin*) in the first moment. If the effect should be in the third moment, from a destroyed (thing), (then it would be) from a disrupted cause

12. Krishnamacharya, Embar, *Tattvasaṃgraha of Śāntarakṣita*, *Tattvasaṃgraha* vv 512-514, p. 175.

of maturation (*vipāka-hetu*), as the effect is explained. There would be the occurrence of simultaneity if (it were) in the first moment; like the co-existent cause (*sahabhūhetu*), it is not suitably enjoined.

The alternative of the destroyed cause is not enjoined because it is not the principle. For it is thus: that if the effect is in the third and subsequent moments is maintained, as it is agreed among the Vaibhāṣikas that the one when it is past produces the effect, then the birth of the effect from a destroyed (thing) would be admitted. This is not our position, because of non-abiding in the reason (*yukti*). There would be the occcurrence of simultaneity perhaps, if the effect were declared in the first moment, as the co-existent cause is declared by those Vaibhāṣikas. This is not enjoined.

It is to be observed that Śāntarakṣita and Kamalaśīla are attacking the Vaibhāṣika school, through the argument that otherwise there would be simultaneity of cause and effect or else disconnectedness of cause and effect. Madhva and his school, in their interpretation of the *sūtra* "*ubhayathā ca doṣāt*" (*Brahma-sūtra* II.2.23) attempt to refute the Buddhist principle, "When this is, that is" (*asmin satīdam bhavati*), which they interpret as the simultaneity of cause and effect. Madhva and his school argue that if cause and effect are simultaneous, then there is an endless series of effects. They ignore the fact, however, that according to Śāntarakṣita and Kamalaśīla, the effect is born in the second moment from a cause which is yet capable and undestroyed, and that thereby the dangers of simultaneity of cause and effect on the one hand and of disconnectedness of cause and effect on the other hand are avoided.

The Buddhist teaching that a cause (*hetu*) possesses no activity (*vyāpāra*) apart from its being (*sattā*) was also misunderstood. Śaṅkara, for instance, in his interpretation of the *sūtra* "*uttarotpāde ca pūrva-nirodhāt*" (*Brahma-sūtra* II.2.20) attempts to refute the supposed Buddhist position that the earlier momentary existence at full development becomes the cause of the later momentray existence. Śaṅkara refutes this supposed position by arguing that such a position is only a roundabout way of saying that something of the first moment passes into the second moment, and that thereby the principle of momentariness is abandoned. Śaṅkara may be referring to the position of Śāntarakṣita and Kamalaśīla that the effect is born in the second moment from a cause which is born in the first moment and is yet undestroyed. Śāntarakṣita and Kamalaśīla have also declared, however, that a cause possesses no activity apart from its being, so that it is not the case that a cause takes birth and subsequently enters into activity. Śāntarakṣita and Kamalaśīla state that the mere existence of the cause is its activity, in answer to the question how a given thing can be a cause if it does not enter activity. They explain that any activity of the cause, after the effect has taken birth, is inapplicable to the effect. The cause, they explain, is that which upon taking birth immediately causes the effect to appear, and the effect appears immediately succeeding the being of the cause. Consequently there is no time for the cause to enter into an activity apart from its own being.

> nanu ya utpādya vyāpāraṃ nāviśet viśeṣotpādārthaṃ sa katham hetuḥ syādityāha—janmātiriktetyādi/
> janmātiriktakālena vyāpāreṇātra kim phalaṃ/
> sattaiva vyāpṛtistasyāṃ satyām kāryodayo yataḥ//520//
> kāraṇasattāsamanantarameva kāryasya niṣpannatvādakiṃcitkara eva kāryasya janmottarakālabhāvī vyāpāraḥ kārye/tathāhi—vyāpāro nāma kāraṇasya ka ucyate/ yadanantarameva kāryamudayamāsādayati kāraṇasattānantarameva ca kāryamudbhavatīti sattaiva vyāpāraśabdavācyā 'stu kiṃ janmātirekiṇā vyāpāreṇa kalpitena//520//[13]

If it be objected that how should that which having taken birth not enter into activity for the sake of the birth of the qualification be a cause it is said:
In an activity belonging to a time separate from birth, is there any effect?
The being is the activity (*vyāpṛti*), since there is the appearance of the effect when this is so.
From the maturation (*niṣpannatva*) of the effect immediately after the being of the cause, any activity of the cause whatsoever at a time later than the birth of the effect is not to be in the case of the effect. Thus it is said; the name activity is given

13. Ibid., Volume I, *Tattva-saṃgraha*, v 520, p. 177.

to the cause. It is that which causes the effect immediately succeeding to appear; immediately following the being of the cause the effect appears; (hence) let the being be expressed (*vācya*) by the word activity; what is there by means of the activity imagined as separate from the birth?

It is then asked how there is the dependence (*apekṣā*) of the effect upon the cause, and how there is the activity of the cause in the effect. It is answered that the dependence consists of the immediate sequence of cause and effect, and that the entity itself is the activity of the cause.

yadyevamasati bhāvānāṃ vyāpāre kathamidamadhīyate kāryasya kāraṇe 'pekṣā kāraṇasya ca kārye vyāpāra ityāha—ya ānantaryetyādi/
ya ānantaryaniyamaḥ saivāpekṣābhidhīyate kāryodaye sadā bhāvo vyāpāraḥ kāraṇasya ca idameva hi kāryasya kāraṇe 'pekṣā yattadanantarabhāvitvaṃ, kāraṇasyāpi kārye 'yameva vyāpāro yatkāryodayakāle sadā sannihitatvam//521//[14]

If this is the case, in connection with entities, how is it thought in the case of the activity, that there is the dependence of the effect upon the cause and that there is the activity of the cause in the effect? It is said:
It is the principle of immediate sequence (*ānantarya*) which is considered dependence.
In the arising of the effect, the entity is the activity of the cause.
For that which is the dependence of the effect upon the cause is the coming into existence (*bhāvitva*) immediately succeeding, that which is the activity of the cause upon the effect is always struck down (*nihata*) at the moment of the arising of the effect.

(d) Destruction (*vināśa*) and Disruption (*pradhvaṃsa*)

The Buddhist doctrine of momentariness, according to which the destruction of a thing is supposedly synonymous with its momentary existence, was the target of attack by Vedāntins. In his interpretation of the *sūtra* "*anusmṛteśca*" (*Brahmasūtra* II.2.24),

14. Ibid., Vol. I, *Tattvasaṃgraha*, v 521, p. 177.

Rāmānuja accuses the Buddhists of denying, for instance, that the hammer is the cause of the destruction of the jar. What the Buddhists explain, however, is that the destruction cannot have for its nature the given thing. Śāntarakṣita and Kamalaśīla note that there are two kinds of destruction: the first is concerned with the momentary existence of *dharmas* and is admitted to have a cause; the second is concerned with the cessation of the nature of an entity, is called disruption and does not possess a cause. Śāntarakṣita and Kamalaśīla deny that the Buddhists are positing causelessness in connection with the first kind of destruction.

tadatra katamaṃ nāśam pare paryanuyuñjate/
kiṃ kṣaṇasthitidharmāṇaṃ bhāvameva tathoditam/
atha bhāvasvarūpasya nivṛttim dhvaṃsasaṃjñitāṃ/
pūrvaparyaṇuyoge hi naiva kiṃcidvirudhyate//374//

dvividho hi vināśo vidheḥ pratiṣedhalakṣaṇaḥ/tathāhi—kṣaṇasthitidharmā bhāva eva calo vinaśyatīti kṛtvā vināśa ityākhyāyate/ yadvā bhāvasvabhāvapracyutilakṣaṇapradhvaṃsāparanāmā vinaśanaṃ vināśa iti/ tatra pūrvasminnāśe yadyayaṃ hetumatvasādhanaparyanuyogaḥ kriyate yathoktairhetubhiḥ, tadā siddhasādhyatā//373//374//

tāmeva siddhasādhyatāṃ yo hītyādinā darśayati—[15]

Thus in this case, what kind of destruction is questioned by others? Is it the entity declared in connection with *dharmas* abiding for a moment? Or is it the cessation which is of the nature of an entity, and which is named disruption (*dhvaṃsa*)? For in the case of objection to the former, it is not opposed at all—

According to the rule, there are two kinds of destruction having the characteristic of negation (*pratiṣedha*). That is to say with reference to the entity which having the characteristic of abiding for a moment and of being mobile is destroyed, after it has been destroyed, in reference to that destruction, it is said that there is the destruction, and that there is the destruction which is annihilation having the alternative name of disruption which is characterized by the loss (*pracyuti*) of the

15. Ibid., *Tattvasaṃgraha*, vv 373-374, p. 137.

nature (*svabhāva*) of an entity. Then, if objection is made because of the reason of procession from a cause in the case of the former destruction through the reasons explained, then it is a demonstrated conclusion.

That existence of a demonstrated conclusion is shown by the statement beginning with the following:

Śāntarakṣita and Kamalaśīla go on to explain that the destruction which is synonymous with the momentary existence of a thing possesses a cause, whereas the other type, disruption does not possess a cause, for it has no connection with the given thing, e.g. the jar. The form of destruction known as disruption can be said to possess the character of "becoming immediately succeeding a thing" (*vastvanantarabhāva*) in a general sense (*sāmānya*), in that it follows its supposed immediate cause, e.g. the blow of the hammer in the case of the jar. In other words, the disruption of the jar-series can be said to have a cause only in the general sense, for the disruption does not possess the nature of the jar.

yo hi bhāvaḥ kṣaṇasthāyī vināśa iti gīyate /
taṃ hetumantamicchāmaḥ parābhāvāttvahetukam //375//
yadyevaṃ kathamahetuko vināśo bhavatāṃ pratīta ityāha—parābhāvāttvahetukamiti /
parasya svakāraṇavyatiriktasyottarakālaṃ mudgarādernāśakasyābhāvādahetukamicchāma iti prakṛtena sambandhaḥ //375// atra caivambhūte vināśe dharmiṇi kādācitkatvātprāgabhūtvā 'tmalābhāditīmau hetū siddhau/ vastvanantarabhāvitvamapi yadi sāmānyena vivakṣitaṃ tadā siddhameva, kāraṇabhūtavastvanantaramasya bhāvaprasiddheḥ/ athātmabhūtavinaśvaravastvanantarabhāvitvamasya vivakṣitaṃ tadā heturasiddha iti darśayati—vastvanantarabhāvitvamityādi/[16]

For that entity, residing (*sthāyin*) for a moment, is called destruction. That we say is possessed of a cause because of the absence of an extrinsic thing.

If it is said, "How is destruction not possessing a cause known by you ?" it is replied: "That is not possessing a cause on account of the absence of an extrinsic (cause). In

16. Ibid., *Tattvasaṃgraha*, v 375, pp. 137-138.

connection with an extrinsic thing we claim the later time of that separated by its own cause to be unpossessed of a cause because of the absence of the destruction of the hammer." Through this statement's having been set forth, there is the connection.

Here in the case of a factual base composed of destruction, of two reasons—because it is occasional, because of obtaining its nature after having previously not existed. If the production immediately succeeding a given thing is declared in the common way, then it is approved, because of the approval of the entity in connection with the immediate succession to a given thing which is composed of the cause. If it is declared in connection with the becoming immediately succeeding a given thing that the destruction is composed (*bhūta*) of its nature (*ātman*) then the reason is not conclusive.

This statement is set forth in the words "The becoming immediately succeeding a given thing" (*vastvanantarabhāvitva*).

It may be noted that the sub-commentators Vādirāja and Jayatīrtha of the Madhva school in their interpretations of the *sūtra* "*pratisaṃkhyā 'pratisaṃkhyā-nirodhāprāptir avicchedāt*" (*Brahma sūtra* II.2.22) argue against what they designate as the destruction with series (*sasaṃtānanāśa*) by elaborating upon Madhva's argument for the non-establishment of destruction (*nāśa*). Madhva argues that there would be an endless series of effects if it could be demonstrated that the cause continues to exist, and that consequently there would be non-establishment of destruction. Śāntarakṣita and Kamalaśīla, however, have simply indicated that this second type of destruction, which they term disruption, is causeless, for it has no connection with the given thing which is supposedly disrupted, e.g. a jar. A hammer cannot be said to be the cause of the destruction of the jar, for destruction cannot have for its nature the given thing, e.g. the jar. The arguments of Madhva and the commentators of his school in connection with the destruction with series do not apply, therefore, to the type of destruction known as disruption, since such destruction can have no connection with a given thing, e.g. the jar. To Rāmānuja's claim that the hammer should be considered as the cause of the destruction of the jar, on the grounds of immediate succession in time (*ānantarya*), the Buddhist would agree with him that in a general sense only the disruption is a "becoming immediately succeeding the given thign" in that it immediately succeeds its cause, e.g. the hammer. But the contention that destruction immediately succeeds the given thing, e.g. the jar, which supposedly constitutes its own nature would be rejected by the Buddhist. Śāntarakṣita and Kamalaśīla then go on to explain that the destruction of a given thing must appear along with that given thing for the given thing has no parts by virtue of which destruction could immediately succeed it. Therefore, Śāntarakṣita and Kamalaśila reject the notion of "becoming immediately succeeding a given thing" in connection with destruction. Otherwise, the destruction would not constitute the nature of a given thing.

> vastvanantarabhāvitvaṃ na tatra tvaṣti tādṛśi /
> calabhāvasvarūpasya bhāvenaiva sahodayāt //376//
> tādṛśīti calavastusvabhāvāvyatirekiṇi / na hi niraṃśavastuno bhāgo 'sti yena tadanantarabhāvitvamasya bhavet / tatsvabhāvavattadavyatirekiṇo nāśasya tanniṣpattāveva niṣpannatvāt / anyathā tatsvabhāvatvameva tasya na syādityuktam // 376 //[17]
>
> The becoming immediately succeeding a given thing (*vastvanantarabhāvitva*) is not present there in such a one, because of the appearance with the entity in connection with the nature of the mobile entity.
> "In such a manner" : in a manner not separate from the nature of the mobile given thing. For there is no part for a given thing without parts by which it (the destruction) should be in connection with the becoming immediately succeeding that (the given thing), because of the emergence of the destruction in the case of the emergence not separate from that like the nature of that (the given thing). Otherwise, it is said that there would not be the existence of that destruction (*tad*) as the nature of that (the given thing).

Rāmānuja also argues that it may be claimed by the Buddhists that the hammer for instance is the cause of the origination of

17. Ibid., *Tattvasaṃgraha*, v 376, p. 138.

a new series, the fragments of the jar. The Vedāntin, in particular Rāmānuja, replies that the origination of a new series is in fact destruction, and that consequently the destruction of a given thing is not intrinsic to it. Kamalaśīla explains, however, that destruction cannot be equivalent to the origination of a new series, because at the time of its supposed beginning, its cause (e.g. the hammer) is absent. Consequently, according to Kamalaśīla such a new series does not even exist.

> atha visadṛśakṣaṇotpādalakṣaṇo dvitīyo vināśo 'bhipretastasyāhetukatvamasiddhaṃ / vastutayā tasya mudgarādikāraṇabalenotpādanābhyupagamāt / ata evāsāvādau na jāyate, svahetormudgarādestadānīmabhāvāt //439//440//[18]
>
> If the second type of destruction having the characteristic of the birth of dissimilar moments is intended, the non-possession of a cause in connection with that is not conclusive, because of the non-maintenance of the birth by the strength of the cause of the hammer in connection with that, by way of the existence of a given thing. Therefore, that is not born at the beginning, because of the absence at that time of its own cause, the hammer.

(e) Remembrance (*smṛti*) and Recognition (*pratyabhijñā*)

In connection with Śaṅkara's argument in his interpretation of the *sūtra* "*anusmṛteśca*" (*Brahma-sūtra* II.2.25) that the judgement of similarity requires a stable subject, it should be noted that a similar argument has been set forth and refuted by Śāntarakṣita and Kamalaśīla. According to the *prima facie* view, the notion that recognition (*pratisaṃdhāna* or *pratyabhijñā*) may be due to similarity (*sādṛśya*) is to be rejected because there is a difference of knowers as well as a difference of knowable at separate moments. If there were not a single knower, according to the *prima facie* view attributed by Śāntarakṣita and Kamalaśīla to the opponent, then it would be the case for instance that one person sees a fruit and another remembers it.

> nanu lūnapunarjātakeśanakhādiṣviva bhede 'pi sādṛśyātpra-

18. Ibid., *Tattvasaṃgraha*, vv 439-440, p.156.

tyabhijñānaṃ bhaviṣyatītyetadāśaṅkyāha—sādṛśyādityādi /
sādṛśyātpratyabhijñānaṃ bhinne keśādike bhavet /
jñāturekasya sadbhāvāddvibhede tvanibandhanaṃ // 494 //
pratisandhānakārī ca yadyeko 'rtho na vidyate /
rūpe dṛṣṭe 'bhilāṣādistatkathaṃ syādrasādiṣu // 495 //

yadi hyeko jñātā bhavettadā syātpratisandhātṛvaśājjñeyasya bhede 'pi sādṛśyakṛtaṃ pratyabhijñānaṃ / dvibhede tu—dvayorjñātṛjñeyayorbhedo dvibhedaḥ, tasminsatyanibandhanameva pratyabhijñānam / api ca—yadi na kaścidekaḥ pratisandhātā puruṣo bhavettadā yadetanmatuluṅgaphalādirūpe dṛṣṭe tadrūpāvinābhāviṣu rasādiṣu smaraṇapūrvamabhilaṣaṇaṃ paribhogāya ca pravṛttistatkathaṃ bhavet / na hyanyena dṛṣṭe 'nyasyābhilāṣādirbhavet /[19]

If it be objected that there will be recognition from similarity even when there is difference as in the case of hair, nails, etc. which are cut and grown again, after consideration it says :

In that hair, etc. are different, there would be recognition because of similarity,
because of the true existence (*sadbhāva*) of one knower. In the case of two-fold difference, the recognition would be baseless.
If there is not the object-entity causing remembrance (*pratisaṃdhāna*)
then when a formation is seen, how would there be longing (*abhilāṣā*) for the taste ?

If there were one knower, then there would be recognition because of the dominion of the one who remembers due to similarity even when there is a difference of the knowable. In the case of two-fold difference—the two-fold difference which is a difference of the two knowers and knowables—in that case recognition would be baseless. Moreover, if there should not be any one person who remembers, then when the formation of citronfruit is seen, then how would there be a going forth for the enjoyment towards the longing preceded by the remembrance in respect to the taste inherent in that

19. Ibid., *Tattvasaṃgraha*, vv 494-495, p. 170-171.

formation ? When it has been seen by the one, there should be no longing for the other.

In reply to this argument, Śāntarakṣita and Kamalaśīla explain that there is in the absolute sense no one who experiences (*anubhavitṛ*) and no one who remembers (*smarttṛ*); otherwise a thing would be remembered by one who experiences it. Remembrance is explained as brought about by a seed deposited in the series through the birth of more and more differentiated moments each following the other through an intense experience. In other words, remembrance is explained on the basis of cause and effect as initiated by experience, in the series. Furthermore, Śāntarakṣita and Kamalaśīla explain that there is a distinction between remembrance (*smaraṇa* or *smṛti*) and recognition (*pratyabhijñā*), and that the latter is always preceded by the former. They conclude by stating that recognition, etc. does not require a single knower (*jñātṛ*), for it can be explained on the basis of mere cause and effect.

keṣāṃcideva cittānāṃ viśiṣṭā kāryakāryitā /
niyatā tena nirbādhāḥ sarvatra smaraṇādayaḥ // 543 //

kāryakāryiteti kāryamasyāstīti kāryi, kāraṇamityarthaḥ / kāryakāryiṇorbhāvaḥ kāryakāryitā / kāryakāraṇabhāva ityarthaḥ / na hi kaścitparamārthataḥ smarttā 'nubhavitā vā 'sti/ yato yenaivānubhūtaṃ sa eva smaratīti syāt / kiṃ tarhi ? yatra saṃtāne paṭīyasā 'nubhavenottarottaraviśiṣṭataratamakṣaṇotpādātsmṛtyādibījamāhitaṃ tatraiva smaraṇādayaḥ samutpadyante, nānyatra pratiniyatatvātkāryakāraṇabhāvasyeti samāsārthaḥ / yathoktam—"anyasmaraṇabhogādiprasaṅgaśca na bādhakaḥ / asmṛteḥ kasyacittena hyanubhūte smṛtodbhava" iti / smaraṇādipūrvakāśca pratyabhijñānādayaḥ prasūyanta ityaviruddhaṃ/ na cāpi kvacidekajñātṛnibandhanāḥ pratyabhijñānādayaḥ siddhāḥ, yenocyate dvibhede tvanibandhanamiti, kāryakāraṇabhāvamātratayā sarvatraiva bhedābhyupagamāt //543//[20]

In connection with some thoughts (*citta*), the differentiated existence of effect and effect-possessor is restricted; therefore, remembrance, etc. is without obstacle.

20. Ibid., *Tattvasaṃgraha*, v 543, p. 144.

The relationship of effect and effect-possessor, etc. The effect-possessor is in connection with that which has an effect; the significance is that it is a cause. The existence of effect and effect-possessor is the relationship of effect and effect-possessor. The significance is that it is the relationship of cause and effect. For in the absolute sense there is no one who remembers, and no one who experiences, since the one by whom it is experienced would be the one who remembers. What then? Where there is the seed of remembrance deposited because of the birth of more and more qualified moments each following the other through an intense experience, there remembrances take birth, and nowhere else, because of the difference in each case of the relationship of cause and effect—this is the meaning of the compound. It has been declared thus : "The occurrence (*prasaṅga*) of the experience and remembrance of another is not an assailant (*bādhaka*) (to our position). In connection with non-remembrance, when (something) has been experienced by that one, is there the birth of it as remembered for anyone whatsoever?

That recognition, etc. is brought forth preceded by remembrance is not contradicted. Nor are recognition, etc. proved to be based on any one knower whatsoever, by virtue of which it is said, "If there were the difference of the two (knowers), it (recognition) would be baseless," because of the principle of difference in all cases by means of the relation of cause and effect only.

For Śāntarakṣita and Kamalaśīla, recognition and remembrance are explained on the basis of cause and effect within the series.

G. ŚAṄKARA'S "CRYPTO"-BUDDHISM

In this section, the question of Śaṅkara's supposed "crypto"-Buddhism will be explored. It will be seen that there are parallels between Śaṅkara's Vedānta and Buddhism, particularly in connection with the doctrine of nescience (*avidyā*) and the doctrine of the two truths, the absolute (*paramārtha*) and the practical (*vyavahāra*). It will be seen that there is a possibility of a historical relationship, too, through the teacher Gauḍapāda (or school by that name). This study of Śaṅkara's "crypto"-Buddhism is divided under six headings : 1) The "Crypto"-Buddhism of Gauḍapāda; 2) Śaṅkara's Relationship to Gauḍapāda; 3) The Characterization of Śaṅkara as "Crypto"-Buddhist; 4) The Two Truths; 5) Nescience; 6) Name-and-Formation in Śaṅkara's Thought.

1. THE "CRYPTO"-BUDDHISM OF GAUḌAPĀDA

There is some evidence that the *Gauḍapāda-kārikās*, on which there is a commentary said to be written by Śaṅkara, reveal strains of Buddhist influence, particularly from the Mādhyamika school. For instance, in verse 4 of the fourth chapter (*prakaraṇa*) there is an attempt to affirm the notion of the non-common origin (*ajāti*).

> 4. bhūtaṃ na jāyate kiñcid abhūtaṃ naiva jāyate/
> vivadanto 'dvayā hy evam ajātiṃ khyāpayanti te//[1]
>
> The existent is not born; whatever is non-existent is not born.
> For, disputing thus the adherents of not-two (*advaya*) proclaim the non-common origin.

According to Bhattacharya the first half of this *kārikā* is undoubtedly based on such a statement as Nāgārjuna's *Mūlamadhyamakakārikā* I.6.

> 6. naivāsato naiva sataḥ pratyayo 'rthasya yujyate/
> asataḥ pratyayaḥ kasya sataśca pratyayena kiṃ//[2]
>
> Neither of an object-entity existing nor of an object-entity not existing is a condition applicable.
> In connection with the non-existing, whose is the condition ?
> In connection with the existing, why by means of a condition?

An interesting term used in the second half of the *kārikā* is "*advaya*," those adhering to the notion of "not-two." Bhattacharya explains that whereas the term *Advaita* signifies non-duality in the sense of non-difference, the term *advaya* signifies "not-two" in the sense of avoidance of the two extremes (*atyanta*) and hence adherence to a middle path (*madhyamā pratipad*). The Buddha as *Advayavādin* (one of the titles for the

1. Bhattacharya, Vidhushekhara, *The Āgamaśāstra of Gauḍapāda*. edited, translated, annotated, (Calcutta : University of Calcutta, 1943), *Āgama-śāstra* IV.4, pp. 101-102.

2. Inada, Kenneth M., *Nāgārjuna, Mūlamadhyamakakārikā* I.6, p. 40.

Buddha as noted by Bhattacharya[3]) expounds the middle path as presented in such a verse as Nāgārjuna sets forth in the *Madhyamaka-vṛtti*—a verse which teaches that there is neither origination nor cessation.

> anirodham anutpādam anucchedam aśāśvatam/
> anekārtham anānārtham anāgamam anirgamam//[4]
>
> (It is) without cessation, without birth, without destruction, not eternal, not having different meanings, not coming, not departing.

The middle path is set forth in another *kārikā*, in Nāgārjuna's *Mūlamadhyamakakārikā*, which states that those of inferior insight cannot comprehend the quiescence (*upaśama*).

> 8. astitvaṃ ye tu paśyanti nāstitvaṃ cālpabuddhayaḥ/
> bhāvānāṃ te na paśyanti draṣṭavyopaśamaṃ śivam//[5]
>
> Those of slight intelligence who see only the existence and non-existence of entities do not see the apparent, benign quiescence.

The notion of the middle path as avoidance of extremes is emphatically set forth in the *Gauḍapāda-kārikā* IV.22, where it is said that nothing can be produced or originated from itself or from another.

> 22. svato vā parato vāpi na kiñcid vastu jāyate/
> sad asat sadasad vāpi na kiñcid vastu jāyate//[6]
>
> No given thing (*vastu*) whatsoever is born either from itself or from another.
> No given thing whatsoever is born existent, non-existent, or both existent and non-existent.

The first half of this *kārikā* seems to be taken from Nāgārjuna's *Mūlamadhyamakakārikā* XXI.13 and I.1.

---

3. Bhattacharya, Vidhushekhara, *The Āgamaśāstra of Gauḍapāda*, p. 102.
4. Ibid., p. 103.
5. Inada, Kenneth M., *Nāgārjuna, Mūlamadhyamakakārikā* V. 8, p.59.
6. Bhattacharya, Vidhushekhara, *The Āgamaśāstra of Gauḍapāda*, *Āgamaśāstra* IV. 22, p. 127.

na svato jāyate bhāvaḥ parato naiva jāyate/
na svataḥ parataś caiva jāyate jāyate kutaḥ//[7]

Neither is an entity born from itself nor from another, nor is it born from both itself and another. Whence is it born?

na svato nāpi parato na dvābhyāṃ nāpyahetutaḥ/
utpannā jātu vidyante bhāvāḥ kvacana kecana//[8]

Nowhere at all are seen born any entities whatsoever, either from themselves, or from others, or from both themselves and others, or from no causes.

The second half of the *Gauḍapāda-kārikā* IV.22 seems to be taken from Nāgārjua's *Mūlamadhyamakakārikā* I.7.

na san nāsan na sadasan dharmo nirvartate yadā/
kathaṃ nirvartako hetur evam sati hi yujyate//[9]

When no *dharma* either existent, non-existent, or both existent and non-existent evolves, how in that case is there applicable an evolver?

A difficulty arises, however, in the occurrence of the term "*ajāti*" (non-common origin). In *Gauḍapāda-kārikā* IV.5, for instance, the term *ajāti* is associated with approval of those who declare it.

khyāpyamānām ajātim tair anumodāmahe vayaṃ/
vivadāmo na taiḥ sārdham avivādaṃ nibodhata//[10]

We applaud the non-common origin being declared by them; we do not contest; listen to our non-dispute with them.

According to Bhattacharya, Gauḍapāda though a Vedāntin is here expressing approval of the Buddhist concept of non-origination (*anutpāda*).

It is to be noted here that Gauḍapāda is a Vedāntist, yet he accepts the doctrine of non-origination of the Advayavādins or Buddhists expressing his approval. He does not see any use

7. Ibid., (citing *Mūlamadhyamakakārikā* XXI 13), p. 127.
8. Ibid., (citing *Mūlamadhyamakakārikā* I.1), p. 127.
9. Ibid., (citing *Mūlamadhyamakakārikā* I.7), p. 128.
10. Ibid., *Āgamaśāstra* IV. 5, p. 187.

disputing with them and invites apparently his Vedāntist followers to listen to him as to why the view cannot be disputed.[11]

It is to be questioned, however, whether the term "*ajāti*" signifies "non-origination," or "non-common origin." If it signifies "non-common origin," then it does not possess Buddhistic connotations but is rather akin to the first type of name-and-formation, the unseparated name-and-formation (*avyākṛta nāma-rūpa*) to be discussed later.

According to Hixon, the text of the *Gauḍapāda-kārikā* is composite in nature and is the result of a syncretistic Mahāyāna-Vedānta movement in sixth-century Bengal—a syncretism inspired more by Mahāyāna than by Vedānta. In this respect, Hixon is expressing the position of Walleser, for whom there existed a philosophical school in the country of Gauḍa until the eighth century, a school which embodied the teachings of the Vedas and the Upaniṣads in the form of a collection of sayings.[12] Bhattacharya thinks that the text requires an author, and that as long as there is no contradiction or incongruity involved in the notion of a single author, one should accept the traditional view of an author named Gauḍa.[13] Bhattacharya, however, does hold the untraditional view that the four *prakaraṇas* of the *Gauḍapāda-kārikās* are four independent treatises put together under the title of *Āgamaśāstra*.[14] According to Hixon, the *Gauḍapāda-kārikās* represent a synthesis of Mahāyāna and Vedānta with emphasis on the Mahāyāna aspect. According to Bhattacharya, however, the author Gauḍapāda was a Vedāntin, whose Vijñānavāda tendencies are traceable to an Upaniṣadic source. Thus according to Bhattacharya even the equation of the dream and waking states made in the *Gauḍapāda-kārikās* is traceable to the *Bṛhadāraṇyaka Upaniṣad* IV.3.14, which contains the following passage :

...atho khalv āhuḥ, jāgarita-deśa evāsyaiṣaḥ; yāni hi eva jāgrat

11. Ibid., p. 107.
12. Ibid., p. lxx.
13. Ibid., p. lxxi.
14. Ibid., p. lvii.

> paśyati, tāni supta iti...[15]
> Now indeed, they say that this (the state of sleep) is the state of waking, for those which he sees when he is awake he (sees) when he is asleep (*supta*)...

According to Bhattacharya, the Upaniṣads are the seeds of the "idealism" he finds in Buddhist Vijñānavāda and in the the *Gauḍapāda-kārikās* or *Āgamaśāstra.*

> This Upaniṣadic seed of idealism being influenced by its elaborate system in Buddhism and the vast literature on it by the Buddhist teachers who flourished before Gauḍapāda, has developed into what we now find in the *Āgamaśāstra.*[16]

According to Bhattacharya, there are two schools of Vijñānavāda: a school of Vedāntins headed by Gauḍapāda, and a school of Buddhists with Maitreya at the head.[17] The difference between the two, according to Bhattacharya, consists in that Vedānta Vijñānavāda emphasizes Ātman and the concept of *māyā*, whereas Buddhist Vijñānavāda denies Ātman, and emphasizes thought (*citta*) and the concept of habit-energy (*vāsanā*).[18] Ultimately, however, according to Bhattacharya, the Brahman of Vedānta and the thought (*citta*) of Vijñānavāda are identical except that whereas the former is "*nitya*" (eternal), the latter is "*dhruva*" (enduring).[19] The word "*nitya,*" Bhattacharya notes, does not allow for change, whereas the word "*dhruva*" does allow for change.[20] According to Wayman, the *Māṇḍūkya-Upaniṣad* and *Gauḍapāda-kārikās* were composed concurrently by members of the Gauḍa school during the early Gupta dynasty (fifth century A.D.), and the members of Gauḍa school may have been Vedāntins who studied at one of the large Buddhist universities in northern India such as Nālandā.[21]

---

15. Radhakrishnan, Sarvepalli, *The Principal Upaniṣads, Bṛhadāraṇyaka-Upaniṣad* IV. 3.14, p. 259.
16. Bhattacharya, Vidhushekhara, *The Āgamaśāstra of Gauḍapāda*, p. cxxxii.
17. Ibid., p. cxxxii.
18. Ibid., p. cxxxiii.
19. Ibid., p. cxlii.
20. Ibid., p. cxl.
21. Hixon, Alexander Paul, *Mahāyāna Buddhist Influence on the Gauḍa School of Advaya Vedānta : An Analysis of the Gauḍapāda-kārikā,* (Unpublished Ph. D. dissertation, Columbia University, 1976).

Although Bhattacharya inclined towards the view that Gauḍapāda was a Vedāntin and that the *Āgamaśāstra* drew its primary inspiration from the Upaniṣads, in particular the *Bṛhadāraṇyaka Upaniṣad,* he nevertheless was aware of the traces of Buddhist influence throughout the work, particularly in the fourth *prakaraṇa.* Throughout the work, concepts, terms, and occasionally phrases seem to be drawn from Buddhist scriptures in what seems to be an attempt to syncretize Mahāyāna Buddhism and Vedānta.

2. ŚAṄKARA'S ASSOCIATION WITH THE GAUḌAPĀDA SCHOOL

a. Śaṅkara's Relationship with the Gauḍapāda School

In this section, Śaṅkara's possible association with the teacher Gauḍapāda (or school by that name) will be studied. It is possible that Śaṅkara's knowledge of Buddhism was obtained from the school or tradition named Gauḍapāda, as well as from the Mīmāṃsā teacher Kumārila, who had earlier attacked the Buddhists in his *Śloka-vārtika.* There is a tradition that the *paramaguru* of Śaṅkara was a figure named Gauḍapāda. Towards the end of the commentary on the *Gauḍapāda-kārikā*, the commentator salutes his paramaguru.

> prajñāvaiśākhavedhakṣubhitajalanidhervedanāmno 'ntarastham bhūtānyālokya magnānyaviratajananagrāhaghore samudre/
> kāruṇyāduddadhārāmṛtamidamarairdurlabhaṃ bhūtahetoryastaṃ pūjyābhipūjyaṃ paramagurumamuṃ pādapātairnato 'smi// (2)[1]

> I salute by prostration at the feet, the *guru* of my *guru*, to be honored among the honorable, who, having looked upon the beings immersed within the ocean terrible with monsters having incessant births, who out of compassion took up the nectar (*amṛta*) having the name of the Veda in the depths of the water stirred by the penetration of the churning-stick of insight (*prajñā*)—this (nectar) hard to obtain by the immortals deposited through a past reason.

Whether or not Śaṅkara wrote the commentary to the *Gauḍapāda-kārikā*, there are references to the *Gauḍapāda-kārikās* in the *Brahmasūtra-bhāṣya* of Śaṅkara. As Mahadevan notes, in his

---

1. Balasubramanyam, T K., *The Works of Śrī Śaṅkarāchārya*, Volume 5, (Srirangam : Sri Vani Vilas Press), containing a translation of *Māṇḍūkyopaniṣatkārikābhāṣyam*, commentary to *Āgama-śāstra* IV. 100, p. 230.

commentary to *Brahma-sūtra* II.1.9, Śaṅkara cites a verse from the *Gauḍapāda-kārikā*.

anādimāyayā supto yadā jīvaḥ prabudhyate/
ajam anidram asvapnam advaitaṃ budhyate tadā//[2]

When a Jīva asleep by means of beginningless *māyā* is awakened,
he is awakened to the Unborn, Sleepless, Dreamless, Non-dual.

The point Śaṅkara is urging in his commentary to *Brahma-sūtra* II.1.9 is that the Self remains unaffected by the states of creation, subsistence, destruction; consequently the Brahman is not affected by the world at the time of *pralaya*. Śaṅkara by introducing the verse from the *Gauḍapāda-kārikā* is equating the macrocosmic states of creation, subsistence, and destruction with the microcosmic states of waking, dream, and sleep, none of which affect the *Turīyā*. Furthermore, in his commentary to the *Brahma-sūtra* I.4.14, Śaṅkara referring to those who know the tradition cites another verse from the *Gauḍapāda-kārikās*.

tathā ca sampradāyavido vadanti—mṛllohavisphulliṅgādyaiḥ sṛṣṭiryā coditānyathā/upāyaḥ so'vatārāya nāsti bhedaḥ kathaṃcana iti/[3]

So also, those knowing the tradition say : "By the characteristic of earth, iron, sparks, etc. the creation (*sṛṣṭi*) which is otherwise enjoined, is the means for the realization "There is no difference in any way whatsoever."

Śaṅkara in his commentary to this *sūtra* is noting that although there are discrepancies in scriptural passages concerning the order of things created, nevertheless they all indicate the Brahman, from which comes the origin, subsistence and destruction of the world.

brūmaḥ—satyapi prativedāntaṃ sṛjyamāneṣvākāśādiṣu
kramādidvārake vigāne na sraṣṭari kiṃcidvigānamasti[4]

2. Bhattacharya, Vidhushekhara, *The Āgamaśāstra of Gauḍapāda*, *Āgamaśāstra* I. 16, p. 7.

3. Balasubrahmanyam, T. K., *The Works of Śrī Śaṅkarāchārya*, Volume I, *Brahmasūtra Bhāshya*, (Srirangam, India : Sri Vani Vilas Press), commentary to *Brahma-sūtra* I.4.14, p. 252.

4. Ibid., Volume I, commentary to *Brahma-sūtra* I.4.14, p. 251.

> In this case, we say : "In every Upaniṣad, although there is conflict occasioned by the order, etc. in connection with space, etc. being created, there is no confiict whatsoever in the case of the creator.

The purpose of the creation-texts, according to Śaṅkara, is not to teach the process of creation, but to teach the Brahman, as is indicated for Śaṅkara by a passage in *Chāndogya Upaniṣad* (VI.8.4).

> darśayati ca sṛṣṭyādiprapañcasya brahmapratipattyarthatām—'annena somya śuṅgenāpo mūlamanvicchādbhiḥ somya śuṅgena tejo mūlamanviccha tejasā somya śuṅgena sanmūlamanaviccha' iti/[5]
>
> It (Scripture) declares the ascertainment of the Brahman to be the purpose in connection with the treatment at length of creation, etc.—"With food as the offshoot, O *Saumya*, search for the root, water. With water as the offshoot (*śuṅga*), O *Saumya*, search for its root, fire. With fire as the offshoot, O *Saumya*, search for its root, the True.

The *Gauḍapāda-kārikā* passage exemplifies what for Śaṅkara is the ultimate truth—that there is no difference (*bheda*) between creator and creation.

> Mṛdādidṛṣṭāntaiśca kāryasya kāraṇenābhedaṃ vaditum sṛṣṭyādiprapañcaḥ śrāvyata iti gamyate[6]
>
> It is understood that by means of examples such as clay, the lengthy treatment of creation etc. is taught in order to declare the non-difference of effect from cause.

Many theories have been adopted to explain Śaṅkara's connection with Gauḍapāda or with the Gauḍapāda school. According to Hacker, as Alston notes, Śaṅkara began as an expositor of the Yoga system but later found the spiritual discipline of Advaita more effective.[7] According to Ingalls, Śaṅkara was brought up in the tradition of difference and non-difference

5. Ibid., p. 252.
6. Ibid., p. 252.
7. Alston, A. J., *Śaṅkara on the Absolute,* Volume I of *A Śaṅkara Source Book*, (London : Shanti Sadan, 1980), p. 48.

(*bhedābheda*) and was later influenced by the school represented in the *Gauḍapāda-karikā.*

> It seems to me likely that Śaṅkara was brought up in the Bhedābheda tradition and that he later turned away from it under the influence of a much more phenomenalistic school that is now represented only by the *Gauḍapāda Kārikās.* But Śaṅkara never went so far in the direction of phenomenalism as Gauḍapāda.[8]

Whaling explains, however, that Śaṅkara's opposition to *bhedābheda* in the *Brahmasūtra-bhāṣya* is no proof that he had earlier been a follower of *bhedābheda.* According to Whaling, it seems more probable that Śaṅkara began as a close follower of Gauḍapāda and then began to react against him.[9] According to Hixon, Śaṅkara's teachings reveal a synthesis of Mīmāṃsā and Gauḍa teachings so that Śaṅkara must have undergone early training under conservative Mīmāṃsā influences and was later exposed to the Gauḍa school.

> But also from the point of view of his philosophical attitudes, it is difficult to see how Shankara could have developed such an intense involvement with the conservative, text-oriented approach to Vedānta unless this reflected training and conditioning from a young age. Be this as it may, however, it is undeniable that Shankara represents a strangely precarious balance between the Mīmāṁsā conservativism and Gauḍa radicalism.[10]

According to Hixon, the writing style of the *Brahmasūtra-bhāṣya* of Śaṅkara has a strong flavor of the Mīmāṃsā school in its concern for interpreting passages so that they appear to have a single purport and in his use of hermeneutical techniques.[11] But in this text, Hixon notes, Śaṅkara also employs the Gauḍa

8. Whaling, Frank, "Śaṅkara and Buddhism," *Journal of Indian Philosophy* 7 (1979), p. 24.
9. Ibid., p. 24.
10. Hixon, Alexander Paul, *An Analysis of the Gauḍapādakārikā*, p. 62.
11. Ibid., p. 61.

approach, inherited from Mahāyāna, of "two texts, two truths."[12]

(b) The Authorship of the *Gauḍapāda-kārikā-bhāṣya*

In order to assess the possible relationship of Śaṅkara with the teacher, Gauḍapāda (or school by that name), it is necessary to approach the question of Śaṅkara's supposed authorship of the commentary to the *Gauḍapāda-kārikas* and the question of Śaṅkara's historical relationship to the school or person that was Gauḍapāda. One of the chief objections to the theory of Śaṅkara's authorship of the commentary to the *Māṇḍūkya-kārikā* is the fact that the author of the commentary to the *Gauḍapāda-kārikās* seems to approve of the subjective idealism of the *Gauḍapāda-kārikās* by which the dream and waking states are equated. Such approval contradicts Śaṅkara's position in the *Brahmasūtra*-bhāṣya, where Śaṅkara refutes what he considers to be the Vijñānavāda position that dream and waking states are equivalent. According to the *Gauḍapāda-kārikās*, the waking and dream states are equivalent in that each state involves the dichotomy of subject and object.

> yathā svapne dvayābhāsaṃ spandate māyayā manaḥ/
> tathā jāgrad dvayābhāsaṃ spandate māyayā manaḥ/[13]
>
> As the mind in dream vibrates having a two-fold appearance, so in the waking state, the mind having a two-fold appearance vibrates through *māyā*.

According to the commentator the dream and waking states are equivalent in that each involves the dichotomy of subject and object.

> kathaṃ punaḥ sato māyayaiva janmetyucyate—yathā rajjvāṃ vikalpitaḥ sarpo rajjurūpeṇāvekṣyamāṇaḥ san, evam manaḥ paramātmavijñaptyātmarūpeṇāvekṣyamāṇaṃ sat grāhyagrāhakarūpeṇa dvayābhāsaṃ spandate svapne māyayā, rajjvāmiva

12. Bhattacharya, Vidhushekhara, *The Āgamaśāstra of Gauḍapāda*, p. lxx.

13. Ibid., p. lxxi.

sarpaḥ; tathā tadvadeva jāgrat jāgarite spandate māyayā manaḥ, spandata ivetyarthaḥ//[14]

How again is it said that there is birth of an existing thing through *māyā*? As a snake imagined in a rope is existent, while addressed under the form of a rope, so the mind is addressed as existent under the formation of the self and the representation (*vijñapti*) of the highest self, and has a two-fold appearance of subject and object. It vibrates in dream through magical display (*māyā*)—like the snake in the rope. "So," in this manner, "awake" in the waking state, the mind vibrates through magical display; "it vibrates," signifies "as though it vibrates."

The commentator's approval here of the equation of dream and waking states is in marked contrast to the position taken by Śaṅkara in the *Brahmasūtra-bhāṣya*, where the dream and waking states are declared to be quite distinct. Śaṅkara in the *Brahmasūtra-bhāṣya* stresses the empirical reality of perception in the waking state.

atrocyate—na svapnādipratyayavajjāgratpratyayā bhavitumarhanti; kasmāt? vaidharmyāt—vaidharmyaṃ hi bhavati svapnajāgaritayoḥ; kiṃ punarvaidharmyaṃ? bādhābādhaviti brūmaḥ bādhyate hi svapnopalabdhaṃ vastu pratibuddhasya[15]

It is said—like the notions of dreams, etc. the notions of the waking state are not able to be. Why? Because of diversity. There is diversity in connection with the dream-state and the waking-state. Why is there diversity? We say, "Because of supplanting and non-supplanting," for a given thing perceived in dream is supplanted for the waking state.

Śaṅkara in his commentary even employs the term "*bādhyate*" to emphasize that the things apprehended as real in the dream-state are supplanted in the waking-state. His position here seems in marked contrast to the position taken by the commentator on the *Gauḍapāda-kārikās*. According to Ingalls, Śaṅkara's position

---

14. Balasubrahmanyam, T. K., *The Works of Śrī Śaṅkarāchārya, Māṇḍūkyakārikā-bhāṣya* III.29.

15. Ibid., Volume II, commentary to *Brahma-sūtra* II.2.29, p. 400.

in the *Brahmasūtra-bhāṣya* has made him liable to the charge of hypocrisy by ancient and modern critics, who are dubious about Śaṅkara's inconsistency.

> Let me next consider Bhāskara's charge of hypocrisy against Śaṁkara. The same charge has been brought forward by a few scholars in modern times also. It may be put most strongly as follows. In arguing against the Vijñānavāda, Śaṁkara seems to argue as a realist. Certainly he seems to insist on the reality of the external thing. On the other hand, when developing his own system of philosophy, he claims not once but a hundred times that the world is unreal, as unreal as the foam on water, as the trick of a magician, as a mirage, as a dream. If not hypocrisy, this is at least a logical contradiction. Or is it?[16]

The ancient commentator Bhāskara, for instance, as Ingalls observes, excoriates Śaṅkara in his own commentary to this *sūtra* for being one of "the *māyāvādins* hanging on to Buddhist doctrine"[17] (*ye tu bauddhamatāvalambino māyāvādinaste...*).[18] It should be noted, however, that the seeming contradictoriness of the positions taken by Śaṅkara in the *Brahmasūtra-bhāṣya* and by the commentator on the *Gauḍapāda-kārikās*, may not indicate philosophical inconsistency. Mahadevan notes that the subjective idealism of the *Gauḍapāda-kārikās* may be simply a device.

> The procedure followed by Gauḍapāda, then, is exactly similar to that adopted by the Absolute Idealists in the West in their criticism of the Realistic doctrines. Subjectivist arguments are advanced only to overthrow Realism. And when this is accomplished, Subjectivism itself is subjected to unsparing criticism; and is finally discarded.[19]

---

16. Ingalls, Daniel H. H., "Śaṁkara's Arguments Against the Buddhists," p. 304.

17. Ibid., p. 294.

18. Dvivedin, Pandit Vindhyesvari Prasad. *Brahma-sūtra With a Commentary by Bhāskarāchārya*, Chowkhamba Sanskrit Series, Numbers 70, 185 and 209. (Banaras : Vidya Vilas Press, 1915), commentary to *Brahmasūtra* II.2.29, p. 124.

19. Mahadevan, T.M.P., *Gauḍapāda : A Study in Early Advaita*, (Madras : University of Madras, 1952), p. 198.

Mahadevan's argument can be extended to the case of the commentary on the *Gauḍapāda-kārikās*; there is no need to regard the equation of dream and waking states in the commentary to the *Gauḍapāda-kārikās* as opposed to the position of the *Brahmasūtra-bhāṣya* if the equation of dream and waking states in the former is simply regarded as a procedural or methodological device. Therefore, the argument of inconsistency is not necessarily sufficient to disprove Śaṅkara's authorship of the traditional commentary to the *Gauḍapāda-kārikās*, or to accuse him of hypocrisy if he were the traditional commentator. Mahadevan cites B. Bosanquet on the value of subjective idealism as a methodological or procedural device to produce dissatisfaction with the world blindly accepted by common sense.

> It is necessary to be wholly dissatisfied with common-sense theory, and with the notion of a ready-made world set up for us to copy in the mind, before the logical analysis of intellectual construction can have interest or meaning for us. And to produce this dissatisfaction is the value of subjective idealism.[20]

According to Alston, modern research, utilizing the methods of Professor Hacker, has removed all reasonable doubt as to the authenticity of Śaṅkara's authorship of the commentary to the *Māṇḍūkya Upaniṣad* with *Gauḍapāda-kārikās*.

In his article, "On the Author of the *Māṇḍūkyopaniṣad*—and the *Gauḍapādīya-bhāṣya*," Mayeda tests the authenticity of the *Gauḍapāda-kārikā-bhāṣya* or *Gauḍapādīya-bhāṣya* by comparing it with the *Brahmasūtra-bhāṣya* in connection with the use of eight terms—*avidyā*, *nāmarūpa*, *māyā*, *Īśvara*, *ānanda*, *vivarta*, *Śiva*, and *Vyāsa*. According to Mayeda, Śaṅkara's stylistic and conceptual peculiarities are so manifest in his use of these particular terms that his works can be distinguished by this method even from the works of his disciples. Mayeda concludes that as a result of his comparison the *Gauḍapādīya-bhāṣya* is in complete agreement with the *Brahmasūtra-bhāṣya* in connection with the usage of these eight terms.[21] Therefore, according to Mayeda, Śaṅkara

20. Ibid., (citing Bosanquet, B., *The Essentials of Logic*, London: MacMillan & Co., 1928, p. 20), p. 199.

21. Mayeda, Sengaku, "On the Author of the *Māṇḍūkyopaniṣad*—and

must be the author of the *Gauḍapādīya-bhāṣya.* Mayeda also mentions four points raised by those who question the authenticity of Śaṅkara's authorship of the *Gauḍapādīya-bhāṣya*: first, that whereas in the *Brahmasūtra-bhāṣya,* Śaṅkara demonstrates knowledge of Buddhism, the author of the *Gauḍapādīya-bhāṣya* seems ignorant of Buddhism; secondly, that the author of the *Gauḍapādīya-bhāṣya* uses Buddhist technical terms used neither in the *Gauḍapāda-kārikās* nor in the *Brahmasūtra-bhāṣya* (for example, the highest Ātman is called *vijñapti*), thirdly, that there are several cases of interpretation which do not look like Śaṅkara's (e.g., the author of the *Gauḍapādīya-bhāṣya* asserts that *asparśayoga* is well known in the Upaniṣads although it is never mentioned in the Upaniṣads); fourthly, that the *Gauḍapādīya-bhāṣya* begins and ends with benedictory stanzas, although benedictory stanzas are seen in comparatively modern works.[22] To Mayeda, the first three objections are closely related in that they have to do with the philosophical standpoint of the author of the *Gauḍapādīya-bhāṣya,* and his consequent principle of interpretation. That philosophical standpoint, according to Mayeda, and that principle of interpretation, represent "advaitinization." The purpose of the *Gauḍapāda-kārikās* for the commentator, according to Mayeda, is to reveal the knowledge of Brahman and so the author interprets it consistently from the Advaitin point of view. Mayeda says of the author of the *Gauḍapādīya-bhāṣya*:

> According to him the objective of the *Gauḍapādīya-kārikā* is the realization of the state of non-duality (*advaitabhāva*), i.e., the realization of the natural state of Ātman (*svasthatā*) and the *Gauḍapādīyakārikā* was meant to reveal the knowledge of Brahman. In other words, the author intends to interpret it consistently from the Advaita point of view.[23]

Mayeda goes on to note that the effect of the *Gauḍapādīya-bhāṣya* was to give the *kārikās* an Advaitic character and that the *Gauḍa-*

---

the *Gauḍapādīya-bhāṣya,*" *Dr. V. Raghavan Felicitation Volume,* (Madras, India : The Adyar Library and Research Centre, 1967-1968), p. 75.

22. Ibid., p. 85-86.
23. Ibid., p. 87.

pādīya-bhāṣya represents a turning point in the Vedānta tradition, which until the time of the *Gauḍapādīya-bhāṣya* had been becoming more Buddhistic.[24] Mayeda seems to assume, however, that each chapter (*prakaraṇa*) of the *Gauḍapāda-kārikās* is more Buddhistic in character than the preceding chapter, that each was written after the preceding, that the *Māṇḍūkya Upaniṣad* was written prior to the *Gauḍapāda-kārikās,* and that there was not one author who composed or compiled the text of the *Gauḍapāda-kārikās,* when he speaks of the *Gauḍapādīya-bhāṣya* as a turning point in a Vedānta tradition becoming progressively more Buddhistic. Furthermore, Mayeda's statement ignores the tradition of the *Brahma-sūtra* and its commentators—a tradition which attempts to refute what it considers to be Buddhist doctrines. Mayeda's point, however, is that the *Gauḍapādīya-bhāṣya* represents an attempt to reinterpret the Buddhistic tendencies of the Gauḍa tradition along Advaita lines, whereas in the *Brahmasūtra-bhāṣya*, Śaṅkara tries to reinterpret a *bhedābheda* text along Advaita lines.

> On the other hand, in the *Gauḍapādīyabhāṣya*, the commentator's knowledge of Buddhism is tacitly used to transmit Buddhist doctrines into Advaitism...[25]

The process of "advaitinization" of the *Gauḍapāda-kārikās,* as well as of other scriptures, according to Mayeda, is responsible for Śaṅkara's seeming ignorance of Buddhism, his idiosyncratic use and interpretation of Buddhist terms and Upaniṣadic passages. According to Mayeda, Śaṅkara had a profound knowledge of Buddhism. What lies behind the commentator's interpretation of a word like "*dharma,*" in *Gauḍapāda-kārikā* IV. 99, in one case as "Ātman" and in another case as "*viṣayāntara*" is not ignorance, according to Mayeda, but intentional misinterpretation. In his commentary to *Gauḍapāda-kārikā* IV.99, the commentator seems to be aware of the meaning of the terms "*dharma*" and "*buddha*" in the Buddhist context, but interprets them in terms of his own purposes.

24. Ibid., p. 88.
25. Ibid., pp. 90-91.

kramate na hi buddhasya jñānam dharmeṣu tāyinaḥ/
sarvadharmās tathā jñānaṃ naitad buddhena bhāṣitam//99//[26]

Interpreting this passage in terms of the "silence" of the Buddha, Bhattacharya translates as follows:

> According to the Buddha who instructs the way known to him (*tāyin*), *jñāna* does not approach the *dharmas* (i.e., it does not relate itself to the objects). But all *dharmas* as well as *jñāna*—this has not been said by the Buddha.[27]

This passage, however, may also be interpreted in terms of the Buddha as protector. Thus another possible translation proceeds as follows:

> The knowledge (*jñāna*) of the protector (*tāyin*) Buddha does not extend to *dharmas*.
>
> Likewise, all *dharmas* (do not extend to) knowledge—this was not spoken by the Buddha.

Swami Gambhirananda's translation, which reflects the traditional commentary, proceeds as follows:

> 99. The knowledge of the enlightened man, who is all-pervasive, does not extend to objects; and so the souls, too, do not reach out to objects. This view was not expressed by Buddha.[28]

The shifting interpretation of the terms "*dharma*" and "*tāyin*" in the traditional commentary should be noted.

> yasmān na hi kramate buddhasya paramārthadarśino jñānaṃ viṣayāntareṣu dharmeṣu dharmasaṃsthaṃ savitarīva prabhā/ tāyinaḥ tāyo 'syāstīti tāyī, saṃtānavato nirantarasya ākāśakalpasyetyarthaḥ; pūjāvato vā prajñāvato vā sarve dharmā ātmāno

---

26. Bhattacharya, Vidhushekhara, *The Āgamaśāstra of Gauḍapāda*, *Āgamaśāstra* IV. 99, p. 212.

27. Ibid., *Āgamaśāstra* IV. 99, p. 212.

28. Gambhirananda, Swami, *Eight Upaniṣads*, Volume II, containing translation of *Māṇḍūkya Upaniṣad* and *Kārikā* and commentary of Śaṅkara. (Calcutta : Advaita Ashram, 1966, reprint), *Āgamaśāstra* IV. 99, p. 401.

'pi tathā jñānavadeva ākāśakalpatvānna kramante kvacidapyarthāntara ityarthaḥ/[29]

For, from that there is the knowledge situated in *dharma* like the light of the sun. In connection with the awakened one (*buddha*) seeing the absolute, (this knowledge) does not extend to *dharmas* or distinct sense-objects.

In the phrase "Of the protector (*tāyin*)," the "protector (*tāyin*)" is in reference to the pervading (*tāya*) by him; the meaning is that it is like the continuous succession without interval that is similar to space. Or the phrase "Of the protector" is in connection with the one endowed with either honour or insight. The significance is that the *dharmas* or Selves (Ātman), likewise, like knowledge, do not extend to distinct object-entities anywhere, because of similarity to space.

Of the commentator's treatment of the term "*dharma*," Mayeda says that what is involved here is intentional misinterpretation, not ignorance.

The term *dharma* in the *Gauḍapādīyakārikā* IV. 99 is no doubt used in a Buddhist sense, i.e. 'a thing' or 'an object of knowledge.' However, the commentator explains it as Ātman. He sometimes does not interpret it. This fact probably does not indicate ignorance of the Buddhist usage of the term, but rather an intentional misinterpretation by the author so as to give the text an Advaitic character.[30]

That Śaṅkara was quite aware of the Buddhist sense of the term *dharma* is according to Mayeda attested by a verse in the *Upadeśasāhasrī* where he uses the term in a Buddhistic sense to refute a Buddhist tenet.[31]

kṣaṇikaṃ hi tad atyarthaṃ dharmamātraṃ nirantaraṃ/
sādṛśyād dīpavat taddhīs tacchāntiḥ puruṣārthatā//[32]

---

29. Balasubrahmanyam, T. K., *The Works of Śrī Śaṅkarāchārya*, Volume 5, commentary on *Āgamaśāstra* IV. 99, p. 229.

30. Mayeda, Sengaku, "On the Author of the *Māṇḍūkyopaniṣad* and the *Gauḍapādīya-bhāṣya*," p. 88.

31. Ibid., p. 90.

32. Balasubrahmanyam, T. K., *The Works of Śrī Śaṅkarāchārya*, Volume 14, *Upadeśasāhasrī* 1.16.23, p. 192.

23. (All) this is indeed the mere *dharma* (element of life) which indeed perishes every moment and arises without intervals. (Though all this is momentary), there arises the recognition that this (is that past one, because of similarity, just as a lamp (at this moment is recognized to be the same as it was at the previous moment on account of similarity). The cessation of (all) this is the aim of life.[33]

The more accurate treatment of the term "*dharma,*" in comparison with its treatment in the commentary to *Gauḍapāda-kārikā* IV. 99 should be noted. The reasonably accurate presentation of the Buddhist explanation of memory in terms of similarity should also be noted. Mayeda also indicates, however, the difference between Śaṅkara's approach to Buddhism in his *Brahmasūtra-bhāṣya,* and the approach of the author of the *Gauḍapādīya-bhāṣya*. In the *Brahmasūtra-bhāṣya* the process of "advaitinization" is directed towards the *bhedābheda* of the *Brahma-sūtras* and its tradition of commentary; the approach towards Buddhism is one of refutation only. Consequently, Mayeda explains, Śaṅkara's commentary, in comparison with those of Bhāskara and Rāmānuja, is far removed from the original significance of the *Brahma-sūtras*.[34] But in the *Gauḍapādīya-bhāṣya*, Mayeda notes, the process of "advaitinization" is directed towards the Buddhist doctrines of the Gauḍa tradition.[35] In this way, Mayeda demonstrates the authenticity of Śaṅkara's authorship of the *Gauḍapādīya-bhāṣya* or the *Gauḍapāda-bhāṣya*, and illumines Śaṅkara's intention towards the work of interpretation—to interpret the texts in an Advaitic way.

---

33. Mayeda, Sengaku, *A Thousand Teachings, Upadeśasāhasrī* I.16.23, p. 151.

34. Mayeda, Sengaku, "On the Author of the *Māṇḍūkyopaniṣad* and the *Gauḍapādīya-bhāṣya,*" p. 90.

35. Ibid., p. 91.

(3) THE CHARACTERIZATION OF ŚAṄKARA AS "CRYPTO"-BUDDHIST

In this section Śaṅkara's supposed "crypto"-Buddhism and his relationship to previous commentators on the *Brahma-sūtras* will be discussed. It must be recalled that Śaṅkara has been regarded by his opponents as a "crypto"-Buddhist. Bhāskara, a later Vedāntic commentator, for instance, refers to "the *māyāvādins* hanging on to Buddhist doctrine."[1]

> ye tu bauddhamatāvalambino māyāvādinaste 'pyanena nyāyena sūtrakāreṇaiva nirastā veditavyāḥ[2]
>
> These *māyāvādins* hanging on to Buddhist doctrines are to be known as refuted by the *sūtrakāra* through this logic.

Bhāskara goes on to excoriate Śaṅkara for attempting to refute Śūnyavāda through the argument that the world cannot be denied except on the basis of the discovery of another truth. Bhāskara accuses Śaṅkara of slyly denying the world on the basis of Ātman.

> atha manyase 'nyasmin sthāyini vastvantare 'sati vijñānamātraṃ neṣyate sati punarātmatattve prapañcāpalāpa iti /[3]
>
> Now you think, "When there is no other permanent thing, no other given thing, consciousness-only (*vijñāna-mātra*) is rejected, but when there is the truth (*tattva*) of the self there is dissolution of the manifold world.

Ingalls interprets this passage as follows :

> "Perhaps you reason thus," he says, "So long as there is no other permanent entity, pure consciousness is to be denied.

---

1. Ingalls, Daniel H. H., "Śaṁkara's Arguments Against the Buddhists," p. 294.

2. Dvivedin, Pandit Vindhyesvari Prasada, editor, *Brahmasūtra With A Commentary by Bhāskarāchārya*, commentary on *Brahma-sūtra* II.2.29, p. 124.

3. Ibid., p. 124.

> But when there is the true Ātman, then we can get rid of the world." Bhāskara goes on to ask, "What sort of logic is this ?"[4]

According to Ingalls, however, Śaṅkara's emphasis in his commentary to *Brahma-sūtra* II.2.29 is on the necessity of something beyond cognition, namely a cognizer.

> Notice, first, that in arguing with the Buddhist idealists Śaṁkara's emphasis is not so much on the necessity of the external world as it is on the necessity of something beyond cognition.[5]

An interesting contribution to the study of Śaṅkara's "crypto"-Buddhism and Śaṅkara's relationship to previous commentators on the *Brahma-sūtras* has been made by Daniel H.H. Ingalls in his articles "Śaṁkara's Arguments Against the Buddhists" (*Philosophy East and West*, Volume III, Number 4, January 1954) and "The Study of Śaṁkarācārya" (*Annals of the Bhandarkar Oriental Research Institute*, Volume XXXIII, 1952). In these articles he concedes that the earliest extant commentary to the *Brahma-sūtras* is the *Brahmasūtra-bhāṣya* of Śaṅkara, written probably early in the eighth century A.D. and that the next earliest commentary is that of Bhāskara, written around 800 A.D. But he also concludes, on the basis of certain evidence, that there must have been an earlier commentary which served as the basis for Śaṅkara's and Bhāskara's later works. The author of this earlier commentary Ingalls simply calls the "Protocommentator."[6] One basis, according to Ingalls, for assuming the existence of a protocommentary is the fact that Bhāskara, Śaṅkara, and commentators of Śaṅkara's *Brahma-sūtra-bhāṣya* refer to a figure called the "*vṛttikāra*," the commentator. In his commentary to *Brahma-sūtra* I.1.9, I.1.23, I.2.23, and III.3.53 (as listed by Dasgupta), Śaṅkara mentions the *vṛttikāra*.[7] Ingalls makes the very interesting observation

---

4. Ingalls, Daniel H. H., "Śaṁkata's Arguments Against the Buddhists" p. 304.

5. Ibid., p, 304.

6. Ibid., p. 293.

7. Das Gupta, Surendranath, *A History of Indian Philosophy*, Volume II, p. 43.

that wherever the supercommentators of Śaṅkara's works indicate that Śaṅkara is departing from the proto-commentary, it is to be noted that Bhāskara upholds the views of the proto-commentator and passionately objects to Śaṅkara's departure.[8] Ingalls thinks that Bhāskara's commentary is based largely on the protocommentary. Ingalls also points out that a large part of Bhāskara's commentary is basically similar to Śaṅkara's. Since Bhāskara had little love for Śaṅkara, whom he often attacks in vitriolic fashion, it cannot be said that Bhāskara was borrowing from Śaṅkara. Rather, it seems better to assume, Ingalls explains, the existence of a common proto-commentary which served as the basis for the work of Śaṅkara and Bhāskara. One instance, according to Ingalls, where the supercommentators mention that Śaṅkara is departing from the views of the *vṛttikāra*, the Protocommentator, occurs at *Brahma-sūtra* I.1.19. The *sūtra* proceeds as follows :

> asminnasya ca tad yogam śāsti[9]
> And, moreover, it (i.e. the scripture) teaches the joining of this with that on that (being fully known).

In his commentary to this *sūtra*, Śaṅkara first presents the view which Govardhana and Ānandagiri, according to Ingalls,[10] attribute to the *vṛttikāra*, or Protocommentator. According to this view, the *ānandamayātman* (self consisting in bliss) is identified with the Paramātman (Highest Self), in that otherwise liberation (*mokṣa*) is not possible. Brahman in itself, Śaṅkara explains, cannot be described as "abounding in bliss." For Śaṅkara, the term *ānandamaya* (consisting of bliss) is no more a description of Brahman than the other members of the series beginning with *anna-maya* (consisting of food). The affix "*-maya*," according to Śaṅkara, denotes modification just as in the case of the other members of the series.

---

8. Ingalls, Daniel H. H., "Śaṁkara's Arguments Against the Buddhists," p. 293.

9. Radhakrishnan, Sarvepalli, *The Brahma Sūtra, Brahma Sūtra* I.1.19, p. 260.

10. Ingalls, Daniel H. H., Śaṁkara's Arguments Against the Buddhists," p. 293.

tasmādaṇumātramapi viśeṣamanāśritya na svata eva priya-śirastvādi brahmaṇa upapadyate / na ceha saviśeṣam brahma pratipipādayiṣitaṃ, vāṅmanasagocarātikramaṇaśruteḥ / tasmā-dannamayādiṣvivānandamaye 'pi vikārārtha eva mayaṭ vijñe-yaḥ na prācuryārthaḥ[11]

Therefore, not without having relied upon qualification even of an atom only, (the statements) beginning with "But pleasure is the head," are not possible of the Brahman itself. Nor is it desired that the qualified Brahman be explained, because of śruti concerned with the transcendence of the range of speech and mind. Therefore, as in the case of "*anna-maya*", so in the case of "*ānanda-maya*" the affix "*mayaṭ*" is to be understood as having the meaning of modification (*vikāra*), not abundance (*prācurya*).

It seems, therefore, that Śaṅkara is relegating the *ānandamaya* to the sphere of empirical or relative (*vyavahāra*) truth, thereby declaring in opposition to the view attributed by Govardhana and Ānandagiri to the *vṛttikāra*, that the *ānandamayātman* (the Self consisting of bliss) and the Paramātman (the Highest Self) are not equivalent in the sense that *ānanda* (bliss) can be considered to be of the nature of the Brahman. Bhāskara, however, as Ingalls notes, accepts the interpretation of the *vṛttikāra* or Protocommentator and criticizes Śaṅkara's interpretation, and says "The proper way to interpret this *sūtra* is the traditionally handed down way." Although Śaṅkara departs from the traditional interpretation of the *vṛttikāra*, however, one must not be too quick to dismiss his interpretations as "parenthetical remarks." Other passages in which Śaṅkara departs from the traditional commentary of the *vṛttikāra* to the refrain of vitriolic criticism on Bhāskara's part are listed as follows : *Brahma-sūtra* I.1.23; I.2.23; I.4.26. There has been much speculation in relation to the identity of the *vṛttikāra* in Śaṅkara's *Brahma-sūtra-bhāṣya*. S. Das Gupta mentions an article by Prof. S. Kuppusvami Śāstri in which he quotes a passage from Veṅkaṭa's *Tattvaṭīkā* on Rāmānuja's commentary on the *Brahma-sūtras*, in which it is said that Upavarṣa is a name of Bodhāyana:

11. Balasubrahmanyam, T. K., *The Works of Śrī Śaṅkarāchārya*, Volume I, commentary to *Brahma-sūtra* I.1.19, p. 62.

vṛttikārasya Bodhāyanasyaiva hi Upavarṣa iti syān nāma.[12] S. Das Gupta goes on to explain that the commentaries on Śaṅkara's *Brahmasūtra-bhāṣya* say that, when he refers to the *vṛttikāra* (or proto-commentator) in *Brahma-sūtra* I.1.9, I.1.23, I.2.23, and III.5.3, he refers to Upavarṣa by name.[13] In only one of these passages, however, does Śaṅkara refer to Upavarṣa by name, that is to say, in his commentary to *Brahma-sūtra* III.3.53.

Rāmānuja also attacks the Vedāntins of Śaṅkara's school. In his attempt to refute the Vijñānavādins, Rāmānuja also attacks those Vedāntins (presumably of Śaṅkara's school) whom he calls "crypto"-Buddhists (*pracchanna-bauddha*) for their supposed position that the absolute (*paramārtha*) is mere knowledge (*jñānamātra*)—a position formulated according to Rāmānuja on the basis of knowledge in a form having both action (*karma*) and agent (*kartṛ*), a subject and an object.

> evaṃrūpeṇa sakarmakeṇa sakartṛkeṇa jñādhātvarthena sarvalokasākṣikamaparokṣamavabhāsamānenaiva, jñānamātrameva paramārthaḥ 'iti sādhayantaḥ sarvalokopahāsopakaraṇaṃ bhavantīti vedavādacchadmapracchannabauddhanirākaraṇe nipuṇataraṃ prapañcitam /[14]

> That, establishing knowledge only as the ultimate in such a form by means of the type of knowledge which has action and agent, and which is appearing as perceptible to all the witnesses in the world, they are a matter of laughter for the world, is developed next in the refutation of the Buddhist hidden by a cover of belief in the Veda.

12. Das Gupta, Surendranath, *A History of Indian Philosophy*, Volume II, p. 43.

13. Ibid., p. 43.

14. Viraraghavacharya, Sri Uttamur T., *Brahmasūtra-Śrībhāshya*, commentary to Brahma-sūtra II.2.27, p. 539.

4. THE TWO TRUTHS

(a) The Two Truths in Relation to Gauḍapāda

A concept which the *Gauḍapāda-kārikās* have in common with Buddhism and which is taken up by Śaṅkara is that of "two truths"—the absolute truth (*paramārtha-satya*) and conventional truth (*saṃvṛti-satya*). It is to be noted that the Upaniṣads also speak of a higher science (*parāvidyā*) and a lower science (*aparā-vidyā*). Associated with the distinction of types of truth is the distinction of spiritual states (*āśrama*). Truth is thereby made provisional in accordance with the needs of the seeker.

> 16. āśramās trividhā hīnamadhyamotkṛṣṭadṛṣṭayaḥ /
> upāsanopadiṣṭeyaṃ tadarthaṃ anukampayā //[1]
>
> There are three types of stages—the lower vision, the middle vision, the superior vision; Therefore the meditative exercise (*upāsanā*) is to be taught out of compassion.

The treatment of *upāsanā* (meditative exercise) here may be the precedent for Śaṅkara's treatment of *upāsanā* as it is described by V. Raghavan in his Introduction to *The Thirty Two Vidya-s*.

> Śaṁkara says that such is man's habitual preoccupation with action that it is difficult to get away from it and hence the upāsanā-s or meditations on aspects of these acts in a higher significance, to be mentally dwelt upon, form one way of slowly abstracting oneself from them...[2]

In *Gauḍapāda-kārikā* IV. 58, the "two truths" are presented through the term "*saṃvṛti*" and the term "*tattva*". In this verse it is said that *dharmas*, which are said to be born, are born only from the standpoint of conventional truth (*saṃvṛti*), not in reality (*tattva*).

---

1. Bhattacharya, Vidhushekhara, *The Āgamaśāstra of Gauḍapāda*, *Āgamaśāstra* III.15, p. 58

2. Aiyar, Narayanaswami, *The Thirty-Two Vidya-s*, Volume 90, Adyar Library Series, (Madras, India : The Adyar Library and Research Centre, 1962, reprint), from Introduction by Professor Raghavan, p. v.

58. dharmā ya iti jāyante saṃvṛtyā te na tattvataḥ /
janma māyopamaṃ teṣāṃ sā ca māyā na vidyate //[3]

In reference to those *dharmas* which are born, they are born by convention not in reality. Their birth is like magical display, and that magical display does not exist.

In the second half of this verse, there appears the term "*māyā*" which is employed in a variety of meanings in the Indian context and which here signifies "magical display." The birth of *dharmas* is declared to be "like magical display." The term "*māyā*" as signifying magical display is employed in other *kārikās* of the *Gauḍapāda-kārikā*, such as *kārikā* 59, fourth chapter (*prakaraṇa*).

59. yathā māyāmayād bijāj jāyate tanmayo 'ṅkuraḥ /
nāsau nityo na cocchedī tadvad dharmeṣu yojanā //[4]

From a seed constituted of a magical display (*māyāmaya*) is born a sprout constituted of the same; that is neither eternal nor attended with destruction. In this way, there is the application to *dharmas*.

The use of the term "*māyā*" in the sense of magical display in the *Gauḍapāda-kārikās* has precedent in Buddhist literature, as for example the following sentence in the *Catuḥśataka* from which the *kārikā* cited above seems to have been drawn.

yathā hi kṛtakād bījāj jāyate taṅmayo 'ṅkuraḥ[5]
For insofar as it takes birth from a created (*kṛtaka*) seed, that sprout is constituted of the same

In *Gauḍapāda-kārikā* IV. 73, the terms "*parikalpita*" (imagined) and "*paratantra*" (dependent) are associated with each other and declared to exist from the standpoint of empirical truth only, not absolute truth.

73. yo 'sti kalpitasaṃvṛtyā paramārthena nāsty asau /
paratantro 'bhisaṃvṛtyā syān nāsti paramārthataḥ //[6]

---

3. Bhattacharya, Vidhushekhara, *The Āgamaśāstra of Gauḍapāda*, *Āgamaśāstra* IV. 58, p. 163.
4. Ibid., p. 164.
5. Ibid., p. 164.
6. Ibid., p. 174.

> That which exists by convention, which is fabricated, does not exist by means of the absolute.
> The dependent (*paratantra*) may exist only by means of convention; it does not exist in reality.

In this *kārikā*, the characteristic of being imagined (*kalpita*) seems to be equated with the characteristic of being dependent (*paratantra*), in that they possess the common quality of existing by means of convention (*abhisaṃvṛti*), not by means of the absolute (*paramārtha*). The relationship among these three terms is explained by Bhattacharya on the basis of Prajñākaramati's statement in the *Bodhicaryāvatāra-pañjikā*.

> It is to be noted that *saṃvṛti* consists in *parikalpita* and *paratantra svabhāvas* and *paramārtha* in *pariniṣpanna*. Thus it is rightly said in the *kārikā* 73 that *paratantra* can exist only in practical truth (*saṃvṛti*) and not in any way in absolute truth. This is fully explained by Prajñākaramati (in his *Bodhicaryāvatārapañjikā*, pp. 354-355) saying that whatever comes into existence (*jāyate*) does so being dependent on the entirety of the cause and conditions (*hetupratyayasāmagrī*), and that which is thus dependent for its existence has not existence in reality, like a shadow on a looking glass.[7]

The point here is that whatever arises dependent on causes and conditions is like a magical display. Prajñākaramati in the *Bodhicaryāvatāra-pañjikā* explains as follows :

> api tu hetupratyayasāmagrīṃ pratītya māyāvad utpadyate[8]
> Dependent on the forest of causes and conditions, it arises like a magical display.

(b) The Two Truths in Relation to Śaṅkara.

One of the strongest parallels to Buddhism in Śaṅkara's works as well as in the *Gauḍapāda-kārikās* is the notion of two truths, the practical (*vyavahāra*) and the absolute (*paramārtha*). The practical in Śaṅkara's writings parallels the conventional (*saṃvṛti*) in Mahāyāna Buddhism. The term "*saṃvṛti*" is derived from the verb "*saṃvṛ*" ("*vṛ*" in the root-form) and signifies

7. Ibid., p. 179.
8. Ibid., p. 179.

enclosure, concealment, covering, even dissimulation. The term "*vyavahāra*" is derived from the verb "*vyavahṛ*" ("*hṛ*" in the root-form) and signifies practice, conduct, and behavior. Both the term "*saṃvṛti*" and the term "*vyavahāra*," however, connote the relative as opposed to the absolute. The notion of two truths provided Śaṅkara with a useful tool for setting forth his Advaita and for the "advaitinization" of the *Brahma-sūtra* tradition. It has already been mentioned that in his commentary to the *Brahma-sūtra* I.4.14, Śaṅkara explains the differences among the creation texts by noting that these differences are secondary in relation to their primary significance of indicating the Brahman as that from which the origin, subsistence, and destruction of the world proceed.

> brūmaḥ—satyapi prativedāntaṃ sṛjyamāneṣvākāśādiṣu kramādidvārake vigāne, na sraṣṭari kiṃcidvigānamasti[9]
> We say : "Although in every Upaniṣad there is a conflict occasioned by the order of things being created, space, etc., there is no conflict whatsoever in the case of the creator."

It must also be noted, however, that even the notion of difference between creator and created is regarded in the commentary to this *sūtra* as in some sense secondary, for in reality the effect is not different from the cause.

> mṛdādidṛṣṭāntaiśca kāryasya kāraṇenābhedaṃ vaditum sṛṣṭyādiprapañcaḥ śrāvyata iti gamyate[10]
> It is understood that the elaboration of creation, etc. is taught in order to declare the non-difference of effect with cause by means of examples of clay, etc.

In another text, the commentary to *Brahma-sūtra* II.1.14, the cause as the Brahman and the effect as the manifold world are declared to be in reality non-different. In his commentary to the previous *sūtra, Brahma-sūtra* II.1.13, Śaṅkara had noted that the distinction between enjoyers and objects of enjoyment is possible in terms of the practical although both are non-differ-

9. Balasubrahmanyam, T. K., *The Works of Śrī Śaṅkarāchārya*, Volume I, commentary to *Brahma-sūtra* I.4.14, p. 251.
10. Ibid., commentary to *Brahma-sūtra* I.4.14, p. 252.

ent on the analogy of the sea and its waves. In his commentary to *Brahma-sūtra* II.1.14, Śaṅkara notes that in reality cause and effect are non-different, and the distinction between the enjoyer and object of enjoyment is practical only.

> abhyupagamya cemaṃ vyāvahārikaṃ bhoktṛbhogyalakṣaṇaṃ vibhāgaṃ syāllokavat iti parihāro 'bhihitaḥ; na tvayaṃ vibhāgaḥ paramārthato 'sti, yasmāttayoḥ kāryakāraṇayorananyatvamavagamyate /[11]
>
> Having maintained the practical distinction having the characteristic of enjoyer and enjoyed, the refutation was set forth in the statement, "It may be, as in worldly experience"; nor is there the distinction in reality since the identity of the two, cause and effect, is understood.

The effect is the manifold world; the cause is the Brahman. The term "*paramārthataḥ*" signifies that "in reality" they are non-different.

> kāryamākāśādikaṃ bahuprapañcaṃ jagat; kāraṇaṃ paraṃ brahma; tasmātkāraṇātparamārthato 'nanyatvaṃ vyatirekeṇābhāvaḥ kāryasyāvagamyate[12]
>
> The effect is the manifold world consisting of space, etc.; the cause is the highest Brahman; it is understood therefore in connection with the effect that there is no difference in reality from the cause, nor is it an entity by way (of being) apart.

The term "*vyavahāra*," which relates to the sphere of the practical, arises in connection with Śaṅkara's refutation of *bhedābheda* in his commentary to *Brahma-sūtra* II.1.14. Śaṅkara has explained that it has been predicated by the scriptures that the embodied Self (*śārīrātman*) has no existence apart from the Brahman (e.g. the *mahāvacana* "*tat tvam asi*," "That thou art"); hence, the practical has no existence apart from the Brahman.

> bādhite ca śārīrātmatve tadāśrayaḥ samastaḥ svābhāviko vyavahāro bādhito bhavati[13]

11. Ibid., Volume II, commentary to *Brahma-sūtra* II.1.14, pp. 307-308.
12. Ibid., Volume II, commentary to *Brahma-sūtra* II.1.14, p. 308.
13. Ibid., commentary to *Brahma-sūtra* II.1.14, p. 310.

If the existence of the embodied Self is supplanted, then the entire natural, practical sphere based on it, is supplanted.

Śaṅkara associates the practical and the principle of manifoldness (*nānātva*) with mistaken knowledge ((*mithyājñāna*), and the principle of unity (*ekatva*) with the true (*pāramārthika*). According to Śaṅkara, the scriptures attest the truth of unity and the falsity of manifoldness, as is seen by the instance of the thief and the ordeal of the heated axe in *Chāndogya Upaniṣad* (VI.16).

> taskaradṛṣṭāntena cānṛtābhisaṃdhasya bandhanaṃ satyābhisaṃdhasya ca mokṣam darśayan ekatvamevaikaṃ pāramārthikaṃ darśayati, mithyājñānavijṛmbhitaṃ ca nānātvam; ubhayasatyatāyāṃ hi katham vyavahāragocaro 'pi janturanṛtābhisaṃdha ityucyate?[14]
>
> Teaching by the example of the thief, the bondage of the false-spoken and the liberation of the true-spoken, it (Scripture) teaches oneness (to be) absolute, and difference (to be) manifested as false knowledge; if both (alternatives) were true, how could a man within the range of the practical be called false-spoken?

Śaṅkara then brings up the possible objection that if the distinctions supporting the injunctions and prohibitions of the scriptures are invalid, then the entire body of doctrine which refers to release would collapse. Furthermore, if the concept of liberation is false, Śaṅkara continues, there is a question whether the truth of the unity of the Self can be maintained in view of the fact that the Self is inseparably connected with the possibility of liberation. Śaṅkara's reply to this possible objection is to explain that the injunctions and prohibitions of the scriptures are true in the practical dimension until the knowledge of absolute truth arises.

> atrocyate—naiṣa doṣaḥ sarvavyavahārāṇāmeva prāgbrahmātmatāvijñānātsatyatvopapatteḥ svapnavyavahārasyeva prāgbodhāt...[15]

---

14. Ibid., commentary to *Brahma-sūtra* II.1.14, p. 310.
15. Ibid., commentary to *Brahma-sūtra* II.1.14, p. 311.

Here it is said : this is not a fault, because of the occurrence of the truth of all practices before the consciousness (*vijñāna*) of Brahman as the Self, like the practices of a dream before awaking.

In this way, Śaṅkara grants those texts which concern injunctions and prohibitions a secondary significance which nevertheless are valid from the standpoint of practical truth. Practical religious observances, according to Śaṅkara, may continue as long as true knowledge has not dawned.

tasmātprāgbrahmātmatāprabodhādupapannaḥ sarvo laukiko vaidikaśca vyavahāraḥ.[16]
Hence, before the realization of Brahman as Ātman, every worldly and Vedic practice is suitable.

A major problem arises in Śaṅkara's work over the ontological status of Īśvara as the creative principle. Śaṅkara insists that the creation, subsistence, and destruction of the world proceed from an intelligent Lord, not non-intelligent *pradhāna* (first principle). He cites a text from the *Taittirīya Upaniṣad* which supports his contention.

'tasmādvā etasmādātmana ākāśaḥ sambhūtaḥ' ityādivākyebhyaḥ nityaśuddhabuddhamuktasvarūpātsarvajñātsarvaśakterīśvarājjagajjanisthitipralayāḥ nācetanātpradhānādanyasmādvā[17]
"From that very Self arose space." Because of the words beginning with this statement, the birth, maintenance, and destruction of the world (proceed) from an eternal, pure, awakened liberated nature (*svarūpa*), from an all-knowing, omnipotent Lord, not from a non-intelligent first principle or from another.

Śaṅkara then raises the possible objection that the duality of creative cause and created effect is in contradiction to the principle of the unity and non-duality of the Self. Śaṅkara replies first by associating Īśvara with the principle of name-and-formation (*nāma-rūpa*) which are fragments of *avidyā* (nescience) and

16. Ibid., Volume II, commentary to *Brahma-sūtra* II.1.14, p. 311.
17. Ibid., Volume II, commentary to *Brahma-sūtra* II.1.14, p. 315.

which cannot be defined either as identical with Brahman or as different from it.

> sarvajñasyeśvarasyātmabhūta ivāvidyākalpite nāmarūpe tattvānyatvābhyāmanirvacanīye saṃsāraprapañcabījabhūte sarvajñasyeśvarasya māyāśaktiḥ prakṛtiriti ca śrutismṛtyorabhilapyete[18]
>
> In the case of name-and-formation, fabricated of nescience, as it were, consisting of the Self of the omniscient Lord, not to be defined as being different or as being that, consisting of the seeds of the manifold world, they are called in Śruti and Smṛti the all-knowing Lord's power of magical display, his nature.

Name-and-formation (*nāma-rūpa*), the figments of nescience are here treated as the germinal power (*bījaśakti*) of the cosmos. In other words, nescience seems to be elevated to the status of an ontological principle which is paralleled in the epistemological realm by the concept of empirical truth. *Avidyā* when it is associated with the germinal power (*bījaśakti*) of the cosmos is thereby being treated as an ontological principle by which the existence of the cosmos is explained (or perhaps, explained away, since nescience is associated with *māyā*, or magical display). If it is asked with what type of knowledge are name-and-formation, the figments of nescience, associated, the reply is that they are associated with the practical standpoint. For the Vedāntin, the epistemological question, "How does one know?" is answered by reference to the two truths, the absolute and the practical. Īśvara is declared by Śaṅkara to owe his qualities to nescience; hence, Īśvara is a reality from the practical standpoint alone, whereas in reality the Self is qualityless. The qualities that we attribute to Īśvara are true, but only from the practical standpoint. In reality, the Self is free from the projections imposed by the limitations (*upādhi*) due to nescience.

> tadevamavidyātmakopādhiparicchedāpekṣameveśvarasyeśvaratvaṃ sarvajñatvaṃ sarvaśaktitvaṃ ca, na paramārthato vidyayā apāstasarvopādhisvarūpe ātmani īśitrīśitavyasarvajñatvādivyavahāra upapadyate;[19]

18. Ibid., Volume II, commentary to *Brahma-sūtra* II.1.14, p. 315.
19. Ibid., Volume II, commentary to *Brahma-sūtra* II.1.14, p. 316.

> Hence the divinity of the Lord, his omniscience and omnipotence are dependent on the limitation of the limiting adjuncts composed of nescience; in reality, in the case of the Self having a nature rid of every limiting adjunct by clear vision (*vidyā*) the practices of omniscience, ruler and ruled are not possible.

The notion of two truths—the practical and the absolute—is seen in Śaṅkara's statement that the *sūtrakāra* (author of the *sūtra*) had devoted the previous *sūtra* (*Brahma-sūtra* II.1.13) to the practical standpoint and the present *sūtra* (*Brahma-sūtra* II.1.14) to the absolute standpoint.

> sūtrakāro 'pi paramārthābhiprāyeṇa 'tadananyatvam' ityāha; vyavahārābhiprāyeṇa tu 'syāllokavat' iti mahāsamudrādisthānīyatāṃ brahmaṇaḥ kathayati; apratyākhyāyaiva kāryaprapañcaṃ pariṇāmaprakriyāṃ cāśrayati.[20]
>
> The *sūtrakāra* says, "The non-difference from that," with the intention of (referring to) the absolute; intending the practical in the *sūtra*, "it (the distinction) may exist, as in worldly experience," he relates the comparison of the great ocean, etc. in connection with the Brahman; not having refuted the manifold world of effect he supports the production of the modification (*pariṇāma*).

Śaṅkara is here subjecting the *Brahma-sūtras* to the process of "advaitinization" by attributing to the *sūtrakāra* the attitude that the distinction between Brahman and the world implied in the previous *sūtra* (*Brahma-sūtra* II.1.3) is valid only until it is supplanted by the state of reality. That Śaṅkara grants some utility, however, to the qualified Brahman even though it is the product of nescience which is synonymous with the practical standpoint is seen in his final comment to this *sūtra*.

> saguṇeṣūpāsaneṣūpayokṣyata iti[21]
> In the case of meditative exercises (*upāsana*) on the qualified (*saguṇa*), it will be useful.

---

20. Ibid., Volume II, commentary to *Brahma-sūtra* II.1.14, p. 316.
21. Ibid., Volume II, commentary to *Brahma-sūtra* II.1.14, p. 317.

5. NESCIENCE (*AVIDYĀ*)

An interesting comparison between Śaṅkara's Vedānta and Mahāyāna Buddhism can be made in connection with the concept of nescience (*avidyā*). For both traditions, nescience is pre-eminent as that which is to be removed. For both traditions, nescience is two-fold in that it possesses a cognitional aspect and a conational aspect. That *avidyā* (nescience) seems to be treated by Śaṅkara as an ontological principle has been noted by Esther Solomon in her book *Avidyā—A Problem of Truth and Reality*. According to Solomon, Śaṅkara hypostasizes *avidyā* and regards it as material (*jaḍa*).

> Śaṅkara hypostasizes *avidyā* to account for the material world, and hence *avidyā* must be regarded as *jaḍa* or material.[1]

According to Solomon, the significance of *avidyā* in Śaṅkara's works consists in that it has a cognitional aspect in addition to the conational aspect which is related to passion and hatred (*rāga-dveṣa*). According to Solomon, the world through *avidyā* is unreal from the cognitional point of view as well as valueless from the conational point of view in Śaṅkara's writings. *Avidyā* (nescience) in Śaṅkara's writings, according to Solomon, is a metaphysical principle just as it was in Mahāyāna thought, where it possesses the cognitional aspect of the hindrance of the knowable (*jñeya-āvaraṇa*) as well as the conational aspect of the hindrance of defilement (*kleśa-āvaraṇa*).

> For Śaṅkara, the world is not only valueless from the conational point of view, but is unreal from the cognitional point of view also. He hypostasizes *avidyā* as a principle responsible for the world phenomena. Thus *avidyā* should be a metaphysical principle in Śaṅkara's philosophy as it was in Mahāyāna thought also.[2]

---

1. Solomon, Esther A., *Avidyā—A Problem of Truth and Reality*, Gujarat University Theses Publication Series—8, (Ahmedabad, Gujarat, India : Gujarat University), p. 233.
2. Ibid., p. 224.

Solomon's use of the term "unreal," as a description of the world seen through *avidyā* may be unfortunate, however, since as she herself has noted, Śaṅkara employed the notion of "two truths" in his works.

> But somehow one important point in Śaṅkara's philosophy has not been sufficiently emphasized. He has propounded his philosophy from two points of view, the higher or the supra-empirical and the lower or empirical.[3]

According to Sengaku Mayeda, it is *avyākṛta-nāma-rūpa* (translated by Mayeda as "unevolved name-and-form" and by Wayman as "unseparated name-and-formation") which is the potentiality of the world's manifoldness in Śaṅkara's works. The function which according to Solomon is carried out by *avidyā* is according to Mayeda carried out by *avyākṛta nāma-rūpa.*

> According to Śaṅkara, originally Unevolved Name-and-Form evolves from Brahman, and in the course of its evolution becomes ether. Therefore, ether evolves indirectly from Brahman. Consequently, his introduction of "Unevolved Name-and-Form" into the Vedānta system may be effective in explaining the manifoldness of the universe, the creation of this material world, and other theoretical difficulties which the monism of the *Brahmasūtra* had to face.[4]

Śaṅkara was aware of the perils of dualism, and so he stressed the notion that the separated name-and-formation (*vyākṛta nāma-rūpa*) is both different and non-different from the unseparated name-and-formation (*avyākṛta nāma-rūpa*), as dirty foam is different and non-different from clear water.

> ...te nāmarūpe 'vyākṛte satī vyākriyamāṇe tasmād etasmād ātmana ākāśanāmākṛtī saṃvṛtte/ tac cākāśākhyaṃ bhūtam anena prakāreṇa paramātmanaḥ sambhūtaṃ, prasannāt salilān malam iva phenaṃ / na salilaṃ na ca salilād atyantabhinnaṃ phenam/ salilavyatirekeṇādarśanāt / salilaṃ

3. Ibid., p. 215.

4. Mayeda, Sengaku, *The Thousand Teachings*, (translation of the *Upadeśasāhasrī* of Śaṅkara), (Tokyo : Tokyo University Press, 1979), Introduction, p. 22.

tu svaccham anyat phenān malarūpāt/evaṃ paramātmā nāmarūpābhyām anyaḥ phenasthānīyābhyāṃ śuddhaḥ prasannas tadvilakṣaṇaḥ/...[5]

In the case of the existence of name-and-formation, not being evolved, from that Self there is the name and form of space when name-and-formation have evolved. In this way, the element called space arose from the highest Self, as dirty foam from clear water. Foam is not excessively different from water, nor is it water, because it is not seen by (being) separate from water. Water is clear, other than foam (which is of) the formation of dirt.

Thus the highest Self is other than both name-and-formation which belong to foam; it is pure, clear, different from it.

Mayeda explains, however, that Śaṅkara's special expression "*avyākṛta nāma-rūpa*" (unevolved name-and-form) was not used by his own pupils, perhaps because the phrase is remote from an illusionistic connotation.[6] He indicates that Padmapāda, one of Śaṅkara's disciples, used the term "*avidyā*" (*or māyā*) for the material cause of the world, for this very reason.[7] It seems that Solomon, therefore, is perhaps construing Śaṅkara's thought through the interpretation of his disciples and successors when she considers nescience to be more ontologically significant in Śaṅkara's writings than unseparated name-and-formation in the sense that nescience is given more responsibility than unseparated name-and-formation for the seeming existence of the cosmos. In contrast with the viewpoint expressed by Solomon, Mayeda holds that the significance of *avidyā* in Śaṅkara's works is conational. He holds that *avidyā* is treated in Śaṅkara's writings as a kind of psychic affection or defilement (*kleśa*), not as the cosmic material from which mistaken knowledge (*mithyājñāna*) arises as was the opinion of Śaṅkara's disciples.

Avidyā is identical with the original error of all being, and *mithyājñāna* (false knowledge) is a synonym of it. In the case of Śaṅkara's followers, however, *avidyā* is the material from which

5. Ibid., *Upadeśasāhasrī* II.1.19, p. 23.
6. Ibid., p. 25.
7. Ibid., p. 25.

all forms of *mithyājñāna* come; *avidyā* is not *mithyājñāna* but the cause of *mithyājñāna*. In Śaṅkara's works, *avidyā* is sometimes treated, like sexual desire (*kāma*), as a kind of psychic affection (*kleśa*) as in the Yoga system. Psychic affection is regarded as a wider concept to which *avidyā* belongs.[8]

In the *Upadeśasāhasrī*, *avidyā* is the first and most dangerous member, according to Mayeda, of the series *avidyā-kāma-karman* (nescience, desire, and action) which are psychic affections. According to the *Upadeśasāhasrī*, the three psychic affections are associated with the intellect (*buddhi*).

ātmāgnerindhanā buddhiravidyākāmakarmabhiḥ
dipitā prajvalatyeṣā dvāraiḥ śrotrādibhiḥ sadā/ /[9]
The fuel of the fire of Self set on fire with nescience, desire, and action is the intellect; it burns through doors such as the ear, etc.

According to the *Brahmasūtra-bhāṣya*, the qualities of *avidyā-kāma-karman* are fictitiously ascribed to the cognizing Self (*vijñānātman*) which in reality is not different from the highest Self (paramātman).

yadyapi vijñānātmā paramātmano 'nanya eva, tathāpyavidy-ākāmakarmakṛtaṃ tasminmartyatvamadhyāropitaṃ bhayaṃ cetyamṛtatvābhayatve nopapadyete/[10]
Although the cognizing Self (*vijñānātman*) is not other than the highest Self, nevertheless fear and mortality brought about by nescience, desire, and action are superimposed (*adhyāropita*) on it; thus immortality and fearlessness are not present.

In Śaṅkara's thought, however, *avidyā* (nescience) also has a cognitional aspect, that is to say, it is concerned with the mutual superimposition of Self and non-Self. Whether *avidyā* can be considered to possess a cognitional aspect in the sense of being an ontological principle, as Solomon maintains, is debatable, but it does seem to possess a cognitional aspect in the epistemological

8. Ibid., p. 78.
9. Balasubrahmanyam, T. K., *The Works of Śrī Śaṅkarāchārya*, Volume 14, *Upadeśasāhasrī* I.15, 21, p. 185.
10. Ibid., Volume I, commentary to *Brahmasūtra* I.2.17, p. 117.

realm as it does in Mahāyāna Buddhism. That is to say, just as nescience (*avidyā*) in the Mahāyāna context is a hindrance to the knowable (*jñeya-āvaraṇa*) in that through it one ascribes self-existence (*svabhāva*) to natures (*dharmas*) and which can be removed only through the insight (*prajñā*) that natures are selfless (*dharma-nairātmya*), so in Śaṅkara's thought, nescience (*avidya*) is mistaken knowledge (*mithyā-jñāna*) in that through it one superimposes a Self (Ātman) on that which is not-Self (*anātman*) and which can be removed by the discrimination (*viveka*) that is clear vision (*vidyā*). The cognitive aspect of nescience for both Śaṅkara and Mahāyāna Buddhism relates to epistemology, in that this aspect of nescience is a barrier to knowledge. The conational aspect of nescience relates to psychology in that this aspect of nescience is a barrier to the mental purification synonymous with the removal of what for the Mahāyāna Buddhist is the hindrance of defilement (*kleśa-āvaraṇa*) and for Śaṅkara is the series nescience, desire, action (*avidya-kāma-karma*). Śaṅkara defines nescience as the mutual superimposition (*adhyāsa*) of Self and non-Self in his *Brahmasūtra-bhāṣya*.

> tametamavidyākhyamātmānātmanoritaretarādhyāsaṃ puraskṛtya sarve pramāṇaprameyavyavahārā laukikāḥ pravṛttāḥ, sarvāṇi ca śāstrāṇi vidhipratiṣedhamokṣaparāṇi/[11]
>
> On account of this very mutual superimposition (*adhyāsa*) of Self and non-Self which is called nescience, all the worldly practices of authority and the sanctionable are produced, as well as all the scriptures having as their chief object injunctions, prohibitions and liberation.

Superimposition is also defined by Śaṅkara in terms of apparent presentation (*ābhāsa*).

> āha—ko 'yamadhyāso nāmeti/ucyate—smṛti-rūpaḥ paratra pūrvadṛṣṭāvabhāsaḥ[12]
>
> It says, "What is this called superimposition?" It is said, "The appearance having the form of memory of something previously seen elsewhere."

11. Ibid., Volume I, commentary to *Brahma-sūtra* I.1.1, p. 3.
12. Ibid., Volume I, commentary to *Brahma-sūtra* I.1.1, p. 2.

Clear vision or wisdom (*vidyā*) is according to Śaṅkara obtained through discrimination.

> tametamevaṃlakṣaṇamadhyāsaṃ paṇḍitā avidyeti manyante/ tadvivekena ca vastusvarūpāvadhāraṇaṃ vidyāmāhuḥ/[13]

> Pandits think that this superimposition having this very definition is nescience. They call clear vision the ascertainment of the nature of the given thing by the discrimination of that.

It is to be noted that Śaṅkara in his definition of *avidyā* equates *avidyā* with the practical or worldly realm. Thus the connection between nescience and the practical realm is to be observed. In Mahāyāna Buddhism, too, conventional truth (*saṃvṛti-satya*) and nescience are equated. For instance, Tsoṅ-kha-pa refers to the following passage from the *Avatāra*-Commentary, as translated by Wayman in his book *Calming the Mind and Discerning the Real.*

> By means of this (nescience which is apprehension as true) the sentient beings are deluded about how the entities are present. Delusion, i.e., nescience, which causes the attribution of own-nature to entities although they do not have it, and has the nature of hindrance so that they see a self-existence—is called "*saṃvṛti.*"[14]

It seems, however, that *saṃvṛti-satya* is associated by Tsoṅ-kha-pa with the hindrance of defilement (*kleśa*). Tsoṅ-kha-pa even states that conventional truth is established by "the power of defiled nescience."

> Accordingly, *saṃvṛti-satya* is established by the power of defiled nescience incorporated in the members of phenomenal life.[15]

In his emphasis upon the hindrance of defilement (*kleśa-āvaraṇa*) and hence the conational aspect of nescience, Tsoṅ-kha-pa differs from the Mahāyāna Yogācāra teacher Asaṅga, who taught two types of nescience as is evident from his inclusion within

---

13. Ibid., commentary to *Brahma-sūtra* I.1.1, p. 3.
14. Wayman, Alex, *Calming the Mind and Discerning the Real*, p. 265.
15. Ibid., p. 265.

the *Cintāmayī bhūmi* the following verses of the *Paramārthagāthā* (translated by Wayman).

> One finds that creatures lie in two categories.
> They are heedless in sense fields; moreover, deviantly setting out
> Truly those caught by delusion are those deviantly setting out.
> While those caught by craving are those heedless in sense fields.[16]

According to Wayman's interpretation of Asaṅga's self-commentary, there are two types of nescience: nescience towards "the *dharmas* possessed of cause" and nescience towards "the suffering possessed of cause."[17] The former is to be eliminated through the realization of the "non-Self of personality" (*pudgala-nairātmya*), the latter through realization of the "non-Self of *dharmas*" (*dharma-nairātmya*). The former is the hindrance of defilement (*kleśa*); the latter is the hindrance of the knowable (*jñeya*). The former are "those caught by craving"; the latter are "those caught by delusion." The two categories of creatures refer on the one hand to the *śrāvakas* and *pratyekabuddhas*, who only remove the hindrance of defilement, and on the other hand, to the *bodhisattvas* who also remove the hindrance of the knowable. Thus Asaṅga states in the *Bodhisattvabhūmi*, as translated by Wayman:

> Among them, the lineage of all the *Śrāvakas* and *pratyekabuddhas* becomes pure through purification of the hindrance of defilement (*kleśa*), not through purification of the hindrance of the knowable (*jñeya*). However, the lineage of the *bodhisattvas* becomes pure not only through purification of the hindrance of defilement, but also through purification of the hindrance of the knowable.[18]

Both in Asaṅga's Yogācāra and in Śaṅkara's Vedānta, there is the concern for the two aspects of nescience, the conational and the

---

16. Wayman, Alex, "Nescience and Insight According to Asaṅga's *Yogācārabhūmi*," to be published in Rahula Volume, pre-publication version, p. 3.
17. Ibid.
18. Ibid., p. 4.

cognitional. Just as Asaṅga prescribes morality (*adhiśīla*) and mind-control (*adhicitta*) for the riddance of the conational aspect of nescience which is the hindrance of defilement (*kleśa-āvaraṇa*), so Śaṅkara prescribes *upāsana* as a means of purification for the riddance of the nescience associated with the series *avidyā-kāma-karman* (nescience, desire, and action). The importance of the morality and mind-control is set forth by Asaṅga in his *Vivaraṇa-saṃgrāhaṇī*, as rendered by Wayman.

> By the instructions of the morality-set and the mind-control set, there is non-lust, non-hatred, and non-delusion. (Thus), the absence of the four waywardnesses belongs to the stage of accumulating (merit) (*sambhāra-mārga*) and to the stage of praxis (*prayoga-mārga*).[19]

Śaṅkara, likewise, emphasizes the importance of *upāsanas* (meditative exercises) for the transition from the habitual preoccupation with action to knowledge. Dr. Raghavan describes Śaṅkara's attitude towards *upāsanas* or meditative exercises.

> Śaṅkara says that such is man's habitual preoccupation with action that it is difficult to get away from it and hence the *upāsanas* or meditations on aspects of these acts in a higher significance, to be mentally dwelt upon, form one way of slowly abstracting oneself from them.[20]

Raghavan is referring to Śaṅkara's explanation of *upāsana* in the Introduction to *Chāndogyabhāṣya*.

> tatra karmābhyāsasya dṛḍhīkṛtatvātkarmaparityāgenopāsana eva duḥkham cetaḥsamarpaṇaṃ kartumiti karmāṅgaviṣayameva tāvadādāvupāsanamupanyasyate/[21]

> Thence, since it is difficult to surrender of the mind in the case of meditative exercise through renunciation of action because of the firm cultivation of the practice of action, meditative exer-

19. Ibid., p. 13.

20. Aiyar, K. Narayanaswami, *The Thirty Two Vidyā-s*, (Madras, India : The Adyar Library and Research Centre, 1962 reprint), Introduction by Raghavan, p. v.

21. Apate, Cimanaji Mahadeva, *Chāndogyopaniṣat*, Ānandāśramasaṃskṛtagranthāvaliḥ, Granthāṅkaḥ : 14, (Ānandāśrama, India, 1890), p. 7.

cise having for its object the parts of the sacrificial rite is certainly suggested at the beginning.

The importance of the *upāsana* for Śaṅkara can be seen in the fact that his mention of the series *avidyā-kāma-karman* (nescience, desire, and action) occurs within the context of a *sūtra* that according to him is concerned with the *Akṣi-vidyā* (the Meditation on the Eye). The *Akṣi-vidyā* has for its subject-matter the following text from *Chāndogya Upaniṣad* IV. 5.1.

1. ya eṣo 'kṣiṇi puruṣo dṛśyate, eṣa ātmā iti hovāca, etad amṛtam abhayam, etad brahmeti. tad yady apy asmin sarpir vodakaṁ vā siñcati, vartmanī eva gacchati.[22]

He said, "This person seen in the eye, this is the self. This is immortality, this is fearlessness, this is the Brahman. Even if one drops either ghee or water on it (the eye), it goes along the rim.

The *sūtra* upon which Śaṅkara is commenting is according to him concerned with the nature of the Self which is identified with the person in the eye. The *sūtra* proceeds as follows:

anavasthiterasambhavācca netaraḥ// (17) //[23]

Because of the instability and because of the impossibility, there is no other.

Śaṅkara associates the series *avidyā-kāma-karman* with the cognizing self (*vijñānātman*) as qualities falsely ascribed to the cognizing Self, although the *vijñānātman* is no other than the highest Lord in reality. Because of its association—albeit false—with these qualities, Śaṅkara explains, the *vijñānātman* cannot be the Self to which the *Akṣi-vidyā* refers. Rather the *Akṣi-vidyā* refers to the highest Lord—not to the shadow-Self (*chāyātman*), not to the cognizing Self, not to the gods.

tasmātparameśvara evāyamakṣisthānaḥ pratyetavyaḥ[24]

---

22. Radhakrishnan, Sarvepalli, *The Principal Upaniṣads, Chāndogya Upaniṣad* IV.15.1, p. 46.

23. Balasubrahmanyam, T. K., *The Works of Srī Śaṅkarāchārya*, Volume I, commentary to *Brahma-sūtra* I.2.17, p. 117.

24. Ibid., Volume I, commentary to *Brahma-sūtra* I.2.17, p. 118.

> The one residing in the eye must be understood as the highest Lord.

Furthermore, in connection with the cognitional aspect of nescience, just as Asaṅga prescribes clear sight (*vidyā*) belonging to the Instruction of insight (*prajñā*) for the realization of the selflessness of all *dharmas* (*dharma-nairātmya*), so Śaṅkara prescribes *vidyā* (clear sight) which occurs by means of *viveka* (discrimination) as a corrective to the mutual superimposition of Self and non-Self. According to Asaṅga, the Instruction of Insight (*prajñā*) embraces three stages so that the term insight is being employed as a category of practices. *Vidyā* (clear sight) is associated with these stages and practices.

> Clear sight (*vidyā*) and liberation (*mukti*) belong to the Instruction of insight set, the stage of vision (*darśana-mārga*), stage of contemplation (*bhāvana-mārga*), and ultimate state (*niṣṭhāgamana-mārga*).[25]

According to Śaṅkara, *vidyā* (clear sight) occurs by means of *viveka* (discrimination) of Self from non-Self.

> tadvivekena ca vastusvarūpāvadhāraṇaṃ vidyāmāhuḥ/[26]
> They call clear vision the ascertainment of the nature of the given thing by the discrimination of that.

But in the case of Śaṅkara's works, it is not as clear whether *vidyā* (clear sight) or *viveka* (discrimination) involves a path as in the case of Asaṅga's works. According to Śaṅkara, the path of the gods (*deva-yāna*) has nothing to do with perfect vision (*samyag-darśana*).

> na tu samyagdarśane tallakṣaṇārthopalabdhirasti[27]
> But when there is perfect vision (*samyag-darśana*) there is not the perception (*upalabdhi*) which has an object-entity possessing the characteristic of that.

In the sub-commentary *Ratnaprabhā*, the characteristic is described

25. Wayman, Alex, "Nescience and Insight According to Asaṅga's *Yogācārabhūmi*," p. 13.

26. Balasubrahmanyam, T. K., *The Works of Śrī Śaṅkarāchārya*, Volume I, Introducton to the Commentary to the *Brahma-sūtrā*, p. 3.

27. Ibid., Volume III, commentary to *Brahma-sūtra* III.3.30, p. 665.

in terms of going (*gatirlakṣaṇam*).[28] Śaṅkara employs examples from daily life to illustrate that perfect vision requires no doing on one's parts.

> lokavacca eṣa vibhāgo draṣṭavyaḥ—yathā loke grāmaprāptau deśāntaraprāpaṇaḥ panthā apekṣyate, na ārogyaprāptau, evamihāpīti[29].
>
> The distinction is to be seen as in the world. For instance, when one reaches a village in the world, the reaching of another place is connived at by means of a path, but when one reaches non-illness, in this very case it is not so.

On the other hand, it is to be noted that Śaṅkara in his introduction to the *Brahmasūtra-bhāṣya*, does sanction the study of the Vedānta texts. Such study requires "doing"; it is not the knowledge itself. Furthermore, Śaṅkara speaks of *Vedānta-mīmāṃsā*, the investigation into the Vedānta. Again, investigation involves effort; it is not the knowledge itself.

> asyānarthahetoḥ prahāṇāya ātmaikatvavidyā-pratipattaye sarve vedāntā ārabhyante/ yathā cāyamarthaḥ sarveṣām vedāntānāṃ, tathā vayamasyāṃ śārīrakamīmāṃsāyāṃ pradarśayiṣyāmaḥ/ vedāntamīmāṃsāśāstrasya vyācikhyāsitasyedamādimaṃ sūtram/[30]
>
> For the sake of the relinquishing of that, the cause of nonsense, and for the acquisition of the clear vision of the unity of the Self, the Vedāntas are begun. That this is the meaning of all the Vedāntas, we will show in this *Śārīrakamīmāṃsā*. Of the *Vedāntamīmāṃsā* text about to be explained the first *sūtra* is as follows:

Furthermore, Śaṅkara speaks of knowledge as an authority by means of which the Brahman is known. The association with *pramāṇa* involves the notion of investigation, which in turn involves effort.

> jñānena hi pramāṇenāvagantumiṣṭam brahma.[31]

28. Bākre, Pandit Mahādeva Śāstrī, *The Brahmasūtra-Shānkarabhāshyam* (Bombay, India : Nirnaya Sagar Press, 1934), (with commentary *Ratnaprabhā, Bhāmatī, Nyāya-nirṇaya*), *Ratnaprabhā* sub-commentary to Śaṅkara's commentary to *Brahma-sūtra* III,3.30, p. 730.
29. Balasubrahmanyam, T. K., *The Works of Śrī Śaṅkarāchārya*, Volume I, commentary to *Brahma-sūtra* III.3.30, p. 665.
30. Ibid., Volume I, Introduction to *Brahmasūtrabhāṣya*, p. 5.
31. Ibid., Volume I, commentary to *Brahma-sūtra* I,1.1, p. 8.

By means of the authority of knowledge the Brahman is declared to be known.

Śaṅkara also terms the comprehension of Brahman the highest end of man (*puruṣārtha*), thereby implying that such comprehension is a goal which requires effort. In any case, such comprehension according to Śaṅkara involves the destruction of *avidyā* in its cognitional aspect. It is to be noted that here nescience is regarded by Śaṅkara as the seed of *saṃsāra*; hence there is some justification for Solomon's theory that *avidyā* represents a cosmological principle in Śaṅkara's thought.

brahmāvagatirhi puruṣārthaḥ, niḥśeṣasaṃsārabījāvidyādyanarthanibarhaṇāt/[32]
The understanding of Brahman is the aim of the person, out of the destruction of evil such as nescience which is the seed of the entire world.

Furthermore, Śaṅkara asks whether the Brahman is already known or not known. He replies that it is known from an etymological viewpoint (in that the root "*bṛh*," to be great, implies such attributes as purity), and from the introspective viewpoint (in that it is the Self of everyone). According to Śaṅkara, introspection reveals the Self.

sarvasyātmatvācca brahmāstitvaprasiddhiḥ sarvo hyātmāstitvaṃ pratyeti, na 'nāhamasmi' iti/ yadi hi nātmāstitvaprasiddhiḥ syāt, sarvo lokaḥ 'nāhamasmi' iti pratīyāt. ātmā ca brahma.[33]

Because of the existence of the Self in all the existence of the Brahman is well-known, for everyone acknowledges the existence of the Self and does not say, "I am not." For if there were no establishment of the existence of the Self, everyone would acknowledge "I am not." The Self is Brahman.

If the Brahman is already known, then there is no need of inquiry. But Śaṅkara goes on to explain that on the other hand the Self is not known, for there is a conflict of opinions in connection with its nature.

yadi tarhi loke brahma ātmatvena prasiddhamasti; tato jñātamevetyajijñāsyatvam punarāpannam; na, tadviśeṣaṃ prati

32. Ibid., Volume I, commentary to *Brahma-sūtra* I.1.1, p. 8.
33. Ibid., Volume I, commentary to *Brahma-sūtra* I.1.1, p. 8.

> vipratipatteḥ.[34]
>
> If the Brahman is well-known in the world by means of the existence of the Self then it is known and the need for inquiry is not obtained. No, we reply, because of divergent positions towards the special properties of it.

Because of the possibility of error, Śaṅkara affirms the necessity of inquiry into Brahman and investigation of Mīmāṃsā texts.

> tasmādbrahmajijñāsopanyāsamukhena vedāntavākyamīmāṃsā tadavirodhitarkopakaraṇā niḥśreyasaprayojanā prastūyate//[35]
> By the commencement with the suggestion of an inquiry into Brahman, an investigation into the texts of the Vedānta is undertaken with the help of the non-opposed logic of it (the Vedānta texts), and with the aim of the most valued.

Therefore, it seems that Śaṅkara, in his emphasis on investigation and inquiry, has provided a "path," like Asaṅga, for the riddance of nescience in its cognitional aspect. According to Asaṅga, the path consists of the practices relating to *prajñā*. According to Śaṅkara, the path consists of investigation into the Vedāntic texts, and the inquiry into the Brahman. It can be seen, therefore, that in his employment of the notion of "two truths," the practical and the absolute, Śaṅkara has inherited much from Buddhism via the tradition of the *Gauḍapāda-kārikās*. In his treatment of *avidyā* (nescience) as two-fold, that is, possessing both a cognitional aspect and a conational aspect, it can be seen that Śaṅkara's teachings parallel those of Buddhism, particularly the Yogācāra Buddhism of Asaṅga.

---

34. Ibid., Volume I, commentary to *Brahma-sūtra* I.1.1, pp. 8-9.
35. Ibid., Volume I, commentary to *Brahma-sūtra* I.1.1, p. 9.

6. NAME-AND-FORMATION IN ŚAṄKARA'S THOUGHT

Related to the question of Śaṅkara's crypto-Buddhism is the topic of the two kinds of name-and-formation—the separated (*vyākṛta*) and the unseparated (*avyākṛta*). As will be observed in the following discussion of Wayman's article, "A Study of the Vedāntic and Buddhist Theory of *Nāma-Rūpa*," the Self of man for Śaṅkara is in fact the *jīva*, or individual, not the *jīvātman*, which he identifies with the Lord (Īśvara). Śaṅkara may have been accused of crypto-Buddhism for denying that there is a self in man to be identified with the Lord, for otherwise man would have created the mountains and rivers. It has been noted that among modern scholars, Mayeda has stressed *avyākṛta nāma-rūpa* as a cosmological principle in Śaṅkara's works, whereas Esther Solomon, in accordance with the approach of Śaṅkara's immediate disciples, has stressed the role of *avidyā* as an ontological principle in Śaṅkara's works. Also, it has been claimed by Hacker, Nakamura, and Mayeda that Śaṅkara's postulation of *avyākṛta nāma-rūpa* (unseparated name-and-formation) is not supported by the scriptures. In his article "A Study of the Vedāntic and Buddhist Theory of *Nāma-Rūpa*," Wayman has shown that Śaṅkara was not unjustified in writing of two kinds of *nāma-rūpa*, for the *Śatapatha Brāhmaṇa* provides some justification for Śaṅkara's treatment of *nāma-rūpa*. Wayman translates the expression "*vyākṛta*" as "separated" rather than "evolved" since the "*vi-*" in the Sanskrit word signifies "separate" or "apart" in the *Ṛgveda* where it was a separable prefix.[1] Wayman notes that the earliest suggestion that *nāma-rūpa* may be of two kinds is contained in *Śatapatha Brāhmaṇa* (XI, 2, 3 in 4-5) which speaks of *nāma-rūpa* as both the "two great monsters (*abhva*) of the Brahman" and the "two great tempting appearances (*yakṣa*) of the Brahman"[2]: "These,

1. Wayman, Alex, "A Study of the Vedāntic and Buddhist Theory of *Nāma-Rūpa*," *Volume in Honour of Professor J. W. de Jong on his Sixtieth Birthday* (Canberra, Australia), p. 624.

2. Ibid., p. 623.

indeed, are the two great monsters (*abhva*) of the Brahman" (*te haite brahmaṇo mahatī abhve*); "These, indeed, are the two great tempting appearances (*yakṣa*) of the Brahman" (*te haite brahmaṇo mahatī yakṣe*).[3] Wayman notes that the usual occurrences of *nāma-rūpa* accord with the latter of these.[4] Śaṅkara in the *Upadeśasāhasrī*, according to Wayman, sets forth two kinds of *nāma-rūpa* in an attempt to solve the problems arising in the *Brahma-sūtras*. These problems also prompted Śaṅkara in his *Brahmasūtra-bhāṣya*, according to Wayman, to write of two kinds of *nāma-rūpa*.

The difficulty, however, as Wayman notes, is that neither the *Chāndogya Upaniṣad*, to which Śaṅkara appeals as authority for his two kinds of *nāma-rūpa*[5] nor the *Brahma-sūtras* themselves speak of two kinds of *nāma-rūpa*. But in a rudimentary way, Wayman explains, the two kinds of *nāma-rūpa*—the unseparated and the separated—are presented in the *Śatapatha Brāhmaṇa*.[6] In his commentary to *Brahma-sūtra* I.4.8, Śaṅkara raises the question whether the *ajā* cited in the *Śvetāśvatara Upaniṣad* IV.5 represents the *pradhāna* of the Sāṅkhyas or something else. The *Śvetāśvatara Upaniṣad* proceeds as follows :

5. ajām ekāṁ lohita-śukla-kṛṣṇām bahvīḥ prajāḥ sṛjamānāṃ sarūpāḥ
ajo hy eko juṣamāṇo 'nuśete jahāty enām bhuktabhogām ajo 'nyaḥ[7]

5. The one unborn, red, white, black, producing much offspring of the same form.
The one unborn (male) lies delighting. Having enjoyed his enjoyment, another unborn leaves her.

Through the principle that doubtful passages are to be explained by recourse to non-doubtful passages, as Wayman notes, Śaṅkara attempts to define the nature of the "*ajā*" (a term which can signify both "the unborn" and "she-goat"). The *Brahma-*

3. Ibid., p. 623.
4. Ibid., p. 623.
5. Ibid., p. 624.
6. Ibid., p. 625.
7. Radhakrishnan, Sarvepalli, *The Principal Upaniṣads, Śvetāśvatara Upaniṣad* IV. 5, p. 732.

sūtras provide one indication, according to Śaṅkara, when it refers (in *Brahma-sūtra* I.4.9) to the elements beginning with light.

I.4.9. jyotir-upakramā tu tathā hy adhīyata eke[8]

These commencing with the light—so it is read in one (text).

According to Śaṅkara, the import of this *sūtra* is that the three colors (red, black, and white) cited in the above-mentioned *Śvetāśvatara Upaniṣad* passage refer to the three elements of fire, earth, and water with which they are paired in the *Chāndogya Upaniṣad* VI.4.1. In the *Chāndogya Upaniṣad* VI.4.1, the three colors are matched with the three elements. In this passage, both the colors (red, white, and black) and the elements (heat, water, food or earth) are placed under the rubric of *rūpa*, which Wayman translates as "formation" due to its close association with the notion of "coloring."[9] The *Chāndogya Upaniṣad* (VI.4.1) proceeds as follows :

I. yad agne rohitaṃ rūpaṃ tejasas tad rūpaṃ, yac chuklam tad apām yat kṛṣṇaṃ tad annasya[10]

This passage may be translated as follows according to Wayman's rendition :

Whatever red formation fire has is a formation of heat, whatever white is a formation of water, whatever black is a formation of food.[11]

Śaṅkara concludes on the basis of this passage that the three colors in the *Śvetāśvatara* passage refer to the three elements, and only in a secondary sense to the Sāṅkhya *guṇas*.

tānyeveha tejobannāni pratyabhijñāyante, rohitādiśabdasāmānyāt, rohitādīnāṃ ca śabdānāṃ rūpaviśeṣeṣu mukhyatvādbhāktatvācca guṇaviṣayatvasya[12]

8. Ibid., *Brahma-sūtra* I.4.9, p. 317.

9. Wayman, Alex, "A Study of the Vedāntic . . .", p. 267.

10. Radhakrishnan, Sarvepalli, *The Principal Upaniṣads, Chāndogya Upaniṣad* VI.4.1, p. 451.

11. Wayman, Alex, "A Study of the Vedāntic . . .", p. 267.

12. Balasubrahmanyam, T. K., *The Works of Śrī Śaṅkarāchārya*, Volume I, commentary to *Brahma-sūtra* I.4.9, p. 242.

> Now those —fire, etc.—are recognized here because of the common property of the words beginning with red, etc., and because the words beginning with red are primary terms in the sense of special formations and because the domain of the attributes is secondary.

But the main passage that is used by Śaṅkara to interpret the above-mentioned *Śvetāśvatara* passage, according to Wayman, is *Śvetāśvatara Upaniṣad* IV.10-11.

> Know then, *prakṛti* is *māyā*, and the great Lord is the holder of *māyā*...the One who rules over every birthplace (*māyāṃ tu prakṛtiṃ vidyān māyinaṃ tu maheśvaram /...yo yoniṃ yoniṃ adhitiṣṭhaty eko...*)[13]

On the basis of this passage and others, Śaṅkara goes on to equate *māyā*, or the power of the Lord, with unseparated name-and-formation, which is antecedent to the state of separated name-and-formation. Śaṅkara concludes that the term *ajā*, on the basis of *Śvetāśvatara Upaniṣad* IV.10-11 and preceding passages, must refer not to the *pradhāna* of the Sāṅkhyas, but to the unseparated name-and-formation (*avyākṛta nāma-rūpa*) equated with *māyā*.

> prakaraṇāttu saiva daivī śaktiravyākṛtanāmarūpā nāmarūpayoḥ prāgavasthā anenāpi mantreṇāmnāyata ityucyate.[14]
>
> Because of the explanation, that divine power having unseparated name-and-formation as the antecedent condition of name-and-formation, is cited by this mantra—thus it is said.

Wayman explains Śaṅkara's equation of *māyā* with the unevolved *nāma-rūpa* as follows :

> Śaṅkara claims that this *māyā* is the divine power having the unevolved *nāmarūpa* that the *Śve. mantra* depicts the prior condition of the (evolved) *nāma-rūpa* (*saiva daivī śaktir avyākṛtanāmarūpā nāmarūpayoḥ prāgavasthānenāpi mantreṇa*).[15]

---

13. Wayman, Alex, "A Study of the Vedāntic . . .", (*Bhāṣya* comments on *Brahma-sūtra* I.4.9, Bombay edition, p. 157), pp. 624-625.

14. Balasubrahmanyam, T. K., *The Works of Śrī Śaṅkarāchārya*, Volume I, commentary to *Brahma-sūtra* I.4.9, p. 242-243.

15. Wayman, Alex, "A Study of the Vedāntic . . ." p. 625.

According to Wayman, Śaṅkara's two kinds of *nāma-rūpa* can be considered as a systematization of the earlier intuition expressed in the *Śatapatha-Brāhmaṇa.*

> Although he does not appeal to *Śatapatha Br.'s* vocabulary, Śaṅkara's two kinds can be considered as a much later formulation, rationalized in a system, of the earlier intuition. If we follow through with this idea, then what was once called "the two great monsters of the Brahman" became the *māyā* (=*prakṛti*) of the great Lord, and what was once called "the two great tempting appearances of the Brahman" became the evolved *nāma-rūpa.*[16]

Wayman hastens to add, however, that the *Śatapatha ṛṣis* would not necessarily have approved of Śaṅkara's application of *avidyā.* Wayman follows Mayeda's summary, based on the *Upadeśasāhasrī,* of an "unevolved" or "unseparated" name-and-formation which is the first emergence from Brahman and which is equivalent to *avidyā* and *māyā,* and of an "evolved" or "separated" name-and-formation which has the name "space" (*ākāśa*) and its configuration (*ākṛti*). But Wayman asks in addition how the first kind of *nāma-rūpa* becomes the second kind.[17] He indicates that the unevolved or unseparated Name-and-Formation is regarded by Śaṅkara as the seed of the world (*jagadbījabhūta*), called also *prakṛti.* He notes, however, that the second kind is pre-existent in the first kind, which becomes the second kind by what the *Brahma-sūtra* calls the process of "transformation" (*pariṇāma*), although as Mayeda explains, the *Brahma-sūtra* itself does not speak of two kinds of *nāma-rūpa.*[18] As Mayeda notes, the followers of Śaṅkara dropped his terminology of an unseparated or unevolved *nāma-rūpa* and instead treated *avidyā* as the cosmological principle of a phenomenal world which is *vivarta* (illusion). Wayman summarizes Mayeda's position towards Śaṅkara's disciples as follows :

> The followers of Śaṅkara did not adopt his terminology of an "unevolved *nāma-rūpa,*" but held that the phenomenal world

16. Ibid., p. 625.
17. Ibid., p. 625.
18. Ibid., p. 625.

> is a transformation of *avidyā* and in regarrd to Brahman (the reality) is a *vivarta* (illusion).[19]

Wayman explains that Śaṅkara's followers may have dropped the notion of a pregenetic *nāma-rūpa* for fear of dualism.

> Since Śaṅkara's pupils refrained from this terminology of an unevolved *nāma-rūpa*, they did not clarify it. The Sāṅkhya can interpret the dual compound *nāma-rūpa*, when 'unevolved,' as their own *Puruṣa* and *Prakṛti*—and the Vedānta cannot tolerate this ![20]

Mayeda's view is that Śaṅkara did not employ the term *vivarta* in an illusionistic sense although he avoided the *pariṇāmavāda* (theory of transformation) of the *Brahma-sūtra*, and that Śaṅkara's own position might be styled an "early *vivartavāda*" which enabled Śaṅkara to avoid Sāṅkhya dualism.[21]

Wayman then goes on to explain what is the "name" and what is the "formation" in the first and second kinds of *nāma-rūpa*. He begins with the "evolved" or "separated" name-and-formation, since it is the more familiar of the two kinds. Of the *rūpa* part of *nāma-rūpa*, Wayman notes that it can be identified with the deceitful *varpas*, or with *vivarta*, or else with the four phenomenal elements.[22] In connection with *nāma*, Wayman cites a passage in the *Chāndogya Upaniṣad* (VI.3.2) where the *jīva-ātman* appears to have been given the role of evolving or separating out the *nāma-rūpa*.

> That divinity thought, 'Well, let me imitate these three divinities with this *jīva-ātman* and evolve (i.e. separate out) the *nāma-rūpa*' (*seyaṃ devataikṣata—hantāham imās tisro devatā anena jīvenātmanānupraviśya nāmarūpe vyākaravāṇīti*).[23]

Wayman explains that the idea of imitating (*anupraviśya*) refers to the duplication of the three divinities in each thing that can be regarded as a *nāma-rūpa*, and that it is the *jīva-ātman* which

19. Ibid., p. 626.
20. Ibid., p. 627.
21. Ibid., p. 626.
22. Ibid., p. 626.
23. Ibid., *Chāndogya Upaniṣad* VI.3.2, p. 626.

carries out the imitation.[24] Wayman notes, however, that according to Śaṅkara, the term *jīva-ātman* always refers to the highest Lord (Parameśvara), or else that this *jīva-ātman* is not different from the highest Lord. Śaṅkara justifies himself, according to Wayman, through the following passage, in the *Brahma-sūtra* (II.4.20).

> saṃjñāmūrtikḷptis tu trivṛtkurvata upadeśāt[25]
> ("But the fashioning of names and material forms belongs to him rendering threefold, according to the precept".)

Wayman notes that Śaṅkara interprets *saṃjñā-mūrti* as the *nāma-rūpa* of the *Chāndogya Upaniṣad* and *kḷpti* as "evolving." and that Śaṅkara insists that the evolving or separating of *nāma-rūpa* as mountains, rivers, etc. can only be carried out by the highest Lord (*parameśvara*). Śaṅkara first equates *saṃjña-mūrti* (names and material forms) with *nāma-rūpa* (name-and-formation), and *kḷpti* (fashioning) with *vyākriyā* (separating), and the *trivṛtkurvata* ("the one rendering three-fold") with the highest Lord.

> saṃjñāmūrtikḷptiriti—nāmarūpavyākriyetyetat; trivṛtkurvata iti parameśvaraṃ lakṣayati, trivṛtkaraṇe tasya nirapavādakartṛtvanirdeśāt —[26]
> "The fashioning of name and material forms"—this is equivalent to the evolving of name and formation; "of the one rendering three-fold" refers to the Highest Lord, because his agency is designated as beyond contradiction in the case of the three-fold rendering.

Śaṅkara argues that only the highest Lord (*Parameśvara*) can evolve such names-and-formations as seen in the natural world.

> yeyaṃ saṃjñākḷptiḥ mūrtikḷptiśca, agniḥ ādityaḥ candramāḥ vidyuditi, tathā kuśakāśapalāśādiṣu paśumṛgamanuṣyādiṣu ca, pratyākṛti prativyakti ca anekaprakārā, sā khalu parameśvarasyaiva tejobannānāṃ nirmātuḥ kṛtirbhavitumarhati[27]

---

24. Ibid., p. 626.
25. Ibid., (citing commentary to *Brahma-sūtra* II.4.20), p. 627.
26. Balasubrahmanyam, T. K., *The Works of Śrī Śaṅkarāchārya*, Volume II, commentary to *Brahma-sūtra* II.4.20, p. 518.
27. Ibid., commentary to *Brahma-sūtra* II.4.20, p. 518.

> This fashioning (*kḷpti*) of name (*saṃjñā*) and fashioning of material form (*mūrti*), seen as fire, lightning, or the moon, as in *kuśa*-grass, *kāśa*-grass, or *palāśa*-grass, or in cattle, deer, human beings, these many types, according to species, according to individual—this work can be of the highest Lord only, the maker of fire, water, earth.

Wayman notes, however, that the passage in the *Chāndogya Upaniṣad* (VI. 32) does not include objects like pots which men create and name, and that Śaṅkara declared natural objects like lightning, animals, etc. to be the second kind of *nāma-rūpa*. The name in the second kind of *nāma-rūpa*, according to Wayman, should therefore be understood as the individual self (Jīva).

> Hence, this *nāma-rūpa* does not signify objects like pots which men make and give names to. Śaṅkara is right: They are the natural objects, creatures, lightning, and the rest. Hence, the 'name' in the name-and-formation should be understood as the individual life or self (called in these texts the Jīva).[28]

Of the first kind of *nāma-rūpa*, the *avyākṛta nāma-rūpa* (the unseparated name-and-formation) Wayman notes that the *Chāndogya* passage already mentioned ("That divinity thought, 'Well, let me imitate these three divinities with this *jīva-ātman*...) provides an indication of the *rūpa* aspect of *nāma-rūpa*. The three divinities, according to Wayman, are specified in *Chāndogya Upaniṣad* VI.4.1-4, as the red heat, the white water, and the dark food. These three are called the three *rūpas* and are the only reality in fire, sun, moon, and lightning. Wayman notes that the same statements are made of these four, to the extent that whatever red formation they have is a formation of heat, whatever white is a formation of water, whatever dark is a formation of food or earth.[29] The *Chāndogya Upaniṣad* passage (VI.4.1) proceeds as follows, in connection with fire (*agni*).

> I. yad agne rohitaṃ rūpam tejasas tad rūpam, yac chuklaṃ tad apām, yat kṛṣṇam tad annasya[30]

---

28. Wayman, Alex, "A Study of the Vedāntic . . . ", p. 627.
29. Ibid., p. 627.
30. Radhakrishnan, Sarvepalli, *The Principal Upaniṣads*, *Chāndogya Upaniṣad* VI.4.1, p. 451.

Wayman translates as follows :

> Whatever red formation fire has is a formation of heat, whatever white is a formation of water, whatever black is a formation of food.[31]

The passage proceeds further to illustrate that fire is only a modification whereas only the three formations are real. The remainder of the passage proceeds as follows :

> ...vācārambhaṇam vikāro nāma-dheyam, trīṇi rūpāṇity eva[32]
> . . . the modification is a usage of speech and a conferral of name (*nāmadheya*). Only the three formations are real (*satya*).[33]

Therefore the reality in all natural entities is the three formations (*rūpa*) of red heat, black earth, and white water.

> Hence, the *jīva-ātman* has limited, or duplicated the three divinities; but when we strip away the usages of speech and discern the reality in those entities, it turns out to be just the three formations. Thus, the 'unevolved formation' is the three *rūpa* divinities of the *Chāndogya*.[34]

Wayman also concludes that the "unevolved name" of the *avyākṛta nāma-rūpa* must be "*jīvātman*," or name of the Lord.[35] He suggests that the appeal to *Agni* (the fire god) in the *Taittirīya Saṃhitā* alludes to the *jīvātman* as "unevolved name."

> mama nāma tava ca jātavedo vāsasī iva vivasānau ye carāvaḥ /
> āyuṣe tvam jīvase vayaṃ yathāyathaṃ vi pariṃ dadhāvahai punas te //[36]
> My name and thine, O all-knower, which like men changing

31. Wayman, Alex, "A Study of the Vedāntic . . . ", p. 627.
32. Radhakrishnan, Sarvepalli, *The Principal Upaniṣads, Chāndogya Upaniṣad* VI. 4.1, p. 451.
33. Wayman, Alex, "A Study of the Vedāntic . . .", p. 627.
34. Ibid., p. 627.
35. Ibid., p. 628.
36. Ibid., (citing *Taittirīya-saṃhitā of the Kṛṣṇa Yajurveda*, published at Pāradi-nagara, 1957, p. 33, 1.5.10), p. 640, footnote 60.

> garments we bear, let us exchange again; thou for life, and we to live.[37]

Wayman explains that "my name" is the Jīva, "thine" is the *jīvātman*, "thou for life" is "for mind, speech, and breath," "we to live" is the partaking in the omniscience of the *jīvātman*.[38]

In reference to the connection between *rūpa* and Brahman, Wayman notes in his article "A Study of the Vedāntic and Buddhist Theory of *Nāma-Rūpa*," that the Śruti mentions three qualities of Brahman, but only one kind of *nāma-rūpa*, the evolved kind. Wayman cites the *Varāha Upaniṣad* which assigns only two portions, among the five, to the world, namely *nāma* and *rūpa*.

> asti bhāti priyam rūpam nāma cety aṃśapañcakam /
> ādyatrayam brahmarūpam jagadrūpam tato dvayam //[39]

Wayman translates this passage as follows :

> For says the Śruti : 'It is, it shines forth, the pleasing, formation, name—these are the five portions. The first three are the nature of Brahman. The two thereafter are the nature of the world.[40]

Wayman notes that this passage seems to agree with the *Chāndogya Upaniṣad* if one takes dark food as the "It is," the red heat as the "It shines forth," and the white water as "the pleasing."[41] In other words, the pregenetic triad of the unevolved *rūpa* is here being applied to the Brahman, so that the Brahman in effect is being associated with *rūpa*. Wayman notes that the *Brahma-sūtra* and Śaṅkara vehemently oppose this view. The *Brahma-sūtra* (III.2.14) declares the Brahman to be *arūpa* (without form).

---

37. Ibid., (citing Keith's translation, p. 80), p. 628.

38. Ibid., (citing Keith's translation, p. 80), p. 628.

39. Wayman, Alex, "A Study of the Vedāntic and Buddhist Theory of *Nāma-Rūpa*," p. 639, footnote 59, (citing Śāstrī, A. Mahādeva, *The Yoga Upaniṣads*, with the commentary of Śrī-Upaniṣad-Brahmayogin, The Adyar Library and Research Center, Madras, 1968).

40. Ibid., p. 628.

41. Ibid., p. 628.

arūpavad eva hi tatpradhānatvāt

For (Brahman) is indeed devoid of form, as this is salient among those (Upaniṣadic) passages.[42]

Wayman also notes that Śaṅkara equates space (*ākāśa*) with the Brahman, and that since Brahman is declared by Śaṅkara to be *arūpa* (without form) therefore space is declared by Śaṅkara to be devoid of *rūpa*. Śaṅkara's position that space is devoid of *rūpa* may have led him to argue with those Buddhists, Vaiśeṣikas, or Sāṅkhyas who considered space to have *rūpa*.

Thus Wayman has shown that there is a rudimentary basis in the *Śatapatha Brāhmaṇa* for Śaṅkara's two kinds of *nāma-rūpa*, the unevolved or unseparated (*avyākṛta*) and evolved or separated (*vyākṛta*). It is also interesting to note that according to Wayman, the Buddhist *nāma-rūpa*, the fourth member of dependent origination (*pratītya-samutpāda*), is to be associated with the second kind, the evolved or separated (*vyākṛta*) kind, of *nāma-rūpa*. The reason is that the Buddhist *nāma-rūpa* is explained as the five personal aggregates (*skandha*). It is to be realized that Wayman has noted that the *nāma* of the second type of *nāma-rūpa* for Śaṅkara is the Jīva, the individual self. In this way, the self of man for Śaṅkara is in fact the Jīva, or individual, not the *jīvātman*, which he identifies as the Lord. Perhaps Śaṅkara's "crypto"-Buddhism consists in his denial that there is a self in man to be identified with the Lord, for otherwise man would have created the mountains and rivers. Wayman also notes the portrayal of *nāma-rūpa* in the "Wheel of Life" as two persons in a boat.

> We shall see that the usual occurrences of the term *nāma-rūpa* go with the second one of two kinds. Certainly such is the case of the Buddhist *nāma-rūpa*, 4th member of Dependent Origination (*pratītya-samutpāda*), explained as the five personality aggregates (*skandha*) in the womb, depicted in the 'Wheel of Life' as two persons in a boat, the two persons noted by Vinītadeva in his *Vinaya* commentary as a woman and a man.[43]

42. Wayman, Alex, "A Study of the Vedāntic . . .", (citing *Brahmasūtra* III.2.14), p. 628.

43. Wayman, Alex, "A Study of the Vedāntic . . .", p. 623.

Part II

A STUDY OF THREE COMMENTARIES TO *BRAHMA-SŪTRA* II.2.18-32

A. INTRODUCTION

In Part II of this work, an attempt will be made to compare the commentaries of Śaṅkara, Rāmānuja, and Madhva in connection with the *Brahma-sūtras* concerned with the refutation of the Buddhists, namely *Brahma-sūtras* II. 2.18-32 in the case of Śaṅkara and Madhva, and *Brahma-sūtras* II. 2.17-30 in the case of Rāmānuja. The similarities and differences among the three commentaries will be noted. Furthermore, an attempt will be made not only to compare the representation of Buddhism by the three Vedāntic figures to positions actually set forth in Buddhist texts, but also to compare the interpretations of the three Vedāntic commentators with each other. It will be observed that the three commentaries to these *sūtras* reveal not only disagreements among the Vedāntic figures themselves but also differences in their perception of Buddhism.

First of all, it is to be noted that Rāmānuja, Madhva and the Madhva school while attempting to refute supposed Buddhist positions were also attempting to refute positions supposedly held by Śaṅkara and his school. In his commentary to the *sūtra* "*nābhāva upalabdheḥ*" (*Brahma-sūtra* II. 2.27), for instance, Rāmānuja seems to attack Śaṅkara as a Buddhist hidden behind the cover of belief in the Veda because of their supposed position that the absolute is mere knowledge—a position formulated according to Rāmānuja on the basis of knowledge in a form having both action and agent, a subject and an object. In its interpretations of this *sūtra*, the school of Madhva also attacks the unqualified non-dualism (*nirviśeṣādvaita*) of Śaṅkara as well as Śūnyavāda Buddhism. It is interesting to note, however, that both Rāmānuja and the Madhva school attack Śaṅkara in their commentaries to a *sūtra* considered by Śaṅkara to be directed against Vijñānavāda Buddhism, namely, the *sūtra* "*nābhāva upalabdheḥ*" (*Brahma-sūtra* II. 2.28 for Śaṅkara). According to Vyāsatīrtha in the *Tātparyacandrikā*, as noted in the section of Part II concerned with Madhva's interpretation of *Brahma-sūtra* II. 2. 28, for both Śaṅkara and Vijñānavāda, consciousness (*vijñāna*) appears as external objects. In the same section of Part II, it is noted that according to Vyāsatīrtha the description of object-entities as devoid of the characteristic of the existent and the non-existent (*sadasadvilakṣaṇa*) set forth by Śaṅkara's school and the description of object-entities as non-existent set forth by the Madhva school are equivalent in that object-entities are perceived as existent by both schools and in that there is no non-existence apart from absence of existence. According to Jayatīrtha, both Śaṅkara and the Buddhists speak of conventional existence which is different from the non-existent. According to Jayatīrtha in the *Nyāya-suddhā*, Madhva's commentary to the *sūtra* "*udāsīnānām api caivaṃ siddhiḥ*" (*Brahma-sūtra* II. 2.27) is directed against the argument of Śaṅkara's follower Śrīharṣa in the *Khaṇḍana-khaṇḍakhādya*. Śrīharṣa had argued that if the existence of a cause is from within, then there is a question whether it will obtain its existence prior to its existence as cause, and that if the existence of a cause is from without, then there is the objection that the cause has no existence of its own. This argument is rejected by Madhva, however, according to Jayatīrtha, as is seen in the section of Part II concerned with Madhva's interpretation of *Brahma-sūtra* II. 2. 27, on the basis that if the void (*śūnya*) were to possess causality, then indifferent things like sky-flowers would possess causality. It is to be observed that Madhva's interpretations of the *Brahma-sūtras* differ radically from those of Śaṅkara and Rāmānuja. In particular, it may be noticed that in his interpretation of *Brahma-sūtras* II. 2. 26-29, Madhva and his school attempt to refute what they consider to be the Śūnyavāda school of Buddhism, whereas Śaṅkara criticizes what he considers to be the Sarvāstivādins and Vijñānavādins, and Rāmānuja criticizes the Sautrāntikas, Sarvāstivādins and Vijñānavādins. As is to be observed, Madhva and his school in their interpretations of the *sūtra* "*udāsīnānām api caivaṃ siddhiḥ*" (*Brahma-sūtra* II. 2.27) seem to criticize the viewpoint of Śaṅkara's follower Śrīharṣa, and in their interpretations of the *sūtra* "*nābhāva upalabdheḥ*" (*Brahma-sūtra* II. 2. 28) they seem to criticize the viewpoints of Śaṅkara. It seems, therefore, that a reason for Madhva's departure from the interpretations of his predecessors Śaṅkara and Rāmānuja may have been the desire to refute Śaṅkara and his school by equating them with Śūnyavāda Buddhism.

Secondly, it is to be noted that Rāmānuja, Madhva and the Madhva school give more attention to the work of the later

Buddhist logicians Śāntarakṣita, Kamalaśīla, and Ratnakīrti, than does Śaṅkara. Rāmānuja, for instance, in his commentary to the *sūtra "anusmṛteśca"* (*Brahma-sūtra* II. 2. 24) seems to devote more attention than Śaṅkara, in the latter's commentary to the *sūtra "pratisaṃkhyā'pratisaṃkhyā-nirodhāprāptir avicchedāt"* (*Brahma-sūtra* II. 2. 22), to Śāntarakṣita's and Kamalaśīla's distinction between the two kinds of destruction, destruction (*vināśa*) as such and disruption (*pradhvaṃsa*). According to Śāntarakṣita and Kamalaśīla, destruction is concerned with the momentary existence of *dharmas* and is admitted to have a cause, and disruption is concerned with the cessation of the nature of an entity and does not possess a cause. For Rāmānuja argues against the Buddhist position of momentariness by noting that the jar requires a visible cause for destruction and must be considered permanent and continuous until a visible extrinsic cause like a hammer intervenes. Rāmānuja in one case, however, attributes to the Buddhists a claim which utterly contradicts their actual position. Kamalaśīla explains, for instance, as has been discussed in the section on the Later Logicians, that destruction cannot be equivalent to the origination of a new series, because at the time of its supposed beginning, its cause (e.g. the hammer) is absent. Rāmānuja, however, as is discussed in the section concerned with the *sūtra "anusmṛteśca"* (*Brahma-sūtra* II.2.24) argues that it may be claimed by the Buddhist that the hammer for instance is the cause of the origination of a new series (e.g. the fragments of the jar). Although such a representation of the Buddhist position represents a distortion, it reveals at least an obscured awareness of the work of Śāntarakṣita and Kamalaśīla. Madhva and his school in their commentaries to the *sūtra "pratisaṃkhyā'pratisaṃhkyānirodhāprāpṭir avicchedāt"* (*Brahma-sūtra* II.2.22) also reveal some awareness of Śāntarakṣita's and Kamalaśīla's position towards the two types of destruction, when the former speak of the destruction with series equivalent to the disruption set forth by Śāntarakṣita and Kamalaśīla and of the destruction without series equivalent to the destruction set forth by Śāntarakṣita and Kamalaśīla. Furthermore, as is to be noted in the discussion of the *sūtra "anusmṛteśca"* (*Brahma-sūtra* II.2.25) Rāmānuja seems to have been somewhat aware of the arguments set forth by Ratnakīrti to the effect that whatever is existent is momentary (e.g. a jar), for a non-momentary thing cannot be efficient. Rāmānuja, for instance, argues in an attempted refutation of the Buddhist position, that efficiency attests the non-momentariness of jars in that momentary things are not capable of activity and are thus inefficient. Madhva, as is to be noted in the discussion of the *sūtra* "*ākāśe cāviśeṣāt*" (*Brahma-sūtra* II.2.24) seems to have been aware of Ratnakīrti's argument when he tries to establish its contrary, namely that whatever is existent is non-momentary as in the case of space. Śaṅkara, however, as is noted in the discussion of the *sūtra* "*uttarotpāde ca pūrvanirodhāt* (*Brahma-sūtra* II.2.20), does seem to have been aware of one argument of Śāntarakṣita and Kamalaśīla to the effect that the cause possesses no activity apart from its being. As though mindful of this argument on the part of Śāntarakṣita and Kamalaśīla, Śaṅkara argues that if the existence of the cause be its activity, then the effect is imbued with the nature of the cause. Consequently, according to Śaṅkara, the principle of momentariness is contradicted, for the effect lasts more than one moment. Śaṅkara seems to be more concerned with the refutation of earlier Buddhist logicians such as Dignāga, even to the extent of citing Dignāga's verse "*yad antar-jñeya-rūpaṃ tad bahirvad avabhāsate*" (the inner form of the knowable which appears as though it were external) in his commentary to the *sūtra* "*nābhāva upalabdheḥ*" (*Brahma-sūtra* II.2.28), which he considers to be directed against the Buddhist Vijñānavādins. As is discussed in the section of Part II concerned with this *sūtra*, Śaṅkara argues that it is the nature of perception to point towards an external object-entity. Of even more concern to Śaṅkara is Dignāga's notion of introspection (*sva-saṃvedana*) which Śaṅkara interprets as the notion that perception is experienced for itself. Śaṅkara argues that perception cannot be experienced in itself, because of the contradictoriness of activity in itself.

Thus, it is seen that in their attempted refutation of Buddhism the three Vedāntins reveal the disagreements among each other's schools, as well as the differences in the Vedāntic perception of Buddhism.

B. *BRAHMA-SŪTRA* II.2.18:

SAMUDĀYA UBHAYAHETUKE 'PI TADAPRĀPTIḤ

1. Śaṅkara's Interpretation

This *sūtra*, "*samudāya ubhayahetuke 'pi tadaprāptiḥ*,"[1] may be translated as follows in accordance with the interpretation of Śaṅkara ; "In the case of the aggregate(s) having two-fold causes, there is non-establishment of that."

In his commentary to this *sūtra* Śaṅkara declares that the purport of the following set of *sūtras* is to repudiate the opinions of the various Buddhist schools, which, according to him teach universal non-permanency or universal destruction. He refers to three schools of Buddhism: The Sarvāstivādins, the Vijñānavādins, the Śūnyavādins. The Sarvāstivādins for Śaṅkara are those who believe that all exists (*kecitsarvāstitvavādinaḥ*).[2] The Vijñānavādins are those who believe that all is ideation-only (*kecidvijñānāstitvavādinaḥ*).[3] The Śūnyavādins are those who believe that all is void (*sarvaśunyatvavādina iti*).[4] Śaṅkara then proceeds to refute the Sarvāstivāda school. The term "*samudāya*" according to Śaṅkara refers to two sets : first, the evolutes (*bhautika*) having as their cause the elements (*bhuta*) of fire, wind, earth, and water; and secondly, the mentals (*caitta*) having as their cause thought (*citta*). According to the Sarvāstivādins, as Śaṅkara represents them, the given thing is both internal and external and includes both the set of elements and evolutes and the set of thought and mentals. The elements include the four beginning with earth etc. There are four types of atoms (*paramāṇu*) according to the Sarvāstivādins, as Śaṅkara represents their position, corresponding to the four elements and these atoms are gathered together into aggregates. The five personal aggregates (*skandha*), as Śaṅkara describes, are gathered together as the inward basis for all that is practical.

---

1. Radhakrishnan, Sarvepalli, *The Brahma Sūtra*, *Brahma-sūtra* II.2.18, p. 378.

2. Balasubrahmanyam, T. K., *The Works of Śrī Śaṅkarāchārya*, Volume II, commentary to *Brahma-sutra* II.2.18, p. 381.

3. Ibid., commentary to *Brahma-sūtra* II.2.18, p. 381.

4. Ibid., commentary to *Brahma-sūtra* II.2.18, p. 381.

tatra ye sarvāstitvavādino bāhyamāntaraṃ ca vastvabhyupagacchanti bhūtaṃ bhautikaṃ ca cittaṃ caittaṃ ca, taṃstavatpratibrūmaḥ / tatra bhūtaṃ pṛthivīdhātvādayaḥ / bhautikaṃ rūpādayaścakṣurādayaśca/catuṣṭaye ca pṛthivyādiparamāṇavaḥ kharasnehoṣṇeraṇasvabhāvāste pṛthivyādibhāvena saṃhanyanta iti manyante/tathā rūpavijñānavedanāsaṃjñāsaṃskārasaṃjñakāḥ pañcaskandhāḥ/te'pyādhyātmaṃ sarvavyavahārāspadabhāvena saṃhanyanta iti manyante/[5]

Hence those who hold the doctrine that all exists conclude that the given thing (*vastu*) is both inward and outward, concerned both with elements and evolutes, with thought and mentals; we reply to them thoroughly. Then, the element is the set beginning with the *dhātu* of earth. The evolute is the set beginning with formation and the set beginning with the eye. They hold that the four (types of) atoms of earth, etc. which have the nature of hardness, liquidity, heat, and motion, are gathered together as the entities of the set beginning with earth. Thereupon, they hold that the five personal aggregates are named formation, perception, feeling, idea, motivation. These are gathered together inwardly by way of being the basis for all that is practical.

Śaṅkara remarks that no cause is established for the existence either of the aggregate of elements and evolutes or of the aggregate of thought and mentals.

tatredamabhidhīyate—yo 'yamubhayahetuka ubhayaprakāraḥ samudāyaḥ pareṣāmabhipretaḥ—aṇuhetukaśca bhūtabhautikasaṃhatirūpaḥ, skandhahetukaśca pañcaskandhīrūpaḥ—tasminnubhayahetuke 'pi samudāye 'bhipreyamāṇe, tadaprāptiḥ syāt—samudāyaprāptiḥ samudāyabhāvānupapattirityarthaḥ;[6]

---

5. Bākre, Mahādeva Śāsrtī, ed., *The Brahmasūtra-Shānkarbhāshyam*, with commentaries by Srigovindānanda, Vācaspati, Ānandagiri (Bombay : Nirnaya Sagar Press, third edition, 1934), commentary to *Brahma-sūtra* II.2.18, pp. 450-451.

6. Balasubrahmanyam, T. K., *The Works of Śrī Śaṅkarāchārya*, Volume II, Śaṅkara's commentary on *Brahma-sūtra* II.2.18, p. 382.

Then it is thought: that aggregate being of two types and having two causes is intended by the others (Buddhists) to be the formation of the collection of elements and evolutes having their causes in the atoms and (to be the) formation of the personal aggregates having their cause in the personal aggregates; in the case of these aggregates having the two causes, as claimed by them, there is non-establishment of that. The significance is that there is objection to the existence of the aggregate.

Śaṅkara notes that the aggregates are devoid of intelligence and reminds us that the Buddhists do not admit of a creative divinity or enjoying soul.

kutaḥ ? samudāyināmacetanatvāt, cittābhijvalanasya ca samudāyasiddhyadhīnatvāt, anyasya ca kasyaciccetanasya bhoktuḥ praśāsiturvā sthitasya saṃhanturanabhyupagamāt[7]

How ? Because of the non-intelligence of the aggregates. And because of the lack of proof of (the being of an) aggregate for the kindling of thought. Because of the non-attainment of any intelligent enjoyer, ruler and permanent joiner whatsoever.

Śaṅkara also objects that if individual atoms cannot enter activity on their own account, then their activity would never cease.

nirapekṣapravṛttyabhyupagame ca pravṛttyanuparamaprasaṅgāt[8]

Because of the impossibility of the cessation of motion in maintaining independent motion.

Through this objection, it appears that Śaṅkara is referring to the two *dharmas* of cessation—the cessation-with-understanding and the cessation-without-understanding — for in the sub-commentary *Ratnaprabhā* it is stated that if the atoms and personal aggregates proceed of themselves, there would be no liberation.

---

7. Ibid., Volume II, commentary to *Brahma-sūtra* II.2.18, p. 382.
8. Ibid., Volume II, commentary to *Brahma-sūtra* II.2.18, p. 382.

na ca kartāramanapekṣyāṇavaḥ skandhāśca svayameva saṃghātārthaṃ pravartanta iti vācyam, anirmokṣaprasaṅgāt/[9]

It is not to be said that the atoms and personal aggregates independent of a doer proceed of themselves for the sake of the aggregate, because of the non-occurrence of liberation.

Śaṅkara then attributes to the Buddhists the position that the aggregation of atoms may be caused by the "*āśaya*," which can signify either the ideation-store or the series. Śaṅkara argues that such a position is indefinable in the case of the identity of the "*āśaya*" with single perceptions, because there are the contradictions inherent in the momentariness of these perceptions. He also argues that such a position is indefinable in the case of the difference of the "*āśaya*" from the single perceptions because of the impossibility of accounting for motion, since the "*āśaya*" is inactive.

āśayasyāpyanyatvānanyatvābhyāmanirūpyatvāt kṣaṇikatvābhyupagamācca nirvyāpāratvātpravṛttyanupapatteḥ[10]

Because of the indefinability of the otherness and non-otherness of the *āśaya* on account of maintaining momentariness, and on account of objection to motion because of inactivity.

The commentators of Śaṅkara's interpretation explain *āśaya* as either series, as in the case of the *Ratnaprabhā*, or as *ālayavijñāna*, as in the case of the *Bhāmatī*. According to the *Bhāmatī*, the *āśaya* is eqivalent to the ideation-store.

āśerate 'smin karmānubhavavāsanā ityāśaya ālayavijñānaṃ tasya[11]

In this case, in reference to the propensities relating to the experience of *karma*, the *āśaya* is the ideation-store.

9. Bākre, Mahādeva Śāstrī, ed., *The Brahmasūtra-Shānkarbhāshyam*, *Ratnaprabhā* sub-commentary to Śaṅkara's *bhāṣya* on *Brahma-sūtra* II.2:18, p. 452.

10. Balasubrahmanyam, T. K., *The Works of Śrī Śaṅkarāchārya*, Volume II, commentary to *Brahma-sūtra* II.2.18, p. 383.

11. Bākre, Mahādeva Śāstrī, ed., *The Brahmasūtra-Shānkarbhāshyam*, *Bhāmatī* sub-commentary to Śaṅkara's *bhāṣya* to *Brahma-sūtra* II.2.18, p. 452.

According to the *Ratnaprabhā*, the *āśaya* is equivalent to the series.

> āśayasyeti/aśerate 'smin rāgādaya ityāśayaḥ saṃtānaḥ, sa kim saṃtānibhyo 'nyo vijñānibhyo nānyo vā/[12]
>
> In this case, in reference to passion etc., the *āśaya* is an uninterrupted series. Is it other than the series or not-other than the perception ?

Śaṅkara then argues that, given these considerations, there is valid objection to the aggregate, and that on the basis of such an aggregate the world cannot be established.

> tasmātsamudāyānupapattiḥ/samudāyānupapattau ca tadāśrayā lokayātrā lupyeta//[13]
>
> Therefore, there is objection to the aggregate. When there is objection to the aggregate, worldly existence having its basis in that, is cancelled.

It is to be noted that Śaṅkara has ignored the various Buddhist positions in connection with causality, including the doctrine of dependent origination. As Yamakami Sogen notes, the Sarvāstivādins claim that atoms can enter into combination through causes and conditions.

> The difficulty raised by Śaṅkara is rather irrelevant. The Sarvāstivādins maintain that the atoms though devoid of intelligence enter into combination with one another owing to causes and conditions, the former of which, technically called *hetu*, are of six sorts and the latter known as *pratyaya*, are of four sorts.[14]

As has been noted in the section of the Introductory Background concerned with Causation (as understood by the Sarvāstivādins and Sautrāntikas), it has been stated in the *Abhidharmakośa* that

---

12. Ibid., *Ratnaprabhā* sub-commentary to Śaṅkara's bhāṣya to *Brahma-sūtra* II.2.18, p. 452.

13. Ibid., Śaṅkara's commentary to *Brahma-sūtra* II.2.18, p. 452.

14. Sogen, Yamakami, *Systems of Buddhistic Thought* (Calcutta: University of Calcutta, 1912), p. 127.

according to the Sarvāstivādins it is by means of conditions having assembled together that the constructed thing is accomplished.[15] Śaṅkara also objects that if the atoms and personal aggregates could enter into activity on their own, there would be no cessation of motion. If Śaṅkara is referring here to the two cessations, the cessation-with-understanding and the cessation-without-understanding, it should be noted as has been explained in the Introductory Background, in the section concerned with Momentariness, the Sarvāstivādins in their interpretation of momentariness held all three times to be real, and that they postulated duration as a characteristic of constructed *dharmas*. Since *dharmas* possess duration in the Sarvāstivāda system, they are able to form aggregates. If the *āśaya* is interpreted in the Sautrāntika sense of a series, then it should be noted, as has been discussed in the section of Part I concerned with Momentariness, that the Sautrāntikas define the four characteristics in terms of the series so that a subsequent moment in the series is the duration of the antecedent. The Sautrāntikas, therefore, are interpreting *dharmas*, as well as their characteristics, in terms of series. They are noting that even aggregates, such as streams and flames, must be interpreted in terms of a series.

2. Rāmānuja's Interpretation

This *sūtra*, "*samudāya ubhayahetuke 'pi tadaprāptiḥ*," may be translated as follows in accordance with the interpretation of Rāmānuja : "In the case of the aggregate having a two-fold cause, there is non-attainment of that." In contrast to Śaṅkara's introduction to the section of his commentary concerned with the refutation of Buddhism, Rāmānuja mentions four schools, including a school that seems to be the Sautrāntikas. It should be noted that Rāmānuja devotes a whole *sūtra* to an attempted refutation of the Sautrāntika school in his commentary to the *sūtra* "*nāsato 'dṛṣṭatvāt*" (*Brahma-sūtra* II.2.25), and a whole *sūtra*, "*sarvathānupapatteśca*" (*Brahma-sūtra* II.2.30) to an attempted refutation of the Śūnyavādins. Thus Rāmānuja concerns himself with only two schools (although he refers to

15. Shastri, Swami Dwarikadasa, *Abhidharmakośam*, *Sphuṭārtha* commentary to *Abhidharmakośa* III.45, p. 248.

Śūnyavāda briefly in his attempted refutation of Vijñānavāda). Rāmānuja classifies three of these schools together on the basis of what he considers their common principle of momentariness, as well as denial of space, Self, etc.

> te caturvidhāḥ—kecit pārthivāpyataijasavāyavīyaparamāṇusaṃghātarūpān bhūtabhautikān bāhyān cittacaittarūpāṃścābhyantarān arthān pratyakṣānumānasiddhān abhyupayanti/anye tu bāhyārthān sarvān pṛthivyādīn vijñānānumeyān vadanti/apare tu, 'arthaśūnyam vijñānameva paramārthasat, bāhyārthāstu svāpnārthakalpāḥ' ityāhuḥ/trayo 'pyete svābhyupagataṃ vastu kṣaṇikamācakṣate/uktabhūtabhautikacittacaittavyatiriktamātmākāśādikaṃ svarūpeṇaiva nānumanvate/[16]
>
> These Bauddhas are of four types. Some maintain the proof by perception and inference of outer object-entities, the four great elements and evolutes having the form of aggregates of atoms of earth, water, fire, and wind, and of inner object-entities, the thought and mentals. Others say that all the outer object-entities such as earth, etc. are to be inferred by consciousness. Others say, "The absolute truth is consciousness devoid of the object-entity, and that outer object-entities are the imaginations of dreams". The three declare the momentary given thing agreed upon among themselves. Apart from the above-mentioned great elements, evolutes, thought, and mentals, the set beginning with Self, space, etc. is not affirmed in their own nature.

It is to be noted that in his attempted refutation of what he considers to be the positions of the Sautrāntikas and Vaibhāṣikas, Rāmānuja takes up questions discussed by the later schools of Buddhism, exemplified by Śāntrakṣita and Kamalaśīla or Ratnakīrti. Rāmānuja also mentions the Śūnyavādins, whose position according to him is that all is void.

> anye tu sarvaśūnyatvameva saṅgirante[17]
> Others, finally, assert that all is void.

16. Viraraghavacharya, Sri Uttamur T., *Brahmasūtra-Śrībhāshya*, commentary to *Brahma-sūtra* II.2.17, pp. 527-528.
17. Ibid., commentary to *Brahma-sūtra* II.2.17, p. 528.

In his description of the two-fold aggregate Śaṅkara mentions the formation which is composed of the five personal aggregates.

> tatredamabhidhīyate—yo 'yamubhayahetuka ubhayaprakāraḥ samudāyaḥ pareṣāmabhipretaḥ—aṇuhetukaśca bhūtabhautikasaṃhatirūpaḥ, skandhahetukaśca pañcaskandhīrūpaḥ[18]
>
> Then it is thought : that aggregate being of two types and having two causes is intended by the others (Buddhists) to be the formation of the collection of elements and evolutes having their causes in the atoms and (to be the) formation of the personal aggregates having their causes in the personal aggregates.

Rāmānuja, however, presents a different version of what for Śaṅkara is the aggregate having its cause in the five personal aggregates. Rāmānuja speaks of the aggregate's having a formation of body, senses, object—a formation which has its cause in the set beginning with the earth.

> yo 'yamaṇuhetukaḥ pṛthivyādibhūtātmakaḥ samudāyaḥ, yaśca pṛthivyādihetukaḥ śarīrendriyaviṣayarūpaḥ samudāyaḥ, tasmin ubhayahetuke 'pi samudāye tatprāptirnopapadyate—jagadātmakasamudāyotpattirnopadyata ityarthaḥ/ paramāṇūnāṃ pṛthivyādibhūtānāṃ ca kṣaṇikatvābhyupagamāt/[19]
>
> That aggregate composed of the great elements or the earth, etc. having as its cause the atoms, that aggregate having a formation of body, senses, sense-object, and having for its cause the earth, etc.—in the case of this aggregate with its two-fold cause the establishment of that is not possible, that is to say, the arising of the aggregate consisting in the earth is not possible, because of the principle of momentariness in connection with the atoms and the great elements beginning with earth.

Rāmānuja's attempted refutation of the Sarvāstivāda doctrine of the aggregates is based on the contradictions posed by the

---

18. Balasubrahmanyam, T. K., *The Works of Śrī Śaṅkarāchārya*, Volume II, commentary to *Brahma-sūtra* II.2.18, p. 382.

19. Viraraghavacharya, Sri Uttamur T., *Brahmasūtra-Śrībhāshya*, commentary to *Brahma-sūtra* II.2.17, pp. 528-529.

doctrine of momentariness also held by that school. Rāmānuja poses the question that if one grants the atoms and the elements to be subject to destruction at every moment, then how could aggregates be formed, and who would come in contact with them? Whereas Śaṅkara employs the argument of the necessity of a conscious agent, Rāmānuja employs the argument that the notions of momentariness and the aggregate are contradictory.

> kṣaṇadhvaṃsinaḥ paramāṇavo bhūtāni ca kadā saṃhatau vyāpriyante; kadā vā saṃhanyante/[20]
>
> When do the atoms perishing in a moment and the great elements engage in combination, when do they combine ?

Like Śaṅkara in his commentary to the *sūtra* "*anusmṛteśca*" (*Brahma-sūtra* II.2.25), Rāmānuja in his commentary to the this *sūtra* (*Brahma-sūtra* II.2.17) also argues for a permanent subject that is able to know what has been contacted or perceived and to appropriate what has been known. It seems that Rāmānuja assumes that to appropriate, to know, and, to touch or have contact requires three separate moments.

> spraṣṭā hi naṣṭaḥ, spṛṣṭaśca naṣṭaḥ; tathā veditā viditaśca naṣṭaḥ/kathaṃcānyena spṛṣṭamanyo vedayate; kathaṃcānyena viditam (anyam) arthamanya upādatte.[21]
>
> The one who contacts is perished, the thing contacted is perished; likewise, the knower and the known are perished. How is one made to know a thing contacted by another ? How does one appropriate an object-entity known by another ?

Rāmānuja also attempts to refute here a possible Sautrāntika objection which is in accordance with the Sautrāntika notion of a series, flow, or stream, which provides a kind of oneness.

> saṃtānānāmekatve 'pi saṃtānibhyasteṣāṃ vastuto vastvantaratvānabhyupagamāt na tannibandhanaṃ vyavahārādikamupapadyate/[22]

---

20. Ibid., commentary to *Brahma-sūtra* II.2.17, p. 529.
21. Ibid., commentary to *Brahma-sūtra* II.2.17, p. 529.
22. Ibid., commentary to *Brahma-sūtra* II.2.17, p. 529.

In the case of the oneness of the series, because of the non-establishment of the existence of a given thing distinct from a given thing in connection with those parts of the series, through the series there exists no basis for the practical sphere.

According to Rāmānuja, the series would be composed of parts, each of which is momentary and perishing; hence, according to Rāmānuja, the notion of the series like the notion of the aggregate is contradicted by the doctrine of momentariness. A difficulty inherent in Rāmānuja's attempted refutation of the notion of the series, however, is that the series cannot be easily broken into discrete parts. Thus in the *Abhidharmakośa*, as is noted in the Introductory Background, in the section concerned with Momentariness, it is mentioned that the duration of a series is the series itself. The series is declared to have a beginning and a cessation. The difficulty is that if the series itself is its own duration, how can it be broken into parts? Thus Rāmānuja's attempted refutation does not seem to take into account the implications of the Sautrāntika interpretation of Momentariness. Rāmānuja also questions the Sarvāstivādins as to how atoms and elements such as earth, etc. being momentary can form aggregates. It seems, however, that Rāmānuja is assuming that aggregates are permanent and motionless. Entities such as a flame or a stream, however, cannot be said to be permanent and motionless. It must be remembered also that according to the Sarvāstivādins, there is a difference between the nature of a *dharma*, and its characteristic, as has been noted in the section on Momentariness.

3. Madhva's Interpretation

This *sūtra*, "*samudāya ubhayahetuke'pi tadaprāptiḥ*," may be translated as follows in accordance with Madhva's interpretation : "In the case of the aggregate with its two-fold cause also, there is non-establishment of that." Madhva's brief commentary proceeds as follows :

paramāṇupuñjavādimatamapākaroti // samudāyasyaikahetukatvaṃ na yujyate// ubhayahetuke'pyanyonyāśrayatvāttadaprāptiḥ anyathā sarvadā samudāyasattvaṃ syāt //[23]

23. Bhikācārya Ainapure and Anantācārya Aṣṭaputre, *Brahmasūtras* with Ānandatīrtha's *Brahmasūtrabhāṣya* and Jayatīrtha Muni's *Tattva-*

He refutes the doctrine of those holding the position of an aggregate of atoms. That one (atom) is the cause of the aggregate is not enjoined. Because there is mutual dependence in the case of the two-fold cause, there is non-establishment of that (the aggregate). Otherwise, there would be the existence of the aggregate endlessly.

Unlike Śaṅkara and Rāmānuja, Madhva in his interpretation of this *sūtra* is concerned with the notion of the aggregate as whole (*avayavin*) distinguished from the part (*avayava*). What characterizes the Sarvāstivāda school, called *Paramāṇupuñjavāda* by Madhva[24] according to B.N.K. Sharma's study of Madhva and his sub-commentators, is the denial of a permanent whole apart from the aggregates of atoms. This summation of the *Paramāṇupuñjavāda* position is expressed by Jayatīrtha in his *Nyāyasudhā*.

aṇusamudāyā eva goghaṭādibodhabodhyā, na tu tadarikto 'vayavī nāmāsti.[25]

The ideas of cattle, jars, etc. are to be understood as the aggregates of atoms; there is nothing having the name "whole" which is not freed from these (aggregates of atoms).

According to B.N.K. Sharma, there is no such thing in this school as the production of a whole through evolution or "atomic combination" in the Vaiśeṣika sense. It is through false imagination that the notion of a "whole" arises.[26] According to B.N.K. Sharma, Madhva's commentary to this *sūtra* exposes the weakness of the *Paramāṇupuñjavāda* point of view, in that the notion of the aggregate is unintelligible if such aggregation does not give us a new whole. A single atom cannot form an aggregate. But in the case of an aggregation of two or more atoms coming together, there occurs the fallacy of mutual dependence, for the atoms cannot be conceived as aggregates unless they have come together and they cannot have come together without forming

---

prakāśikā, MS. form, ff. 126, 101, 108, 46, (Bombay, Gaṇpat Kṛṣṇaji Press, 1883), *Brahmasūtra* II.2.18, with Madhva's commentary, p. 36.

24. Sharma, B.N.K. *The Brahmasūtras and Their Principal Commentaries*, Volume II, (Bombay : Bharatiya Vidya Bhavan, 1974), p. 51.

25. Ibid., (*Nyāya-sudhā* II.2.18), p. 51, footnote 5.

26. Ibid., p. 51.

an aggregate.[27] If the aggregation is conceived as subsisting in several atoms as they lie isolated in space and as conceivable at all times, then there would be no prospect of the dissolution of the aggregate. According to B.N.K. Sharma, Madhva is saying that the difficulty can be solved only by the admission on the part of the Buddhists of "real organized wholes over and above the fleeting atoms of which they are supposed to be constituted."[28] In the case of later Buddhists such as Śāntarakṣita and Kamalaśīla, however, not only is there a denial of the notion of the whole, but also of the notion of the part, as has been noted in the Introductory Background, in the section concerned with the Later Logicians.

Madhva's interpretation of this *sūtra*, according to B.N.K. Sharma, surpasses Śaṅkara's and Rāmānuja's respective interpretations in that Madhva does not need to import the reason for the impossibility of the formation of the aggregates from outside, for he has shown the reason to be embodied within the *sūtra* itself.[29] Whereas Śaṅkara must introduce the absence of an intelligent Self acting as the one who brings about the aggregation and Rāmānuja must introduce the momentariness of atoms and *skandhas*, Madhva simply notes what he considers the unintelligibility of the notion of aggregate. B. N. K. Sharma cites the following passage from Vyāsatīrtha's *Tātparyacandrikā* to explain Madhva's interpretation. According to Vyāsatīrtha, the notion of an aggregate from one atom is contradictory. If the aggregate has two causes and both are separated by an interval, the aggregate would always exist. If the two causes are combined, there is the fallacy of mutual dependence. The key term in Vyāsatīrtha's explanation is "*sūtrarūḍha*," which signifies "brought under the cognizance of the *sūtra*."

> samudāye ekaikahetuke virodhaḥ/ekasmāt samudāya iti vyāhateḥ/ubhayahetukatvapakṣe 'pi samudāye, viralobhayahetuke samudāyaḥ sadā syāt/militobhayahetuke 'nyonyāśrayaḥ iti yuktiḥ sūtrarūḍhā[30]

27. Ibid., pp. 51-52.
28. Ibid., p. 52.
29. Ibid., Volume II, p. 52.
30. Ibid., Volume II, (*Tātparyacandrikā* 915b), p. 65, footnote 54.

When there is the aggregate with a single cause, there is contradiction, because of the contradiction that the aggregate is from one. In the case of the aggregate according to the position of two-fold causation, when both causes are separated by an interval, the aggregate would always exist. When both causes are combined, there is (the fallacy of) mutual dependence (*anyonyāśraya*)—thus it is enjoined and brought under the cognizance of the *sūtra*.

B. N. K. Sharma also notes in accordance with Vyāsatīrtha's explanation that there seems no reason for the use of the expression "*api*" and the use of the locative if the reason for non-aggregation is to be imported from outside as in the case of Śaṅkara's and Rāmānuja's interpretations. B. N. K. Sharma cites a passage from the *Tātparyacandrikā* to explain his point.

tathātve**samudāye ubhayahetuke iti saptamyoḥ, apiśabdasya tadaprāptirityatra tacchabdasya ca vyarthatvāt[31]

In the case of such a condition...Because of the absurdity of terminology in reference to the non-establishment of that, in connection with the word "*api*" and in connection with the two locatives in the expression "in the case of aggregate with its two-fold cause."

31. Ibid., Volume II, (*Tātparyacandrikā* 915b), p. 65, footnote 55.

C. *BRAHMA-SŪTRA* II.2.19 :

"*ITARETARA-PRATYAYATVĀD ITI CEN NOTPATTIMĀTRANIMITTATVĀT*"

1. Śaṅkara's Interpretation

This *sūtra*, "*itaretara-pratyayatvād iti cen notpattimātranimittatvāt*" (*Brahma-sūtra* II.2.19),[1] may be translated as follows in accordance with the interpretation of Śaṅkara: "If it is said that (the aggregate exists) because of mutual conditionality, it is replied that it is not so, because of the efficient causation (*nimittatva*) of the production only (of the subsequent member of the series)."

In his commentary to this aphorism, Śaṅkara charges the Sarvāstivādins with circular reasoning : they suppose that on the basis of the series of dependent origination, the formation of the aggregates can be assumed, and that on the basis of the formation of the aggregates the series of dependent origination can be explained. He attributes to the Buddhists the position that the formation of the aggregates is explained by the mutual causality (*pratyayatva*) of the series of dependent origination, the individual members of which are called *nidānas* (causes).

> yadyapi bhoktā praśāsitā vā kaściccetanaḥ saṃhantā sthiro nābhyupagamyate, tathāpyavidyādīnāmitaretarakāraṇatvādupapadyate lokayātrā; tasyāṃ copapadyamānāyāṃ na kiṃcidaparamapekṣitavyamasti; te cāvidyādayaḥ[2]
>
> Although no intelligence whatever is established as the enjoyer, the ruler, the permanent joiner, nevertheless, the world is made possible because of mutual causation. Since it has been made possible, no other (principle is required). This is the set beginning with nescience...

But Śaṅkara also attributes to the Buddhists the position that the formation of the aggregates must be assumed to account for the series of causes.

---

1. Radhakrishnan, Sarvepalli, *The Brahma Sūtra*, *Brahma-sūtra* II.2.19, p. 379.
2. Balasubrahmanyam, T. K., *The Works of Śrī Śaṅkarāchārya*, Volume II, Śaṅkara's commentary to *Brahma-sūtra* II.2.19, pp. 382-383.

tadevamavidyādikalāpe parasparanimittanaimittakabhāvena ghaṭīyantravadaniśamāvartamāne 'rthākṣipta upapannaḥ saṃghāta iti cet, tanna;[3]

If in the case of the collection beginning with nescience, revolving incessantly like a waterwheel through being mutual, efficient causes and effects, the meaning is given that the aggregate is born we say that it is not so.

Śaṅkara then rejects the position that he attributes to the Buddhists that the series of causes provides an efficient cause for the formation of the aggregates, on the basis that the causes only provide efficient causes for other *nidānas*.

kasmāt ? utpattimātranimittatvāt[4]

Why ? Because of the efficient causation of birth only.

According to Śaṅkara, that nescience is the first link in the chain of dependent origination assumes the prior existence of the aggregates.

nanvavidyādibhirarthādākṣipyate saṃghāta ityuktam; atrocyate—yadi tāvadayamabhiprāyaḥ—avidyādayaḥ saṃghātamantareṇātmānamalabhamānā apekṣante saṃghātamiti; tatastasya saṃghātasya kiṃcinnimittaṃ vaktavyam;[5]

If it be objected that the aggregate is indicated because of its significance by the set beginning with nescience then the reply is, if such is the meaning, that the set beginning with nescience, obtaining its nature by the mediation of the aggregate, requires an aggregate; any efficient cause whatsoever for (the aggregate) is to be declared.

Śaṅkara tries to show that the very existence of an aggregate is impossible in the Sarvāstivāda system on account of the momentariness of all atoms. Then Śaṅkara asks how the causes can be considered to be the efficient causes of the aggregates without which the *nidānas* would be deprived of an abode.

3. Ibid., Śaṅkara's commentary to *Brahma-sūtra* II.2.19, p. 383.
4. Ibid., Volume II, commentary to *Brahma-sūtra* II.2.19, p. 383.
5. Ibid., commentary to *Brahma-sūtra* II.2.19, p. 383.

tacca nityeṣvapyaṇuṣvabhyupagamyamāneṣvāśrayāśrayibhūteṣu ca bhoktṛṣu satsu na saṃbhavatītyuktaṃ vaiśeṣikaparīkṣāyāṃ; kimaṅga punaḥ kṣaṇikeṣvapyaṇuṣu bhoktṛrahite—svāśrayāśrayiśūnyeṣu vābhyupagamyamāneṣu saṃbhavet? athāyamabhiprāyaḥ—avidyādaya eva saṃghātasya nimittamiti, kathaṃ tamevāśrityātmānaṃ labhamānāstasyaiva nimittaṃ syuḥ?[6]

That, in the case of eternal atoms being arrived at, in the case of the existence of the basis and the resident, in the case of the existing enjoyer, has been said to be impossible in the examination of the Vaiśeṣikas. Wherefore then, when the atoms are momentary, when the enjoyer is regarded as unconnected, when the basis and the resident are regarded (*abhyupagamyamāna*) as void, should it (the aggregate) be possible? If this is the meaning, that the set beginning with nescience is an efficient cause for the aggregate, how obtaining its nature by relying upon that (the aggregate) should it (the set beginning with nescience) be an efficient cause for that (the aggregate) ?

Śaṅkara also attributes to the Buddhists the position that since the aggregates follow one another in a series (*saṃtati*) so also nescience etc. which have the aggregates as their basis. Śaṅkara seems to be confusing the Sarvāstivādins with the Sautrāntikas here in his application of the term *saṃtati* (series) to the entire school. Śaṅkara then goes on to indicate what for him are the logical consequences of the unbroken succession of aggregates. Śaṅkara explains that either the aggregates produce aggregates of the same kind, or they produce aggregates of a different kind. In the former case, a man could never be reborn in a different state; in the latter case, he could in an instant be transformed into something else.

atha manyase—saṃghātā evānādau saṃsāre saṃtatyānuvartante, tadāśrayāścāvidyādaya iti, tadāpi saṃghātātsaṃghātāntaramutpadyamānaṃ niyamena vā sadṛśamevotpadyeta, aniyamena vā sadṛśaṃ visadṛśaṃ votpadyeta;[7]

---

6. Ibid., Volume II, commentary to *Brahma-sūtra* II.2.19, p. 383.
7. Ibid., Volume II, commentary to *Brahma-sūtra* II.2.19, p. 384.

If you think that the aggregates follow one another as a series in an endless world, then so also nescience, etc. which have that (the aggregate) as basis; then an aggregate being born distinct from an aggregate is born similar according to rule, or is born either similar or dissimilar according to no rule.

Śaṅkara's last argument in his commentary to *sūtra* 19 is concerned with the question, "Who desires liberation ?" Śaṅkara states that there must be a permanent enjoying soul for whose sake the aggregates are formed, otherwise the aggregates are self-formed and self-subservient. But the Buddhists, Śaṅkara goes on to say, cannot admit such an entity because of the doctrine of Momentariness.

api ca yadbhogārthaḥ saṃghātaḥ syāt sa jīvo nāsti sthiro bhoktā iti tavābhyupagamaḥ; tataśca bhogo bhogārtha eva, sa nānyena prārthanīyaḥ; tathā mokṣo mokṣārtha bhavati mumukṣuṇā nānyena bhavitavyam; anyena cetprārthyetobhayaṃ, bhogamokṣakālāvasthāyinā tena bhavitavyam; avasthāyitve kṣaṇikatvābhyupagamavirodhaḥ[8]

Moreover, that for the sake of the enjoyment of whom the aggregate exists, is not the Jīva; that he is the permanent enjoyer is the principle. Hence, enjoyment is for the sake of enjoyment, and not by another is it to be desired. Thereupon, liberation is for the sake of liberation, and not by another desirous of liberation is it to be. If it should be desired by another, (then) for him residing up to the times of both enjoyment and liberation there must be liberation. In the state of residing there is a contradiction of the principle of Momentariness.

It is important to ask, however, whether the Buddhists and in particular the Sarvāstivādins, actually regard the series of *nidānas* involved in dependent origination as the efficient cause of the aggregates. Or is it rather the case that the Sarvāstivādins interpret dependent origination in terms of the principle "*asmin sati idam bhavati*," (when there is this, that is) ? If such is the case, then it is to be noted that each member of the chain accounts only for a subsequent member. Śaṅkara also argues, in

8. Ibid., Volume II, commentary to *Brahma-sūtra* II.2.19, p. 384.

opposition to the Sautrāntika concept of series, that if aggregates are born from other aggregates in an endless series, then in effect liberation would be desired by one but attained by another. As has been observed in the Introductory Background, however, in the section concerned with the two Cessations, the Sautrāntikas according to the *Sphuṭārtha* declared that the basis subsists only as long as the defilement subsists and then vanishes. It is not the case for the Sautrāntikas that "another" attains liberation; rather it is the case that the basis vanishes.

2. Rāmānuja's Interpretation

This *sūtra*, "*itaretara-pratyayatvād iti cen notpattimātranimittatvāt*," may be translated as follows in accordance with the interpretation of Rāmānuja : "If it be objected that (the aggregate exists) because of mutual causality, it is replied that there is no production because of efficient causation." In his commentary to this *sūtra*, Rāmānuja attributes to the Vaibhāṣika the position that the existence of the chain of dependent origination is itself evidence for the existence of the aggregate.

> etacca sarvam pṛthivyādibhūtabhautikasaṃghātamantareṇa nopapadyate / ataḥ saṃghātabhāvādikamupapannam—iti /[9]
>
> All this is not possible without the aggregate of the evolutes and the elements as earth, etc. Hence, it is said that the entity of the aggregate is proved.

Unlike Śaṅkara, who argues that the *nidānas* beginning with nescience cannot be efficient causes of the aggregates because the causes themselves presuppose the existence of the aggregates, Rāmānuja argues that to declare the causes beginning with nescience to be the causes of the aggregates is like saying that the illusion of silver in a shell is cause of the shell.

> na khalvasthirādiṣu sthiratvādibuddhyātmikā 'vidyā, tannimittāḥ rāgadveṣādayo vā arthāntarasya kṣaṇikasya saṃhatihetutāṃ pratipadyante; śuktikārajatādibuddhirhi na śuktyādyarthasaṃhatiheturbhavati /[10]

---

9. Viraraghavacharya, Sri Uttamur T., *Brahmasūtra-Śrībhāshya*, commentary to *Brahma-sūtra* II.2.18, p. 530.

10. Ibid., commentary to *Brahma-sūtra* II.2.18, pp. 530-531.

> Indeed, neither nescience, composed of such notions as the existence of permanence in the impermanent, nor the set beginning with passion and aversion, which have their efficient causes in that (nescience), arrive at the causation of the aggregate of another momentary object-entity; for the notion of silver in mother-of-pearl is not the cause of the aggregate of the object-entity mother-of-pearl.

It has been noted, however, in the Introductory Background, in the section of this work concerned with Causation, that dependent origination in Buddhism is intended to set forth the interdependence of the *dharmas* composing the aggregates rather than the genesis of *dharma* or aggregates. There is the principle, for instance, "*asmin sati idam bhavati*" (when there is this, that is), which illustrates the dependence of one *nidāna* upon another. It has been shown that Buddhist commentators like Buddhaghoṣa combatted the tendency to consider nescience or *avidyā* (*P. avijjā*) as first principle like the *prakṛti* (*P. pakati*) of Sāṅkhya. Both Śaṅkara and Rāmānuja seem to exhibit a gross misunderstanding of the Buddhist teaching of dependent origination insofar as it is concerned with *dharmas*, when they treat it as the efficient cause of the universe rather than as a principle of interdependence. Furthermore, when Rāmānuja attributes to the Buddhists the position that nescience is the cause of the aggregates, he is misrepresenting their position, in that the *nidānas* are intended not to explain the origin of the world but rather the this-conditioned nature (*idampratyayatā*, or in Pali, *idappaccayatā*) of things. Rāmānuja's final argument in his commentary to this *sūtra* (*Brahma-sūtra* II.2.18) seems to be directed against the Sautrāntikas, in that the Sautrāntika concept "*āśraya*" (basis) is employed by him, and the Sautrāntika concept "*bīja*" (seed) is employed in the sub-commentary *Bhāṣyārthadarpaṇa*. Rāmānuja argues that the one who is nescient, who sees the momentary as permanent, is momentary and perishes; consequently there is no basis for the motivations of passion etc. In this way, Rāmānuja argues, the continuance of motivation, the cause following nescience in the chain of dependent origination, cannot be assumed.

kiṃca yasya kṣaṇike sthiratvabuddhiḥ, sa tadaiva naṣṭa iti kasya rāgādaya utpadyante? saṃskārāśrayaṃ sthiramekaṃ dravyamanabhyupagacchatāṃ saṃskārānuvṛttirapi na śakyā kalpayitum //[11]

Whoever possesses the notion of permanence in a momentary thing, is destroyed; hence in whom will passion, etc. arise? For those not maintaining the one permanent material flow as a basis of the motivations, the continuance of the motivations cannot be declared.

In the sub-commentary *Bhāṣyārthadarpaṇa* there is mentioned the Sautrāntika concept "seed" in connection with this passage. According to the sub-commentary the meeting of the atoms included within the "seed" cannot take place, presumably because of momentariness.

yo hi kartāramekaṃ svīkṛtya kāryam kṣaṇikamapi sthiratvena gṛhītaṃ manyeta tasya kathamapyupāditsādi sampadyate, kartṛkṣaṇikatve tu na kiṃcit siddhyedityāśayenāha *kiṃceti* / atra pratyayopanibandhāsaṃbhavaḥ spaṣṭaḥ / evam hetūpanibandhāsaṃbhavepi hetubhūtabījādyantargatāṇūnāṃ melanāsaṃbhavena grāhyaḥ /[12]

For, in connection with the one who, having accepted the one doer considers the momentary effect apprehended by way of permanence, how is there the readiness to accept ? When there is the momentariness of the doer, nothing whatsoever may be established. He says thus by means of the basis in connection with the phrase "whatsoever". In this case, the non-occurrence of the notion as basis is evident. Thus the non-occurrence of a cause as basis is to be apprehended by means of the non-occurrence of the meeting of the atoms included within the seed etc., composed of them as cause.

It is to be noted that the Sautrāntika outlook towards the basis, however, is different from Rāmānuja's treatment of the concept

---

11. Viraraghavachārya, Sri Uttamur T., *Brahmasūtra Śrībhāshya*, commenttary to *Brahma-sūtra* II.2.18, p. 531.
12. Ibid., commentary to *Brahma-sūtra* II.2.18, p. 531.

of the basis when he argues that the motivations require a basis for their continuance. According to the presentation of the Sautrāntika position in the *Abhidharmakośa*, the basis subsists only as long as the defilements called seeds subsist. When the defilements disappear by the capacity engendered by the path of the cultivation of vision, the basis too disappears.

> āśrayaviśeṣādetatsidhyati/ āśrayo hi āryāṇām darśanabhāvanāmārgasāmarthyāttathā parāvṛto bhavati yathā na punastatpraheyāṇāṃ kleśānām prarohasamartho bhavati / ato 'gnidagdhavrīhivadabījībhūte āśraye kleśānāṃ prahīṇakleśa ityucyate /[13]
>
> That is accomplished because of the special property of the basis. As surely as the germinating capacity in connection with the defilements that are eliminated is no more, so truly the basis has vanished according to the noble ones, because of the capacity (engendered) by the path of cultivation of vision. Hence, when the basis does not form a seed like rice burnt over a fire, it is called, in relation to the defilements, one which has eliminated defilements.

3. Madhva's Interpretation

This *sūtra*, "*itaretara-pratyayatvād iti cen notpattimātranimittatvāt*," (*Brahma-sūtra* II.2.19) may be translated as follows in accordance with the interpretation of Madhva: "If it is objected that (the aggregate exists) because of mutually coordinate cognition (*itaretara-pratyayatva*), it is replied that it is not so, because there is an efficient cause for the birth only (of the aggregates)." Madhva's commentary proceeds as follows:

> sarvadā vidyamānopi samudāyaḥ parasparāpekṣayā vyavahriyata iti cenna // ekakāryamutpādya tasya vinaṣṭatvātparasparapratyayastadapekṣayā vyavahāra iti na yujyate // kāraṇe sati kāryam bhavatyeveti hi tasya niyamaḥ //[14]

---

13. Pradhan, Prof. P., *Abhidharmakośam of Vasubandhu*, (*Abhidharmakośa* II.37), p. 63.

14. Bhikācārya Aināpure and Anantācārya Aṣṭaputre, *Brahmasūtras with Ānandatīrtha's Brahmasūtrabhāṣya*, commentary to *Brahma-sūtra* II.2.19, pp. 36-37.

If it be said that the aggregate even though existing at all times, is designated by means of interrelated consideration (*parasparāpekṣā*), we say that it is not so, because of the destruction of that after having given birth to one effect. As for the convention, with reference to that the mutually coordinated cognition (*parasparapratyaya*) is not possible. For, that given the cause, there is the effect is the principle in connection with that.

In his commentary to this *sūtra*, Madhva supposes that aggregates are formed out of disconnected atoms lying isolated in space. If the atoms are permanent, there would be an unending series of aggregates in accordance with the principle "*kāraṇe sati, kāryam bhavati*" (when there is the cause, there is the effect). This principle is interpreted to signify that as long as the cause exists, the effect continues to be produced infinitely.[15] It may be suggested that the isolated atoms come to be grasped as aggregates when there is interrelated consideration (*parasparāpekṣā*) of the atoms as a group, as Madhva explains.

sarvadā vidyamāno 'pi samudāyaḥ parasparāpekṣayā vyavahriyata iti cenna.[16]

If it be said that the aggregate even though existing at all times, is designated by means of interrelated consideration (*parasparāpekṣā*), we say that it is not so.

Such interrelated consideration is known as "*itaretarapratyaya*" or "*apekṣābuddhi*" and has been described by Jagannātha Tīrtha in the *Bhāṣya-dīpikā*.

itarasahitamitarat itaretarat tasya pratyayaḥ tadviṣayāpekṣābuddhi itaretarapratyayaḥ[17]

One joined with another, one with another—the notion of this is the interdependent cognition (*apekṣābuddhi*) of that sense-object, the mutually coordinate cognition (*itaretarapratyaya*).

15. Sharma, B.N.K., *The Brahmasūtras and Their Principal Commentaries*, p. 54.

16. Ibid., (Madhva's commentary to *Brahma-sūtra* II.2.19), p. 52, footnote 11.

17. Ibid., (*Bhāṣya-dīpikā*), p. 53, footnote 12.

Because such an interdependent cognition (*apeksābuddhi*) need not last permanently, creation and dissolution would be explained. Such interdependent cognition has for its causes mutual proximity and mutual association according to Rāghavendra in his *Tantradīpikā*, as cited by B.N.K. Sharma.

> itaretaretyuktiḥ apekṣābuddhisvarūpopadarśanāya / tadapi anyonyasāhityarūpasāmīpyahetukā seti sūcayitum /[18]

> In reference to "one with another" the reasoning is for the sake of demonstrating the nature of the interdependent cognition (*apekṣābuddhi*). That (the *apekṣābuddhi*, the interdependent cognition) is manifested as having for its cause mutual proximity and mutual association.

There are contradictions in the concept of interdependent cognition or the mutually coordinate notion when it is juxtaposed with a system that teaches momentariness according to the Madhva school. For, as soon as the atoms are grouped into an aggregate, according to Madhva, they perish. Having given birth to the effect (the aggregate), the atoms perish.

> sarvadā vidyamānopi samudāyaḥ parasparāpekṣayā vyavahriyata iti cenna // ekakāryamutpādya tasya vinaṣṭatvātparasparapratyayastadapekṣayā vyavahāra iti na yujyate //[19]

> If it be said that the aggregate even though existing at all times, is designated by means of interrelated consideration, we say that it is not so, because of the destruction of that after having given birth to one effect. As for the convention, with reference to that the mutually coordinated cognition is not possible.

Furthermore, the percipient is also momentary. Then how is it possible for him to perceive the atoms, cognize them in the form "this is one," through interdependent cognition and then convert this knowledge into the judgment referring to the aggre-

18. Ibid., (*Tantradīpikā*), p. 53, footnote 12.
19. Bhikācārya Aināpure and Anantācārya Aṣṭaputre, *Brahmasūtras with Ānandatīrtha's Brahmasūtrabhāṣya*, commentary to *Brahma-sūtra* II.2.19, pp. 36-37.

gate as "cow" or "horse"? B.N.K. Sharma explains that the concept of interdependent cognition requires that the same atoms and the same percipient be the locus of such cognition in contradiction to the principle of Momentariness.[20] B.N.K. Sharma cites a passage from Rāghavendra's *Tattvaprakāśikā-Bhāvadīpa* to explain the contradictions involved in the momentariness of percipient and atoms on the one hand and *apekṣā-buddhi* on the other hand. Rāghavendra explains that the existence of one subject (*ekādhikaraṇatva*) and one sense-object (*ekaviṣayatva*) is difficult to maintain if momentariness is also to be upheld.

> viṣayadvandvātmano'pi kṣaṇikatvamupetya paramāṇudarśanamapekṣābuddhisamudāyavittivyavahārau ityeteṣām ekaviṣayatvamiva ekādhikaraṇatvamapi na yuktamityarthaḥ[21]
>
> That, having approached the momentariness of subject and object in reference to consciousness and the aggregate there is the interdependent cognition (*apekṣābuddhi*) of atoms and viewing—the meaning is that in connection with these the existence of one subject like the existence of one sense-object is inadequate.

It is to be recalled that Rāmānuja in his commentary to *Brahmasūtra* II.2.17 also questioned the possibility of the formation of the aggregates if one grants the momentariness of the knower and the momentariness of the atoms. Perhaps Madhva and the sub-commentators of his school were recalling Rāmānuja's argument when they included a similar argument in connection with their treatment of the concept "*apekṣābuddhi.*" Perhaps Madhva and the sub-commentators were confusing the Buddhist logicians' account of perception and inference with the "*apekṣā-buddhi*" of the Vaiśeṣika school, which actually employed the term. According to Dasgupta's presentation of "*apekṣā-buddhi*" in Praśastapāda's teaching the "*apekṣā-buddhi*" is the relative oscillatory state of mind whereby if one sees two jugs, for instance, one entertains the notion "This is one jug, and that is another jug." The concept of "*apekṣā-buddhi*" in this

20. Sharma, B.N.K., *The Brahmasūtras and Their Principal Commentaries*, p. 53.
21. Ibid., (*Tattvaprakāśikā-Bhāvadīpa*), p. 54, footnote 17.

system is concerned with the category (*padārtha*) of number (*saṃkhyā*).

> The sixth is *saṃkhyā* (number), that entity of quality belonging to things by virtue of which we can count them as one, two, three, etc. The conception of numbers two, three, etc. is due to a relative oscillatory state of the mind (*apekṣā-buddhi*); thus when there are two jugs before my eyes, I have the notion —This is one jug, and that another. This is called *apekṣā-buddhi*; then in the two jugs there arises the quality of twoness (*dvitva*) and then an indeterminate perception (*nirvikalpā-dvitva-guṇa*) of *dvitva* in us and then the determinate perceptions that there are the two jugs. The conceptions of other numbers as well as of many arise in a similar manner.[22]

There is also the difficulty, as B.N.K. Sharma notes in accordance with Madhva's commentary, that if the Buddhist should concede that the atoms which come to be embraced within an aggregate continue to exist, and are not destroyed, then there results the arising of an endless series of aggregates on the basis that given the cause, there is the effect.[23]

> kāraṇe sati kāryaṃ bhavatyeva iti hi tasya niyamaḥ[24]
>
> For that when there is the cause, there is the effect, is the principle in connection with that.

It is also noted by B.N.K. Sharma in accordance with the explanation of Madhva's sub-commentators that the reasons averred by Śaṅkara and Rāmānuja for the impossibility of the formation of the aggregates are such that the objections raised by them in their interpretation of the *sūtra* "*itaretara-pratyayatvād iti cen notpattimātranimittatvāt*" are redundant.[25] Śaṅkara's representation of the Sarvāstivāda teaching as the asser-

---

22. Dasgupta, Surendranath, *History of Indian Philosophy*, Volume I, (Cambridge, England : University Press, 1963, reprint), p. 314.

23. Sharma, B.N.K., *The Brahmasūtras and Their Principal Commentaries* p. 54.

24. Ibid., (Madhva's commentary to *Brahma-sūtra* II.2.19), p. 54, footnote 18.

25. Ibid., p. 66.

tion that aggregates are formed through an incessant chain of causes and effects acting like a water-wheel is redundant, because without the aggregating agent earlier specified by Śaṅkara, and found wanting by him in his interpretation of the previous *sūtra*, there can be no aggregate.

Vyāsatīrtha explains the objection to Śaṅkara's representation of the Buddhist position in his *Tātparyacandrikā*.

> nahi saṃhantuścetanasyābhāvāt saṃghāto na yukta ityukte tvaduktamavidyāsaṃskārajarāmaraṇaśokādīnām anyonyaṃ hetuhetumadbhāvena pūrvāparībhūtatayā ghaṭiyantravadaniśamāvartamānatvarūpamitaretarapratyayatvam śaṅkārham.[26]

> Since it has been said that because of the absence of the consciousness of the aggregating agent, an aggregate is not enjoined, the mutual causation in the form of continuing ceaselessly like a water-wheel by (the successive) truth of the relation of cause and cause-possessor mutually, one after another, in connection with nescience, motivation, decay, death, sorrow, etc. mentioned by you, is open to doubt.

According to Rāghavendra in his *Tātparyacandrikā-prakāśa*, doubt concerning the mutual causality of the causes is set aside by the absence of a stable conscious agent.

> avidyādipratītivyavahārāṇāṃ saṃghātasiddhyadhīnatvena, tasyaivāsaṃbhave 'nyonyahetukatvaśaṅkā dūrāpāsteti bhāvaḥ/[27]

> By means of dependence on the establishment of the aggregate in connection with the conventions of the apprehension of nescience, etc. in the case of the impossibility of that (the conscious agent), doubt regarding mutual causation is set at a distance—such is the purport.

Likewise, Rāghavendra criticizes Rāmānuja for bringing up the objection of the mutuality of cause and effect in connection with the chain of dependent origination when he has already attempted to disprove the aggregates on the basis of the principle of Momentariness.

26. Ibid., (*Tātparyacandrikā*, p. 915b), p. 66, footnote 58.
27. Ibid., (*Tātparyacandrikā-prakāśa*, p. 915), p. 66, footnote 59.

tathā kṣaṇikatvādaṇūnāṃ saṃghāta eva nopapadyata ityukte, punaḥ kathamanyonyahetuhetumadbhāvarupetaretarapratyayatvaṃ śaṅkārham ?[28]

Since it has been said that the aggregate does not arise in connection with the atoms because of momentariness, then how is the mutual conditionality in the form of being mutually causes and cause-possessors open to doubt ?

28. Ibid., (*Tātparyacandrikā-prakāśa*, p. 915), p. 66, footnote 60.

D. *BRAHMA-SŪTRA* II·2·20 :
"*UTTAROTPĀDE CA PŪRVA-NIRODHĀT*"

1. Śaṅkara's Interpretation

This *sūtra*, "*uttarotpāde ca pūrva-nirodhāt,*"[1] (*Brahma-sūtra* II.2.20) may be translated as follows in accordance with the interpretation of Śaṅkara : "And in the case of the birth of the later, because of the cessation of the previous." In his interpretation of this *sūtra,* Śaṅkara attempts to refute the position that each member in the chain of dependent origination gives rise to the succeeding member.

Śaṅkara's argument here against the Sarvāstivādins is based upon the notion that causal efficiency cannot be maintained in the case of momentary existence, for if a thing exists for one moment, there is a question whether the causal efficiency of that moment can be made intelligible. The question arises due to the difficulty that if a thing has disappeared in the previous moment, how can it be the cause of a thing arising in the succeeding moment ? There would thus be no connection between the thing said to be the cause and the thing said to be the effect.

> kṣaṇabhaṅgavādino 'yamabhyupagamaḥ—uttarasmin kṣaṇe utpadyamāne pūrvaḥ kṣaṇo nirudhyata iti; na caivamabhyupagacchatā pūrvottarayoḥ kṣaṇayorhetuphalabhāvaḥ śakyate sampādayitum, nirudhyamānasya niruddhasya vā pūrvakṣaṇasyābhāvagrastatvāduttarakṣaṇahetutvānupapatteḥ.[2]
>
> According to the principle of the one who holds the position of momentary destruction, when the next moment is arising, the previous moment is vanishing. Not by one thus upholding can the existence of the cause and effect of the previous and later moments be accomplished, because of objection to the causation of the later moment on account of refutation through the absence of the previous moment which has vanished or is vanishing.

1. Radhakrishnan, Sarvepalli, *Brahma Sūtra*, *Brahma-sūtra* II.2.20, p. 379.

2. Balasubrahmanyam, T. K., *The Works of Śrī Śaṅkarāchārya*, Volume II, commentary to *Brahma-sūtra* II.2.20, p. 385.

Śaṅkara presents several supposed Buddhist positions on the topic of causality and then proceeds to refute them. One such Buddhist position suggests that the former momentary existence at full development becomes the cause of a later momentary existence. Śaṅkara refutes this argument on the basis that such a position is only a roundabout way of saying that something of the first moment passes into the second moment, and that thereby the principle of Momentariness is trespassed.

> atha bhāvabhūtaḥ pariniṣpannāvasthaḥ pūrvakṣaṇa uttarakṣaṇasya heturityabhiprāyaḥ, tathāpi nopapadyate, bhāvabhūtasya punarvyāpārakalpanāyāṃ kṣaṇāntarasambandhaprasaṅgāt[3]
>
> If it is intended that the entity having a perfected condition in the previous moment is the cause of the later moment, such a thing is not possible, because of the occurrence of connection with a second moment when there is the hypothesis of the further activity of an entity.

Śaṅkara, although he intends this argument to be aimed at the Buddhist realists, may be referring here to the position of Śāntarakṣita and Kamalaśīla in the *Tattvasaṃgraha* (512-514) and *Pañjikā*, as discussed in the Introductory Background, in the section on Later Logicians, that the effect is born in the second moment from a cause which is born in the first moment and is yet undestroyed. It has also been noted, however, that Śāntarakṣita and Kamalaśīla have also declared in the *Tattvasaṃgraha* (520-521) and *Pañjikā*, that a cause possesses no activity apart from its being so that it is not the case that a cause takes birth and subsequently enters into activity. As though mindful of this argument on the part of Śāntarakṣita and Kamalaśīla, Śaṅkara then argues that if the existence (*bhāva*) of the cause be its activity (*vyāpāra*), then the effect is imbued with the nature of the cause. Consequently, Śaṅkara argues, the cause lasts for more than one moment, and the principle of momentariness is trespassed.

---

3. Ibid., Volume II, commentary to *Brahma-sūtra* II.2.20, p. 385.

atha bhāva evāsya vyāpāra ityabhiprāyaḥ tathāpi naivopapadyate, hetusvabhāvānuparaktasya phalasyotpattyasambhavāt, svabhāvoparāgābhyupagame ca. hetusvabhāvasya phalakālāvasthāyitve sati, kṣaṇabhaṅgābhyupagamatyāgaprasaṅgaḥ[4]

If it is intended that the existence is its activity, then it is impossible, because of the impossibility of the arising of an effect which is not imbued with the nature of the cause. And in the case of the principle of the colouring by nature, since there is abiding at the time of the effect (something of) the nature of the cause, there is the occurrence of the renunciation of the principle of momentary destruction.

It has been noted, however, in the Introductory Background, in the section concerned with Early Vijñānavāda, that according to Asaṅga it is the origin (*bhūti*) which is the activity (*kāritra*) of *saṃskāras*, which are doers if examined from the standpoint of the cause and activity if examined from the standpoint of effect. For Asaṅga, it is the birth which is the activity of the cause. The effect cannot be imbued with the nature of the cause when the activity in question is identified with the birth of the cause. Śaṅkara also argues that if the nature of the cause were inherent in the effect, then such a position would be tantamount to saying that the cause is permanent. Sogen criticizes Śaṅkara's reply on the basis that if one grants antecedence to imply causality, the resulting causality is not permanent but merely relative.

Śaṅkara overlooks the plain fact that causality is not a permanent but merely a relative quality. Thus A may be the cause of B, B the cause of C and C the cause of D, without the causality in these cases being identical, just as William may be the father of Edward, Edward that of Charles, and Charles that of James, without the fatherhood in the three cases being identical.[5]

Śaṅkara mentions another position supposedly held by the Buddhists according to Śaṅkara, to the effect that cause and

4. Ibid., Volume II, commentary to *Brahma-sūtra* II.2.20, p. 385.
5. Sogen, Yamakami, *Systems of Buddhistic Thought*, p. 135.

effect can continue to exist without the colouring of the effect by the cause. Śaṅkara replies that such a position would bring about confusion.

> vinaiva vā svabhāvoparāgeṇa hetuphalabhāvamabhyupagacchataḥ sarvatra tatprāpteratiprasaṅgaḥ[6].
>
> There is a stretching of the rule of the attainment of that (the effect) in every case by one maintaining the relationship of cause and effect without the colouring of nature.

Śaṅkara then examines three alternatives for explaining the origination (*utpāda*) and cessation (*nirodha*) of a thing: that origination and cessation constitute either a thing's own form (*svarūpa*), or another state of it (*avasthāntara*), or an altogether different thing (*vastvantara*).

> api cotpādanirodhau nāma vastunaḥ svarūpameva va syātām, avasthāntaraṃ vā, vastvantarameva vā—sarvathāpi nopapadyate[7]
>
> Moreover, let birth and cessation by name be the own-formation of a given thing, another state of it, or other than the given thing—it is impossible in all cases.

In accordance with the first alternative, Śaṅkara explains, if origination and cessation constitute the own-formation of a given thing, then we are led to the absurd conclusion that the given thing, origination, and cessation are equivalent. In accordance with the second alternative, that of difference by condition, Śaṅkara notes, if origination and cessation represent the initial and final stages of the given thing which is the intermediate stage, then the given thing is connected with three moments and is no longer momentary—so that thereby the Buddhist principle of Momentariness is trespassed. In accordance with the third alternative, that of being altogether different from the given thing, then the given thing is altogether disconnected from origination and cessation and must be regarded as everlasting.

---

6. Balasubrahmanyam, T. K., *The Works of Śrī Śaṅkarāchārya*, Volume II, Śaṅkara's commentary to *Brahma-sūtra* II.2.20, p. 385.
7. Ibid., commentary to *Brahma-sūtra* II.1.20, p. 385.

yadi tāvad vastunaḥ svarūpamevotpādanirodhau syātāṃ, tato vastuśabda utpādanirodhaśabdau ca paryāyāḥ prāpnuyuḥ; athāsti kaścid viśeṣa iti manyeta—utpādanirodhaśabdābhyāṃ madhyavartino vastuna ādyantākhye avasthe abhilapyete iti, evamapyādyantamadhyakṣaṇatrayasambandhitvād vastunaḥ kṣaṇikatvābhyupagamahāniḥ; athātyantavyatiriktāvevotpādanirodhau vastunaḥ syātām—aśvamahiṣavat, tato vastu utpādanirodhābhyāmasaṃsṛṣṭamiti vastunaḥ śāśvatatvaprasaṅgaḥ[8]

If the own-formation of a thing, certainly, be birth and cessation, the word "*vastu*" (given thing) and the words cessation and birth would be obtained as convertible terms. If he should think that there is any difference whatsoever, if the two states called beginning and end, in connection with the given thing existing in the middle are spoken about in terms of birth and cessation, there is thus an abandonment of the principle of Momentariness of the given thing because of the connection with the three moments of beginning, middle and end. If the birth and cessation of a given thing be altogether separate like a horse and a buffalo, then (given that) the given thing is unconnected with birth and cessation, there is the occurrence of the permanence of a thing.

The difficulty with this attempted refutation, however, is that the Sarvāstivādins, as has been noted in the Introductory Background, in the section on Momentariness, regarded birth, duration, decay and impermanence to be the only characteristics of the *dharma* to be distinguished from the nature of the *dharma*. Thus none of the three alternatives which Śaṅkara, as described above, attributes to the Sarvāstivādins actually apply to them. Śaṅkara also attributes another position to some Buddhist realists to the effect that the origination and cessation of a given thing signify merely the perception and non-perception of a given thing. This supposed position is refuted by Śaṅkara on the basis that perception and non-perception are attributes of the perceiving mind only and that thus the given thing would be everlasting.

8. Ibid., Volume II, commentary to *Brahma-sūtra* II.2.20, pp. 385-386.

yadi ca darśanādarśane vastuna utpādanirodhau syātām. evamapi draṣṭṛdharmau tau na vastudharmaviti vastunaḥ śāśvatatvaprasaṅga eva[9]

If seeing and non-seeing with reference to a given thing be the birth and cessation, then (given that) these are the characteristics of a seer, not the characteristics of a given thing. Thus there again is the occurrence of the permanence of a given thing.

It is difficult to say, however, whether such an idealistic position befits those to whom Śaṅkara himself attributes the position of the reality of the external object.

2. Rāmānuja's Interpretation

This *sūtra*, "*uttarotpāde ca pūrva-nirodhāt*," may be translated as follows in accordance with the interpretation of Rāmānuja: "And in the case of the birth of the later, because of the cessation of the previous." In his commentary to this *sūtra*, Rāmānuja basically repeats the argument employed by Śaṅkara to the effect that the preceding moment, because it has disappeared, cannot be the cause of a subsequent moment, in that non-existence cannot be a cause or else anything might originate at any time. Rāmānuja again attempts to employ an argument based on momentariness in order to prove the self-contradictoriness of Buddhist teachings.

itaśca kṣaṇikatvapakṣe jagadutpattirnopapadyate; uttarakṣaṇotpattivelāyāṃ pūrvakṣaṇasya vinaṣṭatvāt tasyottarakṣaṇam prati hetutvānupapatteḥ/abhāvasya hetutve, sarvaṃ sarvatra sarvadotpadyate/[10]

Hence in the case of the doctrine of Momentariness, the arising of the world is not possible, because there is objection to the causality of the previous moment towards the later moment on account of the destruction of the previous moment at the time of the arising of the later moment. In the case of the causality of an absent thing all things would arise at all places at all times.

---

9. Ibid., Volume II, commentary to *Brahma-sūtra* II.2.20, p. 386.

10. Viraraghavacharya, Sri Uttamur T., *Brahmasūtra-Śrībhāshya*, commentary to *Brahma-sūtra* II.2.19. p. 531.

Like Śaṅkara, Rāmānuja also portrays as a Buddhist position the notion that the very existence of a cause constitutes its causal activity. But whereas Śaṅkara replies to this supposed Buddhist position by arguing that as long as the effect is imbued with the cause, the principle of Momentariness is violated, Rāmānuja replies that if the mere existence of a cause were to constitute causality, there would be no real causality for anything could arise. Furthermore, whereas Śaṅkara is concerned with the implications of momentariness for the Buddhist concept of dependent origination in the sense that each *nidāna* contributes to the rise of the next, Rāmānuja is concerned with the implications of the doctrine of Momentariness for causality in general. According to Śaṅkara, as has been discussed above, the effect would be imbued with the cause.

> atha bhāva evāsya vyāpāra ityabhiprāyastathāpi naivopapadyate, hetusvabhāvānuparaktasya phalasyotpattyasambhavāt...[11]
>
> If it is intended that the existence is its activity, such a thing is impossible, because of the impossibility of the arising of an effect which is not imbued with the nature of the cause.

According to Rāmānuja, the effect could be anything if such a position were valid.

> atha pūrvakṣaṇavartitvameva hetutvamityucyate—evaṃ tarhi kaścideva ghaṭakṣaṇaḥ taduttarakālabhāvināṃ sarveṣāmeva gomahiṣāśvakuḍyapāṣāṇādīnāṃ trailokyavartināṃ hetuḥ syāt//[12]
>
> If it be said that the causality is the existence of the previous moment, then any moment whatsoever of a jar would be the cause of all entities of a moment subsequent to it—whether of cattle, bulls, chairs, stones, etc., existing in the three worlds.

The difficulty with Rāmānuja's argument, however, is that his characterization relates neither to the position of the Sarvsāti-

---

11. Balasubrahmanyam, T. K., *The Works of Srī Sankarachayra*, Volume II, commentary to *Brahma-sūtra* II.2.20, p. 385.

12. Viraraghavacharya, Sri Uttamur T., *Brahmasūtra-Śrībhāshya*, commentary to *Brahma-sūtra* II.2.19, p. 531.

vādins nor to that of the Sautrāntikas. As has been noted, Śāntarakṣita and Kamalaśīla did hold that the existence of the cause is its activity and Asaṅga held that the origin is the activity. Such positions do not necessarily correspond, however, to Rāmānuja's characterization of the Buddhist position as an identification of the entity of the cause with its causality.

3. Madhva's Interpretation

This *sūtra*, "*uttarotpāde ca pūrvanirodhāt*" (*Brahma-sūtra* II.2·20), may be translated as follows in accordance with Madhva's interpretation : "And in the case of the birth of the later, because of the cessation of the earlier." Madhva's interpretation of this aphorism differs from those of Śaṅkara and Rāmānuja in that Madhva takes up the question of the production of the effect (i.e. aggregates) which is unlike the cause (i.e. unitary atoms). Madhva's commentary proceeds as follows :

> kāryotpattāveva kāraṇasya vināśācca na viśeṣakāryotpattiḥ//[13]
>
> There is no production of an unlike effect from the destruction of the cause in the case of the birth of the effect.

According to B. N. K. Sharma, the dogma of the advocate of Momentariness is "*uttarotpāde ca pūrvanirodhaḥ*" (cessation of the preceding upon the birth of the subsequent). This statement for Sharma represents a commitment to the position that a cause is capable only of producing a like effect: *kāraṇasya sadṛśakāryajanana eva sāmarthyāt* (because of the capacity of the birth only of a like effect in connection with the cause). Having produced the like effect, the cause ceases to be; consequently there is no place for the production of an unlike effect. The production of aggregates of atoms from unaggregated ones, as notes B. N. K. Sharma in accordance with the explanation of Trivikrama Paṇḍita, would be the production of an unlike effect (*visadṛśakāryotpatti* or *viśeṣakāryotpatti*).[14] Such a production would represent a contradiction with the supposed Buddhist principle of the non-production of an unlike effect. Trivikrama Paṇḍita

13. Bhikācārya Aināpure and Anantācārya Aṣṭaputre, *Brahmasūtras with Ānandatīrtha's Brahmasūtrabhāṣya* commentary to *Brahma-sūtra* II.2.20, p. 37.

14. Sharma, B.N.K., *The Brahmasūtras and Their Principal Commentaries*, p. 54.

explains the impossibility of the formation of the aggregates in his *Tattva-pradīpa*.

> ekaṃ sadṛśaṃ kāryamutpādya tasya vinaṣṭatvānna visadṛśakāryotpattiḥ/ataścāsaṃyuktayoḥ paramāṇvorna saṃyuktāvutpadyeyātām/[15]
>
> From the destruction of that having given birth to one similar effect, there is not the arising of a dissimilar effect. Hence in the case of a pair of unaggregated atoms, a pair of aggregated ones would not take birth.

It is noted by B. N. K. Sharma that the terms "*pūrva*" and "*uttara*" in the *sūtra* refer respectively to the cause and effect, and that, in accordance with Jagannātha Tīrtha's explanation in the *Bhāṣyadīpikā*, the effect is to be understood in the sense of "like effect" (*sadṛśakārya*) and the locative case in "*uttarotpāde*" signifies the incapacity of the cause to produce an unlike effect.[16]

> kāryaśabdaḥ sadṛśakāryaparaḥ/viṣayasaptamīyaṃ/sāmarthyāditi śeṣaḥ/na tu visadṛśakāryotpattau/anyathā ghaṭāt paṭotpattiprasaṅga ityeva śabdārthaḥ/[17]
>
> The word "effect" signifies not other than a similar effect. There is the locative case in the sense of "with regard to" (*viṣayasaptamī*). The remainder signifies "from capacity", not in the case of the birth of a dissimilar effect. The meaning is that otherwise there would be the occurrence of the birth of the cloth from the pot.

It is noted by Sharma that the text of Madhva's commentary, "*kāryotpattāveva kāraṇasya vināśācca na viśeṣakāryotpattiḥ*"[18] (There is no production of an unlike effect from the destruction of the cause in the case of the birth of the effect) can be split into halves.

(i) (*Sadṛśa*)-*kāryotpattāveva kāraṇasya* (*sāmarthyāt*) *na viśeṣakāryotpattiḥ* and

---

15. Ibid., (*Tattvapradīpa* II.2.19), p. 54, footnote 19.
16. Ibid., p. 55.
17. Ibid., (*Bhāṣyadīpikā*), p. 55, footnote 20.
18. Ibid., (Madhva's commentary to *Brahma-sūtra* II.2.20), p. 55.

(ii) *kāraṇasya (sadṛśamekam kāryam utpādya) vināśācca na viśeṣakāryotpattiḥ*[19]

(1) Because of the capacity of the cause in the case of the production of the effect, there is no production of an unlike effect.

(2) Because of the destruction of the cause having given birth to a like effect, there is no production of an unlike effect.

B. N. K. Sharma notes that the latter half is intended to counter another supposed defense of the advocate of Momentariness to the effect that having produced a like effect, the cause may after doing so produce an unlike effect.[20] The latter half of Madhva's commentary, according to B. N. K. Sharma, nullifies the objection of the advocate of Momentariness by indicating that the cause, once it has produced its like effect, ceases to be effective, because of its destruction.[21] The locative form "*uttarotpāde*," notes B. N. K. Sharma, is to be taken in the sense of locative absolute in accordance with the explanation of Jagannātha Tīrtha in the *Bhāṣyadīpikā*.

atra pakṣe uttarotpāda iti satisaptamī[22]

Here in reference to the half "*uttarotpāde*" there is a locative absolute.

According to Jayatīrtha in the *Nyāya-sudhā*, however, as noted by B.N.K. Sharma, the Buddhist may supposedly argue that the point is not that a cause has the capacity to produce only a like effect but that the cause is merely competent to produce an effect which is like or unlike the cause in accordance with unseen factors (*adṛṣṭa*).[23]

kāraṇaṃ kāryajananasvabhāvameva. adṛṣṭādisahakārisamavadhānāttu tatsadṛśaṃ visadṛśam vā janayiṣyatīti[24]

The cause has the nature of giving birth to the effect; because of the meeting of the unseen and auxiliaries, it will give birth to a like or an unlike effect.

---

19. Ibid., p. 55.
20. Ibid., p. 55.
21. Ibid., p. 55.
22. Ibid., (*Bhāṣyadīpikā*), p. 56, footnote 2.
23. Ibid., p. 55.
24. Ibid., (*Nyāya-sudhā*, p. 392), p. 55, footnote 22.

Jayatīrtha in his *Nyāya-sudhā* argues that this position does not provide an explanation for the production of an unlike effect, as aggregates of atoms from unaggregated atoms, for it may be asked how the unseen (*adṛṣṭa*) factor produces an unlike effect.

> ata āha—adṛṣṭamapi tasyaiva viśeṣāpādakaṃ kutaḥ ? yasya kasyāpi yatkiṃcidviśeṣam utpādayet//[25]
>
> Here it says: how is the unseen producing a difference in connection with that ? In connection with what should it produce any difference whatsoever ?

B.N.K. Sharma also notes that Śaṅkara's interpretation of this *sūtra* to the effect that at the time of the production of the subsequent thing, the former has already ceased to be, renders the latter half of the next *sūtra* ("*yaugapadyamanyathā*"[26]—"or else simultaneity") redundant. The reason is that if there were no cessation of the cause at the time of the production of the effect then there would be simultaneity. This criticism of Śaṅkara's position is explained in a passage from Vyāsatīrtha's *Tātparya-candrikā* cited by B. N. K. Sharma.

> 'yaugapadyamanyathā' ityasya 'uttarotpāde ca pūrvanirodhāt' iti tṛtīyena gatārthatā/ tatrāpi, 'anyathā yaugapadyaṃ syāt' iti vipakṣe bādhakavivakṣāṃ vinā uttarotpāde pūrvanirodhasy-āsiddheḥ/[27]
>
> There is meaninglessness in connection with this statement, "Or else simultaneity," through the third *sūtra*, "Because of the cessation of the previous in the case of the birth of the later," in this case because of the establishment of the cessation of the earlier in birth of the later without the opposing desire to say in a counter-statement, "Otherwise there would be simultaneity."

Whether the production of only a like effect from a cause is a Buddhist maxim is questionable. First, in connection with the Sarvāstivāda notion of aggregates, it is not clear whether the Vaibhāṣikas considered the atoms of material flow to be in any sense the cause of the aggregates. It has also been noted that

25. Ibid., (*Nyāya-sudhā*, p. 392), p. 55, footnote 23.
26. Radhakrishnan, Sarvepalli, *The Brahma Sūtra*, p. 380.
27. Sharma, B.N.K., *The Brahmasūtras and Their Principal Commentaries*, (*Tātparyacandrikā*, p. 915), p. 67, footnote 63.

Śāntarakṣita and Kamalaśīla even deride the notion of the "atom". Furthermore, if it were a Buddhist maxim that the cause may produce only a like effect, how could one explain the variety of cause and condition discussed in the Introductory Background, in the section on Causality? It is questionable whether the notion of the aggregate can be rejected on the basis of the supposed Buddhist maxim that a cause can produce only a like effect.

E. *BRAHMA-SŪTRA* II.2.21:

"*ASATI PRATIJÑOPARODHO YAUGAPADYAM ANYATHĀ*

1. Śaṅkara's Interpretation

This *sūtra*, "*asati pratijñoparodho yaugapadyam anyathā*,"[1] (*Brahma-sūtra* II.2.21), may be translated as follows in accordance with the interpretation of Śaṅkara: "If (the cause) is not, there is contradiction of the declaration or else simultaneity." This *sūtra* for Śaṅkara represents a corollary of the preceding *sūtra*. Śaṅkara mentions that it has been shown that a former momentary thing, having disappeared, cannot be the cause of a subsequent thing. He notes that if the Buddhist should assert that an effect arises even when there is no cause, the Buddhist would be contradicting his own principle that thought and mentals arise in conjunction with the four conditions.

> athāsatyeva hetau phalotpattiṃ brūyāt tataḥ pratijñoparodhaḥ syāt—caturvidhān hetūn pratītya cittacaittā utpadyanta itīyam pratijñā hīyeta; nirhetukāyāṃ cotpattāvapratibandhātsarvaṃ sarvatrotpadyeta[2]

> He may claim the arising of the effect even when there is no cause; hence, there would be contradiction of the declaration. If having resorted to four types of causes, the thought and mentals are born, this declaration would be abandoned. When there is arising without cause anything whatsoever may be born because of the lack of connection (of cause and effect).

Śaṅkara, however, also explains that if one were to suppose that the antecedent were to last until the succeeding, then they would be simultaneous. But the theory of Momentariness would thereby be denied.

> athottarakṣaṇotpattiryāvattāvadavatiṣṭhate pūrvakṣaṇa iti brūyāt, tato yaugapadyaṃ hetuphalayoḥ syāt; tathāpi pratijñoparodha eva syāt—kṣaṇikāḥ sarve saṃskārā itīyaṃ pratijñoparudhyeta//[3]

---

1. Radhakrishnan, Sarvepalli, *The Brahma Sūtra*, *Brahma-sūtra* II.2.21, p. 380.
2. Balasubrahmanyam, T. K., *The Works of Śrī Śaṅkarāchārya*, Volume II, commentary to *Brahma-sūtra* II.2.21, p. 386.
3. Ibid., Volume II, commentary to *Brahma-sūtra* II.2.21, p. 386.

> If one should say that the previous moment so much as reaches down into the birth of the later moment, then there would be the simultaneity of cause and effect. Hence, there is contradiction of the declaration. That all *saṃskāras* are momentary—this declaration would be contradicted.

It has been noted, however, in the Introductory Background, in the section on Causation, that the Sarvāstivādins and Sautrāntikas both held that all constructed things are dependently originated. Consequently they could not have held the position that an effect may arise even when there is no cause. Even the doctrine of "causeless destruction" held by the Sautrāntikas proves the rule of causation, for the destruction in this case is not an effect, but a corollary of momentariness. It has also been noted, in the section on Momentariness in the Introductory Background, that the Sarvāstivādins reconciled momentariness with causal continuity through the distinction of the *dharma* and its characteristics, and that the Sautrāntikas reconciled momentariness with causal continuity through their emphasis on the series.

2. Rāmānuja's Interpretation

This *sūtra*, "*asati pratijñoparodho yaugapadyam anyathā*," (*Brahma-sūtra* II.2.20) may be translated as follows in accordance with Rāmānuja's interpretation: "(If the cause) is not, there is contradiction of the declaration, or else simultaneity." In his commentary to this *sūtra*, Rāmānuja employs arguments basically similar to those of Śaṅkara, namely that the Buddhist must give up the notion of causality, or else admit the simultaneity of cause and effect in contradiction to the principle of Momentariness. If there is an effect without cause resulting from the assignation of cause and effect to separate moments, Rāmānuja avers, then anything could arise at any time in contradiction to the principle of dependent origination. If the cause after its own birth continues to exist at the moment of the production of the effect, then there is simultaneity in contradiction to the principle of Momentariness.

> asatyapi hetau kāryamutpadyate cet—sarvaṃ sarvatra sarvadotpadyetetyuktaṃ / na kevalamutpattivirodha eva, pratijñā

ca bhavatāmuparudhyeta, 'adhipatisahakāryālambanasamanantarapratyayāścatvāro vijñānotpattau hetavaḥ' iti vaḥ pratijñā / adhipatiḥ indriyam / atha pratijñānuparodhāya ghaṭakṣaṇe sthita eva ghaṭakṣaṇāntarotpattiriṣyate—tathā ca sati dvayoḥ kāryakāraṇayorghaṭakṣaṇayoryaugapadyenopalabdhiḥ prasajyeta / na ca tathopalabhyate / kṣaṇikatvapratijñā caivam hīyate // kṣaṇikatvaṃ sthitam eveti cet—indriyasamprayogajñānayoryaugapadyaṃ prasajyeta // 20 //[4]

If it be objected that when there is no cause, an effect is born, then it is said that all things would be born at all times and at all places. There is not only the contradiction of production, but the declaration would be contradicted by you. The declaration is as follows: "There are four causes—the dominant, the auxiliary, the support, the immediately preceding condition—for the production of perception." The dominant condition relates to the sense-organs. If for the sake of the non-contradiction of the declaration when the moment of the jar abides the birth of a second moment of the jar is declared, then, if this is the case, there follows the ascertainment by means of the simultaneity of moments of the jar as cause and effect. It is not so ascertained. The declaration of momentariness is thus abandoned. If it be objected that momentariness abides, then there follows the simultaneity of the knowledge in association with the sense-organ.

3. Madhva's Interpretation

This *sūtra*, "*asati pratijñoparodho yaugapadyam anyathā*," (*Brahma-sūtra* II.2.21) may be translated as follows in accordance with Madhva's interpretation : "If (the cause) is not, there is contradiction of the declaration or else simultaneity." Madhva's commentary proceeds as follows :

kāraṇe vinaṣṭe kāryamutpadyate cettatkāryamiti pratijñāhāniḥ/ tatkāle kāraṇamasti cedvināśakāraṇābhāvādyaugapadyaṃ sarvakāryāṇām //[5]

---

4. Viraraghavacharya, Sri Uttamur T., *Brahmasūtra-Śribhāshya*, Volume II. commentary to *Brahma-sūtra* II.2.20, p. 532.

5. Bhikācārya Ainapure and Anantācārya Aṣṭaputre, *Brahmasūtras with Ānandatīrtha's Brahmasūtrabhāṣya*, commentary to *Brahma-sūtra* II.2.21, p. 37.

If it be said that when the cause is destroyed, the effect arises, in reference to that effect there is abandonment of the declaration. If it be said that there is anything in reference to the cause at the time of that, there is simultaneity of all the effects because of the absence of the destruction of the cause.

According to B.N.K. Sharma, what Madhva and the sub-commentators of his school attempt to refute in their interpretation of this *sūtra* is the notion of ceaseless change and constant production perceived by them to be involved in momentariness.[6] The view of the advocate of Momentariness is examined from two sides, according to B.N.K. Sharma's study of Madhva's commentary.[7] Is the effect produced after the cessation of the cause ? Then it cannot be said to be the effect of that cause and there would be abandonment of the principle "*asmin sati, idam bhavati*" (when there is the cause, there is the effect). If it is produced at the same time as the cause, then the cause must be conceded a life of at least two moments in order to arise and then give birth to the effect. At this stage, Madhva carries the argument further than Śaṅkara and Rāmānuja, for he argues that in this latter case, there is no reason why the cause should be destroyed in subsequent moments. Consequently it would be competent to produce further effects in subsequent moments and so on *ad infinitum.* It is to be noticed that an argument similar to Ratnakīrti's argument discussed in the section of this work concerned with the Later Logicians is employed here against the Buddhists. The dilemma is expressed as follows by Madhva.

kāraṇe vinaṣṭe karyamutpadyate cet, tatkāryamiti pratijñāhāniḥ / tatkāle kāraṇamiti cet vināśakāraṇābhāvāt yaugapadyaṃ sarvakāryāṇām /[8]

If it be said that when the cause is destroyed the effect arises, in reference to that effect there is abandonment of the declaration. If it be said that there is anything in reference to the cause at the time of that, there is simultaneity of all the effects because of the absence of the destruction of the cause.

6. Sharma, B.N.K.; *The Brahmasūtras and Their Principal Commentaries*, p. 57.

7. Ibid., p. 57.

8. Ibid., (Madhva's commentary to *Brahma-sūtra* II.2.21), p. 57, footnote 29.

The consequence of the production of an endless series of effects if there is the simultaneity of cause and effect is explained by Jayatīrtha in the *Tattva-prakāśikā*.

> kṣaṇikasya dvikṣaṇāvasthāne taduttarasya vināśakāraṇābhāvāt punastasmāt kāryotpattayaḥ syuḥ tebhyaśca tatheti sarvakāryāṇāṃ yaugapadyam syāt.[9]

> Because of the absence of the destruction of the cause in connection with the later in the case of the abiding for two moments of the momentary thing, again therefore there would be the arising of effects; from them there would be the simultaneity of all the effects.

In Madhva's argument that an endless series of effects would result from simultaneity of cause and effect, one is reminded of Ratnakīrti's similar argument for momentariness as discussed in the Introductory Background, in the section on Later Logicians. Ratnakīrti bases his argument for momentariness on the danger of the production of an endless series of effects from a non-momentary cause. It is to be noted, however, that the Sarvāstivādins were able to reconcile causal continuity with momentariness through the distinction of *dharma* and its characteristics and that the Sautrāntikas were also able to reconcile these two positions through their notion of the series. It should also be noted that according to Asaṅga the origin of a momentary *saṃskāra* is its activity. It is not the case for Asaṅga that a *saṃskāra* is born and then acquires its activity. Likewise, according to Śāntarakṣita, the existence of the cause is its activity.

9. Ibid., (*Tattva-prakāśikā* II.2.21), p. 57, footnote 28.

F. *BRAHMA-SŪTRA* II.2.22 :

"*PRATISAṂKHYĀ 'PRATISAṂKHYĀ-NIRODHĀPRĀPTIR AVICCHEDĀT*"

1. Śaṅkara's Interpretation

This *sūtra, "pratisaṃkhyā 'pratisaṃkhyā-nirodhāprāptir avicchedāt,"*[1] (*Brahma-sūtra* II.2.22) may be translated as follows in accordance with Śaṅkara's interpretation : "There is no establishment of cessation-with-understanding and cessation-without-understanding, because of uninterruptedness." Śaṅkara first attributes to the Buddhist realists the position that there are three unconstructed *dharmas* which are the cessation-with-understanding (*pratisaṃkhyā-nirodha*), the cessation-without-understanding (*apratisaṃkhyā-nirodha*), and space (*ākāśa*). He attributes to the Buddhist realists the position that these are nonplaceable (*avastu*), insubstantial (*abhāvamātra*), indefinable (*nirupākhya*). The cessation-with-understanding, according to Śaṅkara's representation of the Sarvāstivāda position, is the destruction preceded by the mind and is opposed by the cessation-without-understanding. Space, according to Śaṅkara's representation of the Sarvāstivāda position, is the mere absence of hindrance (*āvaraṇābhāvamātra*).

> api ca vaināśikāḥ kalpayanti—buddhibodhyaṃ trayādanyatsaṃskṛtaṃ kṣaṇikaṃ ceti; tadapi ca trayaṃ—pratisaṃkhyāpratisaṃkhyānirodhau ākāśaṃ cetyācakṣate; trayamapi caitat avastu abhāvamātraṃ nirupākhyamiti manyante; buddhipūrvakaḥ kila vināśo bhāvānām pratisaṃkhyānirodho nāma bhāṣyate; tadviparīto 'pratisaṃkhyānirodhaḥ; āvaraṇābhāvamātramākāśamiti /[2]
>
> Moreover, the destructionists think that (whatever is) to be understood by the mind and is other than the three is constructed and momentary. Therefore, it declares three : the cessation-with-understanding, the cessation-without-under-

---

1 Radhakrishnan, Sarvepalli, *The Brahma Sūtra*, *Brahma-sūtra* II.2.22, p. 380.

2. Balasubrahmanyam, T. K., *The Works of Śrī Śaṅkarāchārya*, Volume II, commentary to *Brahma-sūtra* II.2.22, p. 387.

standing, and space. They think that the three are non-placeable, insubstantial, and indefinable; the destruction, preceded by the mind, of entities is indeed spoken of as the cessation-with-understanding by name; its opposite is spoken of as the cessation-without-understanding; space is spoken of as the absence of hindrance.

Śaṅkara's argument in his commentary to this *sūtra* is based upon the notion that the continuity of the series of dependently originated *dharmas* connot be broken, so that neither the series nor the individual members can be interrupted.

> pratisaṃkhyāpratisaṃkhyānirodhayoḥ aprāptirasambhava ityarthaḥ; kasmāt ? avicchedāt[3]
>
> There is non-attainment of the cessation-with-understanding and the cessation-without-understanding. The meaning is that it is impossible. How? Because of non-interruption.

The series cannot be broken because the *nidānas* (causes) are related to each other as cause and effect.

> etau hi pratisaṃkhyāpratisaṃkhyānirodhau saṃtānagocarau vā syātāṃ, bhāvagocarau vā; na tāvatsaṃtānagocarau vā sambhavataḥ, sarveṣvapi saṃtāneṣu saṃtānināmavicchinnena hetuphalabhāvena saṃtānavicchedasyāsambhavāt[4]
>
> For let these, the cessation-with-understanding and the cessation-without-understanding, be within the range of a series or within the range of entities. Certainly, within the range of a series (the two cessations) are not possible, because of the impossibility in the case of the series of the interruption of the series through the relationship of cause and effect not separated from the series.

Śaṅkara notes in reference to the *nidānas* that a dependently originated *dharma* must be inseparably connected with its previous states.

> nāpi bhāvagocarau sambhavataḥ—na hi bhāvānāṃ niranvayo

3. Ibid., Volume II, commentary to *Brahma-sūtra* II.2.22, p. 387.
4. Ibid., commentary to *Brahma-sūtra* II.2.22, p. 387.

nirūpākhyo vināśaḥ sambhavati, sarvāsvapyavasthāsu pratyabhijñānabalenānvayyavicchedadarśanāt[5]

Even within the range of the entity they are not possible. For an unconnected, indefinable destruction is not possible because there is viewing of other non-interruption of the connection through the strength of recognition in every situation.

It has been noted, however, in the Introductory Background, in the section concerned with the Unconstructed *Dharmas*, that neither the cessation-with-understanding nor the cessation-without-understanding for the Sarvāstivādins signifies the annihilation of *dharmas*. The cessation-with-understanding refers to the attainment of contact with *sāsrava dharmas*. The cessation-without-understanding refers to the obstruction of *dharmas* not born. For the Sautrāntikas, however, as has been noted in the section on Unconstructed *Dharmas*, the cessation-with-understanding is the cessation of all traces. Furthermore, according to the Sautrāntikas, the basis disappears when the defilements are eliminated. It may be the case, however, that Śaṅkara is referring to Śāntarakṣita's and Kamalaśīla's distinction between destruction and disruption discussed in the section on the Later Logicians. Of these, only the former possesses a cause in that destruction is synonymous with momentariness which is intrinsic to *dharmas*, whereas in the latter, disruption is causeless in that it is extrinsic to *dharmas* (e.g. the break-up of a jar upon the occasion of an encounter with a hammer).

2. Rāmānuja's Interpretation

This *sūtra*, "*pratisaṃkhyā 'pratisaṃkhyā-nirodhāprāptir avicchedāt*," (*Brahma-sūtra* II.2.21) may be translated as follows in accordance with the interpretation of Rāmānuja : "There is no establishment (*prāpti*) of cessation-with-understanding and cessation-without-understanding because of non-interruptedness." In his commentary to this *sūtra*, Rāmānuja employs arguments basically similar to those of Śaṅkara in emphasizing that there can be no absolute destruction or destruction without a

5. Ibid., Volume II, commentary to *Brahma-sūtra* II.2.22, p. 387.

residue. Rāmānuja's descriptions of the two cessations (*nirodha*) seem to refer more pointedly than Śaṅkara's descriptions, however, to the *Tattvasaṃgraha*'s distinction between destruction synonymous with momentariness and disruption which relates to extrinsic factors like a hammer in the case of a jar that has been smashed. Such is the case despite the fact that this *sūtra* is regarded by both Śaṅkara and Rāmānuja to be directed against the Buddhist realists. Rāmānuja refers to a gross destruction such as the blow of a hammer which brings about the destruction of the jar-series, and to a subtle destruction which takes place every moment. Rāmānuja avers that absolute destruction is not possible.

> evam tāvat asata utpattirnirastā; sato niranvayavināśo 'pi nopapadyata ityucyate / kṣaṇikatvavādibhirmudgarābhighātādyanantarabhāvitayopalabdhiyogyaḥ sadṛśasaṃtānāvasānarūpaḥ sthūlo yaḥ, sadṛśasaṃtāne pratikṣaṇabhāvī copalabdhyanarhaḥ sūkṣmaśca yaḥ niranvayo vināśaḥ pratisaṃkhyānirodhāpratisaṃkhyānirodhaśabdābhyāmabhidhīyete, tau na sambhavata ityarthaḥ / kutaḥ? avicchedāt—sato niranvayavicchedāsambhavāt /[6]
>
> Thus certainly, the production of the non-existent is refuted; that the unconnected destruction of an existent is not possible is explained. That unconnected destruction which is gross, having the form of the cessation of the series of similar things, capable of the ascertainment, produced immediately from the blow of the hammer, by those upholding momentariness, and (that destruction) which is subtle, not capable of perception, existing every moment in a series of similar things, are thought to be the cessation-with-understanding and the cessation-without-understanding; that these two are not possible is the meaning. Why ? Because of the non-interruptedness, because of the impossibility of unconnected destruction of an existent.

Rāmānuja claims that it has elsewhere been declared in the attempt to demonstrate the non-otherness of effect to cause, that

6. Viraraghavacharya, Sri Uttamur T., *Brahmasūtra-Śrībhāshya*, commentary to *Brahma-sūtra* II.2.21, p. 533.

birth and destruction are only the occurrences of different conditions of a stable, unitary material flow.

> asambhavaśca, 'sata utpattivināśau nāma avasthāntarāpattireva; avasthāyogi tu dravyamekameva sthiram' iti kāraṇādananyatvaṃ kāryasyopapādayadbhirasmābhiḥ (śārī. 2.1.15) "tadananyatvam" ityatra pratipāditaḥ /[7]
>
> It is impossible. In the statement, "The occurrence of another condition is called the birth and destruction of an existent; it is a stable, unitary material flow joined with condition," the non-otherness from that is established by us proving the non-otherness of effect to cause.

It may be objected by the Buddhist, Rāmānuja continues, that unconnected destruction is inferred from the example of the extinguished flame. Rāmānuja replies that as the clay of a jar is seen to enter into another state when the jar is smashed, so in the case of the flame the occurrence of another condition must be inferred, although that condition may be a subtle condition.

> nirvāṇasya dīpasya niranvayavināśadarśanāt anyatrāpi vināśo niranvayo 'numīyata iti cet—na;ghaṭaśarāvādau mṛdādidravyānuvṛttyupalabdhyā sato dravyasyāvasthāntarāpattireva vināśa iti niścite sati pradīpādau sūkṣmadaśāpattyā 'pyanupalambhopapatteḥ tatrāpyavasthāntarāpattikalpanasyaiva yuktatvāt //[8]
>
> If it is objected that the unconnected destruction is inferred elsewhere because of the viewing of the unconnected destruction of the extinguished flame, it is replied that it is not so. The reason is that it is associated with the assumption of the occurrence of another condition there in connection with the event of the non-ascertainment of the occurrence of a subtle state in the case of a flame, etc., since it is determined that a destruction is the occurrence of another condition of the material flow of an existent by means of the perception of the continuation of clay when there is the destruction of the pot.

---

7. Ibid., commentary to *Brahma-sūtra* II.2.21, p. 533.
8. Ibid., commentary to *Brahma-sūtra* II.2.21, p. 533.

3. Madhva's Interpretation

This *sūtra*, "*pratisaṃkhya 'pratisaṃkhyā-nirodhāprāptir avicchedāt*," (*Brahma-sūtra* II.2.22) may be translated, in accordance with Madhva's interpretation, as follows : "There is no establishment of cessation-with-understanding and cessation-without-understanding, because of uninterruptedness." Madhva's commentary proceeds as follows :

> kāraṇe sati kāryam bhavatyeveti niyamānnissaṃtānaḥ sasaṃtānaśca vināśo na yujyate //[9]
>
> Because of the principle that given the cause, there is the effect, the destruction-with-series and the destruction-without-series is not enjoined.

In comparison with Śaṅkara and Rāmānuja, according to B.N.K. Sharma, Madhva in his interpretation of this *sūtra* is concerned with destruction as such, rather than unconnected destruction (*niranvaya vināśa*) or destruction-without-residue.[10] The non-interruptedness (*aviccheda*) of the *sūtra* is interpreted by Madhva and his school as a reference to the possibility of an endless series of effects if the cause continues to exist. According to B.N.K. Sharma, Madhva in his commentary to this *sūtra* refutes the two types of destruction in *Kṣaṇabhaṅgavāda* : the transcendental and the empirical.[11] The former, notes B.N.K. Sharma,[12] has been designated by Madhva as *nissaṃtāna-nāśa* which has been explained by Jayatīrtha as "that destruction every moment without the series" (*saṃtānam antareṇa yaḥ pratikṣaṇavināśaḥ*). The other is the destruction whereby the continuity is broken (*sasaṃtāna-nāśa*), as takes place when a pot is shattered by the blow of a stick. In connection with the former, *nissaṃtānanāśa*, there is the objection as noted by B.N.K. Sharma in accordance with the explanation of Jayatīrtha in the

9. Bhikācārya Aināpure and Anantācārya Aṣṭaputre, *Brahmasūtras with Ānandatīrtha's Brahmasūtrabhāṣya*, commentary to *Brahma-sūtra* II.2.22, p. 38.

10. Sharma, B.N.K., *The Brahmasūtras and Their Principal Commentaries*, p. 60.

11. Ibid., p. 58.

12. Ibid., p. 58.

Tattva-prakāśikā, that as the cause must be there at the time of the origination of the effect, and as the same moment will be the cessation of the effect, the cause as existing at the moment of the cessation of the effect would be producing another effect, and so on endlessly.[13]

pratikṣaṇaṃ kāraṇaṃ kāryaṃ nirvartya naśyatīti vaktavyaṃ / tatra svakāryaviyogakāle kāraṇaṃ sadeveti kāryamutpādayet/ kāraṇe sati kāryaṃ bhavatyeveti niyamābhyupagamāt / tad-utpattyanantaraṃ caivamiti kathaṃ pratikṣaṇam nāśo yujyeta?[14]

It is to be declared that the cause having brought about the effect is destroyed every moment. Then, at the time of separation of its own effect, the cause should continuously give birth to the effect, because of the maintenance of the principle that even when there is the cause, there is the effect. In reference to the birth of that (the effect) without interval, how should there be enjoined destruction at every moment ?

In connection with the destruction whereby the continuity is broken as a pot by the blow of a stick, it is noted by B.N.K. Sharma[15] in accordance with the explanation of Vādirāja in the *Tattva-prakāśikā-gurvarthadīpikā* that since it is the same atoms which form and break up the aggregate at every moment, these same atoms must be present at the time of the disruption in that otherwise it would be impossible to bring about their aggregation at the next moment. In other words, there would be constant regrouping with no room for dissociation.

viralaparamāṇavo nibiḍatayā puñjībhūya kāryakarā bhavanti/ idameva samudāyarūpakāryajanakatvaṃ nāma, nānyat / ta eva ca kṣaṇe kṣaṇe tatra tatra viralībhavanti punaḥ puñjībhavanti ca / tatra teṣāmeva viralībhāvo nāśaḥ, puñjībhāvastu utpattiriti parasya hṛdayam /

idaṃ cānupapannaṃ—teṣāmeva paramāṇūnāṃ vināśāya svakāryaviyogakāle sattvaṃ vaktavyam / anyathā, kārya-kāraṇabhāvāyogāt / sataśca nibiḍapuñjībhāvākhyakāryakara-

13. Ibid., p. 58.
14. Ibid., (*Tattva-prakāśikā* II.2.22), p. 58, footnote 30.
15. Ibid., p. 58.

tvarūpakāryajanakatvaniyamāt, paunaḥpunyena nibiḍataiva syāt / viralitāyāḥ kadāpi nāvasara iti na sasaṃtānanāśopapattiriti[16]

The loose atoms, by being compacted, having gathered together are efficacious. This has the name of the generation of the effect having for its formation the aggregate, and no other. At every moment and place they are dissociating and gathering. Hence the essence for you is that destruction is the state of dissociating in connection with them; the state of gathering together is the arising of another.

This is not accepted. Existence must be ascribed at the time of separation of its own effect for the sake of destruction in connection with these atoms. It is otherwise, because of the non-conjunction of the entities of cause and effect. Because of the principle of the generation of the effect having the form of efficaciousness named the compact state of gathering in connection with an existing thing, it would again be compacted. Since there would be no opportunity for dissociating, there is no acceptance of destruction with the series.

The concept of destruction with the series is invalidated by other arguments also, as described by B.N.K. Sharma[17] in accordance with the explanation of Jayatīrtha in the *Tattva-prakāśikā*. The existence of something like a pot must be granted at the time of its destruction. If it exists, the atoms composing it will produce another effect (of aggregated atoms), and consequently there would be no destruction of the series. If the series is unreal, the units composing it would be unreal. Furthermore, it must be asked whether the aggregate is the same as its constituents or different from them. It cannot be the same, for atoms are invisible and the pot is visible. If it is different from them, then the Buddhist has admitted a whole distinct from the parts, because of the need for a support for such notions as jars. Atoms cannot be the support for such notions, because the atoms are multiple and beyond the senses.

16. Ibid., (*Tattva-prakāśikā-gurvarthadīpikā*, p. 81), p. 58, footnote 31.
17. Ibid., p. 58.

nāpyanyaḥ / sato hi ghaṭasyātyantiko nāśaḥ / ato 'sau sattvāt kāryamutpādayedeva; kāraṇe sati kāryaṃ bhavatyeveti niyamāt / tatkāryam caivameveti kathaṃ saṃtānocchedāvasara iti bhāvaḥ / saṃtāno nitya eveti cenna / pralayānupapatteḥ / viviktatayā pralayopapattiriti nirastaṃ / saṃtānasya nityatve kṣaṇikatvavirodhaḥ / avāstavatvānnāsau kṣaṇika iti cenna / saṃtānināmapi tathātvaprasaṅgāt / nahi santi saṃtānino, na saṃtāna iti yuktam / etena samudāyasyāvāstavatvaṃ parāstam / samudāyo 'pi samudāyimātram? tadatirikto vā? nādyaḥ, virodhāt / dvitīye, sa evāvayavī / avāstavatve ghaṭādibuddhīnāṃ nirālambanatvāpātāt / paramāṇava evālambanamiti cenna / teṣāmanekatvāt; atīndriyatvācceti /[18]

It is not so, from another point of view. Destruction is in close proximity to an existent thing, the pot. Hence, from existence those (atoms) would give birth to an effect, because of the principle that when there is the cause, there is the effect. The meaning is that since there is the effect of those, how is there the opportunity for the destruction of the series? If it is objected that the series is eternal, it is not so, because of the objection of destruction. That there is the occurrence of destruction by means of separation is rejected. In the case of the eternality of the series, there is opposition to momentariness. If it is said that that (the series) is not momentary because it is not like a given thing, it is not so, because of the occurrence of such a condition in connection with the constituents of the series. For, that the series (is) not (a given thing) and the constituents of the series (are given things) is not enjoined. Therefore, the non-existence of the aggregate as a given thing is rejected. Is the aggregate only related to the aggregate or is it separated from it ? The first is not the case, because of opposition. In the case of the second, that (aggregate) would be a whole because of the occurrence of the non-existence of a support for the notions of pot, etc., in the case of non-existence as a given thing. If it be said that atoms are the support, it is not so, because of the multiplicity of them (the atoms), because of their existence beyond the senses.

---

18. Ibid., (*Tattvaprakāśikā* II.2.22), p. 59, footnote 32.

In connection with the argument employed by Madhva and the commentators of his school against what they designate as the destruction without series, it should be noted that again this school is employing an argument similar to Ratnakīrti's argument that there would be an endless series of effects from non-momentary causes. Again, however, Asaṅga's verse in the *Paramārtha-gāthā* is to be recalled, to the effect that the origin of a momentary *saṃskāra* is either doer or activity insofar as it is considered from the standpoint of cause and effect. There is no question involved here whether the doer would consume its activity or exert further activity to produce an effect, for the origin is the activity and that activity is the doer. Cause and effect in this case are only standpoints from which the origin is to be considered. In connection with the argument employed by Madhva and the sub-commentator of his school against what they designate as the destruction with series, it should be noted that Śāntarakṣita and Kamalaśīla in the *Tattva-saṃgraha* and *Tattva-saṃgraha-pañjikā* respectively have indicated that this second type of destruction, which they term disruption is causeless, as has been discussed in the section of this work concerned with the Later Logicians. In that section, it was explained that disruption for Śāntarakṣita and Kamalaśīla does not possess a cause, for it has no connection with the given thing (*vastu*) which is supposedly disrupted, e.g. a jar. A hammer cannot be said to be the cause of the destruction of the jar, for destruction cannot have for its nature the given thing, e.g. the jar. The arguments of Madhva and the commentators of his school in connection with the destruction with series do not apply, therefore, to the type of destruction known as disruption, since such destruction can have no connection with a given thing (*vastu*), e.g. the jar. It should also be observed in reference to the cessation-with-understanding and the cessation-without-understanding as they are presented in the Sarvāstivāda and Sautrāntika systems, that these two cessations are concerned with spiritual systems, not with destruction, although Madhva, Ramānuja, and Śaṅkara attribute to the Buddhists the position that the two cessations and destruction are associated. These two cessations are discussed in the Introductory Background, in the section concerned with the Unconstructed *Dharmas*.

In comparison with Śaṅkara and Rāmānuja, notes B. N. K. Sharma, Madhva simply interprets *Brahma-sūtra* II.2.22 as referring to destruction as such, not as referring to the destruction without a residue. In contrast Śaṅkara argues in opposition to the Buddhists that there can be no destruction without a residue. B. N. K. Sharma concludes that Śaṅkara has imported the notion of non-residual destruction for purposes of criticism.[19] Śaṅkara argues that such a non-residual destruction is not possible.

> nahi bhāvānāṃ niranvayo nirupākhyo vināśaḥ[20]
>
> For the unaccompanied indefinable destruction of entities is not possible.

Madhva, on the other hand, considers destruction as such.

---

19. Ibid., p. 67.
20. Bākre, Mahādeva Śāstrī, editor, *The Brahmasūtra-Shānkarbhāshyam*, commentary to *Brahma-sūtra* II.2.19, p. 459.

G. *BRAHMA-SŪTRA* II.2.23 :
"*UBHAYATHĀ CA DOṢĀT*"

1. Śaṅkara's Interpretation

This *sūtra*, "*ubhayathā ca doṣāt*," (*Brahma-sūtra* II.2.23)[1] may be translated as follows in accordance with the interpretation of Śaṅkara : "And in both cases because of fault." In his commentary to this *sūtra*, Śaṅkara tries to trap his "Sarvāstivādin" between the horns of a dilemma. He claims that the two kinds of *nirodha* (cessation) must take place either as a result of *samyag-jñāna* (right knowledge), or of its own accord. Then he lays the trap. If the two kinds of *nirodha* (cessation) are the result of perfect knowledge, then the doctrine of Momentariness by which all *dharmas* appear and disappear of themselves is abandoned. If the two kinds of *nirodha* occur without a cause, then the Buddhist "path" is useless.

> yo 'yamavidyādinirodhaḥ pratisaṃkhyānirodhāntaḥpāti paraparikalpitaḥ, sa samyagjñānādvā saparikarāt syāt; svayameva vā—pūrvasmin vikalpe nirhetukavināśābhyupagamahānipra-saṅgaḥ; uttarasmiṃstu mārgopadeśānarthakyaprasaṅgaḥ/evamubhayathāpi doṣaprasaṅgādasamañjasamidaṃ darśanam/[2]
>
> That which is the cessation of the set beginning with nescience, which is included in the cessation-with-understanding, which is assumed (by them)—let it exist either because of perfect knowledge or because (it is) attended by a retinue or by itself. Through the first assumption, there is the occurrence of the abandonment of the principle of causeless destruction. In the latter case, there is the occurrence of the meaninglessness of the teaching of the path. Thus in both cases, because of the occurrence of defect, this is not a correct vision.

It seems that Śaṅkara is referring here to the Sautrāntika doctrine of causeless destruction discussed in the Introductory Background, in the section concerned with Causation. According to this

1. Radhakrishnan, Sarvepalli, *The Brahma Sūtra*, *Brahma-sūtra* II.2.23, p. 381.
2. Balasubrahmanyam, T. K., *The Works of Śrī Śaṅkarācharya*, Volume II, commentary to *Brahma-sūtra* II.2.23, p. 388.

doctrine, the destruction synonymous with momentariness is causeless because it is an absence and because only an entity can possess a cause. The Sautrāntikas also held, however, as has been discussed in the section of the Introductory Background concerned with Unconstructed *Dharmas*, that the defilements are eliminated by the paths of cultivation and vision.

tatpraheyāṇāṃ darśanabhāvanāmārgapraheyāṇām[3]

"Of those (defilements) to be eliminated" signifies those to be eliminated by the paths of vision and cultivation."

It has also been observed that according to the *Abhidharmakośa*, the cessation-with-understanding is equivalent to the cessation of the traces and birth already originated (*utpannānuśayajanma-nirodha*). Although the Sautrāntikas declare that the defilements are eliminated by the paths of vision and cultivation, it is not clear whether they regard these paths as causes of the cessation of the traces.

2. Rāmānuja's Interpretation

This *sūtra*, "*ubhayathā ca doṣāt*," (*Brahma-sūtra* II.2.22) may be translated, in accordance with Rāmānuja's interpretation, as follows : "And in both cases, because of fault." In his commentary to this *sūtra*, Rāmānuja argues with the Buddhists from a cosmological point of view, whereas Śaṅkara discusses the issues raised by the two cessations in connection with the question whether cessation is caused by true knowledge or is without cause. Rāmānuja, however, tries a different approach. He represents the Buddhist position as either origination from emptiness (tuccha) or passing away into emptiness and then shows the absurdity of both.

kṣaṇikatvavādibhirabhyupetā tucchādutpattiḥ utpannasya tucchatāpattiśca na sambhavatītyuktaṃ; tadubhayaprakārābhyupagatau doṣaśca bhavati/[4]

---

3. Shastri, Swami Dwarikadasa, *Abhidharmakośam* (*Sphuṭārtha* commentary to *Abhidharmakośa* II.37), p. 215.

4. Viraraghavacharya, Sri Uttamur T., *Śrībhāshya*, commentary to *Brahma-sūtra* II.2.22, p. 533.

> It is said that the arising from emptiness upheld by one adhering to the position of momentariness, and the entering into emptiness by the arisen thing are not possible; therefore, in maintaining both sorts of positions there is fault.

If there were origination from emptiness, according to Rāmānuja, then all effects would be composed of emptiness.

> tucchādutpattau tucchātmakameva kāryaṃ syāt/[5]
>
> In this case of arising from emptiness the effect would be composed out of emptiness.

If there were destruction of an existent thing (*sat*), according to Rāmānuja, the entire world would pass into emptiness only to arise again and be composed of emptiness. In this way, Rāmānuja refutes both supposedly Buddhist positions.

> sato niranvayavināśe sati, ekakṣaṇādūrdhvaṃ kṛtsnasya jagatastucchatāpattireva syāt/
>
> paścāt tucchāt jagadutpattau anantaroktaṃ tucchātmakatvameva syāt/ata ubhayathāpi doṣāt na bhavaduktaprakārāvutpattinirodhau//[6]
>
> If there were absolute destruction of an existent, after one moment there would be entry into emptiness of the entire world. Afterwards, when there is the arising of the world from emptiness, as is said above, it would be composed of emptiness. Thus because of fault in both cases, there are not the two kinds, arising and cessation, claimed by you.

The only difficulty with this argument of Rāmānuja is that the Buddhists do not claim origination from emptiness or passing into emptiness. Rāmānuja may be referring to the Sautrāntika teaching of *abhūtvā bhāva utpāda* (birth is the existence subsequent to non-existing) and *bhūtvā abhāva* (absence subsequent to existing). But to say that existence is subsequent to non-existence and *vice-versa* is not to say that existence arises out of non-existence or that existence passes into non-existence. Other-

5. Ibid., commentary to *Brahma-sūtra* II.2.22, p. 533.
6. Viraraghavacharya, Sri Uttamur T., *Śrībhāshya*, commentary to *Brahma-sūtra* II.2.22, p. 534.

wise, the Sautrāntika teaching could have been expressed as "*abhāvād-bhāva*" (entity from absence) or "*bhāvād-abhāva*" (absence from entity).

3. Madhva's Interpretation

This *sūtra*, "*ubhayathā ca doṣāt*" (*Brahma-sūtra* II.2.23) may be translated in accordance with Madhva's interpretation as follows : "And in both cases, because of fault." Madhva's interpretation proceeds as follows :

> kāraṇe sati kāryam bhavatyeveti niyame sarvadā kāryabhāvānna kāryakāraṇaviśeṣaḥ// aniyame kāryānutpattiḥ//[7]
>
> Because of the existence of the effect endlessly in the case of the principle, "When there is the cause, there is the effect," there is no distinction of cause and effect. If there is no such principle, there is no production of the effect.

Whereas in Śaṅkara's interpretation of this *sūtra* it is asked whether the cessation of nescience occurs as a result of right knowledge or of its own accord, and Rāmānuja in his interpretation of the *sūtra* attempts to prove that on the basis of momentariness the world would be plunged into emptiness, Madhva in his interpretation seems to examine a Buddhist argument supporting momentariness. According to B. N. K. Sharma, Madhva in his interpretation of this *sūtra* examines the argument based on presumption (*arthāpatti*)[8] in support of the principle of Momentariness. That argument is found in Ratnakīrti's *Kṣaṇabhaṅgasiddhi* discussed in the section concerned with the Later Logicians. Ratnakīrti's argument basically concerns the undesirable contingency of an endless series of effects if the cause does not cease to exist after the first moment, since to be real is to be efficient. Madhva attempts to refute the argument by demonstrating that the doctrine is dependent upon a principle which is self-contradictory : "When there is the cause, there is the effect" (*kāraṇe sati kāryam bhavati*). According to Jayatī-

---

7. Bhikācārya Aināpure and Anantācārya Aṣṭaputre, *Brahmasūtras with Ānandatīrtha's Brahmasūtrabhāṣya*, commentary to *Brahma-sūtra* II.2.23, p. 38.

8. Sharma, B.N.K., *The Brahmasūtras and Their Principal Commentaries*, p. 59.

rtha in the *Tattvaprakāśikā*, as explained by B.N.K. Sharma, the advocate of Momentariness is asked by Madhva and his school whether the law propounded by the Buddhist, "When there is the cause, there is the effect" (*kāraṇe sati kāryam bhavati*) is true or not.[9] If it is true, then effect is simultaneous with the cause, as the left and right horns of a bull. Thus it may not be possible to distinguish which is the cause and which is the effect, just as it may not be possible to distinguish which is the right horn of a bull and which is the left. An infinite cycle occurs whereby the cause is itself an effect of an effect which is its cause. Consequently, there is no distinction of cause and effect. In this manner, the principle "When there is the cause, there is the effect" (*kāraṇe sati idam bhavati*) is shown to be self-contradictory. Yet, if it is granted that the principle is not true, the doctrine of Momentariness is contradicted. If it is not true that when there is the cause, there is the effect, then since the cause does not possess efficiency at the time of the birth of the effect, the cause ceases to be existent, for to be existent is to be efficient. If it is not efficient, it is not momentary.[10] Jayatīrtha in the *Tattvaprakāśikā* first describes the *prima facie* view in connection with momentariness which he attributes to the Buddhists, and then proceeds to refute it.

tathāpi na satām bhāvānāṃ kṣaṇikatā śakyā niṣeddhum// arthakriyākāritvaṃ khalu sattvaṃ nāma//na ca tatkṣaṇikatām antareṇopapannam// yadyādyakṣaṇe ghaṭo ghaṭāntaramutpādya na svayaṃ naśyati tadā ghaṭāntaramapi tathetyanantakāryāpattiḥ// ato 'rthakriyākāritvasattvasiddhau kṣaṇikatvameṣṭavyam bhāvānāmityāśaṅkām pariharatsūtramupanyasya vyācaṣṭe// ubhayatheti// arthakriyākāritvaṃ sattvaṃ tadanyathānupapattyā kṣaṇikatvam bhāvānāmiti vadan praṣṭavyo jāyate// kāraṇe sati kāryam bhavatyeveti niyamo 'sti na veti// yadyasti tadā kāryasyāpi yāvatkāraṇabhāvitvāt savyetaragoviṣāṇavanna kāryakāraṇabhāvaḥ// niyamābhāve tatkāle 'rthakriyākāritvābhāvenā 'sattvāpattyā na kadāpi tataḥ kāryotpatti syāttathā ca kṣaṇikatā vyāhanyata iti bhāvaḥ// na ca vācyaṃ

9. Ibid., p. 59.
10. Ibid., p. 59.

kathaṃ tarhi ghaṭādisattvavyavastheti// jalāharaṇādiyogyatayaiva tadupapatteḥ//23//[11]

Thereupon, the refutation of the momentariness of existent entities is not possible. Efficiency is indeed called existence, and is not possible without momentariness. If the first moment of the jar having given birth to the second moment, does not perish of itself, then there is the occurrence of endless effects in reference therefore to the second jar-moment.

Having laid down this *sūtra* abandoning the uncertainty that the momentariness of entities is to be declared when efficiency is manifested as existence he explains the matter. "In both cases." Declaring in reference to the momentariness of entities by means of the objection that it is otherwise from that because of existence as efficiency the thing in question is born. The principle "When there is the cause there is the effect" (*kāraṇe sati kāryam bhavati*) is true, or is not true. If it is true, then because of the existence of the effect all the way to the cause the relationship of cause and effect is like the right and left horns of a bull. By means of the occurrence of non-existence through the absence of efficiency at the time when there is the absence of (this) principle, there is no birth at any time of the effect, and thereupon momentariness is to be abandoned—such is the meaning. Nor is it to be asked how there is the establishment of the existence of the jar, etc. because of the acceptance by the qualification of fetching water.

Whether the statement, "When this is, that is" (*asmin satīdam bhavati*) can be interpreted to signify the simultaneity of cause and effect is to be questioned. It has been noted, in the section concerned with Causation, that according to the *Abhidharmakośa* III.28, the principle "When this is, that is" is set forth in order to reveal the succession of birth and of members. Furthermore, it has been noted that in the same passage, it is declared that a thing can proceed from its condition either

---

11. Bhikācārya Aināpure and Anantācārya Aṣṭaputre, *Brahmasūtras with Ānandatīrtha's Brahmasūtrabhāṣya, Tattvaprakāśikā* sub-commentary on Madhva's *bhāṣya* on *Brahma-sūtra* II.2.23, p. 38.

immediately or gradually after an interval. In neither case, however, is a thing considered to be simultaneous with its condition. In addition, it has been observed in the Introductory Background, in the section concerned with Later Logicians, that according to Śāntarakṣita and Kamalaśīla, the effect is born in the second moment from a cause which is yet capable and undestroyed. If the effect were born in the first moment, according to Śāntarakṣita and Kamalaśīla, there would occur simultaneity of cause and effect. If the effect were born in the third moment, according to Śāntarakṣita and Kamalaśīla, when the effect is destroyed, there would occur disconnectendness of cause and effect. By saying that the effect is born in the second moment, therefore, Śāntarakṣita and Kamalaśīla attempt to avoid the dangers of simultaneity and disconnectedness of cause and effect.

In Śaṅkara's interpretation of this *sūtra*, the question is posed whether the destruction of nescience, etc. occurs as a result of right knowledge (*samyag-jñāna*) or of its own accord. In the first case, there results a contradiction of the supposed Buddhist maxim that destruction occurs without a cause, as has been discussed above. In the second case, the noble eightfold path would be unnecessary. B. N. K. Sharma remarks that such criticism goes astray, in that Śaṅkara's own commentary attests that destruction of nescience, etc. is brought under *pratisaṃkhyā-nirodha* by the Buddhist.[12] Rāmānuja in his discussion of the *sūtra* attempts to prove that on the basis of the principle of Momentariness, the world would be plunged into emptiness (*tucchatva*)), as has been discussed above. B.N.K. Sharma remarks that Rāmānuja does not set forth two alternatives in his interpretation, as would be required to justify the use of "*ubhayathā*" in the *sūtra*.[13]

12. Sharma, B.N.K., *The Brahmasūtras and Their Principal Commentaries*, p. 67.

13. Ibid., p. 68.

H. *BRAHMA-SŪTRA* II.2.24 : "*ĀKĀŚE CĀVIŚEṢĀT*"

1. Śaṅkara's Interpretation

This *sūtra*, "*ākāśe cāviśeṣāt*," (*Brahma-sūtra* II.2.24)[1] may be translated as follows in accordance with the interpretation of Śaṅkara : "And in the case of space, because of non-distinction". Śaṅkara's argument in his commentary of this *sūtra* is that space is a given thing just as the cessation-with-understanding and the cessation-without-understanding. He attributes to the Buddhists the position that the triad of space, the cessation-with-understanding, and the cessation-without-understanding are indefinable and announces his intention to refute the indefinability of space.

> yacca teṣāmevābhipretaṃ nirodhadvayamākāśaṃ ca nirupākhyamiti—tatra nirodhadvayasya nirupākhyatvaṃ purastānnirākṛtam; ākāśasyedānīṃ nirākriyate/ ākāśe cāyukto nirupākhyatvābhyupagamaḥ, pratisaṃkhyāpratisaṃkhyānirodhayoriva vastutvapratipatteraviśeṣāt/[2]
>
> In connection with these, it is said (by the Buddhists) that the pair of cessations and space are indefinable; in this case the indefinability of the pair of cessations has been previously refuted. Now the indefinability of space is refuted. In the case of space, the principle of indefinability is not suitable because of non-distinction in the acknowledgement that like cessation-with-understanding and cessation-without-understanding, space is a given thing.

Śaṅkara refutes what he considers to be the Sautrāntika notion of space as mere absence of material flow with hindrance (*sapratighadravyābhāvamātra*) when he notes that the absence of hindrance indicates the need for that by which the absence of hindrance is distinguished. He employs the example of birds flying in the sky : how can one distinguish the space occupied

1. Radhakrishnan, Sarvepalli, *The Brahma Sūtra*, *Brahma-sūtra*, II.2.24, p. 381.
2. Balasubrahmanyam, T. K., *The Works of Śrī Śaṅkarāchārya*, Volume II, commentary to *Brahma-sūtra* II.2.24, p. 388.

by one bird from the space occupied by another unless *ākāśa* were a given thing?

> apica āvaraṇābhāvamātramākāśamicchatām, ekasminsuparṇe patatyāvaraṇasya vidyamānatvāt suparṇāntarasyotpitsato 'navakāśatvaprasaṅgaḥ; yatrāvaraṇābhāvas tatra patiṣyatīti cet—yenāvaraṇābhāvo viśeṣyate, tattarhi vastubhūtamevākāśaṃ syāt, na āvaraṇābhāva mātram;[3]
>
> Moreover, let it be asked if space is the mere absence of hindrance because of the presence of hindrance in the case of this one bird flying, there is the occurrence of the lack of space in connection with another bird desirous of flying. If (it be said that) where there is absence of hindrance, there it will fly, it is replied that by whatever the absence of hindrance is distinguished, that space therefore must be a given element not the mere absence of hindrance.

In this way, Śaṅkara attempts to refute what he considers to be the Sautrāntika notion that *ākāśa* is the mere absence of material flow with hindrance or the mere absence of hindrance (*āvaraṇābhāvamātra*).

Śaṅkara also refers to passages saying, for instance, that wind has for its basis *ākāśa* (space). Such passages, for Śaṅkara indicate that for the Buddha, *ākāśa* is a given thing. Śaṅkara refers to the passage in Buddhist scriptures as follows :

> saugate hi samaye 'pṛthivī bhagavaḥ kiṃsaṃniśrayā' ityasmin praśnaprativacanapravāhe pṛthivyādīnāmante, 'vāyuḥ kiṃsaṃniśrayaḥ' ityasya praśnasya prativacanam bhavati—'vayurākāśasaṃniśrayaḥ' iti; tadākāśasyāvastutve na samañjasaṃ syāt tasmādapyayuktamākāśasyavastutvam/[4]
>
> In the Buddhist scripture, it is asked "What basis, O Lord, has the earth?" In this series of questions and answers inside the set beginning with earth it is asked, "What basis has the wind ?" The reply to this question is the statement, "Wind has space as basis." Thus, if space is not a given thing the

3. Ibid., Volume II, commentary to *Brahma-sūtra* II.2.24, p. 388.
4. Ibid., Volume II, commentary to *Brahma-sūtra* II.2.24, pp. 388-389.

statement is not correct. Therefore, that space is not a given thing is unsuitable.

Śaṅkara also criticizes the Vaibhāṣikas for supposedly declaring the three unconstructed *dharmas* to be indefinable (*nirupākhyam*) and non-placeable (*avastu*) and yet eternal (*nityam*). Śaṅkara avers that a thing that is non-placeable cannot be declared to be eternal.

api ca nirodhadvayamākāśaṃ ca trayamapyetannirupākhyamavastu nityaṃ ceti vipratiṣiddhaṃ; na hyavastuno nityatvamanityatvaṃ vā sambhavati, vastvāśrayatvāddharmadharmivyavahārasya; dharmadharmibhāve hi ghaṭādivad vastutvameva syāt, na nirupākhyatvam //[5]

Moreover, if (it be said that) the triad of the pair of cessations and space are indefinable, non-placeable and eternal, it is refuted. For the eternity or non-eternity of a given thing is not possible because there is the basis of a given thing in connection with the practice of factual base and feature. In the case of the relationship of factual base (*dharmin*) and feature (*dharma*), as pots, etc., there must be existence as given things, not indefinability.

Śaṅkara's criticism of the notion of space as mere absence of hindrance, which he attributes to the Buddhist realists, seems to refer both to Sarvāstivāda and Sautrāntika doctrines. As has been noted in the section of the Introductory Background concerned with the Unconstructed *Dharmas,* the Sautrāntikas defined space as that having for its measure (*mātra*) the absence of the tangible (*spraṣṭavyābhāvamātramākāśam*) and the Sarvāstivādins defined it as that which has the nature of non-hindrance (*anāvaraṇasvabhāvamātramākāśam*). The fact that the Sautrāntikas have defined space in terms of the absence of hindrance and that the Sarvāstivādins have defined it in terms of that having the nature of non-hindrance is not to say that these Buddhist schools have declared space to be indefinable. Śaṅkara's example of the two birds does not apply either to the Sarvāstivādins or to the Sautrāntikas, in that neither declares space to be "mere

5. Ibid., Volume II, commentary to *Brahma-sūtra* II.2.24, p. 389.

absence". The "*abhāvamātra*" of the Sautrāntika definition refers to the fact that according to the Sautrāntikas space is that which has the characteristic of being insubstantial, of having absence for its measure. It may also be asked whether to the extent that these Buddhist schools regard space not to be a given thing, they do so only because they do not regard space to be necessary in the sense that it causes the birds to fly. According to Śaṅkara, the Buddhists are claiming that the triad of space, cessation-with-understanding, and cessation-without-understanding are indefinable. It has been observed, however, in the section concerned with the Unconstructed *Dharmas*, that these three have been defined. Śaṅkara claims furthermore that according to the Buddhists, the above-mentioned triad is eternal. It is to be noted, however, that the Sarvāstivādins and Sautrāntikas characterize these three as unconstructed.

2. Rāmānuja's Interpretation

The *sūtra*, "*ākāśe cāviśeṣāt*," (*Brahma-sūtra* II.2.23) may be translated as follows in accordance with the interpretation of Rāmānuja : "And in the case of space, because of non-distinction." In his commentary to this *sūtra*, Rāmānuja represents the Buddhist position in connection with space in terms similar to those of Śaṅkara. He attributes to the Buddhists the position that space is indefinable (*nirupākhya*), empty (*tuccha*), mere absence (*abhāva*). It has been noted in the section of this work concerned with Śaṅkara's commentary to this *sūtra*, that both the Sautrāntikas and the Sarvāstivādins have in fact defined space. The Sarvāstivādins have defined space in terms of its having the nature of non-hindrance (*anāvaraṇasvabhāva*). The Sautrāntikas have defined it as that which has for its measure (*mātra*) the absence of the tangible (*spraṣṭavyābhāvamātramākāśam*). In either case, space has been defined; thus it cannot be said that either the Sautrāntikas or Sarvāstivādins claim the indefinability (*nirupākhyatva*) of space. In reply to this supposed Buddhist position, however, Rāmānuja employs a slightly different argument from that employed by Śaṅkara. Whereas Śaṅkara claims that space can be inferred from the presence of sound, Rāmānuja claims that space must be regarded as definable because it is apprehended as a form of presence like earth.

ākāśe ca nirupākhyatā na yuktā bhāvarūpatvenābhyupagatapṛthivyādivat ākāśasyāpi abādhitapratītisiddhatvaviśeṣāt /[6]

In the case of space also indefinability is not enjoined, because of the special property of the validity of the non-supplanted apprehension of space, as earth, etc. maintained to be a form of presence.

Rāmānuja goes on to argue that space cannot be defined in terms of absence. Like Śaṅkara he employs the example of the two birds flying to indicate that the notion of space is related to that of place as is used by Śaṅkara when he tries to demonstrate that space is a given thing. But Rāmānuja goes on to indicate three possible ways to speak of space in terms of absence and demonstrates the absurdity of all three: space as absence prior to and subsequent to the earth, etc., space as mutual absence, space as absolute absence.

pṛthivyādeḥ prāgabhāvaḥ, pradhvaṃsābhāvaḥ, itaretarābhāvaḥ atyantābhāvo vā ākāśaḥ; sarvathā 'pyākāśapratītyanupapattiḥ syāt / prāgabhāvapradhvaṃsābhāvayorākāśatve, pṛthivyādiṣu vartamāneṣu ākāśapratītyayogāt nirākāśaṃ jagat syāt / itaretarābhāvasyākāśatve 'pi, itaretarābhāvasya tattadvastugatatvena teṣāmantarāle ākāśapratītirna syāt / atyantābhāvastu pṛthivyādīnāṃ na saṃbhavati /[7]

Whether space be the prior absence or the subsequent absence, in connection with earth, etc. the mutual absence, or the absolute absence, in all cases there would be objection to the apprehension of space, etc. In the case of the existence of space through prior absence and subsequent absence, because of the impossibility of the apprehension of space in the existing earth, etc., the world would be without space. In the case of the existence of space in connection with mutual absence, there would not be the apprehension of space in their intermediate region through the containment in this and that

---

6. Viraraghavacharya, Sri Uttamur T., *Brahmasūtra-Śrībhāshya*, commentary to *Brahma-sūtra* II.2.23, p. 534.
7. Ibid., commentary to *Brahma-sūtra* II.2.23, p. 534.

given thing by the mutual absence. Absolute absence in connection with earth, etc. is not possible.

It has been observed, however, that the Sautrāntikas hold the position that space has for its measure the absence of the tangible (*spraṣṭavyābhāvamātra*). The "*abhāvamātra*" of the Sautrāntika definition is a reference to the fact that space is insubstantial. It is not the case for the Sautrāntikas that space is "mere absence." Rāmānuja also argues that since absence is only a quality of existing things, space cannot be said to be indefinable.

abhāvasya vidyamānapadārthāvasthāviśeṣatvopapādanācca ākāśasyābhāvarūpatve 'pi na nirupākhyatvam /[8]

Because it is established that absence is a special condition of the category of the existing, even if space is a form of absence, there is no indefinability.

As has been noted, however, the Buddhists do not claim space to be indefinable.

3. Madhva's Interpretation

This *sūtra*, "*ākāśe cāviśeṣāt*," (*Brahma-sūtra* II.2.24) may be translated in accordance with Madhva's interpretation of it, as follows : "And in the case of space, because of non-distinction." Madhva's commentary proceeds as follows :

dīpādiṣu viśeṣadarśanāt kṣaṇikatvenānyatrāpi kṣaṇikatvamanumīyate cedākāśādiṣvaviśeṣadarśanādanyatrāpi tadanumīyeta//[9]

If it is objected that by means of momentariness on account of the view of differences in the lamp, etc. momentariness is inferred elsewhere, (then) because of the view of non-differences in space, etc. that is inferred elsewhere.

Whereas Śaṅkara and Rāmānuja in their interpretations of this *sūtra*, attempt to refute the supposed Buddhist characterizations of space, Madhva attempts to refute the Buddhist doctrine of Momentariness in relation to which space is employed by him

8. Ibid., commentary to *Brahma-sūtra* II.2.23, p. 535.

9. Bhikācārya Ainapure and Anantācārya Aṣṭaputre, *Brahmasūtras with Ānandatīrtha's Brahmasūtrabhāṣya*, commentary to *Brahma-sūtra* II.2.24, p. 39.

as a counter-example. According to B.N.K. Sharma, Madhva in his commentary to this *sūtra* argues against an inferential argument supposedly preferred by the Buddhist, that whatever is existent is momentary.[10] Jayatīrtha in the *Tattva-prakāśikā*, as cited by B.N.K. Sharma, explains Madhva's point of view.

> mā bhūdarthāpattyā kṣaṇikatvasiddhiḥ / yat sat, tat kṣaṇikaṃ, yathā dīpādi; saṃtaścāmi bhāvā ityanumānena setsyati /[11]
>
> By means of implication (*arthāpatti*), there is not proof of momentariness. "Whatever is, that is momentary, like lamps, etc.; these are existent entities"—by this inference he will repel.

According to B.N.K. Sharma, Madhva interprets this *sūtra* to be setting forth the thesis that whatever is, is non-momentary, like space (*yat sat, tad akṣaṇikam, yathā ākāśaḥ*).[12]

> The *sūtra*, "*ākāśe cāviśeṣāt*" (Brahma-sūtra II.2.24), counters this inference by pointing out that it is open to us to infer that things are not momentary but stable, like *ākāśaḥ*.[13]

Here we are reminded of Rāmānuja's thesis in the *Śrī-bhāṣya*, that whatever is non-permanent is non-existent, non-efficient.

> yadasthāsnu tadasat, anarthakriyākāri ca[14]

B.N.K. Sharma goes on to explain that according to Madhva's school the Buddhist thinks that since the flame of the lamp reveals the presence of contrary attributes (*viruddhadharmādhikaraṇa*) like variation of heat and light, there is a series of different flames, not one flame, whereas the *siddhāntin* attests that variation does not necessarily militate against oneness, for the perception of variation simply indicates the presence of different stages.[15]

---

10. Sharma, B.N.K., *The Brahmasūtras and Their Principal Commentaries*, (*Tattvaprakāśikā* II.2.24), p. 60.
11. Ibid., p. 60, footnote 33.
12. Ibid., p. 60.
13. Ibid., p. 60.
14. Viraraghavacharya, Sri Uttamur T., *Brahmasūtra-Śribhāshya*, commentary to *Brahma-sūtra* II.2.24, p. 536.
15. Sharma, B.N.K., *The Brahmasūtras and Their Principal Commentaries*, pp. 60-61.

dvitīye, dīpādiviśeṣaṇadarśanasya brahmatvaprasaṅga iti bhāvaḥ / viruddhadharmādhyāso bādhakamiti cenna / tasya kālādibhedenopapatteḥ/ nahi tādṛśe 'nyatvamasmatsammatam/ anyathā, ekakṣaṇe 'pi bhāvabhedaprasaṅgāt / etena pradīpo 'pi vyākhyātaḥ.[16]

In the second case, there is the occurrence of the existence of illusion in connection with the sight of the distinctions in the lamp—such is the sense. If it is objected that the superimposition of opposite features is in opposition, it is not so, because of the appearance by means of difference of time, etc. For it is not agreed among us that there is otherness for anybody whatsoever. It is otherwise, because of the occurrence of difference in the entity at one moment. Therefore the lamp is explained.

The relation between the flame and the different stages of burning is one of difference and non-difference, as is true of a river, a ripening fruit, the maturing body, as is attested by Madhva in the *Bhāgavata-tātparya.*

dehadīpanadīvāriphalādīnāṃ pṛthaksvataḥ /
bhedābhedau parijñeyau.[17]

In connection with the body, lamp, flowing river, fruit, etc.
separately of themselves
Difference and non-difference are to be ascertained.

That the flame is a unity is established by recognition (*pratyabhijñā*), as is shown in Madhva's commentary to the next *sūtra*, to be discussed. In any case, space, unlike the flame of a lamp, does not reveal any difference of modification (*pariṇāmabheda*).

kṣaṇikatāsādhakasya pariṇāmabhedāderākāśe 'bhāvācca.[18]

In the case of space, because of the absence of differences, etc. of modification establishing momentariness.

B.N.K. Sharma notes in accordance with the Madhva school that there is a difficulty for the Buddhist advocate of Moment-

16. Ibid., (*Tattvaprakāśikā* II.2.25), p. 61, footnote 40.
17. Ibid., (*Bhāgavata-tātparya* XI.22.44), p. 60, footnote 34.
18. Ibid., (*Nyāya-sudhā* p. 395b), p. 60, footnote 36.

ariness in connection with space. Since space is other than the five personal aggregates, it cannot be momentary. Yet the Buddhist cannot pretend that space does not possess reality. So the inference that whatever exists is momentary is contradicted in the instance of space, and is open to the fallacy of *prakaraṇa-sama* (an assertion by two opponents of some argument which has the same force pro and con).[19]

> It is not possible for the Buddhist to infer *Ākāśa* to be '*Kṣaṇika*,' as it is other than the *Pañcaskandhas*. The inference of unreal momentariness from the predicate of existence will thus be open to the fallacy of *Prakaraṇasama*. The Buddhist cannot pretend that *Ākāśa* does not possess any reality.[20]

The only difficulty with the preceding argument is that it is not clear whether the Buddhist would agree with Madhva and his school that space is existent in the same sense that a jar is existent. For both the Sautrāntika and Sarvāstivādins, space is an unconstructed *dharma* to be distinguished from constructed *dharmas*. Furthermore, notes B.N.K.Sharma, in accordance with Śaṅkara's explanation the Buddhist theory reduces space to a mere absence of covering bodies (*mūrtadravya*).[21]

> āvaraṇābhāvamātramākāśamiti[22]
> ...in reference to space as the mere absence of hindrance

Madhva, however, as noted by B.N.K. Sharma, argues in his *Anuvyākhyāna* that space cannot be so reduced for the conception of absence is always with reference to a factual base (*dharmin*), or counter-correlative (*pratiyogī*). Space, however, is presented without a factul base or counter-correlative.[23]

> sadharmipartiyogitvamabhāvasya niyāmakaṃ/
> tau vinā na hyabhāvaśca kvaciddṛṣṭaḥ kadācana//
> adharmipratiyogitvamākāśasyāvagamyate//[24]

19. Ibid., p. 60.
20. Ibid., p. 60.
21. Ibid., p. 60.
22. Bākre, Mahādeva Śāstrī, *The Brahmasūtra-Shānkarbhāshyam*, (commentary to *Brahma-sutra* II.2.22), p. 450.
23. Sharma, B.N.K., *The Brahmasūtras and Their Principal Commentaries*, p. 61.
24. Ibid., (*Anvvyākhyāna* II.2.24), p. 61, footnote 38.

The existence with factual base, existence of a counter-correlative are defining in connection with absence.
Without these two, there is no absence anywhere, at any time.
Existence with factual base, existence of a counter-correlative, are not conceived in connection with space.

In this way, Madhva tries to show that space cannot be an absence. As has been observed in the section of the Introductory Background concerned with the Unconstructed *Dharmas*, the Vaibhāṣikas do not define space in terms of absence, but in terms of having a nature, for they declare space to have the nature of non-hindrance (*anāvaraṇasvabhāvamākāsam*). The Sautrāntikas, however, do define space in terms of absence when they declare space to be that which has for its measure the absence of the tangible (*spraṣṭavyābhāvamātramākāśam*). Yet even they declare a factual base and a counter-correlative when they mention the tangible or the obstacle of which space is the absence.

kim tarhi spraṣṭavyābhāvamātramākāśaṃ/ tadyathā hyandhakāre pratighātamavindata ākāśamityāhuḥ[25]

How then ? Space is only the absence of the tangible. In such a manner as follows, not finding an obstacle in the dark, they say that this is space.

According to B. N. K. Sharma, the seventh and eighth *sūtras* (*Brahma-sūtra* II.2.24-25, respectively) have been considered by Rāmānuja and Śaṅkara to be establishing different propositions.[26] The first of these *sūtras* according to both Śaṅkara and Rāmānuja refutes the supposed Buddhist position that space is indefinable as are the two cessations. According to Śaṅkara, space is not indefinable because it is a given thing.

ākāśe cāyukto nirupākhyatvābhyupagamaḥ, pratisaṃkhyāpratisaṃkhyānirodhayoriva vastutvapratipatteraviśeṣāt/[27]

---

25. Pradhan, Prof. P., *Abhidharmakośabhāśyam of Vasubandhu*, (*Abhidharmakośa* II.55), p. 92.

26. Sharma, B.N.K., *The Brahmasūtras and Their Principal Commentaries*, p. 68.

27. Balasubrahmanyam, T.K., *The Works of Śrī Śaṅkarāchārya*, Volume II, commentary to *Brahma-sūtra* II.2.24, p. 388.

In the case of space, the principle of indefinability is not suitable because of non-distinction in the acknowledgement that like cessation-with-understanding and cessation-without-understanding, space is a given thing.

The next, *sūtra*, "*anusmṛteśca*," (*Brahma-sūtra* II.2.25), is interpreted by Śaṅkara to be establishing the permanence of the Self, because of the single agency of the one perceiving and the one remembering.

> api ca vaināśikaḥ sarvasya vastunaḥ kṣaṇikatāmabhyupayan upalabdhurapi kṣaṇikatāmabhyupeyāt; na ca sa sambhavati; anusmṛteḥ—anubhavam upalabdhimanūtpadyamānaṃ smaraṇam-evānusmṛtiḥ: sā copalabdhyekakartṛkā satī sambhavati,[28]
>
> Moreover, the destructionist, admitting momentariness in connection with every given thing should admit momentariness in connection with the perceiver. That is not possible, because of remembrance. Remembrance (*anusmṛti*) is recollection (*smaraṇa*) not arising as the perception of an experience. In this case, the single agency of the perception would be possible.

Rāmānuja employs this same *sūtra*, "*anusmṛteśca*," to establish the stability of the given thing.

> tadevamiti, sarvaṃ vastujātamatītakālānubhūtaṃ pratyabhijñāyate/[29]
>
> Every given thing experienced as born in past time is recognized in the saying, "This indeed is that."

B. N. K. Sharma notes, in accordance with the argument of Vyāsatīrtha in the *Tātparyacandrikā*, that the two *sūtras* were intended, from Madhva's point of view, to set forth the stability (*sthiratva* or *sthāyitva*) of external objects and experiencing Selves.[30] In this way, B. N. K. Sharma notes, there would be no need for the importation (*adhyāhāra*) of separate predicates (i.e., the indefinability of space, the permanence of the Self respectively) for the propositions of the two *sūtras*.

---

28. Ibid., commentary to *Brahma-sūtra* II.2.25, p. 389.

29. Viraraghavacharya, Sri Uttamur T., *Brahmasūtra-Śrībhāshya*, commentary to *Brahma-sūtra* II.2.24), p. 535.

30. Sharma, B.N.K., *The Brahmasūtras and Their Principal Commentaries*, p. 68.

saptamāṣṭamayoḥ kṣaṇabhaṅgavirodhisthāyitvarūpaikasādhyānvayasyāṣṭamasthacaśabdānuguṇasya sambhave pṛthak sādhyādhyāhārāyogāt[31]

Because of the joining in the seventh or eighth *sūtras* of the importation of the thing to be proved, separately, when there is the possibility, in accordance with the word "and" situated in the eighth *sūtra*, of the connection of a single thing to be proved in the form of stability in opposition to momentariness.

31. Ibid., (*Tātparyacandrikā*, p. 917b), p. 68, footnote 70.

I. *BRAHMA-SŪTRA* II.2.25 : "*ANUSMṚTEŚCA*"

1. Śaṅkara's Interpretation

This *sūtra*, "*anusṁṛteśca,*" (*Brahma-sūtra* II.2.25)[1] may be translated as follows in accordance with the interpretation of Śaṅkara : "And because of remembrance." In his commentary of this *sūtra*, Śaṅkara argues for the existence of a permanent subject through the phenomenon of remembrance (*anusmṛti*). In this way, Śaṅkara tries to refute the theory of Momentariness. First Śaṅkara explains that remembrance can take place only if it refers to the same subject who previously made the perception, for no one thinks, "I remember; another person made the observation."

> api ca vaināśikaḥ sarvasya vastunaḥ kṣaṇikatāmabhyupayan upalabdhurapi kṣaṇikatāmabhyupeyāt; na ca sā sambhavati; anusmṛteḥ—anubhavam upalabdhimanūtpadyamānaṃ smaraṇameva anusmṛtiḥ; sā copalabdhyekartṛkā satī sambhavati, puruṣāntaropalabdhiviṣaye puruṣāntarasya smṛtyadarśanāt;[2]

> Moreover, the Destructionist, admitting momentariness in connection with every given thing should admit momentariness in connection with the perceiver. That is not possible, because of remembrance. Remembrance is recollection (*smaraṇa*) not arising as the perception of an experience. In this case, the single agency of the perception would be possible, because it is not seen that there is the remembrance for one man, when there is the sense-object which is the perception of another man.

Śaṅkara concludes that the necessity of one subject connected with two moments disproves the theory of Momentariness.

> tatraivaṃ satyekasya darśanasmaraṇalakṣaṇakṣaṇadvayasambandhe kṣaṇikatvābhyupagamahāniraparihāryā vaināśikasya

---

1. Radhakrishnan, Sarvepalli, *The Brahma Sūtra* Brahma-sūtra II.2.25, p. 381.

2. Balasabramanyam, T. K., *The Works of Śrī Śaṅkarāchārya,* Volume II, Commentary to *Brahma-sūtra* II.2.25, p. 389.

syāt/ tathā anantarāmanantarāmātmana eva pratipattiṃ pratyabhijānannekakartṛkām ā uttamāducchvāsāt, atītāśca pratipattīḥ ā janmana ātmaikakartṛkāḥ pratisaṃdadhānaḥ, kathaṃ kṣaṇabhaṅgavādī vaināśiko nāpatrapeta?[3]

When there is in relation to one (agent) the connection of two moments having the characteristics of seeing and recollection, then there must be the severance and the abandonment of the principle of Momentariness by the destructionist. Hence, recognizing the successive cognition of a single agent of the soul up to the last breath, and the attribution that the past cognition from birth is of a single agent, how is the destructionist not ashamed to be an advocate of momentary destruction ?

Śaṅkara argues that if the Buddhist were to say that it is only the similarity of two cognitions that causes the notion of a permanent subject, he would reply that the cognition of similarity is based upon two different things. Therefore, concludes Śaṅkara, the existence of a permanent subject capable of grasping the two things as similar is a necessity. Thus again the theory of Momentariness is disproved for Śaṅkara.

sa yadi brūyāt sādṛśyādetatsampatsyata iti, tam pratibrūyāt—tenedaṃ sadṛśamiti dvayāyattatvātsādṛśyasya, kṣaṇabhaṅgavādinaḥ sadṛśayordvayorvastunorgrahīturekasyābhāvāt sādṛśyanimittaṃ pratisaṃdhānamiti mithyāpralāpa eva syāt; syāccetpūrvottarayoḥ kṣaṇayoḥ sādṛśyasya grahītaikaḥ, tathā satyekasya kṣaṇadvayāvasthānātkṣaṇikatvapratijñā pīḍyeta[4]

If he should say that because of similarity this (seeming single agency) will take place, one should reply to him: "Therefore, in connection with similarity because of the dependence on two in the statement 'this is similar to that' and because of the lack of one given thing and of one apprehender for the two similar things in reference to the advocate of momentary destruction, that similarity is the efficient cause of recollection must be false clatter. If there must be one apprehender of

3. Ibid., Volume II, commentary to *Brahma-sūtra* II. 2. 25, p. 390.
4. Ibid., commentary to *Brahma-sūtra* II.2.25, p. 390.

the similarity of the earlier and later moments, (then) because of the situation of two moments in connection with one (agent), the declaration of Momentariness would be trespassed.

Śaṅkara also notes that the notion of similarity cannot be an altogether new notion unconcerned with the two terms, "this" and "that." If it were an altogether new notion, the expression "this is similar to that" would be meaningless.

pratyayāntarameva cetsādṛśyaviṣayaṃ syāt, 'tenedam sadṛśam' iti vākyaprayogo 'narthakaḥ syāt, sādṛśyam ityeva prayogaḥ prāpnuyāt[5]

It there should be another notion having for its domain similarity, then the employment of the statement "This is similar to that" would be meaningless. The employment of the statement "There is similarity" would obtain.

Śaṅkara also notes that the recognition "this is that" is not always equivalent to the judgment "this is like that." He explains, in other words, that all cases of identity are not necessarily similarity.

na cāyaṃ sādṛśyātsaṃvyavahāro yuktaḥ; tadbhāvāvagamāt, tatsadṛśabhāvānavagamācca/[6]

And the common practice is not enjoined from similarity because of the conception of the entity as that, not because of the conception of the entity as similar to that.

Śaṅkara admits that in connection with external things doubts arise, but the conscious subject never has doubts about whether it is itself or only similar to itself. Here Śaṅkara argues on the basis of what for him constitutes the heart of his system.

upalabdhari tu saṃdeho 'pi na kadācidbhavati—'sa evāhaṃ syāṃ tatsadṛśo vā'iti; ya 'evāhaṃ pūrvedyuradrākṣaṃ sa evāhamadya smarāmi' iti niścitatadbhāvopalambhāt/[7]

5. Ibid., Volume II, commentary to *Brahma-sūtra* II.2.25, p. 391.
6. Ibid., commentary to *Brahma-sūtra* II.2.25, p. 391.
7. Ibid., Volume II, commentary to *Brahma-sūtra* II.2.25, p. 391.

> But in the case of the perceiver there is no doubt whatsoever of the form, "I am that or merely similar to that." The reason is that there is obtained the certain feeling: "I who saw yesterday remember today."

It is interesting to note that, according to Ingalls, Śaṅkara's commentary on this *sūtra* is directed against the Buddhist logicians (whom Ingalls terms "idealists"), since the doctrine equating identity with similarity is not a tenet of the Vaibhāṣikas.

> It is worth noting that the Buddhist objection here is idealist rather than realist. This doctrine that what we call identity is in fact similarity is not pressed by the sarvāstivādins. On the other hand, it is basic to the logic of Dharmakīrti and the Buddhist idealists.[8]

Ingalls' contention, however, that Śaṅkara's commentary to *Brahma-sūtra* II.2.25 is directed mainly towards the logicians is thrown into doubt by a passage in the *Upadeśasāharsī*. In the *Upadeśāsāhasrī* (I.16.23-26), Śaṅkara seems to attribute the argument of similarity to both the Bāhyārthavādins (among whom he fails to distinguish Sautrāntikas from Vaibhāṣikas) and the Vijñānavādins, at least according to Sengaku Mayeda. First, Śaṅkara deftly summarizes the Buddhist argument of similarity.

> kṣaṇikaṃ hi tadatyarthaṃ dharmamātram nirantaraṃ/
> sādṛśyāddīpavattaddhīstacchāntiḥ puruṣārthatā//[9]
>
> 23. (All) this is indeed the mere *dharma* (element of life) which indeed perishes every moment and arises without intervals. (Though all this is momentary,) there arises the recognition that this (is that past one) because of similarity, just as a lamp (at this moment is recognized to be the same as it was at the previous moment on account of similarity). The cessation of (all) this is the aim of life.[10]

Then Śaṅkara mentions two schools of Buddhists. The first school according to Śaṅkara postulates the existence of *dharmas*

8. Ingalls, Daniel H.H., "The Study of Śaṃkarācārya," *ABORI* 33, 1952, 1-14,

9. Ibid., Volume 14, "*Vivekacūḍāmaṇiḥ* and *Upadeśasāhasrī*," (Srirangam: Sri Vani Vilas Press), *Upadeśasāhasrī* I.16.23, p. 192.

10. Mayeda, Sengaku, *The Thousand Teachings*, *Upadeśasāhasrī* I.16. 23, p. 151.

such as *rūpa* which are manifested by that which is other than themselves. The second school according to Śaṅkara postulates the existence of consciousness. For Mayeda, the first school represents the Bāhyārthavādins in Śaṅkara's view; the second represents the Vijñānavādins in Śaṅkara's view.[11]

> svākārānyāvabhāsyaṃ ca yeṣāṃ rūpādi vidyate/
> yeṣāṃ nāsti tataścānyatpūrvāsaṃgatirucyate//[12]

> 24. According to some (Buddhists), there exist (the external objects) such as form-and-color, the forms of which are manifested by one other than themselves. According to other (Buddhists) nothing else exists but this (consciousness). (Now) the improbability of the former (theory) is explained.[13]

According to Mayeda, this verse signifies that for Śaṅkara both the Bāhyārthavādins and the Vijñānavādins employed the argument of similarity, in that stanza 24 suggests that stanza 23 may introduce tenets held by both the Bāhyārthavādins and Vijñānavādins.[14] Therefore it seems that Śaṅkara considered the argument of similarity to be the property of both the Bāhyārthavādins and the Vijñānavādins. It should be noted, however, that whatsoever Buddhist school is the target of Śaṅkara's attempted refutation on the basis of the existence of a stable perceiver manifested in perception, many Buddhist figures, from Dignāga and Dharmakīrti in the earlier period to Śāntarakṣita and Kamalaśīla in the later period, were concerned with the phenomenon of remembrance and its connotations.

The phenomenon of memory (*smṛti*) and remembrance (*anusmṛti*) adduced by Śaṅkara as evidence of the perceiving subject (*upalabdhṛ*), however, is for Dignāga and the Buddhist logicians evidence only for the existence of introspection (*svasaṃvedana*) and self-intuition (*svasaṃvitti*), as has been discussed in the section

11. Ibid., p. 158.
12. Balasubrahmanyam, T K., *The Works of Śrī Śaṅkarāchārya*, Volume 14, *Upadeśasāhasrī* I.16.24, p. 193.
13. Mayeda, Sengaku, *Thousand Teachings*, *Upadeśasāhasrī* I.16.24, p. 151.
14. Ibid., p. 158, footnote 16.

on the Buddhist Logicians in the Introductory Background. It is also to be noted that an argument similar to Śaṅkara's, to the effect that if there were not a single knower (*jñātṛ*) then it would be the case that one person sees a fruit and another remembers it, has been subjected to refutation by Śāntarakṣita and Kamalaśīla, as has been discussed in the section on the Later Logicians. In reply to this argument, Śāntarakṣita and Kamalaśīla explain that there is in the absolute sense no one who experiences and no one who remembers; otherwise a thing would be remembered by the one who experiences. Remembrance (*smaraṇa* or *smṛti*) is explained as brought about by a seed deposited in the series through the birth of more and more differentiated moments each following the other through an intense experience.

2. Rāmānuja's Interpretation

This *sūtra*, "*anusmṛteśca*" (*Brahma-sūtra* II. 2. 24) may be translated, in accordance with Rāmānuja's commentary, as follows: "And because of recognition." Whereas Śaṅkara in his commentary to this *sūtra* focusses on the oneness of the witness (*sākṣin*) who transcends two moments in the phenomenon of remembrance, Rāmānuja focusses on the aspect of recognition (*pratyabhijñā*) in *anusmṛti* as revealed in the thought, "This is just that."

> anusmaraṇam—pūrvānubhūtavastuviṣayaṃ jñānaṃ; pratyabhijñānamityarthaḥ/ tadevedamiti, sarvaṃ vastujātamatītakālānubhūtaṃ pratyabhijñāyate/[15]
>
> Remembrance is knowledge which has for its sphere the given thing experienced in the past; the significance of *anusmṛti* is recognition. Every given thing experienced as born in past time is recognized in the statement, "This indeed is that."

In other words, whereas Śaṅkara focusses on the phenomenon of remembrance and the witnessing subject, Rāmānuja focusses

15. Viraraghavacharya, Sri Uttamur T., *Brahmasūtra-Śrībhāshya*, commentary to *Brahma-sūtra* II.2.24, p. 535.

on the phenomenon of recognition and the identity of the given thing. Rāmānuja does refer, however, to the argument of the one knower in order to attempt to dismiss the argument of similarity, according to which what is now perceived is only similar to what was perceived before. Rāmānuja argues like Śaṅkara that even the judgement of similarity requires a permanent knower able to span two moments.

> na ca bhavadbhirjvālādiṣviva sādṛśyanibandhano 'yamekatvavyāmoha iti vaktuṃ śakyaṃ; vyāmuhyato jñāturekasyānabhyupagamāt/ na hyanyānubhūtenaikatvaṃ sādṛśyaṃ vā svānubhūtasyānyo 'nusaṃdhatte/[16]
>
> Nor can it be said by you that there is a deception of oneness having for its foundation similarity as in the case of flames, etc., because of the non-maintenance of one knower who is being deceived. One cannot ascertain in connection with that experienced by one's Self, the similarity or oneness in terms of that experienced by another.

It has been noted in the section concerned with Śaṅkara's commentary to this *sūtra*, that the Buddhist logician Dignāga considered *smṛti* to be evidence not of a permanent witness, but of self-intuition (*sva-saṃvitti*). Rāmānuja notes that perhaps there is valid authority for holding that in the case of fire there are successive flames, but he argues that in the case of a jar one has no right to assume successive jars. Then Rāmānuja depicts what he considers to be the Buddhist position that perception and inference both demonstrate the momentariness of things. He attributes to the Buddhists the position in connection with inference that momentariness is attested by efficiency and existence. The Buddhist supposedly concludes that since the last moment of the jar is perishable, the previous moments of the jar are perishable, because they exist.

> yadapi cedamucyate—pratyakṣānumānābhyāṃ ghaṭādeḥ kṣaṇikatvaṃ sidhyati/ pratyakṣaṃ tāvat vartamānārthaviṣayam, avartamānādvastuno vyāvṛttaṃ svaviṣayamavagamayati, nīlamiva pītat/ evam ca bhūtabhaviṣyadbhyāṃ vartamānasya vast-

16. Ibid., commentary to *Brahma-sūtra* II.2.24, p. 535.

vantaratvamavagataṃ bhavati,' anumānamapi—arthakriyākāritvāt satvācca ghaṭādiḥ kṣaṇikaḥ; yat akṣaṇikaṃ śaśaviṣāṇādi, tat anarthakriyākāri, asacca,' tathā antyaghaṭakṣaṇatvād pūrvaghaṭakṣaṇasattvāni vināśīni, ghaṭakṣaṇasattvāt, antyaghaṭakṣaṇasattvavat iti[17]

This is said, that the momentariness of the pot, etc., is proved by perception and inference. Perception in the first place causes its own object having for its own sphere the meaning of the present, to be known apart from the given thing, from the non-present as blue from yellow. Thus the distinction of present from past and future is comprehended. Inference (shows that) because of efficiency and because of existence, the pot, etc. is momentary; that which is not momentary such as the horn of a hare is not efficient, not existent. Thereupon, because of the existence of the last moment of the jar the existence of the previous moments of the jar are perishable because as moments of the jar they are existent like the last moment of the jar.

In the first place, it is to be questioned whether Rāmānuja's presentation of the Buddhist's argument from perception is correct, for according to the Buddhist logician Dignāga, perception is free from conceptual construction.

pratyakṣam kalpanāpoḍham[18]

Perception is free from conceptual construction.

Conceptual construction is defined in the *Tattva-saṃgraha-pañjikā* as the association of the thing perceived with name (*nāma*), genus (*jāti*), etc.

nāma-jāty-ādi-yojanā[19]

The association of name, and genus, etc.

Since for the Buddhists perception is free from conceptual construction, it is questionable whether they would take the position that perception sets forth a present thing as different from a non-

---

17. Ibid., commentary to *Brahma-sūtra* II.2.24, pp. 535-536.
18. Hattori, Masaaki, *Dignāga, on Perception*, pp. 81 footnote 1.25.
19. Ibid., p. 81, footnote 1.25.

present one, in that such a process represents the association of a particular genus with the object-entity. In any case, Rāmānuja attempts to refute what he has stated to be the Buddhist position, based on perception and inference. In connection with perception, he notes that the object associated with the present need not be a different thing from the non-present object, but is merely associated with present time. In connection with inference, he elaborates the position, in contrast to the Buddhists, that whatever is existent must be non-momentary, for whatever is non-permanent is not existent as the horns of a hare.

> kiṃca pratyakṣagamyā vartamānasyāvartamānāt vyāvṛttirna vartamānasya vastvantaratvamavagamayati; api tu vartamānakālayogitāmātraṃ/ na ca tāvatā vastvantaratvaṃ siddhyati; tasyaiva kālāntarayogasambhavāt/ yattu sattvādarthakriyākāritvācceti kṣaṇikatve hetudvayamuktaṃ—tat abhimataviparītasādhanatvādviruddhaṃ/ sattvādarthakriyākāritvād vāghaṭādi sthāsnu; yadasthāsnu tadasat, anarthakriyākāri ca, yathā śaśaviṣāṇamityapi hi vaktuṃ śakyam/[20]
>
> Moreover, the deliverance of the present from the non-present accessible through perception does not make known the distinction of the present, but only the conjunction with the present time. Certainly, the existence of another given thing is not proved because of the possibility of conjunction with another time in connection with it. In the case of momentariness, because of efficiency and existence, that which is said to have a two-fold reason is opposed because it leads to the opposite of what is intended. The pot, etc., is permanent because of existence and because of efficiency. That which is not permanent is not existent, inefficient, just as is said in reference to the horns of a hare.

Ratnakīrti's argument in favor of momentariness has been examined in the Introductory Background, in the section concerned with Buddhist Logicians. This work is being cited because according to Surendranath Dasgupta, Hindu writers after Ratnakīrti refer to his work in reference to the doctrine of efficiency.

---

20. Viraraghavacharya, Sri Uttamur T., *Brahmasūtra-Śrībhāshya*, commentary to *Brahma-sūtra* II.2.24, p. 536.

> Whenever Hindu writers after Ratnakīrti refer to the Buddhist doctrine of *arthakriyākāritva* they usually refer to this doctrine in Ratnakīrti's sense.[21]

It should be noted that according to Ratnakīrti, as explained by Dasgupta, the term *arthakriyākāritva* signifies efficiency, and is the characteristic definition of existence.

> But with Ratnakīrti (950 A.D.) the word *arthakriyākāritva* has an entirely different sense. It means with him efficiency of producing any action or event, and as such it is regarded as the characteristic definition of existence (*sattva*). Thus he says in his Kṣaṇabhaṅga-siddhi, pp. 20, 21, that though in different philosophies there are different definitions of existence or being, he will open his argument with the universally accepted definition of existence as *arthakriyākāritva* (efficiency of causing any action or event).[22]

It should be noted, however, that Rāmānuja misrepresents the Buddhist position, therefore, when he speaks of inference on the basis of two reasons in connection with the Buddhist position, for according to Ratnakīrti existence is equivalent to efficiency. In the *Kṣaṇabhaṅgasiddhi Vyatirekātmikā*, Ratnakīrti argues by means of the pervasion (*vyāpti*) composed of difference (*vyatireka*) that whatever exists is momentary, in that whatever is existent or efficient can be shown to be momentary. Rāmānuja also argues that efficiency proves the non-momentariness of jars in that momentary things are not capable of activity, and are thus inefficient, that is to say, incapable of producing effects.

> kiṃca arthakriyākāritvamakṣaṇikatvameva sādhayet/ kṣaṇadhvaṃsino hi vyāpārāsambhavādarthakriyākāritvaṃ na sambhavatītyuktaṃ/[23]

> Moreover, efficiency leads only to non-momentariness. It is said that efficiency is not possible because of the impossibility of activity in connection with a thing having momentary destruction.

---

21. Dasgupta, Surendranath, *A History of Indian Philosophy*, Volume I, (Cambridge, England: University Press, 1963, reprint), p. 163 footnote 3.
22. Ibid., Volume I, p. 163, footnote 3.
23. Viraraghavacharya, Sri Uttamur T., *Brahmasūtra-Śrībhāshya*, commentary to *Brahma-sūtra* II.2.24, p. 536.

It has been mentioned, however, in the section of this work concerned with the Early Vijñānavādins in the Introductory Background, that this problem mentioned by Rāmānuja was answered by Asaṅga in the *Paramārtha-gāthā* (5) and commentary where it is said that the origin of *saṃskāras* is their activity, and that origin is looked upon as agent and activity insofar as they are examined from the standpoint of cause or effect. Rāmānuja's argument is vitiated by the fact that according to the Buddhists, the very origin or existence of momentary *saṃskāras* is their activity. It has also been observed in the section concerned with the Later Logicians, that the very existence of the cause is its activity. Then Rāmānuja goes on to argue against the Buddhist position of momentariness by noting that the jar requires a visible cause for destruction and must be considered permanent and continuous until a visible cause like a hammer intervenes. In other words, Rāmānuja is arguing that the destruction is not intrinsic to a given thing as is the case with momentary things, but is extrinsic.

> tathā 'ntyaghaṭakṣaṇasya hetuto nāśadarśanāditare 'pi ghaṭakṣaṇāḥ hetvapekṣavināśāssyuriti ā mudgarādihetūpanipātāt sthāsnutvameva[24]
>
> Moreover, since there is the very sight of the destruction because of the cause in connection with the last moment of the jar, the moments of the pot would perish in dependence upon that cause; hence, there is permanence until the occurrence of the cause of the hammer, etc.

Then Rāmānuja argues that it cannot be said by the Buddhists that extrinsic things like hammers are not the causes of the destruction of the jar but the causes of the origination of a new series, for destruction only means the origination of new series. If destruction were different from the origination of a new series, Rāmānuja argues, it would be reasonable to conclude on the basis of immediate succession that an extrinsic thing like the hammer is the cause of destruction.

> na ca vācyaṃ na mudgarādayo vināśahetavaḥ, api tu kapālādivisadṛśasaṃtānotpattihetava iti; kapālatvāvasthāpattireva

24. Ibid., commentary to *Brahma-sūtra* II.2.24, p. 536.

ghaṭādīnāṃ vināśa ityupapāditatvāt / kapālotpattivyatiriktatvābhyupagame 'pi vināśasya vināśahetutvameva mudgarāderānantaryāt yuktam /[25]

It should not be said that hammers, etc. are not the causes of destruction, but that they are the cause of the arising of a dissimilar series of the fragments of the pot because it has been established that the destruction of the pots, etc. is the occurrence of the condition of the fragments of the pot. When it is maintained that there is a separation of the birth of the pot-fragments from the destruction (of the pot), (the hammer) is enjoined to be the cause of destruction because of the immediate succession of the hammer.

Rāmānuja is attacking the Buddhist doctrine of Momentariness, according to which the destruction of a thing is synonymous with its momentary existence. Rāmānuja is accusing the Buddhists of denying, for instance, that the hammer is the cause of the destruction of the jar. What the Buddhists explain, however, is that the destruction cannot have for its nature the given thing. Śāntarakṣita and Kamalaśīla note that there are two kinds of destruction: the first is concerned with the momentary existence of *dharmas* and is admitted to have a cause; the second is concerned with the cessation of the nature of an entity, is called disruption and does not possess a cause. Śāntarakṣita's and Kamalaśīla's positions relating to destruction and disruption have been discussed in the section concerned with the Later Logicians. When Rāmānuja claims that the hammer should be considered as the cause of the destruction of the jar, on the grounds of immediate succession in time, the Buddhist would agree with him that in a general sense only the disruption is a "becoming immediately succeeding the given thing" (*vastvanantarabhāvitva*) in that it immediately succeeds its cause, e.g. the hammer. But the contention that destruction immediately succeeds the given thing, e.g. the jar, which supposedly constitutes its own nature would be rejected by the Buddhist. Rāmānuja also argues that it may be claimed by the Buddhists that the hammer for instance is the cause of the origination of a new

25. Ibid., commentary to *Brahma-sūtra* II.2.24, p. 536.

series, the fragments of the jar. Rāmānuja replies to this supposed position by claiming that the origination of a new series is in fact destruction, and that consequently the destruction of a given thing is not intrinsic to it. Kamalaśīla explains, however, as is set forth in the section concerned with the Later Logicians, that destruction cannot be equivalent to the origination of a new series, because at the time of its supposed beginning, its cause (e.g. the hammer) is absent. Consequently, according to Kamalaśīla such a new series does not even exist. Rāmānuja adds one more argument to demonstrate the absurdity of the Buddhist doctrine of Momentariness. He argues that inference requires a permanent subject who is able to ascertain and to remember the terms of the pervasion, and that a subject is unable to complete the inference.

> kiṃca pramātṛprameyayoḥ kṣaṇikatvaṃ vadadbhirvyāptyavadhāraṇatatsmaraṇapūrvakānumānābhyupagamo 'pi duśśakaḥ / tathā-idam kṣaṇikamityādipratijñāpūrvakahetūpanyāsādikamapi nopapadyate bhavatāṃ; pratijñopakramakṣaṇa eva vakturvinaṣṭatvāt; na hyanyenopakrāntamajānadbhiranyaiḥ samāpayituṃ śakyam //24//[26]

> Moreover, by one claiming the momentariness of the cognizing subject and the sanctionable, the maintenance of inference preceded by the remembrance and ascertainment of the pervasion is impossible. Thereupon, the assignment by you of reasons preceded by the declaration. "This is momentary," is not possible, because of the destruction of the speaker at the moment of the commencement of the declaration; what is begun by one cannot be completed by another, (who is) ignorant.

It must be recalled, however, that the Buddhists do not deny memory, but that, according to the Buddhist logician Dignāga, memory is indicative of the existence of self-intuition (*svasaṃvitti*), not of a permanent subject.

3 Madhva's Intepretation

This *sūtra*, "*anusmṛteśca*" (*Brahma-sūtra* II.2.25) may be

26. Ibid., commentary to *Brahma-sūtra* II.2.24, p. 536.

translated, in accordance with Madhva's interpretation, as follows: "And because of recognition." Madhva's commentary proceeds as follows:

> tadevedamiti pratyabhijñānācca // pratyabhijñāyā bhrāntitve viśeṣadarśanasyāpi bhrāntitvam //[27]
>
> Because of the recognition (*pratyabhijñā*) "This is that." If there is the illusion in connection with recognition, then there is illusion in connection with the beholding of differences.

Whereas Śaṅkara in his interpretation of this *sūtra* adduces the phenomenon of remembrance as evidence for the stable perceiver in order to refute the theory of Momentariness, Madhva like Rāmānuja, according to B.N.K. Sharma, employs the phenomenon of remembrance interpreted as recognition in order to refute the momentariness of things and the Self.[28] Madhva adopts a different approach, however, from that of Śaṅkara and Rāmānuja in that he attempts to demonstrate that the Buddhists' argument from recognition leads to a contradiction of their own position. In reply to the Buddhist's supposed assertion that recognition insofar as it affirms the oneness of things like the flames of the burning lamp, is to be branded as illusory, Madhva states that even the perception of differences in the burning lamp is to be branded as illusory.

> Pratyabhijñāyā bhrāntitve viśeṣadarśanasyāpi bhrāntitvam.[29]
>
> If there is illusion in connection with recognition, then there is illusion in connection with the beholding of differences.

It is to be noted, however, that Dignāga has defined perception to be free of conceptualization (*pratyakṣaṃ kalpanāpoḍham*); in consequence, judgments concerning the oneness of the fire properly belong to the realm of inference in Dignāga's system. The relation of the flame to its variation, as has been mentioned in the discussion of Madhva's interpretation of the *sūtra*, "*ākāśe*

---

27. Bhikācārya Ainūpure and Anantācārya Aṣṭaputre, *Brahmasūtras with Ānandatīrtha's Brahmasūtrabhāṣya*, commentary to *Brahma-sūtra* II.2.25, p. 39.

28. Sharma, B.N.K., *The Brahmasūtras and Their Prinicipal Commentaries*, p. 61.

29. Ibid., commentary to *Brahma-sūtra* II.2.25, p. 61.

cāviśeṣāt" (*Brahma-sūtra* II.2.24) is one of difference and non-difference. The recognitive judgement, as B.N.K. Sharma notes, is not falsified by the perception of different stages.[30] Jayatīrtha explains in the *Nyāya-sudhā*, according to B.N.K. Sharma, that when there is the recognitive judgement "this indeed is that" (*tad eva'idam*) or "I indeed am he" (*sa eva aham*) concerning the identity of the person or thing as it was and as it is at the time of recognition only the emphatic element "indeed" (*eva*) does not hold true, but that when such a recognitive judgement concerns the relation of a given person or thing to two moments, both the affirmation of identity and the emphatic element are true.[31]

> nanu bhavanmate 'pi pratyabhijñā bhrāntireva / pariṇāmavāde pūrvottaravastuno bhedābhedāṅgīkārāt / tadevedamiti ca pratyabhijñayātyantabhedasyāvagāhanāt/ ucyate—yadi hi pūrvottarakālabhāvinorabhedaḥ pratyabhijñānaviṣayo 'ṅgīkriyate, tadā sāvadhāraṇasya pratyabhijñānasya bhramatve 'pi, "tadidam" iti tu na bhramaḥ / tenaiva sthāyitvasiddheḥ / yadā tu kālādidvayasambandho viṣayaḥ tadā sāvadhāraṇamapi na bhrama iti /[32]

> It may be objected that, in your opinion, recognition is an illusion, because of the agreement of difference and non-difference of the antecedent and subsequent given thing in the case of the system advocating transformation, and because of the immersion in excessive non-difference in the recognition "This indeed is that." It is replied: For if the sense-object of recognition is agreed upon as non-difference of the entities of the antecedent and subsequent times, then in the case of the existence of illusion in connection with restricted recognition, the statement "this is that" is not illusion, because of the establishment of permanence through it. When there is the sense-object connected with the two times, then that which is restricted (e.g. the emphatic element) is not illusion.

Another supposed argument of the Buddhist advocate of

30. Ibid., p. 61.
31. Ibid., p. 62.
32. Ibid., (*Nyāya-sudhā*, p. 394), p. 62, footnote 42.

Momentariness is presented by Jayatīrtha in his *Nyāya-sudhā* to the effect that perception establishes the reality of a thing in reference to the present and not to the future or past. Such a position is also attributed to the Buddhists by Rāmānuja in his interpretation of the *sūtra "anusmṛteśca"* (*Brahma-sūtra* II.2.24). Jayatīrtha explains as follows:

> nanu, pratyakṣaṃ kṣaṇikatāmarthānāmavagamayati/ taddhi vartamānamātragocaramarthasya vartamānamātrakṣaṇasambandhinīṃ sattāmavagāhate; na pūrvottarakṣaṇasambandhinīmapi/ tat kathaṃ kṣaṇikatvamarthānāmaprāmāṇikamiti/[33]
>
> It may be objected that perception teaches the momentariness of object-entities. For, that (object-entity) is absorbed in existence connected with the moment of the present only, in connection with the object-entity within the range of the present only—existence which is not connected with the previous and subsequent moments. Then how can it be said that the momentariness of object-entities is not authorized?

Jayatīrtha replies to this supposed objection by explaining that if what is meant by momentariness is simply the connection with a given moment, then there is nothing detrimental to the notion of a stable (sthāyin) object-entity.

> ucyate—kimidaṃ kṣaṇikatvam nāma? kiṃ kṣaṇasambandhitvaṃ? kiṃ vā kṣaṇamātra evotpattivināśavattvaṃ? yadvā kṣaṇāntarāsambandhitve satyekakṣaṇasambandhitvam? ādyastviṣṭa eva; sthāyino 'pyarthasya ekakṣaṇasattāsvīkārāt[34]
>
> The reply is as follows. What is this having the name momentariness? Is it connection with a moment? And is there anything similar to destructiveness in origination in only a moment? Or is it the connection with one moment, when there is the non-connection with another moment? The first (alternative) is preferred, because of the acceptance of the existence of one moment in connection with the stable object-entity.

The point here, notes B.N.K. Sharma in accordance with Jayatīrtha's explanation, is that perception does not reveal a given

33. Ibid., (*Nyāya-sudhā*, p. 393), p. 62, footnote 43.
34. Ibid., (*Nyāya-sudhā*, p. 393), p. 62, footnote 44.

thing being originated or destroyed, but only as existing at the time. Perception, in other words, reveals a given thing as existing in the present, not in past or future.[35]

> yogyānupalambhasyaivāsattvāvagamakatvāt/
> na ca pūrvottarakālayartitā pratyakṣayogyā/[36]
>
> Because there is made known the non-existence in connection with the non-ascertainment of the perceptible. Not perceptible by perception are those not brought about in previous or subsequent moments.

It is to be noted that Dignāga, since he has declared the separation of the authority of perception and inference, would agree that perception does not establish name and genus of a given thing in its inherent character, for perception is defined as that which is free from conceptual construction. The attribution of existence to a thing that will be, or that has been, or that is "before the eyes" (*pratyakṣa*) would represent for Dignāga a process of inference which is characterized by the application of name, genus, etc. Jayatīrtha goes on to argue, however, as notes B. N. K. Sharma, that although perception is limited to the present, recognition is able to comprehend a given thing's existence both in the present and in the past.[37]

> astu vā ādyaḥ pakṣaḥ/ kasyacit pratyakṣasya vartamānamātragrāhitve 'pi tadevedamiti pratyabhijñālakṣaṇasya tadabhāvāditi[38]
>
> Let it be the first alternative, because there is the absence of that (arising at a particular moment) in connection with the characteristic of the recognition, "this is that," although there is the seizure of the present only in any perception whatsoever.

A further series of arguments is presented by B. N. K. Sharma in accordance with the explanation of Trivikrama Paṇḍita in the *Tattvapradīpa*, in attempted refutation of the Buddhists' refuta-

35. Ibid., p. 62.
36. Ibid., (*Nyāya-sudhā*, p. 394b), p. 62 footnote 45.
37. Ibid., p. 63.
38. Ibid., (*Nyāya-sudhā*, p. 394b), p. 63, footnote 46.

tion of the identity of a thing in recognition in favor of similarity. In reply to the Buddhist, it is noted that the perception of similarity between two momentary things requires an identical perceiver in the two moments.[39] It is to be noted that Śaṅkara argued in this way in his interpretation of the *sūtra* "*anusmṛteśca*" (*Brahma-sūtra* II. 2. 25). But since the perceiver is momentary also, how would he apprehend that two things are similar and that their identity is illusory? Such a recognition would require the annexation of the *saṃskāra* transferred by the first perception to the second perception. But since cause and effect relate to different times how would such an annexation be effected? In this way, the recognition of similarity cannot be established according to Trivikrama Paṇḍita in the *Tattva-pradīpa.*

> pūrvadṛṣṭasya vastuna uttarakāle 'bhāvāddhi tadevedamiti pratyabhijñā bhrāntiḥ kalpyate/ pūrvadraṣṭuruttarakālamabhāve kathaṃ tatsadṛśamidamiti tatsādṛśyapratītiḥ, tadevedamiti bhrāntiśca syāt? apratītau sādṛśyasya, sādṛśyāt pratyabhijñeti duruktaṃ syāt/ na ca kṣaṇabhaṅguraḥ puruṣa prācyapāścātyaikyaviṣayāṃ pratyabhijñāṃ bhrāntiṃ jānīyāt/ kathaṃ ca bhinnakālīnasya kāraṇasya saṃskārārpakatvaṃ kārye syāt? yena, sādṛśyasiddhirāśāsyate? kṣaṇavināśino 'saṃkhyā bhāvāḥ, tatsādṛśyahetavaḥ saṃskārāḥ, tatsaṃtānaśceti garīyasīyaṃ kalpanā/ kiṃ caikasaṃtānasaṃskārāṇāṃ mithaḥ sādṛśyamantareṇa tannimittaṃ vastusādṛśyaṃ notpadyeta[40]

> For, because of the absence of the given thing seen previously, at a subsequent moment, the recognition "This is that," is considered as an illusion. In the case of absence at a later time of the previous seer, how would there be the apprehension of the similarity to that as represented in the statement "This is similar to that" and of the statement "This is that" as illusion? That there is recognition because of similarity, when there is non-apprehension of similarity is improperly claimed. Nor would a person changing in a moment know as illusion the recognition having one sense-object antecedently and subsequently. How would there be an effect having the annexation

39. Ibid., p. 63.
40. Ibid., (*Tattva-pradīpa*, II.2.25), p. 63, footnote 47.

of the *saṃskāras* in connection with the cause related to a different time? In this way, will the proof of similarity be expected? In reference to the entities reckoned as perishing in a moment, the *saṃskāras* having for their causes similarity to that, the series of these—these are extremely grave assumptions. Would there not arise the similarity to a given thing having that (given thing) as efficient cause, without the similarity, alternately relating to the *saṃskāras* of one series?

In connection with Jayatīrtha's argument that the judgement of similarity requires a stable perceiver (*draṣṭṛ*) just as the judgement of the illusoriness of identity, it should be noted that a similar argument has been presented by Śāntarakṣita and Kamalaśīla as has been explained in the section on Later Logicians in the Introductory Background. Śāntarakṣita and Kamalaśīla explain that remembrance is brought about by a seed deposited in the series through the birth of more and more differentiated moments each following the other through an intense experience. It is also to be recalled that for Dignāga, as has been discussed in the section of this work concerned with the Buddhist Logicians, remembrance is explained on the basis of self-intuition. It is also to be noted that recognition for Dignāga, insofar as it represents the application of name, genus, etc. would fall under the authority of inference, not perception, which is free of conceptualization. In this way, in Dignāga's system also, the need for a stable perceiver in order to account for remembrance and recognition is removed. It should also be noted that Śāntarakṣita and Kamalaśīla have in effect replied to Jayatīrtha's argument that recognition through similarity on the basis of the transfer of *saṃskāras* from cause to effect is to be rejected because cause and effect belong to different times.

It has been mentioned in the discussion of Madhva's refutation of the last *sūtra*, "*ākāśe cāviśeṣāt*" (*Brahma-sūtra* II.2.24) that B.N.K. Sharma explains, in accordance with the explanation of Vyāsatīrtha in the *Tātparyacandrikā*, that these two *sūtras* (*Brahma-sūtra* II.2.24-25) are intended to establish the stability (*sthiratva*) of objects and of experiencing Selves. Thus B.N.K. Sharma notes that Śaṅkara has unnecessarily restricted the scope of this *sūtra* to the permanence of the experiencing subject, in order to account for memory. Śaṅkara, according to B.N.K.

Sharma, should have interpreted "*anusmṛti*" as recognition both in the sense of the statement "*sa eva aham*" (I indeed am he) and in the sense of the statement "*tad eva idam*" (this indeed is that).[41] B.N.K. Sharma cites as reason for his criticism the argument of Vyāsatīrtha in the *Tātparyacandrikā*, to the effect that the Momentariness advocated by the Buddhist is inimical to the stablity (*sthiratva*) of matter as well as of souls.

'sa evāham' 'tadevedam' ityātmānātmasādhāraṇyena pratyabhijñānena vipratipannasya sarvasya sthāyitvasya sākṣāt sādhanasambhave (smṛtyanubhavayoḥ sāmānādhikaraṇyānyathānupapattyā) ātmamātrasthāyitvasādhanasyāyogāt/[42]

Because of the impossibility of the argument of stability in connection only with the Self, through the objection otherwise, of the condition relating to the same object pertaining to the *smṛti* and personal experience, when there is the possibility of establishing a truth openly in connection with every false stability by recognition and by the universality of Self and non-Self in the statements" I am he," and "This is that."

41. Ibid., pp. 68-69.
42. Ibid., (*Tātparyacandrikā*, p. 917b), p. 69, footnote 73.

J. *BRAHMA-SŪTRA* II. 2. 26: "*NĀSATO 'DṚṢṬATVĀT*"

1. Śaṅkara's Interpretation

This *sūtra*, "*nāsato 'dṛṣṭatvāt*," (*Brahma-sūtra* II.1.26)[1] may be translated in accordance with Śaṅkara's interpretation, as follows : "Because of non-observation, not from a non-existent." Śaṅkara explains that those who deny permanent causes are forced to assert that entity springs from absence (*abhāvādbhāva*). In his commentary to this *sūtra*, Śaṅkara criticizes the notion of the springing into existence of an entity from absence—a notion which he attributes to the Buddhists. Perhaps Śaṅkara is referring here to the Sautrāntika position "*abhūtvā bhāva utpāda*," the position that birth is existence subsequent to non-existing as has been explained in the section on Momentariness in the Introductory Background. Whether the notion of an entity's springing from absence, which Śaṅkara attributes to the Buddhist realists, however, is equivalent to the Sautrāntika notion "*abhūtvā bhāva utpāda*" (birth as existence subsequent to non-existing) is questionable. Śaṅkara attributes this predicament to those whom he calls Vaināśikas (destructionists), but there is no evidence that he distinguished between the teachings of the Vaibhāṣikas and the teachings of the Sautrāntikas.

> itaścānupapanno vaināśikasamayaḥ yataḥ sthiramanuyāyikāraṇamanabhyupagacchatām abhāvādbhāvotpattirityetadāpadyate; darśayanti cābhāvādbhāvotpattim—'nānupamṛdya prādurbhāvāt' iti[2]
>
> Hence, the destructionist doctrine is not accepted, since by those maintaining a permanent lasting cause the birth of an entity from absence is fallen into. They teach the arising of an entity from absence (as follows:) "Because of manifestation, not without having been destroyed."

---

1. Radhakrishnan, Sarvepalli, The *Brahma Sūtra*, *Brahma-sūtra* II, 2.26, p. 382.
2. Balasubrahmanyam, T.K., *The Works of Śrī Śaṅkarāchārya*, Volume II, commentary to *Brahma-sūtra* II.2.26, pp. 391-392.

The Buddhists also aver, according to Śaṅkara, that if effects could emerge from unchanged causes, then all effects would originate from all causes at once.

> vinaṣṭāddhi kila bījādaṅkura utpadyate, tathā vinaṣṭātkṣīrād-dadhi, mṛtpīṇḍācca ghaṭaḥ; kūṭasthāccetkāraṇātkāryamut-padyeta, aviśeṣātsarvaṃ sarvata utpadyeta; tasmādabhāva-grastebhyo bījādibhyo 'ṅkurādīnāmutpadyamānatvādabhāvād-bhāvotpattiḥ—iti manyante[3]

> From a destroyed seed, indeed, is born a sprout, likewise from destroyed milk curd, from a lump of clay a pot. If an effect should arise from a permanent cause, from non-qualification everything would arise all at once. They think, therefore, that because of sprouts arising from seeds absorbed into absence there is the birth of an entity from an absence.

Śaṅkara argues that if an existent can arise out of absence, then anything can arise out of anything. Śaṅkara employs four arguments to disprove the Sautrāntika position "*abhūtvā bhāva utpāda*," the position that birth is existence subsequent to non-existing. First, he notes that particular effects cannot be linked to particular causes since absence is one and the same.

> nābhāvādbhāva utpadyate; yadyabhāvādbhāva utpadyeta, abhāvatvāviśeṣātkāraṇaviśeṣābhyupagamo 'narthakaḥ syāt[4]

> Not from absence does an entity arise. If an entity should arise from an absence, from the non-qualification of absence the principle of the qualification of the cause would be meaningless.

Secondly, Śaṅkara argues that if there were different types of absences, they would have to be treated as entities, and that absences cannot be causes.

> yadi punarabhāvasyāpi viśeṣo'bhyupagamyeta—utpalādīnā-miva nīlatvādi, tato viśeṣavattvādevābhāvasya bhāvatvam—utpalādivatprasajyeta; nāpyabhāvaḥ kasyacidutpattihetuḥ syāt; abhāvatvādeva, śaśaviṣāṇādivat[5]

3. Ibid., commentary to *Brahma-sūtra* II.2.26, p. 392.
4. Ibid., Volume II, commentary to *Brahma-sūtra* II.2.26, p. 392.
5. Ibid., commentary to *Brahma-sūtra* II.2.26, p. 392.

If the qualification of an absence should be again maintained, because of the blueness, as for instance, of lotuses, then as though from qualification the existence of absence would result as though it (absence) were lotuses, etc. Nor is there an absence which would be the cause of arising, of anything whatsoever, from absence, like the horns of a hare.

Thirdly, Śaṅkara argues that if existence could spring from absence, all effects would be afflicted with absence, in that all effects are seen to have the nature of their causes.

abhāvācca bhāvotpattāvabhāvānvitameva sarvaṃ kāryaṃ syāt; na caivaṃ dṛśyate, sarvasya ca vastunaḥ svena rūpeṇa bhāvātmanaivopalabhyamānatvāt[6]

In the case of the birth of an entity from absence, every effect would be endowed with absence. This is not seen, because of the observation that the Selves of the entities are with their own-formations, in connection with every given thing.

Fourthly, Śaṅkara argues that in those cases where a particular distinction takes place, as in the case of seeds, the effect issues forth from the cause insofar as it is not destroyed, as sprouts from the undestroyed particles of seed.

yeṣvapi bījādiṣu svarūpomardo lakṣyate, teṣvapi nāsāvupamṛdyamānā pūrvāvasthā uttarāvasthāyāḥ kāraṇamabhyupagamyate, anupamṛdyamānānāmevānuyāyināṃ bījādyavayavānāmaṅkurādikāraṇabhāvābhyupagamāt[7]

In the case of those seeds among which appears the destruction of their own-formation the cause of the later condition is not the preceding condition being destroyed because of the principle that an entity is the cause of sprouts, etc. through the parts of seeds which are not destroyed and are stable.

Thus Śaṅkara concludes that since entities are not seen to arise from absences such as the horns of a hare, but from entities, the position "*abhāvādbhāva*" (existence of an entity from absence) is disproved.

---

6. Ibid., Volume II, commentary to *Brahma-sūtra* II.2.26, p. 392.
7. Ibid., commentary to *Brahma-sūtra* II.2.26, p. 393.

tasmādasadbhyaḥ śaśaviṣāṇādibhyaḥ sadutpattyadarśanāt, sadbhyaśca suvarṇādibhyaḥ sadutpattidarśanāt, anupapanno 'yamabhāvādbhāvotpattyabhyupagamaḥ/[8]

Therefore, because the birth of existents from non-existent things—the horns of hares, etc.—is not seen, and because the birth of existents from existents—gold, etc.—is seen, this principle of the birth of entities from absence is inadequate.

It is to be noted, however, that despite their superficial similarity, the notions "*abhāvādbhāva*" (existence from absence) and "*abhūtvā bhāva utpāda*" (birth as existence subsequent to non-existing) are not equivalent, for the notion that birth is (the existence of) an entity subsequent to non-existing as in the case of the doctrine "*abhūtvā bhāva utpāda*" is not equivalent to the statement that an entity (springs from) absence as in the case of the notion "*abhāvādbhāva*" which Śaṅkara attributes to the Buddhists.

2. Rāmānuja's Interpretation

This *sūtra*, "*nāsato 'dṛṣṭatvāt,*" (*Brahma-sūtra* II.2.25) may be translated as follows in accordance with Rāmānuja's interpretation : "Not from a non-entity, because of non-existence." Whereas Śaṅkara in his interpreation of this *sūtra* attempts to refute what seems to be the Sautrāntika notion "*abhūtvā bhāva utpāda*' (birth as the existence subsequent to non-existing), Rāmānuja in his interpretation of this *sūtra* attempts to refute what he considers to be the Sautrāntika position towards perception and inference. The argument that according to the principle of Momentariness, nothing can become an object of cognition because of the non-abiding of the object-entity at the moment of cognition, the Sautrāntika would reply, according to Rāmānuja's presentation of their position, that to be an object of cognition means only to be the cause of the origination of the cognition. The Sautrāntika goes on to explain that the cause of cognition is an object of cognition through the fact that it imparts its own imagery to the cognition. In this sense, the sense-organs are not considered to be the causes of cognition. The Sautrāntika argues

8. Ibid , Volume II, commentary to *Brahma-sūtra* II.2.26, p. 393.

that even a thing that has perished can contribute its own imagery to the cognition.

> evaṃ tāvat vaibhāṣikasautrāntikayorbāhyārthāstitvavādinoḥ sādhāraṇāni dūṣaṇāni uktāni; tatra yaduktaṃ—samprayuktasyārthasya jñānotpattikāle 'navasthitatvānna kasyacidarthasya jñānaviṣayatvaṃ sambhavatīti—tatra sautrāntikaḥ pratyavatiṣṭhate—na jñānakāle 'navasthānamarthasya jñānaviṣayatvahetuḥ; jñānotpattihetutvameva hi jñānaviṣayatvaṃ/na caitāvatā cakṣurādeḥ jñānaviṣayatvaprasaṅgaḥ, svākārasamarpaṇena jñānahetoreva jñānaviṣayatvābhyupagamāt/jñāne svākāraṃ samarpya vinaṣṭo 'pyartho jñānagatena nīlādyākāreṇānumīyate/[9]
>
> So far the rule common to both of those holding the position of the existence of the outer object-entity, namely the Vaibhāṣikas and Sautrāntikas have been mentioned. Then it is said that because of the non-abiding of the conjoined object-entity until the birth of the cognition, the existence of the object of cognition is impossible for any object-entity whatsoever. Then the Sautrāntika replies, "The non-abiding of the object-entity until the time of the cognition is not the cause of being the object of cognition. To be the cause of the birth of cognition is to be the object of cognition. Nor certainly is there the adherence of the existence of the object of cognition to the set beginning with the eye, because of the principle that the cause of cognition is the object of cognition by means of imparting its own imagery. Having imparted its own imagery to the cognition, the object-entity having perished is inferred by the imagery of blue, etc. included within the cognition.

Rāmānuja then portrays the Sautrāntika to be arguing against the adherents of the ideation-store through the objection that past cognitions cannot account for later cognitions, for it cannot be explained how a cognition of yellow can arise in the midst of a series of blue cognitions. Rāmānuja's Sautrāntika declares

9. Viraraghavacharya, Sri Uttamur T., *Brahmasūtra-Śribhāshya* commentary to *Brahma-sūtra* II.2.25, p. 529.

to the Yogācāra that the variety of cognitions can only be explained by the variety of things.

> na ca pūrvapūrvajñānenottarottarajñānākārasiddhiḥ nīlajñānasaṃtatau pītajñānānutpattiprasaṅgāt/ato 'rthakṛtameva jñānavaicitryam-iti[10]
>
> Nor is the imagery of the later cognition authenticated by the birth of the earlier cognition, because of the occurrence of the birth of the cognition of yellow in a series of cognitions of blue. Hence it is said that the variety of cognitions is caused by the object-entity.

To this claim which he attributes to the Sautrāntikas, Rāmānuja replies that the imagery (*ākāra*) of object-entities cannot be the imagery of object-entities that have perished and are non-existent, for when the factual base (*dharmin*) disappears, its attributes (*dharma*) cannot undertake a progression towards another object-entity. Furthermore, Rāmānuja argues, it cannot be averred by the Sautrāntikas that a reflection (*pratibimba*) carries over into the cognition, for reflections are of permanent things not of attributes. Rāmānuja concludes that the variety of cognitions can only be explained on the basis of permanence (*avasthāna*), not on the basis of the doctrine of Momentariness. The Sautrāntika, then, according to Rāmānuja, fails in his attempt to reconcile the momentariness of the object-entity (*artha*) with our experience of a variety of cognitions.

> atrocyate—nāsato 'dṛṣṭatvāt—iti/ yo 'yaṃ jñāne nīlādirākāra upalabhyate, sa vinaṣṭasyāsato 'rthasyākāro bhavituṃ nārhati; kutaḥ ? adṛṣṭatvāt—na khalu dharmiṇi vinaṣṭe taddharmasyārthāntare kramaṇaṃ dṛṣṭam/ pratibimbādikamapi sthirasyaiva bhavati/ tatrāpi na dharmamātrasya/ ato 'rthavaicitryakṛtaṃ jñānavaicitryamarthasya jñānakāle 'vasthānādeva bhavati//25//[11]
>
> It is said, "Not from a non-existent, because of the non-observation." That imagery of blue, etc., which is perceived in cognition cannot be the imagery of a perished, non-existent

10. Ibid., commentary to *Brahma-sūtra* II.2.25, p. 537.
11. Ibid, commentary to *Brahma-sūtra* II.2.25, p. 537.

> object-entity. Why ? Because it has not been observed. Nor in the case of a perished factual base is a passing over of that attribute to another object-entity seen. That concerned with the reflection is also in connection with the permanent not with the mere attribute. Hence, because of the abiding of the object-entity until the time of cognition, the variety of cognitions is caused by the variety of the object-entity.

Rāmānuja here is referring to the concept of *ākāra* about which there was dispute among Buddhists concerning the question whether perception is with imagery (*sākāra*) or without imagery (*nirākāra*). Rāmānuja attributes to the Sautrāntikas the position that the imagery of an object-entity is imparted (*samarpya*) to the cognition, and rejects their supposed position by arguing that the features of a factual base connot be transferred to another object-entity. As has been discussed in the section concerned with the Buddhist Logicians, however, Alex Wayman has delineated the issues involved in the *nirākāra-sākāra* controversy in his article "Reflections on the Study of Buddhist Logic." In that article, Wayman cites a passage from the "Guided Tour" of Tsoṅ-kha-pa which discusses the imagery as a resemblance of the feature when one fastens upon the external entity as a given thing. It seems that there is no question of the "passing over (*kramaṇa*) of the features of the object-entity which is the factual base, because it is introspective perception (*svasaṃvedana-pratyakṣa*) which grasps the imagery as a reflection of an external feature without discursive thought. Furthermore, it is to be noted that Rāmānuja's representation of the Buddhist position as the claim that to be the cause of the birth of cognition (*jñānotpattihetu*) is to be object of cognition (*jñānaviṣaya*) is contradicted by the first verse of Dignāga's *Ālambana-parīkṣā*, as translated by Alex Wayman.

> (1) Although atoms are the cause of sensory representation, they do not appear therein; so its sense-object (*viṣaya*) is not the atoms, like a sense organ (has objects).[12]

---

12. Wayman, Alex, "Yogācāra and the Buddhist Logicians," *Journal of the International Association of Buddhist Studies*, Volume II, Number I, (1979), p. 69.

It appears, then, that Rāmānuja misrepresents the Buddhists when he claims that they declare the cause of the origination of cognition to be the object of cognition, and that they declare the imparting of the features of an object-entity to the cognition. It should also be noted that the object-entity for the Buddhists is not the cause of the cognition, but the inner form of the knowable which appears as though it were external.

yad antar-jñeya-rūpaṃ tu bahirvad avabhāsate so'rthaḥ[13]

(6) The form of the inner knowable, which appears as though it were external, is the object...[14]

3. Madhva's Interpretation

This *sūtra*, "*nāsato 'dṛṣṭatvāt*," (*Brahma-sūtra* II.2.26) may be translated in accordance with Madhva's interpretation, as follows : "Not from a non-existent, because of non-observation." Madhva's commentary proceeds as follows :

śūnyavādamapākaroti // adṛṣṭatvānnāsataḥ kāraṇatvaṃ yujyate //[15]

He refutes Śūnyavāda. Because of non-observation, causation from a non-existent is not enjoined.

In contrast with the approach of Śaṅkara and Rāmānuja, who are concerned in their interpretations of this *sūtra* with the refutations of the Buddhist realists of the Sarvāstivāda and Sautrāntika schools, Madhva and his school devote this *sūtra*, *Brahma-sūtra* II.2.26, and the subsequent four *sūtras* to an attempted refutation of the Mādhyamika school of Buddhism or Śūnyavāda. B. N. K. Sharma explains, in accordance with Jayatīrtha's explanation in the *Nyāya-sudhā*, that in his interpretation of this *sūtra*, Madhva is refuting the notion that the void (*śūnya*) is the cause of the world since it is pure non-being (*asat*). Jayatīrtha argues that in our experience causation takes place from being (*sat*) not non-being (*asat*).

---

13. Hattori, Masaaki, *Dignāga on Perception*, p. 102, foonote 1.61.
14. Wayman, Alex, "Yogācāra and the Buddhist Logicians," p. 69.
15. Bhikācārya Aināpure and Anantācārya Aṣṭaputre, *Brahmasūtras with Ānandatīrtha's Brahmasūtrabhāṣya*, commentary to *Brahma-sūtra* II.2.26, p. 40.

ataḥ sarvaviśeṣavinirmuktatvena gaganakusumasamānāt śūnyājjagato bhāvo janma nopapadyate / sato bhavataḥ kāryasya kvacit asato janirna dṛṣṭā yataḥ[16]

Hence, because of equality to a sky-flower by means of the fact that it is freed from all qualifications, an entity does not arise from the void at birth in connection with the world, since no birth whatsoever is seen from the non-existent in connection with an existent, existing effect.

That causation takes place from being and not from non-being in our experience applies not only to perception, but also to other authorities, like inference which depend on perception, as Jayatīrtha explains in the *Nyāya-sudhā*.

pratyakṣasyānumānopajīvyatvāt / ato 'numānādyabhāvasyānuktāvapi lābhāt, 'adṛṣṭatvāt' ityevoktam.[17]

Because of the dependence (*upajīvyatva*) of inference (*anumāna*) on perception. Hence, because of the acquisition (*lābha*) since nothing is said (*ukti*) leading to the absence (*abhāva*) of inference (*anumāna*) it is said "because it is not observed" (*adṛṣṭatvāt*).

It is to be observed that Madhva and his school are equating the void of the Mādhyamikas with non-being. According to B. N. K. Sharma, however, it is to be noted that the definition of *śūnya* as consisting of the negation of absence and presence (*bhāvābhāvapratiṣedhātmaka*) given in Sthiramati's commentary to the *Madhyāntavibhaṅga* is the same as the definition given of *asat* by Rāghavendra of the Madhva school in the *Tattvaprakāśikā Bhāvadīpa*.[18] According to Sthiramati, *śūnya* has the characteristic of negation of absence and presence.

tatra lakṣaṇaṃ bhāvābhāvapratiṣedhātmakaṃ śūnyatāyāḥ[19]

---

16. Sharma, B.N.K., *The Brahmasūtras and Their Principal Commentaries*, (*Nyāya-sudhā*, p. 401), p. 72, footnote 5.
17. Ibid., (*Nyāya-sudhā*, p. 102b), p. 72, footnote 6.
18. Ibid., pp. 71-72.
19. Ibid., (Sthiramati's commentary on *Madhyānta-vibhaṅgasūtra* C.O.S.24, p. 38), p. 72, footnote 3.

In that case, there is the characteristic composed of the negation of absence and presence in connection with voidness.

According to Rāghavendra in the *Tattvaprakāśikā-Bhāvadīpa*, non-existence is the non-possession of all attributes. For Rāghavendra, non-existence seems to be equated with the void.

śūnyaṃ saditi pareṇāṅgīkāre 'pi sarvadharmarāhitye sati asattvamavarjanīyamityāpādya dūṣaṇamidam iti dhyeyam[20]

It ought to be considered that this vitiating thing is to be obtained : that non-existence is not to be avoided when there is the non-possession of all attributes in the case of agreement by others that the void is true.

Jayatīrtha explicitly equates the void with non-existence.

atra sarvatra śūnyasyāsattvamāpādya duṣaṇābhidhānamiti draṣṭavyam[21]

It is to be seen that having obtained the non-existence in connection with the void here in every case there is the designation of a vitiating thing.

It seems, therefore, that like Śaṅkara and Rāmānuja, Madhva and his school are equating the void of the Mādhyamikas with "*asat*," which although defined as non-possession of all characteristics by Rāghavendra is nevertheless treated by Jayatīrtha in the *Nyāya-sudhā* as the non-existent in that it is opposed to the existent. In this way, Madhva and his school, like Rāmānuja and Śaṅkara, are liable to the charge of over-pervasion (*ati-vyāpti*) by reason of the presence (*bhāva*) and the absence (*abhāva*) which was levelled at the realists (called the *vastu-sat-padārtha-vādin*) by Tsoṅ-kha-pa, discussed in the section of the Introductory Background concerned with the Mādhyamikas. Since the realists do not distinguish the means (*dharmas* devoid of self-existence or *svabhāva*) from the extremes (the absence of the *dharma*, or the presence of the *dharma* with self-existence or *svabhāva*), they are susceptible to the charge of over-pervasion. Madhva, like Śaṅkara and Rāmānuja, represents the Mādhyamikas to be nihilists when they are in fact advocates of "the middle path."

20. Ibid., (*Tattvaprakāśikā-Bhāvadīpa* II.2.27), p. 72, footnote 4.
21. Ibid., (*Nyāya-sudhā*, p. 401), p. 71, footnote 4.

This *sūtra* is interpreted by Śaṅkara and Rāmānuja to be part of the *samudāyādhikaraṇam* directed against the Sautrāntikas. According to Śaṅkara, this *sūtra* criticizes the Bāhyārthavādins (those advocating the position that there is an external object-entity) for maintaining the genesis of an entity from absence.[22] B. N. K. Sharma notes, however, in accordance with the explanation of Vyāsatīrtha in the *Tātparyacandrikā* that Śūnyavāda which supposedly advocates the causality of the non-existent is the target of this *sūtra.*[23]

> avaśyanirasanīyasya śūnyavādinā svayamevāṅgīkṛtasya satkāraṇatvasya nirāsasambhave, vaibhāṣika (sautrāntika) mate 'rthādāpannasya nirāsāyogāt[24]
>
> Because of the impossibility of refutation in connection with that obtained from the object-entity of the Vaibhāṣika opinion, when there is the possibility of refutation in connection with the existence of the cause as non-existence agreed upon by the Śūnyavādins among themselves and which is necessarily to be rejected.

The term "*abhāva*" here is being used by Śaṅkara in the sense of "*asat,*" the non-existent, notes B. N. K. Sharma in accordance with the explanation of Vācaspati who cites the instance of production from a hare's horn to illustrate the causality of "*abhāva.*"[25]

> tatredamucyate—'nāsato 'dṛṣṭatvāt' iti/nābhāvāt kāryotpattiḥ, kasmāt ? adṛṣṭatvāt/nahi śaśaviṣāṇādaṅkurādīnāṃ kāryāṇām-utpattiḥ dṛśyate[26]
>
> There this is said : "Not from a non-existent, because of non-observation." There is not the production of an effect from an absence. Why? Because it is not observed. For the production of effects, such as sprouts, etc. from the horns of a hare is not observed.

22. Ibid., p. 67.
23. Ibid., p. 64.
24. Ibid., (*Tātparyacandrikā*, p. 917), p. 64, footnote 17.
25. Ibid., p. 69.
26. Ibid., (*Bhāmatī*), p. 69, footnote 75.

K. *BRAHMA-SŪTRA* II.2.27:

"*UDĀSĪNĀNĀM API CAIVAṂ SIDDHIḤ*"

1. Śaṅkara's Interpretation

This *sūtra, "udāsīnānām api caivaṃ siddhiḥ,"* (*Brahma-sūtra* II.2.27)[1] may be translated, in accordance with Śaṅkara's interpretation, as follows : "And even in connection with the indifferent, there would be accomplishment."

In his commentary to this *sūtra*, Śaṅkara carries out a *reductio ad absurdum* of the position "*abhāvādbhāva*" (the existence of an entity from absence) which he attributes to the Buddhists. He notes that if this theory were true, then no one would have to exert himself to attain any end, since ends could be attained without means.

> yadi cābhāvādbhāvotpattirabhyupagamyeta, evaṃ satyudāsīnānāmanīhamānānāmapi janānāmabhimatasiddhiḥ syāt, abhāvasya sulabhatvāt/[2]
>
> If the birth of an entity from absence should be maintained, there would be the perfection of the desired for lazy listless people, because of the easy attainment of absence.

On the basis of the position "*abhāvādbhāva,*" (the existence of) of an entity from absence, even final release could be attained without effort, Śaṅkara charges.

> svargāpavargayośca na kaścitkathaṃcitsamīheta/[3]
>
> Either for heaven or for escape, no one whatsoever would desire in any way whatsoever.

As has been noted, however, the notion "*abhāvādbhāva,*" (the existence of) an entity from absence, is not a Buddhist position.

2. Rāmānuja's Interpretation

This *sūtra, "udāsīnānām api caivaṃ siddhiḥ,"* (*Brahma-sūtra*

---

1. Radhakrishnan, Sarvepalli, *The Brahma Sūtra, Brahma-sūtra* II.2.27, p. 383.
2. Balasubrahmanyam, T. K., *The Works of Śrī Śaṅkarācharya,* Volume II, commentary to *Brahma-sūtra* II.2.27, p. 393.
3. Ibid., Volume II, commentary to *Brahma-sūtra* II.2.27, p. 394.

II.2.26) may be translated as follows in accordance with the interpretation of Rāmānuja: "Even in connection with the indifferent, there would be the accomplishment." Like Śaṅkara in his commentary to this *sūtra*, Rāmānuja attacks the Buddhist doctrine of Momentariness by carrying out a *reductio ad absurdum*. Rāmānuja avers that if one affirms the theory of Momentariness associated with the doctrine of causeless destruction (*ahetuka-vināśa*), and according to him, with the production from a non-existent, one would be forced to admit absurd alternatives. If there were momentary disruption, according to Rāmānuja, then nothing would continue—not even clear vision or the motivations and nothing whatsoever would be achieved by effort. In this way, there would be the accomplishment by the indifferent.

> evam kṣaṇikatva-asadutpatti-ahetukavināśādyabhyupagame udāsīnānām-anudyuñjānānāmapi sarvathārthasiddhiḥ syāt/iṣṭaprāptiraniṣṭanivṛttirvā prayatnādibhiḥ sādhyate/kṣaṇapradhvaṃse hi sarveṣāṃ bhāvānām pūrvapūrvaṃ vastu, tadgato vā viśeṣaḥ saṃskārādiko vidyādirvā uttaratra na kaścidanuvartata iti prayatnādisādhyaṃ na kaścidasti/ evam sati ahetukasādhyatvāt sarvasiddhīnām, udāsīnānāmapyaihikāmuṣmikaphalaṃ mokṣaśca siddhyeta/[4]

In the case of the maintenance of (the doctrines of) causeless destruction, production from a non-existent, momentariness, there would be the accomplishment of the aim in connection with the indifferent, and the effortless. By means of effort, etc. there is attained the reach of the desired and the turning back from the undesired. For since when there is momentary disruption in connection with all entities, nothing whatsoever continues—not the previous given thing, not the qualification of the motivations having disappeared through that, not the later (entities as) clear vision—nothing whatsoever is achieved by effort.

If this is the case, because of the accomplishment without

4. Viraraghavacharya, Sri Uttamur T., *Brahmasūtra-Śrībhāshya*, commentary to *Brahma-sūtra* II.2.26, p. 538.

> cause of all the perfections, liberation and the fruit of this and the other world would be accomplished by the indifferent.

It has been noted, however, in the section concerned with the Unconstructed *Dharmas* that for the Sarvāstivādins the unconstructed is the effect which is disjunction having the characteristic of cessation-with-understanding, but that it is no cause in that it is without birth.

> asaṃskṛtaṃ pratisaṃkhyānirodhalakṣaṇaṃ visaṃyogaphalaṃ bhavati/ na ca tasya hetuḥ, ajanyatvāt/[5]

> The effect which is disjunction having the characteristic of cessation-with-understanding is unconstructed. It (the unconstructed) has no cause, on account of birthlessness.

The disjunction which is the effect is attained through the *dharma* of reach (*prāpti*). But it is not a constructed *dharma* which is subject to destruction. Thus as has been noted in the section on the Unconstructed *Dharmas*, although the cessation-with-understanding does not have the path as its cause, yet it is an effect of the path through the medium of the *dharma* of reach. In this way, the path is declared to be meaningful by the Sarvāstivādins, for the reach of the disjunction which is the cessation-with-understanding is not to be attained by the indifferent. Likewise, the cessation-with-understanding for the Sautrāntikas represents the cessation of the traces (*anuśaya*). This cessation is not subject to destruction. Furthermore, as has been noted, the Sautrāntikas explain the continuation of elimination of the defilements by reference to the basis (*āśraya*) which vanishes when the defilements are eliminated through the paths of vision and cultivation.

3. Madhva's Interpretation

This *sūtra*, "*udāsīnānām api caivaṃ siddhiḥ*" (*Brahma-sūtra* II.2.27) may be translated, in accordance with Madhva's interpretation, as follows : "And even in connection with indifferent things, there would thus be manifestation." Madhva's commentary proceeds as follows :

5. Shastri, Swami Dwarikadasa, *Abhidharmakośa, Abhidharmakośa* II. 55, pp. 317-319.

asataḥ kāraṇatve udāsīnānāṃ heyopādeyabuddhivarjitānāṃ khapuṣpādīnāmapi sakāśāt kāryasiddhiḥ// caśabdānna ced-anyatrāpi na syāt// aviśeṣāt//[6]

When there is causation in connection with a non-existent thing, there is the manifestation of the effect from the presence of indifferent things like sky-flowers, etc. avoiding the notions of abandonment or appropriation. If it were objected that it is not so, it would not be otherwise on account of the word "*ca*" because of the non-distinction of the two.

The Śūnyavādin, however, as B. N. K. Sharma notes in accordance with the explanation of Jayatīrtha,[7] may argue that it is possible to establish the non-existent as a cause through a process of indirect reasoning, inference through conjecture (*āśaṅkyānumāna*). The argument is set forth in Śrīharṣa's *Khaṇḍanakhaṇḍakhādya* to the effect that if the existence of a cause is from within, then there is a question where it will obtain its existence prior to its existence as cause, and that if the existence of a cause is from without then there is the objection that the cause has no existence of its own.

antarbhāvitasattvaṃ cetkāraṇaṃ tadasattaḥ/nāntarbhāvit-asattvaṃ cetkāraṇaṃ tadasattaḥ/[8]

If it is said that the cause has existence caused to be from within, it is from a nonexistent. If it is said that the cause has existence not caused to be from within, it is from a non-existent.

Jayatīrtha explains in the *Nyāya-sudhā* that the Śūnyavādin supposedly is arguing that if the cause is shown not to be existent then it must be non-existent.

kāraṇasya hi sattve niṣiddhe 'sata eva janma setsyatīti āśaṅk-

6. Bhikācārya Ainăpure and Anantācārya Aṣṭaputre, *Brahmasūtras with Ānandatīrtha's Brahmasūtrabhāṣya*, commentary to *Brahma-sūtra* II.2.27, p. 40.

7. Sharma, B.N.K., *The Brahmasūtras and Their Principal Commentaries*, p. 72.

8. Ibid., (Śrīharṣa : *Khaṇḍanakhaṇḍakhādya*, p. 55, Chowkhamba Sanskrit Series, 1914), p. 72.

yānumānānāṃ tarkapratighātaṃ vaktuṃ sūtram udāsīnānām iti?[9]

The *sūtra* is (presented) to declare the obstacle of logic through indifferent things in connection with the indirect inference that when the existence of the cause is put aside, the birth from a non-existent is established.

This supposed argument of the Śūnyavādin, however, is rejected in this *sūtra*, according to Madhva's interpretation of it, in that if the void were to possess causality, then such things as sky-flowers would possess causality. The word "*ca*" (and) indicates that there is no distinction between sky-flowers and non-existent in case it is objected that the void—here interpreted as non-existent—has causality.

asataḥ kāraṇatve udāsīnānāṃ heyopādeyabuddhivarjitānāṃ khapuṣpādīnāmapi sakāśāt kāryasiddhiḥ/ caśabdāt na cedanyatrāpi (i.e. bauddhābhimataśūnyādapi) na syāt, aviśeṣāt.[10]

When there is causation in connection with a non-existent thing, there is the manifestation of the effect from the presence of indifferent things like sky-flowers, etc. avoiding the notions of abandonment or appropriation. If it were objected that it is not so, it would not be otherwise on account of the word "*ca*" because of the non-distinction of the two.

Vyāsatīrtha in the *Tātparyacandrikā* explains that since the thesis of causation from the non-existent is to be rejected on the basis of the example of sky-flowers, the opposite thesis, the preferred is established.

kiṃcaivamihābhāve 'pi kāryotpattau bādhakamuktaṃ syāt natvasataḥ kāryotpattau/ tatra ceṣṭāpattiḥ, kvacidanīhamānānāmapi iṣṭasiddheḥ/ tato varamudāsīnaśabdena heyopādeyabuddhyaviṣayakhapuṣpādīn lakṣayitvā, tebhyaḥ kāryasiddhyāpādanaṃ/tena kāraṇatvasya sākṣāt siddheḥ.[11]

---

9. Sharma, B.N.K., *The Brahmasūtras and Their Principal Commentaries*, (*Nyāya-sudhā*, p. 402b), p. 72, footnote 8.

10. Ibid., (commentary to *Brahma-sūtra* II.2.27), p. 70, footnote 78.

11. Ibid., (*Tātparyacandrikā*, p. 918b), p. 70, footnote 79.

Moreover, in the case of the rise of the effect, when there is absence here, it would be called absurd since there is no arising of an effect from a non-existent thing. Hence, there is occurrence of the preferred alternative, because of the proof of the preferred in connection with certain indifferent things. Hence, having indicated sky-flowers, etc. not having for their sense-object the notions of appropriation or avoidance by the inclusive term indifferent, in connection with these there is the establishment of the proof of the effect, because of the proof in the presence of the existence of the cause.

It may be argued by the Śūnyavādin, however, as B. N. K. Sharma notes in accordance with the explanation of Jayatīrtha in the *Nyāya-sudhā* that the position of the void as cause applies to primordial creation but not to subsequent developments in the conventional sphere dependent on time, agent, etc.[12]

nanvādisṛṣṭāveva śūnyāt kāryotpādaṃ brūmo na sarvadā—anyadā tu, kartrādikāraṇagaṇādeva/[13]

It may be objected that we speak of the birth of the effect from the void in the case of the first creation not continuous but as occurring once, because of the multitude of causes and agents.

B.N.K. Sharma notes, however, in accordance with Jayatīrtha's explanation, that Madhva reads the "*dṛṣṭatvāt*" (because of observation) of the preceding *sūtra* without the negative to signify that agent, material cause etc. applies to the primordial creation as well as subsequent stages.[14]

na puruṣaḥ sataḥ ādikālīnasya kāryasya kartānumātavyaḥ / kutaḥ dṛṣṭatvāt / adhunātanānāṃ kāryāṇāṃ puruṣakartṛtvasya niścitatvāt / iti prathamasūtraṃ prakārāntareṇa vyākhyātaṃ bhavati / sūtrabhāṣyayoḥ puruṣagrahaṇamupādānādyupalakṣaṇam /[15]

---

12. Ibid., p. 73.
13. Ibid., (*Nyāya-sudhā*, p. 402), p. 73, 10
14. Ibid., p. 73.
15. Ibid., (*Nyāya-sudhā*, p. 402), p. 73, footnote 11.

> Nor is a person not to be inferred as the agent in connection with the effect in reference to an existent effect related to primordial time. Why ? Because of observation. Because of the existence of certainty in connection with the existence of the person, and agent in relation to present effects. Thus the first *sūtra* is explained by another method. In connection with the two *sūtra*-commentaries, there is the characteristic of person, grasping, and appropriation.

Śaṅkara interprets this *sūtra* to mean that if the existent could spring from the non-existent, even lazy and inactive people could reap benefits without effort. B.N.K. Sharma notes that in the world lazy and inactive people do sometimes reap benefits and that therefore Madhva's interpretation of this *sūtra* is more pertinent.[16]

16. Ibid., p. 70.

L. *BRAHMA-SŪTRA* II.2.28:

"*NĀBHĀVA UPALABDHEḤ*"

1. Śaṅkara's Interpretation

This *sūtra*, "*nābhāva upalabdheḥ*" (*Brahma-sūtra* II.2.28)[1] may be translated as follows in accordance with the interpretation of Śaṅkara : "There is no absence, because of perception." In this *sūtra*, Śaṅkara attempts to repudiate the Vijñānavāda school of Buddhism, to which he attributes the position of ideation only. According to Śaṅkara, the Vijñānavāda position consists in the notion that even if external things should exist, the process of cognition could only take place in connection with the mind.

> tasmiṇśca vijñānavāde buddhyārūḍhena rūpeṇāntastha eva pramāṇaprameyaphalavyavahāraḥ sarva upapadyate, satyapi bāhyārthe buddhyārohamantareṇa pramāṇādivyavahārāna-vatārāt /[2]
>
> In the case of the doctrine of consciousness, the arrangement of authority, sanctionable, authority-as-result occurs situated internally by means of a formation connected with the mind. The reason is the non-appearance of the arrangement of the set beginning with authority without a connection with the mind (even) when there is an external object-entity.

It should be noted that Alex Wayman suggests in his forthcoming book on Buddhist logicians that the terms *pramāṇa*, *prameya*, and *pramāṇa-phala* should be translated respectively as authority (*pramāṇa*), sanctionable (*prameya*), and authority-as-result (*pramāṇa-phala*). In any case, the Vijñānavāda position according to Śaṅkara should be characterized by a denial that the arrangement of authority, sanctionable, and authority-as-result occurs apart from the mind. In the next sentence Śaṅkara attributes to the Vijñānavādins the position that no outward object-entity exists apart from consciousness.

---

1. Radhakrishnan, Sarvepalli, *The Brahma Sūtra*, *Brahma-sūtra* II.2.28, p. 383.
2. Balasubrahmanyam, T. K., *The Works of Śrī Śaṅkarāchārya*, Volume II, commentary to *Brahma-sūtra* II.2.28, p. 394.

kathaṃ punaravagamyate—antastha evāyaṃ sarvavyavahāraḥ na vijñānavyatirikto bāhyo 'rtho 'stīti; tadasambhavādityāha[3]

How again is it admitted that the whole arrangement is internally situated and that there is no outer object-entity separated from consciousness ? It is said : "Because of the impossibility of that."

According to Śaṅkara in his commentary to this *sūtra*, the supposed Buddhist denial of an independent object-entity is supported by five arguments. First, the supposed Vijñānavādin notes that the existence of the object-entity as composed of atoms or an aggregate of atoms is untenable, for we cannot cognize them directly. Furthermore, if object-entities are different from atoms, they can no longer be said to consist of atoms, and if they are identical with atoms they cannot he said to be aggregates.

sa hi bāhyo 'rtho 'bhyupagamyamānaḥ paramāṇavo vā syuḥ, tatsamūhā vā stambhādayaḥ syuḥ; tatra na tāvatparamāṇavaḥ stambhādipratyayaparicchedyā bhavitumarhanti, paramāṇvābhāsajñānānupapatteḥ, nāpi tatsamūhāḥ stambhādayaḥ, teṣāṃ paramāṇubhyo 'nyatvānanyatvābhyāṃ nirūpayitumaśakyatvāt /[4]

For that outer object-entity being maintained should either be atoms or a collection of them, i.e. posts, etc. Thence certainly atoms cannot be defined by the notions of posts, etc. because of objection to knowledge through the appearance of atoms. Nor are there collections of them (atoms), such as posts, etc., because of the impossibility of ascertaining them (posts, etc.) by means of otherness or non-otherness from atoms.

Secondly, the supposed Vijñānavādin argues that the variety of cognitions is explained only by the variety of sense-objects; hence, he argues, the formation of the sense-objects is determined by cognitions so that in effect the existence of external object-entities becomes gratuitous. In other words, the supposed

3. Ibid., Volume II commentary to *Brahma-sūtra* II.2.28, p. 394.
4. Ibid., Volume II, commentary to *Brahma-sūtra* II.2.28, pp. 394-395.

Vijñānavādin argues that since cognitions are observed to have the same formation as their sense-objects, it can therefore be claimed that sense-objects have a formation similar (sārūpya) to their cognitions. If such is the case, according to Śaṅkara's representation of Vijñānavāda, then the hypothesis of the independent object-entity is unnecessary.

> aṅgīkṛte ca tasmin viṣayākārasya jñānenaivāvaruddhatvādapārthikā bāhyārthasadbhāvakalpanā[5]
>
> When this is admitted, the conception of the real being of an outer object-entity is superfluous because of the containment by cognition of the imagery of the sense-object.

Ingalls summarizes this second argument as follows :

> This particularization being, so to speak, completely enclosed in the knowledge, there is no need of our positing anything outside the knowledge. The particularization need actually be only of the cognition, not of the thing.[6]

Thirdly, the supposed Vijñānavādin of Śaṅkara argues on the basis of the simultaneity of the ascertainment of sense-object and perception that the two are identical.

> api ca sahopalambhaniyamādabhedo viṣayavijñānayorāpatati ;[7]
>
> Moreover, because of simultaneous perception there happens the non-difference of sense-object and perception.

The above statement of Śaṅkara reminds us of the following verse of Dharmakīrti's *Pramāṇa-vārttika* quoted in Vācaspati Miśra's *Bhāmatī* and in the *Sarva-darśanasaṃgraha.*

> Sahopalambha-niyamād abhedo nīla-tad-dhiyoḥ/
> Bhedaś ca bhrānti-vijñānair dṛśyetendau ivādvaye//[8]

Ingalls translates this verse as follows :

5. Ibid., Volume II, commentary to *Brahma-sūtra* II.2.28, p. 395.

6. Ingalls, Daniel H. H., "Śaṅkara's Arguments Against the Buddhists," p. 300.

7. Balasubrahmanyam, T.K., *The Works of Śrī Śaṅkarāchārya*, Volume II, commentary to *Brahma-sūtra* II.2.28, p. 300.

8. Ingalls, Daniel H.H., "Śaṅkara's Arguments Against the Buddhists," p. 300.

Blue and the cognition of blue are not different entities, for the one invariably occurs with the other. One should recognize their difference as due to false cognition, like (the double moon seen by an astygmatic) in the moon, which is single.)[9]

According to Ingalls, the argument of the simultaneity of cognition and content, attributed by Śaṅkara to the Vijñānavādins, is derived from this verse of Dharmakīrti.[10] It is interesting to note the similarity in terminology (i.e. the phrase "sahopalambha-niyamādabhedo) as well as the difference in terminology (i.e. Śaṅkara's substitution of "*viṣayavijñānayoḥ*" for Dharmakīrti's "*nīla-tad-dhiyoḥ*), in the statements of Śaṅkara and Dharmakīrti. Fourthly, the supposed Vijñānavādin argues that consciousness is to be considered as similar to a dream in that just as images occur in dreams without the presence of corresponding object-entities, so in waking life they occur without external object-entities.

> svapnādivaccedaṃ draṣṭavyam—yathā hi svapnamāyāmarīcyudakagandharvanagarādipratyayā vinaiva bāhyenārthena grāhyagrāhakākārā bhavanti; evam jāgaritagocarā api stambhādipratyayā bhavitumarhantītyavagamyate, pratyayatvāviśeṣāt/[11]
>
> For as the notions of *gandharvanagara*, mirage-water, magic, dreams, have the imagery of subject and object without an object-entity, so it is admitted that notions of posts, etc. within the waking realm are able to be (without an object-entity), because of the qualification of being notions.

Fifthly, the supposed Vijñānavādin argues that the variety of notions can be explained by the presence of *vāsanā*—habit-energies or propensities—left by previous actions.

> kathaṃ punarasati bāhyārthe pratyayavaicitryamupapadyate? vāsanāvaicitryādityāha[12]

---

9. Ibid., p. 300.
10. Ibid., p. 300
11. Balasubrahmanyam, T. K., *The Works of Śrī Śaṅkarāchārya*, Volume II, commentary to *Brahma-sūtra* II.2.28, p. 395.
12. Ibid., Volume II, commentary to *Brahma-sūtra* II.2.28, p. 395.

Again, how when there is no outer object-entity does the variety of notions occur? The variety of habit-energies is declared.

These are the five arguments which Śaṅkara's supposed Vijñānavādin employs to demonstrate the absence of an external object-entity.

tasmādapyabhāvo bāhyārthasyeti[13]

Therefore, it is said that there is absence of the outer object-entity.

It is interesting to examine Śaṅkara's attempted refutation of Vijñānavāda as a revelation of his own philosophical position. Śaṅkara's position is set forth in the first few sentences of the *siddhāntin's* refutation of the *prima facie* position. Śaṅkara repeats the *sūtra* and develops the theme that there is an external object-entity on the ground of perception itself.

brūmaḥ—nābhāva upalabdheriti/na khalvabhāvo bāhyasyārthasyādhyavasātuṃ śakyate; kasmāt ? upalabdheḥ—upalabhyate hi pratipratyayaṃ bāhyo 'rthaḥ—stambhaḥ kuḍyaṃ ghaṭaḥ paṭa iti; na copalabhyamānasyaivābhāvo bhavitumarhati;[14]

We say, "There is no absence, because of perception." The absence, indeed, of an outer object-entity cannot be ascertained.
Why ? Because of perception.
The outer object-entity is perceived in accordance with the notion as post, wall, pot, or cloth. The absence of a thing being perceived is not possible.

Śaṅkara criticizes Dignāga's notion of "the inner form of the knowable" (*antar-jñeya-rūpa*) as the object-entity (*artha*). Śaṅkara cites a verse from Dignāga's *Ālambanaparīkṣā* which defines the object-entity as the inner form of the knowable which appears as though it were external.

---

13. Ibid., Volume II, commentary to *Brahma-sūtra* II.2.28, p. 396.

14. Balasubrahmanyam, T.K., *The Works of Śrī Śaṅkarāchārya*, Volume II, commentary to *Brahma-sūtra* II.2.28, p. 396.

antarjñeya/rūpaṃ tu bahirvad avabhāsate so'rthaḥ[15]

6. The form of the inner knowable, which appears as though it were external, is the object...[16]

Śaṅkara objects that the very fact that the Vijñānavādins say "as though it were external (*bahirvad*)" betrays their acceptance of the external object-entity.

atašca evameva sarve laukikā upalabhante, yat pratyācakṣāṇā api bāhyamartham evamācakṣate—'yadantarjñeyarūpaṃ tadbahirvadavabhāsate' iti—te 'pi hi sarvalokaprasiddhāṃ bahiravabhāsamānāṃ saṃvidam pratilabhamānāḥ, pratyākhyātukāmāśca bāhyamarthaṃ 'bahirvat' iti vatkāraṃ kurvanti; itarathā hi kasmāt 'bahirvat' iti brūyuḥ[17]

For this reason all worldly ones so perceive, that those contesting explain of the outer object-entity that that which is the inner form of the knowable appears as if external. They are participating in an understanding appearing to be external well-known to the whole world; desirous of refuting the external object-entity they apply the affix "as if" (*Vat*) as in "as if external" (*bahirvat*). Otherwise, how should they say "as if external"?

Śaṅkara here is employing the argument from identity of objective reference against what he considers to be the Vijñānavādins's position on the inner form of the knowable. The argument from identity of objective reference simply states that our perception takes the form "A is B" not the form "A is like B."

na hi kāścidupalabdhimeva stambhaḥ kuḍyaṃ cetyupalabhate; upalabdhiviṣayatvenaiva tu stambhakuḍyādīn sarve laukikā upalabhante[18]

---

15. Hattori, Masaaki, *Dignāga, On Perception,* quoted from *Tattvasaṃgraha-pañjikā*, p. 102, footnote 1.61.

16. Wayman, Alex, "Yogācāra and the Buddhist Logicians," p. 69.

17. Balasubrahmanyam, T. K., *The Works of Śrī Śaṅkarāchārya* Volume II, commentary to *Brahma-sūtra* II.2.28, pp. 396-397.

18. Ibid., Volume II, commentary to *Brahma-sūtra* II.2.28, p. 396.

> No one whatsoever perceives, "This is a perception," but rather, "This is a post or a wall." By way of the existence of the sense-object of perception all worldly ones perceive a post or a wall.

As has been observed in the section of the Introductory Background concerned with the Vijñānavādins and the Logicians, the Mīmāṃsaka Prabhākara had employed the argument from identity of objective reference by noting that human beings declare "*ayaṃ gauḥ*" (this is a cow), not "*idam gotvavad dravyam*" (this material flow is like a cow). Ingalls explains this argument and considers it to be unique to Śaṅkara.

> No one apprehends a post or a wall as an apprehension, but only as an object of apprehension, namely, a post or a wall. This is almost the same as the argument in favor of true identity that I have pointed out above and that I tried to show is original with Śaṅkara. When we recognize something, we recognize that A is B, not that A is like B.[19]

It seems, however, that this argument of the identity of objective reference was previously employed by Prabhākara of the Mīmāṃsā school. In any case, Śaṅkara notes in the *Brahma-sūtra-bhāṣya* that the external object-entity must be admitted on the ground of the nature of perception, for our perception takes the form "this is A" not the form "this is like A." Śaṅkara is thus employing the argument of the identity of objective reference. If the Buddhist should argue, Śaṅkara continues, that the object-entity is said to be "as if" external on the ground of the impossibility of external things, Śaṅkara answers that the possibility or impossibility of things is to be determined on the basis of the *pramāṇa* (authority).

> nanu bāhyasyārthasyāsambhavāt bahirvadavabhāsate ityadhyavasitaṃ; nāyaṃ sādhuradhyavasāyaḥ, yataḥ pramāṇapravṛttyapravṛttipūrvakau sambhavāsambhavāvavadhāryete, na punaḥ sambhavāsambhavapūrvike pramāṇapravṛttyapravṛttī[20]

19. Ingalls, Daniel H. H., "Śaṅkara's Arguments Against the Buddhists," p. 301.

20. Balasubrahmanyam, T.K., *The Works of Śrī Śaṅkarāchārya* Volume II, commentary to *Brahma-sūtra* II.2.28, p. 397.

It may be objected that it is ascertained that it appears as if external because of the impossibility of the outer object-entity. This is not a correct ascertainment, on the grounds that possibility and impossibility are determined having as precedents the emergence and non-emergence of authority; the emergence and non-emergence (of authorities) (do not have) possibility and impossibility as precedents.

In opposition to the supposed Vijñānavādin's argument that since sense-objects correspond to our cognitions of them, therefore the hypothetical sense-object is unnecessary, Śaṅkara answers that if there were no sense-objects there would be no cognition of them.

na ca jñānasya viṣayasārūpyādviṣayanāśo bhavati, asati viṣaye viṣayasārūpyānupapatteḥ, bahirupalabdheśca viṣayasya;[21]

Nor is there destruction of the sense-object because of the similar formation of the sense-object to the cognition because of objection to a formation similar to a sense-object when there is no sense-object, because of the perception of the sense-object as eternal.

Furthermore, in opposition to the supposed Vijñānavādin's argument of the simultaneity of notion and sense-object—a doctrine which states for example that since blue and the notion of blue occur simultaneously, therefore they are identical—Śaṅkara avers that the simultaneous perception of notion and sense-object proves only that the sense-object constitutes the means to the notion. The term "*sahopalambhaniyama*" indicates simultaneity as well as concomitance.

ata eva sahopalambhaniyamo 'pi pratyayaviṣayayorupāyopeyabhāvahetukaḥ, na abhedahetukaḥ—ityabhyupagantavyam[22]

Therefore, the principle of simultaneous perception is caused by the relationship of sense-object and notion as means and

21. Ibid., Volume II, commentary to *Brahma-sūtra* II.2.28, p. 397.
22. Ibid., Volume II, commentary to *Brahma-sūtra* II.2.28, p. 397.

end respectively and is not caused by non-difference of sense-object and notion—thus it is to be maintained.

The argument from simultaneity of notion and sense-object has been mentioned in the section of the Introductory Background concerned with the Buddhist Logicians. The argument refers to a verse of Dharmakīrti's *Pramāṇavārttika* quoted in Vācaspati Miśra's *Bhāmatī* and in the *Sarva-darśana-saṃgraha*—a verse cited above. Śaṅkara goes on to argue that there is a distinction between the sense-object and its notion on the basis of the distinction between qualification (*viśeṣaṇa*) and qualified (*viśeṣya*). One cognizes a pot and then a cloth. The difference does not reside in the cognition which is qualified, but in the qualification which in this case are the jar and the cloth.

> api ca ghaṭajñānam paṭajñānamiti viśeṣaṇayoreva ghaṭapaṭayorbhedaḥ, na viśeṣyasya jñānasya[23]
>
> Moreover, as to the cognition of the pot, and the cognition of the cloth, the distinction resides in the qualifications of jar and cloth, not in the cognition (which is the) qualified.

According to Śaṅkara, the difference of the qualified from the two qualifications is attested by the presence of the two qualifications, and the difference of the two qualifications from the qualified is attested by the presence of the qualified. Therefore, according to Śaṅkara, the object-entity and its cognition are different.

> yathā śuklo gauḥ kṛṣṇo gauriti śauklyakārṣṇyayoreva bhedaḥ, na gotvasya; dvābhyāṃ ca bheda ekasya siddho bhavati; ekasmācca dvayoḥ; tasmādarthajñānayorbhedaḥ;[24]
>
> Just as in connection with a white cow and a black cow, the difference is of the whiteness and blackness, not of the cowness. From the two, the difference of the one is proved; from the one, the (difference) of the two (is proved). Therefore there is a difference of object-entity and cognition.

23. Ibid., Volume II, commentary to *Brahma-sūtra* II.2.28, p. 397.
24. Ibid., Volume II, commentary to *Brahma-sūtra* II.2.28, p. 398.

Śaṅkara here is saying that the reality of the external object-entity is attested through the fact that cognition itself remains constant; the difference in cognition resides only in the variety of object-entities which qualify cognition. A further argument is then urged by Śaṅkara—the key argument of the witness, as Śaṅkara begins his attempted refutation of the Vijñānavāda concept of *svasaṃvedana* (introspection). Śaṅkara explains that two perceptions due to their momentariness, cannot apprehend each other or be apprehended by each other.

> api ca dvayorvijñānayoḥ pūrvottarakālayoḥ svasaṃvedanenaiva upakṣīṇayoḥ itaretaragrāhyagrāhakatvānupapattiḥ[25]
>
> There is objection to the mutual subject-object (relationship) of two perceptions, having two different times, which are destroyed upon introspection (*svasaṃvedana*).

Consequently for Śaṅkara many Buddhist doctrines involving difference or distinction between perceptions (*vijñāna*), such as the distinction of individuals and classes, cannot be upheld for there is no permanent subject to do the comparison. As has been noted in the section on Vijñānavāda and the Logicians, Wayman explains in his review article on Chatterjee's book *The Yogācāra Idealism,* however, that Vijñānavāda particularly in the *Madhyānta-vibhaṅga*' conceives reality in terms of a dualistic cosmology which rivals that of Sāṅkhya. It replaces *puruṣa* with the "imagination of unreality" (*abhūtaparikalpa*) and *prakṛti* with voidness (*śūnyatā*).

Śaṅkara then attacks the Vijñānavāda concept of *svasaṃvedana* (introspection) by which according to Śaṅkara, each cognition is of an essentially self-illuminating nature like a lamp. For Śaṅkara, the presence of a perception indicates the presence of an external object-entity. He accuses the Vijñānavādins of denying the external object-entity on the grounds that it is not of a luminous nature like a lamp, as is the perception.

> vijñānamanubhūyata iti cet, bāhyo 'pyartho 'nubhūyata eveti yuktamabhyupagantum; atha vijñānaṃ prakāśātmakatvātpradīpavatsvayamevānubhūyate, na tathā bāhyo 'pyartha

25. Ibid., Volume II, commentary to *Brahma-sūtra* II.2.28, p. 398.

iti cet—atyantaviruddhāṃ svātmani kriyāmabhyupagacchasi—agnirātmānaṃ dahatītivat;[26]

If it is objected that perception is experienced, then it is proper to maintain thus that even the outer object-entity is experienced. If it is objected that perception is experienced in itself like a lamp because it consists of light, and that accordingly an outer object-entity is not (so experienced), then you maintain an excessively contradictory activity in itself, like a fire that burns itself.

Śaṅkara goes on to say that a perception apart from an object-entity cannot be experienced, for a process residing in itself is inconceivable.

na cārthavyatiriktamapi vijñānaṃ svayamevānubhūyate, svātmani kriyāvirodhādeva/[27]

Perception is not experienced for itself apart from the object-entity, because of the contradictoriness of activity in itself.

Śaṅkara then goes on to charge his supposed Vijñānavādin of adherence to the position that perceptions apprehend themselves and have no need to be apprehended by a witness apart from themselves. The supposed Vijñānavādin upholds his position through two arguments: first, the danger of infinite regression in that an apprehending agent would again in turn require an apprehending agent; secondly, the notion that perceptions, like lamps, have light as their nature.

nanu vijñānasya svarūpavyatiriktagrāhyatve, tadapyanyena grāhyaṃ tadapyanyena—ityanavasthā prāpnoti; api ca pradīpavadavabhāsātmakatvājjñānasya jñānāntaraṃ kalpayataḥ samatvādavabhāsyāvabhāsakabhāvānupapatteḥ kalpanānarthakyamiti tadubhayamapyasat[28]

If it is objected that in connection with perception when it is apprehended separate from its own formation, that (perception) is to be apprehended by another, and that

26. Ibid., Volume II, commentary to *Brahma-sūtra* II.2.28, p. 398.
27. Ibid., Volume II, commentary to *Brahma-sūtra* II.2.28, p. 399.
28. Ibid., Volume II, commentary to *Brahma-sūtra* II.2.28, p. 399.

> (perception) by another, an infinite regression would obtain. Moreover, for one assuming in connection with cognition another cognition because it is composed of light like a lamp, (it may be objected that) the assumption is meaningless because of objection to the relationship of illumination and illuminated on account of equality. That is false both ways.

Of the first argument, Śaṅkara, explains that the witnessing Self is of the nature of the knowing subject and consequently it has no need of being apprehended. In this way, infinite regression is avoided. Furthermore, Śaṅkara is introducing what for Ingalls is Śaṅkara's "heaviest artillery"—the argument that there must be something beyond cognition, namely a cognizer.

> ...tadubhayamasat vijñānagrahaṇamātra eva vijñānasākṣiṇo grahaṇākāṅkṣānutpādādanavasthāśaṅkānupapatteḥ, sākṣipratyayayośca svabhāvavaiṣamyādupalabdhrūpalabhyabhāvopapatteḥ.[29]

> That is false both ways: because there is objection to the fear of infinite regression, on account of the non-birth of the need for the apprehension of the witness to the perception in the case of the mere apprehension of the perception; because it is a demonstrated conclusion that there is a perceiver and perceived; on account of the diversity of the self-existence of the witness and the notion.

Then Śaṅkara states his major theme—the self-evident nature of the witnessing Self.

> svayaṃsiddhasya ca sākṣiṇo 'pratyākhyeyatvāt.[30]

> Because of the non-refutation of the self-proved witness.

Then Śaṅkara, after having demonstrated that a conscious agent involves no infinite regression, proceeds to affirm the necessity of a conscious agent in refutation of the second argument of the supposed Vijñānavādin which states that perceptions are self-luminous like lamps. Śaṅkara continues the ima-

---

29. Ibid., Volume II, commentary to *Brahma-sūtra* II.2.28, p. 399.
30. Ibid., commentary to *Brahma-sūtra* II.2.28, p. 399.

gery of the lamp and asserts that without a conscious agent the perceptions can be said to manifest themselves no better than a thousand lamps in impenetrable rock.

kiṃcānyat—pradīpavadvijñānamavabhāsakāntaranirapekṣaṃ svayameva prathate—iti bruvatā apramāṇagamyaṃ vijñānamanavagantṛkamityuktaṃ syāt—śilāghanamadhyasthapradīpasahasraprathanavat[31]

By one saying that perception manifests itself without reference to another illuminating agent like a lamp, it is said that perception is intelligible without an authority, and is without a knowing agent, like the manifestation of a thousand lamps situated in the middle of a dense rock.

Śaṅkara's supposed Vijñānavādin then argues that for both the Vedāntin and the Vijñānavādin the perception implies the formation of an experience in connection with perception. Śaṅkara refutes this charge by noting that for the Vedāntin an ulterior conscious agent is needed for the perception to be manifest.

bāḍhamevam—anubhavarūpatvāttu vijñānasyeṣṭo naḥ pakṣastvayā anujñāyata iti cet, na; anyasyāvagantuścakṣuḥsādhanasya pradīpādiprathanadarśanāt; ato vijñānasyāpyavabhāsyatvāviśeṣātsatyevānyasminnavagantari prathanaṃ pradīpavadityavagamyate[32]

If it is objected that it is admitted by you that because of the formation of experience in connection with perception, our position is agreeable (to you), it is replied that it is not so because of the observation firstly, that lamps etc. (are) in association with the eye as means, (and that they are in association with) another knowing agent. Hence it is understood that because of the qualification that the perception is illuminated, there is the manifestation only when there is a knowing agent, like a lamp.

Śaṅkara's supposed Vijñānavādin then argues that the Vedāntin

---

31. Ibid., Volume II, commentary to *Brahma-sūtra* II.2.28, p. 399.
32. Ibid., Volume II, commentary to *Brahma-sūtra* II.2.28, p. 399.

when he affirms a self-evident Self is actually affirming the Vijñānavāda tenet of the self-manifested perception. Śaṅkara then refutes this charge by explaining that the Self of the Vedāntins is one and permanent, while the perceptions of the Buddhist are momentary and fleeting.

> sākṣiṇo 'vagantuḥ svayaṃsiddhatāmupakṣipatā, svayaṃ prathate vijñānamityeṣa eva mama pakṣastvayā vācoyuktyantareṇāśrita iti cet, na; vijñānasyotpattipradhvaṃsānekatvādiviśeṣavattvābhyupagamāt;[33]

> If it is objected by you advancing the self-provedness of the knowing agent and the witness, that the perception manifests itself and that this doctrine of ours is resorted to by another connection of words, it is replied that it is not so, because of the principle that perception is possessed of the qualifications of birth, destruction, and multiplicity.

Thus according to Śaṅkara, perceptions require a separate agent to become manifest.

> ataḥ pradīpavadvijñānasyāpi vyatiriktāvagamyatvamasmābhiḥ prasādhitam[34]

> Hence that there is a separate knowing agent for the perception, as in the case of the lamp, is established by us.

It is evident that Śaṅkara in this section of his commentary on *Brahma-sūtra* II.2.28 is affirming the witness by attempting to refute positions that seem to oppose it. The "Self" of the Vijñānavādins, however, has been discussed in the section concerned with Vijñānavāda and the Buddhist Logicians, where the dualistic cosmology of imagination of unreality (*abhūta-parikalpa*) and voidness (*śūnyatā*) as explained by Wayman is discussed. Śaṅkara also cites the supposed Vijñānavādin's argument of infinite regression which he assumes is directed against the notion of the Self. The supposed Vijñānavādin argues that if a perception were to be apprehended by another perception there would ensure an infinite regression.

---

33. Ibid., Volume II, commentary to *Brahma-sūtra* II.2.28, pp. 399-400.
34. Ibid., commentary to *Brahma-sūtra* II.2.28, p. 400.

nanu vijñānasya svarūpavyatiriktagrāhyatve, tadapyanyena grāhyaṃ tadapyanyena—ityanavasthā prāpnoti[35]

It may be objected that in connection with perception, that when it is apprehended separate from its own formation that (perception) is to be apprehended by another, and that by another, an infinite regression would obtain.

Śaṅkara replies to his supposed Vijñānavādin that the witnessing Self and the notion are of two different natures related to each other as perceiver and perceived, and that consequently there results no infinite regression.

sākṣipratyayayośca svabhāvavaiṣamyādupalabdhrūpalabhyabhāvopapatteḥ[36]

Because it is a demonstrated conclusion that there is a perceiver and perceived on account of the diversity of self-existence of witness and notion.

As has been noted in the section on the Buddhist Logicians, however, according to Dignāga in the *Pramāṇa-samuccaya*, it is only when the subject (*grāhaka*), and the object (*grāhya*), and self-intuition (*svaṣaṃvitti*) are seen as separate that the notion of self-intuition of perception becomes inconceivable. Dharmakīrti, as has been noted, also sets forth as mistaken the three-fold division of the indivisible *vijñāna*.

It has been noted in the section of the Introductory Background concerned with Vijñānavāda and the Logicians, that there is in fact no denial of the independent reality of the external object in the works of the Vijñānavādins or the Logicians. Śaṅkara represents the Vijñānavāda position as an assertion that the arrangement of authority, sanctionable, and authority-as-result occurs internally by means of a formation connected with the mind. In other words, Śaṅkara represents the Vijñānavāda position as an assertion that the object-entity is not required. In fact, Asaṅga has stated in his commentary to the *Paramārtha-gāthā*, however, that perception arises from a sense-basis and that the sense-object is not needed. Śaṅkara

35. Ibid, Volume II, commentary to *Brahma-sūtra* II.2.28, p. 399.
36. Ibid., Volume II, commentary to *Brahma-sūtra* II.2.28, p. 399.

argues that perception requires an object external to it. It is to be observed, however, that Vasubandhu spoke in terms of the doctrine of Representation-Only (*Vijñapti-mātratā*) which emphasizes the mind's ability to create its own world, and entitled his masterpiece the *Vijñapti-mātratā-siddhi*.

2. Rāmānuja's Interpretation

This *sūtra*, "*nābhāva upalabdheḥ*," (*Brahma-sūtra* II.2.27) may be translated, in accordance with Rāmānuja's interpretation, as follows : "There is no absence, because of perception." In his commentary to this *sūtra*, Rāmānuja, like Śaṅkara, attacks positions which he considers to be typical of the Vijñānavādins. Rāmānuja devotes this and two other *sūtras* to an attempted refutation of the Vijñānavādins. He attacks the Vijñānavādins for upholding, according to his representation, the notion that there can be knowledge (*jñāna*) apart (*vi-*) from the object-entity (*artha*). In other words, he attempts to refute them by arguing, like Śaṅkara, that the nature of cognition points towards an object-entity apart from that cognition, as well as towards a knowing subject (*jñātṛ*).

> jñānātiriktasyārthasyābhāvo vaktuṃ na śakyate / kutaḥ ? upalabdheḥ / jñāturātmano 'rthaviśeṣavyavahārayogyatāpādanarūpeṇa jñānasyopalabdheḥ / evame(mi)va hi sarve laukikāḥ pratiyanti—'ghaṭamahaṃ jānāmi' iti /[37]
>
> The absence of an object-entity separate from knowledge, cannot be claimed. Why ? Because of perception, that is to say, because of the perception in connection with knowledge in the form of producing the capacity for the practice of distinct things and of the knowing Self. For all worldly ones acknowledge thus, "I cognize a pot."

In his attempt to refute the Vijñānavādins, however, Rāmānuja also attacks those Vedāntins (presumably of Śaṅkara's school) whom he calls "crypto"-Buddhists (*pracchanna-bauddha*) for their supposed position that the absolute (*paramārtha*)

37. Viraraghavacharya,, Sri Uttamur T., *Brahmasūtra-Śrībhāshya*, commentary to *Brahma-sūtra* II.2.27, p. 539.

is mere knowledge (*jñānamātra*)—a position formulated according to Rāmānuja on the basis of knowledge in a form having both action (*karma*) and agent (*kartṛ*), a subject and an object.

evaṃrūpeṇa sakarmakeṇa sakartṛkeṇa jñānadhātvarthena sarvalokasākṣikamaparokṣamavabhāsamānenaiva, 'jñānamātrameva paramārthaḥ' iti sādhayantaḥ sarvalokopahāsopakaraṇaṃ bhavantīti vedavādacchadmapracchannabauddhanirākaraṇe nipuṇataraṃ prapañcitam /[38]

That, establishing knowledge only as the absolute in such a form by means of the type of knowledge which has action and agent, and which is appearing as perceptible to all the witnesses in the world, they are a matter of laughter for the world, is developed next in the refutation of the Buddhist hidden by a cover of belief in the Veda.

Rāmānuja then attempts to refute the Buddhist principle of the simultaneous perception, for instance, of blue and the thought of it by arguing first that the notion of association implies distinct things, and secondly, that cognition, which has the nature of bringing about the capacity for the practice (*vyavahāra*), cannot be said to be non-identical with the thought.

yattu, "sahopalambhaniyamādabhedo nīlataddhiyoḥ" iti—tat svavacanaviruddhaṃ; sāhityasyārthabhedahetukatvāt / tadarthavyavahāra-yogyataikasvarūpasya jñānasya tena sahopalambhaniyamaḥ tasmādavailakṣaṇyasādhanamiti ca hāsyam/[39]

The statement, "There is a non-difference of blue and the thought of blue, because of the principle of simultaneous perception, is self-contradictory, because of the effecting of difference of object-entity by association. That in connection with cognition having one nature through capacity for the practice in reference to that object-entity, there is the principle of simultaneous perception with that (the object-entity), and that therefore there is proof of non-difference is laughable.

Saṅkara in his attempted refutation of the principle of simul-

38. Ibid., commentary to *Brahma-sūtra* II.2.27, p. 539.
39. Ibid., commentary to *Brahma-sūtra* II.2.27, p. 539.

taneous occurrence argues that simultaneous occurrence only indicates that the sense-object is the means of the cognition.

ata eva sahopalambhaniyamo 'pi pratyaya-viṣayayorupāyopeyabhāvahetuko nābhedahetuka ityabhyupagantavyam /[40]

Therefore, it is to be maintained that the principle of simultaneous perception is caused by the relationship of notion and sense-object as ends and means respectively, and it is not caused by their non-difference.

Rāmānuja then attempts to dismiss the Vijñānavāda notion of *vāsanā* (habit-energy) on the basis that it is in contradiction with the doctrine of Momentariness. Rāmānuja argues, like Śaṅkara, that the former moment which has disappeared cannot be the cause of cognition at a later moment.

niranvayavināśinām jñānānāmanuvartamānasthirākāravirahāt vāsanā ca durupapādā / vinaṣṭena pūrvajñānenānutpannamuttarajñānam katham vāsyate ? ato jñānavaicitryamapyarthavaicitryakṛtameva/[41]

Because of the abandonment of the accompanying permanent aspect by the cognitions having unconnected destruction, the habit-energies are not established. How can the later unarisen cognition be produced by the previous cognition having been destroyed? Hence the variety of cognitions is effected by the variety of object-entities.

Rāmānuja goes on to explain that the special characteristics of the cognition depend on the relationship with this and that thing. In this way, Rāmānuja introduces his own position towards the concept of knowledge : that knowledge is related to the object-entity by means of conjunction for it is itself a material flow and yet is at the same time an attribute of the self. He compares knowledge to the light of a lamp in that light is both a material flow and an attribute of the lamp.

tattadarthavyavahārayogyatāpādanarūpatayā sākṣātpratīyamānasya jñānasya tattadarthasambandhāyattam tattadasādhāra-

40. Bākre, Mahādeva Śāstrī, ed., *The Brahmasūtra-Shānkarbhāshyam*, commentary to *Brahma-sūtra* II.2.28, p. 472.

41. Viraraghavacharya, Sri Uttamur T., *Brahmasūtra-Śrībhāshya*, commentary to *Brahma-sūtra* II.2.27, p. 540.

ṇyaṃ/sambandhaśca saṃyogalakṣaṇaḥ/jñānamapi hi dravyameva/prabhādravyasya pradīpaguṇabhūtasyeva, jñānasyāpyātmaguṇabhūtasya dravyatvamaviruddhamityuktam/ato na bāhyārthābhāvaḥ/27/[42]

In connection with the cognition being recognized clearly by the nature of producing the capability for the practice in reference to that object-entity the special property of this and that depends on the relation to this and that (object-entity). The relation is conjunction. Knowledge is a material flow. As in connection with the material flow of light which is the attribute of the lamp, so in connection with the knowledge which is the attribute of the Self, it is said that its being a material flow is not contradicted. Hence, there is no absence of the outer object-entity.

3. Madhva's Interpretation

This *sūtra*, "*nābhāva upalabdheḥ*." (*Brahma-sūtra* II.2.28) may be translated, in accordance with Madhva's interpretation, as follows : "There is no absence, because of observation." Madhva's commentary proceeds as follows:

na ca jagadeva śūnyamiti vācyaṃ//dṛṣṭatvāt//[43]

That the world is not void is declared, because of observation.

Unlike Śaṅkara and Rāmānuja, Madhva interprets this aphorism to be directed against the Śūnyavādins. B.N.K. Sharma notes in accordance with the explanation of Jayatīrtha in the *Tattvaprakāśikā*[44] that at this point the Śūnyavādin argues further that there is no difficulty in conceiving the non-existent to be cause when it is misapprehended because of convention as the phenomenal world which is only an appearance (*vivarta*) of Śūnya, as is the case when we perceive silver in our illusions.

---

42. Ibid., commentary to *Brahma-sūtra* II.2.27, p. 540.

43. Bhikācārya Aināpure and Anantācārya Aṣṭaputre, *Brahmasūtras with Ānandatīrtha's Brahmasūtrabhāṣya*, commentary to *Brahma-sūtra* II.2.28, p. 41.

44. Sharma, B.N.K., *The Brahmasūtras and Their Principal Commentaries*, p. 73.

bhavedetaddūṣaṇaṃ yadi śūnyatātvāt paramārthato mṛdo ghaṭa iva jagadupapadyate/na caitadasti/saṃvṛtivaśāt śūnyameva jagadākāreṇa vivartata ityabhyupagamāt/nahi śūnye jagadadhyastamityatroktadoṣaprasaraḥ/asata eva rajatākāreṇa pratīyamānatvādityāśaṅkāṃ pariharat sūtraṃ paṭhitvā vyācaṣṭe—nābhāva upalabdheriti/[45]

If this vitiating thing should be, then the world would arise like a clay pot in reality from voidness. It is not so, because of the principle that the void appears from the will of the conventional under the aspect of the world. For, in the case of the void, there is the appearance of fault said here, that the world is superimposed. Refuting the suspicion that there is the admission of the non-existent in the aspect of silver, having read the *sūtra*, he interprets as follows : "There is no absence, because of perception."

It is to be noted, however, that the void of the Mādhyamikas is not equivalent to the non-existent and that to characterize the void as such is to be liable to the charge of over-pervasion as has been discussed in the section on Mādhyamikas. B.N.K. Sharma explains, in connection with Madhva's interpretation of this *sūtra*, that Madhva and his school reply to these supposed objections of the Śūnyavādin by noting that our perception of the reality of the world cannot be treated as illusion like the silver in the shell unless it has been supplanted by another cognition.[46] If our perception is to be considered illusory on the basis that it is a cognition, then it should be possible to recognize silver in the shell as an illusion even at the very outset of falling into such an error. That this *sūtra* is intended to refute the notion of the falsity of external objects is noted by B.N.K. Sharma in accordance with the commentaries of the Madhva school,[47] for if the author of the *sūtra* had held the world to be false or indescribable he could not have contrasted the experience of it in the waking state with the dream state as is done in the next *sūtra*.[48] If the difference between waking state and dream

45. Ibid., (*Tattvaprakāśikā* II.2.28), p. 73, footnote 12.
46. Ibid., pp. 73-74.
47. Ibid., p. 79.
48. Ibid., p. 79.

state mentioned by the author of the *sūtra* is based, as Śaṅkara holds, on the notion that the perception of the waking state cannot be supplanted in the practical situation, then the position of the Vijñānavādin cannot be refuted by Śaṅkara, notes B.N.K. Sharma, for the Vijñānavādin also specifies two truths—absolute (*parinispanna*) and dependent (*paratantra*).[49] It seems to be the case, therefore, that in the interpretation of this *sūtra*, Madhva and his school are attacking the unqualified non-dualism (*nirviśeṣādvaita*) of Śaṅkara and his school as well as the Śūnyavādins. B.N.K. Sharma, in accordance with the explanation of Vyāsatīrtha in the *Tātparyacandrikā*[50] notes that for both Śaṅkara and Vijñānavāda, consciousness (*vijñāna*) appears as external objects.

> vijñānavivarta iti mate 'dhiṣṭhānabhūtajñānasya mithyābhūtabāhyārthātmanā dhīḥ tattvato bāhyārthābhāvaśca dvayoḥ sama eva[51]
>
> By the nature of the outer object-entity composed of the false in connection with the cognition composed of the support of the opinion "Consciousness appears," the thought of the two that there is absence of the outer object-entity in reality. is alike.

B. N. K. Sharma also notes, in accordance with the explanation of Vyāsatīrtha in the *Tātparyacandrikā*, that the advocate of Śaṅkara's school may object that for the Vijñānavādin object-entities are non-existent whereas for Śaṅkara they are devoid of the characteristic of the existent and the non-existent.

The advocate of the Madhva school would reply that whether object-entities are considered as non-existent or devoid of the existent and non-existent they are perceived as existent and that there is no non-existence apart from absence of existence (*sattva*).[52] In this way, the Madhva school attacks the Śaṅkarite notion of "*sadasadvilakṣaṇa*" (devoid of the existent and the non-existent).

---

49. Ibid., p. 79.
50. Ibid., p. 79.
51. Ibid., (*Tātparyacandrikā*, p. 920), p. 79, footnote 15.
52. Ibid., p. 79.

nanu tasyārtho 'tyantāsan/ mama tu, sadasadvilakṣaṇa iti cenna/ tathāpi svapnavaidharmyoktyayogāt/ sattvānubhava-virodhasyobhayatra sāmyāt/ sattvābhāvādanyasyāsattvasyā-bhāvācca[53]

It may be objected in connection with that that the object-entity is ultimately non-existent. If it is objected that according to you, there is the characteristic of neither existence nor non-existence, we reply that it is not so, because therefore of the impossibility of the claim of divergence from the dream-state, because of the similarity in either case of the contradiction of awareness of the existent, because of the absence of non-existence other than in connection with the absence of existence.

Jayatīrtha explains that both the schools of Śaṅkara and the Vijñānavādins speak of conventional existence which is different from the non-existent and of efficiency.

aparokṣadhīviṣayatvārthakriyākāritvādirūpasya saṃvṛtikasatt-varūpasya ca sadvailakṣaṇyasya paramate 'pi bhāvāt/[54]

Because of the presence in connection with the opinion of the other of the divergence from non-existence of the form of conventional existence, in the form of the existence of the not imperceptible, the sense-object, of thought, of efficiency, etc.

Both the schools of Śaṅkara and Vijñānavāda deny absolute existence to the conventional sphere according to Vyāsatīrtha.

paramārthasattvādirūpasya ca tasya tvanmate 'pyabhāvāt[55]

Because of the absence in connection with unbelief in its possession of the form of absolute reality.

In this way, the Madhva school attacks Śaṅkara's unqualified non-dualism and Śaṅkara's attempted refutation of the Vijñāna-vādins. By equating Śaṅkara's system with the school he is

---

53. Ibid., (*Tātparyacandrikā*, p. 920), p. 79, footnote 16.
54. Ibid., (*Tātparyacandrikā*, p. 920), p. 80, footnote 17.
55. Ibid., (*Tātparyacandrikā*, p. 920), p. 80, footnote 18.

attempting to refute, the school attacks Śaṅkara. Thus the Madhva school in its interpretation of this *sūtra "nābhāva upalabdheḥ"* (*Brahma-sūtra* II.2.28), and in its interpretation of the next *sūtra. "vaidharmyācca na svapnādivat,"* attacks both Śaṅkara and Śūnyavāda. It is to be recalled, however, that Madhva equates the void with the non-existent, and is thus liable to the charge of over-pervasion.

M. *BRAHMA-SŪTRA* II.2.29:

"*VAIDHARMYĀC CA NA SVAPNĀDIVAT*"

1. Śaṅkara's Interpretation

This *sūtra*, "*vaidharmyāc ca na svapnādivat*," (*Brahma-sūtra* II. 2.29)[1] may be translated, in accordance with Śaṅkara's interpretation, as follows : "And because of divergence, it is not like a dream." In his commentary to this *sūtra*, Śaṅkara attributes to the Vijñānavādins the position that knowledge (*vijñāna*) is separate (*vi-*) from the object. According to Śaṅkara, the Vijñānavādin argues that just as in the dream-state, there are ideas but no objects to correspond to them, so in the waking state there are ideas but no objects to correspond to them.

> yaduktaṃ bāhyārthāpalāpinā—svapnādipratyayavajjāgaritagocarā api stambhādipratyayā vinaiva bāhyenārthena bhaveyuḥ pratyayatvāviśeṣāditi, tatprativaktavyam;[2]
>
> It is said by one denying the outer object-entity, that the notions of posts, etc. within the range of the waking-state, like the notions of the dream-state, should be without an outer object-entity, because of the qualification of being notions. This is to be answered.

According to Śaṅkara, however, the dream-state and the waking state cannot be considered as alike. First, Śaṅkara argues, the contents of the dream-state are negated by the waking state whereas the contents of the waking state are never negated.

> bādhyate hi svapnopalạbdhaṃ vastu pratibuddhasya[3]
>
> A given thing perceived in the dream is supplanted in the waking state.
>
> naivaṃ jāgaritopalabdhaṃ vastu stambhādikam kasyāñcidapyavasthāyāṃ bādhyate[4]

---

1. Radhakrishnan, Sarvepalli, *The Brahma Sūtra*, *Brahma-sūtra* II.2.29, p. 385.
2. Balasubrahmanyam, T. K., *The Works of Śrī Śaṅkarāchārya*, Volume II, commentary to *Brahma-sūtra* II.2.29, p. 400.
3. Ibid., Volume II, commentary to *Brahma-sūtra* II.2.29, p. 400.
4. Ibid., commentary to *Brahma-sūtra* II.2.29. p. 400.

Thus a given thing perceived in the waking state, such as posts, etc. is never supplanted in any situation whatsoever.

Secondly, Śaṅkara argues that since there is a difference between perception and remembrance, then the dream state, being associated with remembrance, differs from the waking state, which is associated with perception.

api ca smṛtireṣā, yatsvapnadarśanaṃ; upalabdhistu jāgaritadarśanaṃ; smṛtyupalabdhyośca pratyakṣamantaraṃ svayamanubhūyate arthaviprayogasamprayogātmakam—[5]

Moreover, what is seen in dreams is remembrance. What is seen in the waking state is perception. The distinction of remembrance and perception is experienced in itself directly and consists of the association and non-association with an object-entity.

Whether the Vijñānavādins are postulating the similarity of the waking state and the dream state in order to deny the external object is a question that has been examined in the Introductory Background, in the section concerned with Early Vijñānavāda. In stanza 15 of the *Viṃśatikā*, as has been discussed, the question of the similarity of the waking state and the dream state arises.

pratyakṣabuddhiḥ svapnādau yathā sa ca yadā tadā/
na so 'rtho dṛśyate tasya pratyakṣatvaṃ matam//16//[6]

The idea of direct perception is as in a dream, etc. When it (perception) is there, then the object-entity is not seen. (How is there) the opinion that there is the direct perception of it (the object-entity)?

The point here is that on account of momentariness, mental perception does not operate at the same time as sensory perception but a moment afterward. It may then be questioned how there can be mental perception when sensory perception

5. Ibid., Volume II, commentary to *Brahma-sūtra* II.2.29, p. 400.
6. Lèvi, Sylvain, *Vijñaptimātratāsiddhi*, *Viṃśatikā* 16, pp. 8-9.

has vanished. In other words, does mental perception have the same object as sensory perception?

Śaṅkara claims, as noted, that there is a difference between perception and remembrance. According to Śaṅkara, perception is the direct presentation of an object-entity, as when a father directly beholds his son, rather than merely remembers him.

iṣṭaṃ putraṃ smarāmi, nopalabhe, upalabdhumicchāmīti[7]

I remember a son, I do not perceive him, I desire to perceive him

According to the *Viṃśatikā*, mental perception involves the representation of an object, not presentation. Both mental perception and remembrance occur subsequent to the fading out of sensory perception.

uktam yathā tadābhāso vijñaptiḥ smaraṇam tataḥ/[8]

It has been said that the representation is an appearance of that; hence, there is memory.

Perception, at least of the mental sort is being compared in the *Viṃśatikā* to the dream state in that both occur at some remove from their objects, not because, as Śaṅkara claims, the *Viṃśatikā* is denying that there is an object external to the mind. The analogy of the dream is employed in the *Viṃśatikā* only to emphasize the temporal gap that exists between sensory perception and mental perception which is subsequent to the former no less than remembrance.

2. Rāmānuja's Interpretation

This *sūtra*, "*vaidharmyāc ca na svpanādivat*," (*Brahma-sūtra* II.2.28) may be translated in accordance with Rāmānuja's interpretation, as follows : "And because of divergence, it is not like a dream." Like Śaṅkara, Rāmānuja argues in opposition

---

7. Balasubrahmanyam, T. K., *The Works of Śrī Śaṅkarāchārya*, commentary to *Brahma-sūtra* II.2.29, p. 400.

8. Lèvi, Sylvain, *Vijñaptimātratāsiddhi*, *Viṃśatikā* 17, p. 9.

to the supposed Vijñānavāda equation of the dream state with the waking state, that these two states cannot be equated for the cognition of the dream state is born from organs impaired by drowsiness.

> svapnajñānavaidharmyāt jāgaritajñānānāmarthaśūnyatvaṃ na yujyate vaktuṃ/ svapnajñānāni hi nidrādidoṣaduṣṭakaraṇajanyāni, bādhitāni ca; jāgaritajñānāni tu tadviparītānīti teṣāṃ na tatsāmyam/[9]
>
> It is not possible to declare the voidness of the object-entity of cognitions of the waking state because of the divergence from the cognitions of the dream. For, the cognitions of dream born from organs defective by the fault of sleep are supplanted; the cognitions of the waking state are opposite to that; in connection with these it is not equal to that.

He adds furthermore that if all cognitions are void then the inference drawn by the Buddhists that the dream state is to be equated with the waking state is also void, and that if all cognitions are possessed of an object-entity, then dream-cognitions possess an object-entity.

> sarveṣāṃ ca jñānānāmarthaśūnyatve, bhavadbhiḥ sādhyo 'pyartho na siddhyati; nirālambanānumāna(jñāna)syāpyarthaśūnyatvāt/ tasyārthavattve jñānatvasyānaikāntyāt sutarāmarthaśūnyatvāsiddhiḥ//28//[10]
>
> If all cognitions are void of object-entity, the object to be attained by you is not accomplished, because it is void of meaning in connection with the support of the inference. Furthermore if possessed of an object-entity, there is no manifestation void of an object-entity because of the non-exclusiveness of cognition.

As has been noted in the section concerned with Vijñānavāda and the Buddhist Logicians, however, the idea of direct percep-

9. Viraraghavacharya, Sri Uttamur T. *Brahmasūtra-Śrībhāshya*, commentary to *Brahma-sūtra* II.2.28, pp. 540-541.

10. Ibid., commentary to *Brahma-sūtra* II.2.28, pp. 540-541.

tion is compared to a dream because there is the defining activity of the mental perception and the cessation of the eye-perception, so that consequently the object-entity is not seen.

3. Madhva's Interpretation

This *sūtra*, "*vaidharmyāc ca na svapnādivat*" (*Brahmasūtra* II.2.29) may be translated, in accordance with Madhva's interpretation, as follows : "And because of divergence, it is not like a dream." Madhva's commentary proceeds as follows :

> na ca dṛṣṭasyāpi svapnādivadabhāvaḥ//tasyottarakāle svapno-yaṃ nāyaṃ sarpa ityādyanubhavāt//na cātra tādṛśapramāṇa-masti//[11]
>
> There is no absence, as in a dream, of the seen, because of the (following) experience, (for instance), at a subsequent time : "This is not a snake. This is a dream." There is no authority in this case for such a thing.

B.N.K. Sharma notes, in connection with Madhva's commentary to this *sūtra* that at this point the Śūnyavādin turns to illusory experiences such as dreams, the snake in the ropė, etc. to establish his thesis that our perception of the word is illusory, like the perception of a dream.[12] It is replied that there is no cognition supplanting the perception of the world.[13] B.N.K. Sharma also notes, in accordance with the explanation of Madhva, and of Jayatīrtha in the *Tattvaprakāśikā* that even in connection with dreams, it is only the fact that the objects in the dream state are equated with objects of the waking state at the time of dreams that is false and that comes to be supplanted.[14] According to Madhva in his interpretation

11. Bhikācārya Ainãpure and Anantācārya Aṣṭaputre, *Brahmasūtras with Ānandatīrtha's Brahmasūtrabhāṣya*, commentary to *Brahma-sūtra* II.2-29. p. 41.

12. Sharma, B.N.K., *The Brahmasūtras and Their Principal Commentaries*, p. 74.

13. Ibid., p. 74.

14. Ibid., p. 75.

of *Brahma-sūtra* II.2.3, the illusion in dream consists in seeing the opposite of the waking state (i.e. dream) as the waking state.

> yadanyathātvam jāgrattvam sā bhrāntiḥ[15]
>
> That the opposite side of the case is as the waking state is illusion.

According to Jayatīrtha, the ascertainment of the objects of the dream state as belonging to the waking state is illusion.

> pratītaṃ svapnaviṣayāṇāṃ jāgratpadārthatvam eva bādhyata iti tatpratītir bhrāntirastu/na svapnapratītiriti bhāvaḥ/[16]
>
> The existence of the objects of the waking state ascertained in connection with the objects of dream is supplanted. Such ascertainment is illusion. That there is no such ascertainment in dream is the purport.

Trivikrama Paṇḍita in his *Tattvapradīpa* explains that the example of the dream is not sufficient to establish that all is illusion, and that falsity of object-entities is not established by the error of regarding the objects in a dream as objects in the waking state, or by the illusion of the snake in the rope, etc.

> na caikadeśabhrāntitvena sarvabhrāntitvam/ataḥ sādhyavikalaḥ svapnadṛṣṭāntaḥ/na tajjāgrattvavat rajjusarpavadvā mithyātvaṃ vācyam/tasya nedam jāgaritaṃ, nāyaṃ, sarpaḥ iti viparītapramāṇenābhāvānubhavāt/[17]
>
> All is not illusion by means of the existence of illusion in one place. Hence, the example of the dream is insufficient in guidance. Nor should falsity like (the seeming existence of the) waking state or like the snake in rope be proclaimed because of the experience of absence by means of opposite authority

15. Ibid., (Madhva's commentary to *Brahma-sūtra* II.2.3), p. 75, 14.
16. Ibid., (*Tattva-prakāśikā*), p. 75, 14.
17. Ibid., (*Tattvapradīpa* II.2.29), p. 75, 15.

to the effect that, in connection with these (examples), this is not the waking state, this is not a snake.

It is to be noted however, that Madhva and his school are liable to the charge of over-pervasion in claiming that the Śūnyavādins aver the absence of the seen.

N. *BRAHMA-SŪTRA* II.2.30 :

"*NA BHĀVO 'NUPALABDHEḤ*

1. Śaṅkara's Interpretation

This *sūtra*, "*na bhāvo 'nupalabdheḥ*" (*Brahma-sūtra* II.2.30)[1] may be translated, in accordance with Śaṅkara's interpretation, as follows : "There is no entity, because of non-perception". In his commentary to this *sūtra*, Śaṅkara attributes to the Vijñānavādins the position that knowledge can be explained on the basis of habit-energies, without any reference to external object-entities.

> yadapyuktaṃ—vināpyarthena jñānavaicitryaṃ vāsanāvaicitryādevāvakalpata iti tatprativaktavyam; atrocyate—na bhāvo vāsanānām-upapadyate, tvatpakṣe 'nupalabdherbāhyānām-arthānām[2]

> It is said that the variety of cognitions is explained without an external object-entity because of the variety of habit-energies. This is to be answered. It is said : the entity of the habit-energies does not occur, in the case of your position, because of the non-perception of external object-entities.

According to Śaṅkara, the habit-energies could not originate if no external object entities were perceived, for the hypothesis of a beginningless series of habit-energies could only lead to an infinite regression.

> anupalabhyamāneṣu tvartheṣu kiṃnimittā vicitrā vāsanā bhaveyuḥ? anāditve 'pyandha-paramparānyāyenāpratiṣṭhaivānavasthā vyavahāralopinī syāt, nābhiprāyasiddhih.[3]

> But when the object-entity is not being perceived how should the various habit-energies have efficient causes ? In the case of beginninglessness there would be an unending and infinite regression cancelling the practical world through the logic of

1. Radhakrishnan, Sarvepalli, *The Brahma Sūtra*, *Brahma-sūtra* II.2.30, p. 386.

2. Balasubrahmanyam, T. K., *The Works of Śrī Saṅkaracharya*, commentary to *Brahma-sūtra* II.2.30, p. 401.

3. Ibid., Volume II, commentary to *Brahma-sūtra* II.2.30, p. 401.

an uninterrupted series in the dark; your intention would not be perfected.

For Śaṅkara, the existence of the object-entity external to the mind is established on the basis of two arguments : first, that the habit-energies cannot originate independently of the perception of external object-entities, and secondly that the perception of external object-entities can take place without the habit-energies.

> api ca vināpi vāsanābhirarthopalabdhyupagamāt, vinā tvarthopalabdhyā vāsanotpattyanabhyupagamāt arthasadbhāvamevānvayavyatirekāvapi pratiṣṭhāpayataḥ[4]
>
> Moreover, (the arguments of) difference and affirmation establish the true existence of the object-entity, because of the principle of the perception of the object-entity without habit-energies, and because of the non-principle of the arising of habit-energies without perception of the object-entity.

Furthermore, according to Śaṅkara a habit-energy is a kind of qualification which requires a basis. Śaṅkara accuses the Vijñānavādins of denying such a basis.

> api ca vāsanā nāma saṃskāraviśeṣāḥ; saṃskārāśca nāśrayamantareṇāvakalpante, evaṃ loke dṛṣṭatvāt; na ca tava vāsanāśrayaḥ kaścidasti, pramāṇato 'nupalabdheḥ[5]
>
> Moreover, habit-energies by name are qualifications of motivations. And motivations are not explained without a basis, because they are seen in the world. There is no basis whatsoever for your habit-energy because of authority and lack of perception (of them).

Śaṅkara attributes to the Vijñānavādins the position that knowledge is without an object-entity. It has been shown, however, that the concept of habit-energy is closely allied with the concept of the ideation-store which is not necessarily hospitable to idealism. It has been mentioned, in the section concerned with Early Vijñānavāda in the Introductory Background, that

4. Ibid., Volume II, commentary to *Brahma-sūtra* II.2.30, pp. 401-402.
5. Ibid., Volume II, commentary to *Brahma-sūtra* II.2.30, p. 402.

according to de La Vallée Poussin, both the fact that images develop within the *ālaya-vijñāna* which are archetypes and which are ulterior objects of sense-perception, and the fact that one can explain the difference between the perception of a single moon and the questionable perception of a double moon, are hardly compatible with idealism. Furthermore, it has been observed in the section concerned with Early Vijñānavāda that the notions of the ideation-store and habit-energy are primarily associated with the notions of action and fruit. The *ālaya-vijñāna* is even defined in the *Mahāyāna-saṃgraha* of Asaṅga, as translated by Etienne Lamotte, in terms of the doctrine "*vipāka*," translated by him as "retribution." The ideation-store is the perception of the ripened karma of all the seeds. When Śaṅkara argues, therefore, that there is no birth of the habit-energies without the perception of the object-entity, he is neglecting the fact that the habit-energies are associated with the notions of action and effect. It can be seen, therefore, that the notions of ideation-store and habit-energy are not intended by the Vijñānavādins to establish an idealism although Śaṅkara, claims that such was the intention of the Vijñānavādins. Rather these notions are intended by the Vijñānavādins to explicate the processes of action (*karman*) and maturation (*vipāka*). It is evident that Śaṅkara's attack on Vijñānavāda for replacing the external object-entity with habit-energy is not warranted.

2. Rāmānuja's Interpretation

This *sūtra*, "*na bhavo 'nupalabdheḥ*," (*Brahma-sūtra* II.2.29), may be translated in accordance with Rāmānuja's interpretation as follows: "There is no entity, because of non-perception." In his commentary to this *sūtra*, Śaṅkara attempts to refute the Vijñānavāda concept of habit-energy by noting that if external object-entities are not recognized, then there is no basis for the habit-energy. Rāmānuja, in his commentry to this *sūtra*, attempts to refute what he portrays as the Vijñānavāda notion that cognition is possible without a corresponding object-entity. Here he explains that without a corresponding object entity cognition is void. Furthermore, he goes on to explain, even dream-cognitions are not void.

na kevalasyārthaśūnyasya jñānasya bhāvaḥ sambhavati/kutaḥ kvacidapyanupalabdheḥ / na hyakartṛkasyākarmakasya vā jñānasya kvacidapyanupalabdhiḥ/svapnajñānādiṣvapi nārtha-śūnyatvamiti khyātinirūpaṇe pratipāditam//[6]

The existence of cognition having only a void object-entity is not possible. Why ? Because of the non-perception of such a thing. There is no preception of a cognition having no action or having no agent. That there is no voidness of the object-entity even in dream-cognition, etc. has been set forth in the investigation of the idea.

According to Rāmānuja even dream-cognition relates to something that is real. In his commentary to *Brahma-sūtra* I.1.1, Rāmānuja declares that the Lord creates certain things in dreams in accordance with the state of the creature.

svapne ca prāṇināṃ puṇyapāpānuguṇaṃ bhagavataiva tattat-puruṣamātrānubhāvyāḥ tattatkālavāsanāḥ tathābhūtāścārthāḥ sṛjyante/[7]

In a dream certain beings and object-entities which are to be experienced by this and that person only, and which have a conclusion at such and such time, are created by the Lord in accordance with the merits and demerits of living creatures.

According to Rāmānuja all consciousness relates to an object-entity, because in his opinion the scriptures teach that everything is contained in everything else.

yathārthaṃ sarvavijñānamiti vedavidāṃ mataṃ/
śrutismṛtibhyaḥ sarvasya sarvātmatvapratītitaḥ//[8]

It is the opinion of the knowers of the Veda that all perception is in accordance with an object-entity, because of the recognition of the existence of the nature of everything in everything, according to Śruti and Smṛti.

---

6. Viraraghavacharya, Sri Uttamur T., *Brahmasūtra-Śrībhāshya*, commentary to *Brahma-sūtra* II.2.29, p. 541.
7. Ibid., commentary to *Brahma-sūtra* I.1.1, p. 135.
8. Ibid., commentary to *Brahma-sūtra* I.1.1, p. 132.

Rāmânuja is referring here to the doctrine of three-fold creation, which according to him is set forth in such a passage as *Chāndogya Upaniṣad* (VI.4.1), where it is declared that fire partakes of heat, water, and food.

> yad agne rohitaṃ rūpam tejasas tad rūpam, yac chuklam tad apām yat kṛṣṇam tad annasya[9]

Alex Wayman translates this passage as follows :

> Whatever red formation fire has is a formation of heat, whatever white is a formation of water, whatever black is a formation of food.[10]

Furthermore, as has been noted in the section on Vijñānavāda and the Buddhist Logicians, however, the logician Dignāga does not claim that cognition is possible without a corresponding object-entity, but claims rather that the inner form of the knowable which appears as though it were external is the object-entity (*yad-antarjñeya-rūpaṃ tu bahirvad avabhāsate so 'rthaḥ*).

3. Madhva's Interpretation

This *sūtra*, "*na bhāvo 'nupalabdheḥ*," (*Brahma-sūtra* II.2.30) may be translated, in accordance with Madhva's interpretation, as follows: "There is no consciousness, because of non-perception." Madhva's commentary proceeds as follows :

> vijñānavādamapākaroti//na vijñānamātraṃ jagattathānubhavābhāvāt//[11]

> He refutes Vijñānavāda, on account of the absence of the consciousness that the world is accordingly consciousness-only.

In their interpretations of this *sūtra*, Madhva, as well as Śaṅkara and Rāmānuja, criticizes the Vijñānavādins. Whereas Śaṅkara

9. Radhakrishnan, Sarvepalli, *The Principal Upaniṣads, Chāndogya Upaniṣad* IV.4.1, p. 451.

10. Wayman, Alex. "A Study of the Vedāntic and Buddhist Theory of *Nāma-Rūpa*," p. 15.

11. Bhikācārya Aināpure and Anantācārya Aṣṭapatre, *Brahmasūtras with Ānandatīrtha's Brahmasūtrabhāṣya*, commentary to *Brahma-sūtra* II.2.30, p. 41.

criticizes the notion of habit-energies on the grounds of non-perception of their object-entities, and Rāmānuja criticizes the notion that there are cognitions without corresponding object-entities, Madhva interprets "*bhāvaḥ*" in the sense of consciousness or awareness and attacks the Vijñānavāda notion of the world as consciousness. This *sūtra* and the following are devoted by Madhva and the Madhva school to a refutation of Vijñānavāda, which holds the position, according to Jayatīrtha in the *Nyāya-sudhā* as cited by B.N.K. Sharma, that the knowable is not different from knowledge.

> jñānameva jñeyākāraṃ, na jñeyam nāma jñānādbhinnamastītyarthaḥ[12]
>
> Knowledge is the aspect of the knowable; that called the knowable is not different from knowledge.

Vyāsatīrtha explains in the *Tātparyacandrikā* that the term "*bhāva*" is intended to draw attention to the existent form of the agent, that it refers to "*jñāna*", that the positive nature of the terminology indicates the *prima facie* view to be refuted.

> atrāpi sūtre kartṛsādhanabhāvaśabdena sadrūpaṃ jñānamucyate/ vijñānavāde jñānādanyasyāsattvāt/ jñānamityanuktvā, 'bhāva' ityuktistu, nāsato 'dṛṣṭatvāt iti śūnyavādinaṃ pratyukto doṣo nāsmākamiti pūrvapakṣotthānārthamiti draṣṭavyam/[13]
>
> In this *sūtra*, by the word "*bhāva*" denoting an "agent", knowledge having an existent form is mentioned, because of the non-existence in Vijñānavāda of something other than knowledge. The word "knowledge" is not uttered, but the word "*bhāva*" is uttered. The Śūnyavādin is answered under the statement, "Not from a non-existent thing, because of observation." It is to be seen that the fault is not ours, that the meaning is in support of the *prima facie* view.

Jayatīrtha also explains, as noted by B.N.K Sharma, that the word "*bhāva*" is used to denote "consciousness" or "aware-

12. Sharma, B.N.K., *The Brahmasūtras and Their Principal Commentaries*, (*Nyāya-sudhā*, p. 410), p. 76 footnote 1.
13. Ibid., (*Tātparyacandrikā*, p. 519b), p. 76, footnote 2.

ness" and that the prefix "*anu*" simply manifests the meaning latent in the root "*bhava*."[14]

> bhavateranubhavārthatvāt/ upasargā hi dhātulīnasyārthasya vyañjakā eva/[15]
>
> Because there is the meaning "awareness" in connection with "*bhava*", for affixes are indicative of the meaning latent in the root (*dhātu*).

Jayatīrtha further explains the Vijñānavāda position to be that since the attainment of an object is pervaded by knowledge shining forth it is to be explained in terms of knowledge shining forth.

> jñānaṃ hi prakāśate/tena prakāśamānatvasya jñānatvena vyāptau siddhāyāṃ, nīlāderapi prakāśamānasya jñānatvasiddhirityarthaḥ/[16]
>
> For knowledge shines forth. Since the complete attainment of an object is pervaded by the existence of knowledge of that which is shining forth, the complete attainment of an object is the existence of the knowledge of the blue, etc. shining forth.

In his *Tattvaprakāśikā*, Jayatīrtha mentions the principle of simultaneous ascertainment, according to which as Dharmakīrti describes, blue and the cognition of it, for example, are not different.[17]

The advocates of the Madhva school then reply to these supposed positions of the Vijñānavādins. As B.N.K. Sharma explains, the perception of objects as different from consciousness cannot be regarded as misapprehension, for there is no supplanting cognition to the contrary.[18] B.N.K. Sharma also

---

14. Ibid., p. 76.
15. Ibid., (*Nyāya-sudhā*, p. 410), p. 76, footnote 3.
16. Ibid., (*Nyāya-sudhā*, p. 410), p. 77, footnote 4.
17. Ingalls, Daniel H.H., "Śaṁkara's Arguments Against the Buddhists," *Philosophy East and West*, Volume III, Number 1, (January 1954), p. 300.
18. Sharma, B.N.K., *The Brahmasūtras and Their Principal Commentaries*, p. 77.

notes that if the non-difference of cognition and its object were to be established by inference based on "simultaneous occurrence", there would occur the fallacy of interdependence, as is explained by Jayatīrtha in the *Tattvaprakāśikā*.

> anumānasyaiva bādhakatve sphuṭamitaretarāśrayatvam/[19]
>
> In the case of the existence of opposition in connection with inference, the (fallacy of) taking refuge with each other is manifest.

B.N.K. Sharma explains that the inference of non-difference between cognition and its object would be established only when it is proved that the perception of difference is error-ridden, but that the perception of difference as error-ridden can be established only when the inference leading to the non-difference of cognition and its object is proved.[20] Furthermore, as Jayatīrtha argues in the *Tattvaprakāśikā*, the notion of simultaneity, supposedly employed by the Buddhists to prove non-difference of cognition and its object, implies difference, for there can be simultaneity only between two different things.

> sahopalambhādabheda iti pratijñāhetvoḥ virodhaśca/sāhityasya bheda evopapatteḥ[21]
>
> In reference to the non-difference because of simultaneous ascertainment, there is contradiction because of the thesis and the reason on account of the acceptance of the difference in connection with simultaneity.

There is also the other argument of the Vijñānavādins based on the premise that whatever shines forth is consciousness.

> na ca, yatprakāśate tadvijñānaṃ/ yathā jñānaṃ/prakāśante ca nīlādaya iti yuktam[22]
>
> That which shines forth is consciousness, as for instance knowledge. That blue, etc. shines forth is enjoined.

---

19. Ibid., (*Tattvaprakāśikā* II.2.30), p. 77, footnote 6.
20. Ibid., p. 77.
21. Ibid., (*Tattvaprakāśikā* II.2.30), p. 77, footnote 7.
22. Ibid., (*Tattvaprakāśikā* II.2.30), p. 77, footnote 8.

The difficulty with this argument as B.N.K. Sharma notes in accordance with the explanation of Jayatīrtha in the *Tattva-prakāśikā*, is that the reason—that it shines forth—is absent in the example--cited (i.e. knowledge or *jñānam*), for knowledge cannot become an object of its own awareness.[23]

> 'prakāśata' iti vijñānaviṣayatvābhyupagame svavṛttivirodhena, dṛṣṭānte sādhanābhāvaḥ[24]
>
> By the contradition of self-dependence in the case of the principle in connection with the existence of the object of consciousness, there is the absence of proof in the example that it shines forth.

Furthermore, B.N.K. Sharma notes in accordance with the argument of Jayatīrtha in the *Tattvaprakāśikā* and of Vyāsatīrtha in the *Tātparyacandrikā*, the antecedent non-existence of knowledge and conventional truth which is a "covering" of truth, although they "shine forth" in a sense as objects of knowledge, cannot be regarded as "consciousness" for they are opposed to consciousness.[25] According to Jayatīrtha, ignorance represents a deviation from "consciousness," the thing to be established.

> ajñāne vyabhicāraśca[26]
>
> In the case of ignorance, there is deviation.

Vyāsatīrtha exclaims that the absence of knowledge cannot be regarded as knowledge.

> naca jñānābhāvādirapi jñānam! virodhāditi bhāvaḥ[27]
>
> Nor does knowledge accrue from the absence of knowledge! That there is opposition is the purport.

In the section of the Introductory Background concerned with Vijñānavāda and the Buddhist Logicians, however, it has been noted that although the Madhva school attributes to the

23. Ibid., pp. 77-78.
24. Ibid., (*Tattvaprakāśikā* II.2.30), p. 78, footnote 9.
25. Ibid., p. 78.
26. Ibid., (*Tattvaprakāśikā* II.2.30), p. 78, footnote 9.
27. Ibid., (*Tātparyacandrikā* p. 919), p. 78, footnote 10.

Vijñānavādins the position that the knowable is not different from knowledge, the Vijñānavādins do not deny that there is an object external to the mind. It has also been observed that according to Dignāga and Dharmakīrti the three-fold division of perception into subject, object, and self-intuition (*svasaṃvitti*) represents in the first place a distorted or wayward vision and are in reality not separate. It is in this context that Jayatīrtha's argument is to be examined. Jayatīrtha argues that knowledge is not an instance of "shining forth" in that knowledge cannot be an object to itself. But Jayatīrtha's argument assumes the separation of object, subject, and self-intuition. Furthermore, there is Vyāsatīrtha's and Jayatīrtha's argument that the antecedent non-existence of knowledge (*jñānaprāgabhāva*) and conventional truth (*saṃvṛti-satya*) which is a "covering" of truth, although they are objects of knowledge, yet cannot be regarded as "consciousness" (*vijñāna*) because they are opposed to "consciousness". It is to be noted here that there is a distinction between the concept and the conceptualized. Whether the concepts of ignorance (*ajñāna*), antecedent non-existence of knowledge (*jñānaprāgabhāva*), and convention (*saṃvṛti*) are opposed to consciousness (*vijñāna*) is to be questioned.

In his interpretation of the *sūtra*, Śaṅkara attempts to refute the supposed position of the Vijñānavādin that our cognitions can be explained on the basis of habit-energies (*vāsanā*) without external objects by arguing that the existence of habit-energies has been made impossible by the non-perception of external objects. B.N.K. Sharma notes here that such an interpretation is not adequate, because it involves the importation of the subject to be disproved (i.e. the habit-energies, "*vāsanā*"), and because the reason provided in the *sūtra* (i.e. "because of non-perception," "*anupalabdheḥ*") is not directly connected with the subject (i.e. *vāsanā*) imported by Śaṅkara and needs to be connected with another subject (i.e. the object-entity, "*artha*") to be supplied.[28] Furthermore, there is a difficulty in that Śaṅkara seems to be saying that the existence (*sattvam*) of object-entities determines their perception when he argues that if object-entities are not perceived, there cannot be habit-energies.

28. Ibid., p. 80.

> arthopalabdhinimittā hi pratyartham nānārūpā vāsanā bhavanti/ anupalabhyamāneṣu tvartheṣu kiṃnimittā vicitrā vāsanā bhaveyuḥ?[29]
>
> For the habit-energies having for their efficient causes the perception of object-entities are different formations in accordance with the object-entity in every case. If the object-entities are not being perceived, would the various habit-energies have efficient causes?

If the existence of object-entities determines their perception, however, as B.N.K. Sharma notes in accordance with the explanation of Vyāsatīrtha in the *Tātparyacandrikā*,[30] then the perception of things is as impossible in a system, like Śaṅkara's affirming the indescribability (*anirvacanīyatva*) of object-entities as it is in a system, like Vijñānavāda, which (as Vyāsatīrtha represents) teaches the non-existence (*asattva*) of object-entities.

> asattvenānupalabdhiṃ vadatā, lāghavena sattvameva upalabdhau tantramiti vaktavyatayā, anirvācyapakṣe 'pi doṣasāmyāt[31]
>
> Because of similarity of fault in the case of the position of indescribability, by means of the blameworthiness through carelessness for the statement that existence is the thread in the case of the perception by one asserting the non-perception through non-existence.

It is to be questioned, however, whether the Vijñānavādins are asserting the non-existence of object-entities.

---

29. Bākre, Mahādeva Śāstrī, editor, *The Brahmasūtra-Shānkarbhāshyam*, Commentary to *Brahma-sūtra* II.2.30, p. 477.
30. Sharma, B.N.K., *The Brahmasūtras and Their Principal Commentaries*, p. 80.
31. Ibid., (*Tātparyacandrikā*, p. 921 b), p. 80, footnote 21.

O. *BRAHMA-SŪTRA* II.2.31:

"*KṢAṆIKATVĀC CA*"

1. Śaṅkara's Interpretation

This *sūtra*, "*kṣaṇikatvāc ca*," (*Brahma-sūtra* II.2.31)[1] may be translated in accordance with Śaṅkara's interpretation, as follows: "And because of momentariness." In his commentary to this *sūtra*, Śaṅkara argues that the ideation-store (*ālaya-vijñāna*) cannot be the locus or abode of the *vāsanā* (habit-energy), since the ideation-store itself is momentary.

> yadapyālayavijñānaṃ nāma vāsanāśrayatvena parikalpitaṃ, tadapi kṣaṇikatvābhyupagamādanavasthitasvarūpaṃ sat, pravṛttivijñānavanna vāsanānāmadhikaraṇaṃ bhavitumarhati[2]

> That ideation-store (*ālaya-vijñāna*) by name, which is determined by way of being the basis of the habit-energies, which is an existent and has an impermanent self-formation because of the principle of Momentariness, is not able to be the receptacle of the habit-energies, as is the case with the external perceptions.

It may be noted here, however, in response to Śaṅkara, that the concept "basis" (*āśraya*) and momentariness (*kṣaṇikatva*) are not necessarily incompatible. For example, a stream can be said to be the basis of the instants of water. Furthermore, even though it is claimed that one can never enter the same stream twice, one still continues to speak of "that" stream. In fact, Wayman notes that the term "*saṃtati*" (flow or stream) was used in later Buddhism in association with "*citta*" (*thought*) to indicate the transmigrating entity. "*Citta*" (thought) is in its turn associated with *karma* (action).

> Later Buddhism used the expression "*cittasaṃtāna*" or "*citta-saṃtati*" (both: stream of thoughts) for the transmigrating entity. Thus, the words "*karma*" and "*citta*" are

1. Radhakrishnan, Sarvepalli, *The Brahma Sūtra*, *Brahma-sūtra* II.2.31, p. 386.
2. Balasubrahmanyam, T. K., *The Works of Śrī Śaṅkarāchārya*, commentary to *Brahma-sūtra* II.2.31, p. 402.

doctrinally equivalent to indicate the transmigrating entity.[3]

Śaṅkara continues to argue for the witnessing Self, that except on the basis of the witnessing Self remembrance (*smṛti*) cannot be explained.

> na hi kālatrayasambandhinyekasminnanvayinyasati kūṭasthe vā sarvārthadarśini deśakālanimittāpekṣavāsanādhānasmṛtipratisaṃdhānādivyavahāraḥ sambhavati[4]
>
> For when there is not one connected with the three times, when there is not a connecting agent, when there is not a permanent seer of all object-entities, the practice of recollection, remembrance subject to habit-energies dependent on efficient cause, time, place, is not possible.

For the Buddhist logician Dignāga, however, the phenomenon of recollection (*smṛti*) attests to the existence of self-intuition (*sva-saṃvitti*) and introspection (*svasaṃvedana*), as has been discussed in the section on Buddhist Logicians in the Introductory Background. According to Dignāga, one cannot remember that one cognized something except on the basis of self-intuition. As has been explained in the section on Buddhist Logicians, according to Dignāga and Dharmakīrti the distinction between subject, object, and self-intuition is the result of wayward vision. Consequently, they do not postulate a witnessing Self (*sākṣin*), at least in the same sense as Śaṅkara postulates in the following passage of the *Brahmasūtrabhāṣya.*

> sākṣipratyayayośca svabhāvavaiṣamyādupalabdhrupalabhyabhāvopapatteḥ[5]
>
> Because it is a demonstrated conclusion that there is a perceiver and perceived on account of the diversity of the self-existence of witness and notion.

Śaṅkara continues to argue that if the ideation-store is declared to be permanent, then the tenent of Momentariness is contra-

3. Wayman, Alex, review of *The Yogācāra Idealism*, p. 66.
4. Balasubrahmanyam, T. K., *The Works of Śrī Śaṅkarāchārya*, Volume II, commentary to *Brahma-sūtra* II.2.31, p. 402.
5. Ibid., Volume II, commentary to *Brahma-sūtra* II.2.28, p. 399.

dicted. If the tenet of Momentariness is upheld, Śaṅkara urges, then the arguments he has brought forth earlier against the Sautrāntikas and Vaibhāṣikas apply also to the Vijñānavādins

> sthirasvarūpatve tvālayavijñānasya siddhāntahāniḥ/ api ca vijñānavāde 'pi kṣaṇikatvābhyupagamasya samānatvāt, yāni bāhyārthavāde kṣaṇikatvanibandhanāni dūṣaṇānyudbhāvitāni—'uttarotpāde ca pūrvanirodhāt' ityevamādīni, tānīhāpyanusaṃdhātavyāni/[6]
>
> When there is a permanent nature there is abandonment of the principle in connection with the ideation-store. Moreover, in the case of Vijñānavāda, because of equality with the principle of Momentariness those objections are to be investigated which have been brought forth in connection with momentariness as in the statements beginning with the saying "Because of the cessation of the preceding when there is birth of the subsequent" in reference to those adhering to an external object-entity.

Śaṅkara's charge, that if the ideation-store is declared to be permanent, then the tenet of Momentariness is contradicted, ignores the fact that according to the *Madhyānta-vibhaṅga*, as has been explained earlier, the "imagination of unreality" (*abhūta-parikalpa*), to which the ideation-store (*ālayavijñāna*) is allied, is complementary to the principle of the "void" (*śūnyatā*). As Alex Wayman explains, "both the 'imagination of unreality' and 'voidness' are real, co-exist, and are yet distinct."[7] The "imagination of unreality" represents the covering process by which "voidness" or the *dharmadhātu* is covered with transient *dharmas*. The co-existence of the two, the principle of "voidness" and the principle of "the imagination of unreality" reveals that for Vijñānavāda the principles of the eternal absolute and the changing phenomenal were not mutually exclusive. The "imagination of unreality" as formal cause, to which is allied the ideation-store cannot be considered except in association with "voidness" as material cause. It may

---

6. Ibid., Volume II, commentary to *Brahma-sūtra* II.2.31, p. 402.
7. Wayman, Alex, *Yogācāra and the Buddhist Logicians* p. 66.

also be noted that the principles of abidingness and change need not be incompatible, as in the example of a "stream". It is evident, therefore, that if the principle of the ideation-store is seen in the context of Buddhist teachings, then Śaṅkara's representation of it—upon which he attempts his refutation—is inaccurate. But whether the positions which Śaṅkara attributes to the Vijñānavādins are actually descriptive of Vijñānavāda or not, Śaṅkara's attempted refutation is of unparalleled importance in revealing Śaṅkara's own positions : his insistence upon the external object-entity and, above all, his emphasis upon the teaching of the witnessing Self.

In his commentary to this *sūtra*, Śaṅkara also briefly dismisses the Mādhyamika school. He characterizes their position as nihilism, that is to say, as denial of the phenomenal world, and dismisses the school on the basis that the phenomenal world cannot be denied unless one has discovered another truth.

> śūnyavādipakṣastu sarvapramāṇavipratiṣiddha iti tannirākaraṇāya nādaraḥ kriyate/ na hyayaṃ sarvapramāṇasiddho lokavyavahāro 'nyattattvamanadhigamya śakyate 'pahnotum, apavādābhāve utsargaprasiddheḥ//[8]

> Since the position of those adhering to the Void is prohibited by all the authorities nothing is to be done for the sake of repudiation. For the convention of the world approved by all the authorities cannot be denied when another reality has not been approached; for by the absence of exception the general rule is proved.

It is evident that Śaṅkara's brief dismissal of the Mādhyamika school leaves much to be said. That the Mādhyamika school did not adopt the position of nihilism is amply affirmed by its texts. As has been discussed in the section on the Mādhyamikas to accuse the Mādhyamikas of nihilism is to be liable to the charge of over-pervasion.

---

8. Balasubrahmanyam, T.K. *The Works of Śrī Śaṅkarāchārya*, Volume II, commentary to *Brahma-sūtra* II.2.31, p. 402.

2. Madhva's Interpretation

This *sūtra, "kṣaṇikatvāc ca"*, (*Brahma-sūtra* II.2.31) may be translated in accordance with Madhva's interpretation, as follows : "And because of momentariness." Madhva's commentary proceeds as follows :

jñānaṃ kṣaṇikamarthānāṃ ca sthāyitvamuktam// ataśca naikyam//[9]

The momentary cognition, the stability of object-entities has been mentioned. Hence, there is no oneness.

Whereas Śaṅkara argues that the ideation-store cannot be the basis of the habit-energies because the ideation-store is momentary, Madhva argues as noted by B. N. K. Sharma in accordance with the explanation of Jayatīrtha in the *Nyāya-sudhā* that there cannot be identity between cognition and object-entities. The reason is that cognition is momentary and internal and object-entities are external as well as having been shown to be non-momentary.

atra kṣaṇikatvākṣaṇikatvalakṣaṇaviruddhadharmādhyāsaṃ bhedahetum vadatā āntarabāhyatvādiraneko viruddhadharmasaṃsarga upalakṣito bodhyaḥ[10]

By one asserting as reason the difference having the superimposition of contradictory features characterized by momentariness and non-momentariness, the association of contradictory features, multiple because of inferiority and externality is thought to be characterized.

It must be realized, however, that Dignāga declared a distinction between the inherent character and the generalizing character. As Wayman has noted in his article, "Yogācāra and the Buddhist Logicians", what is real is the inherent character (*svalakṣaṇa*) which is causal and has the sense-organ as coopera-

---

9. Bhikācārya Aināpure and Anantācārya Aṣṭaputre, *Brahmasūtras with Ānandatīrtha's Brahmasūtrabhāṣya*, commentary to *Brahma-sūtra* II.2.31, p. 42.

10. Sharma, B.N.K., *The Brahmasūtras and Their Principal Commentaries*, (*Nyāya-sudhā*, p. 411b), p. 80, footnote 12.

ting capacity and that on top of this inherent character the mind adds "shape" (*ākāra*). It has also been noted, in the section concerned with Vijñānavāda and the Buddhist Logicians that they considered knowledge (*jñāna*) to be separate (*vi-*) from the object, although the object-entity has been defined as the inner form of the knowable which appears as though it were external.

In his interpretation of this *sūtra*, Śaṅkara attempts to refute the position of Vijñānavādins that the ideation-store can be the basis of the habit-energies by arguing that the ideation-store is itself momentary and therefore cannot be a basis. The difficulty with Śaṅkara's interpretation, as noted by B. N. K. Sharma[11] in accordance with the explanation of Vyāsatīrtha is that such an objection would be applicable to other schools of Buddhism, and not merely to Vijñānavāda.

> vijñānavādyasādhāraṇasyārtho jñānākara ityasya dūṣaṇasambhave, kṣaṇikatvaprayuktasaṃskārābhāvasya baudhamatasādhāraṇasya uktyayogāt[12]

> Because of the impossibility of the statement of the absence of the above-mentioned motivations due to momentariness—an absence which is common to all those of the Buddhist persuasion—since there is the possibility of fault that the aspect to knowledge has for its meaning (something) which is common to the Vijñānavādins, etc.

11. Ibid., p. 81.
12. Ibid., (*Tātparyacandrikā*, p. 921b), p. 81, footnote 23.

P. *BRAHMA-SŪTRA* II.2.32:

"*SARVATHĀNUPAPATTEŚCA*"

1. Śaṅkara's Interpretation

This *sūtra,* "*sarvathānupapatteśca,*" (*Brahma-sūtra* II.2.32)[1] may be translated in accordance with Śaṅkara's interpretation, as follows : "Because of objection on all sides." In his commentary to this *sūtra*, Śaṅkara declares that Buddhism has been refuted in that from whatsoever point of view Buddhism is tested, it gives way.

> kim bahunā? sarvaprakāreṇa—yathā yathāyaṃ vaināśikasamaya upapattimatvāya parīkṣyate tathā tathā—sikatākūpavadvidīryata eva; na kāṃcidapyatropapattiṃ paśyāmaḥ; ataścānupapanno vaināśikatantravyavahāraḥ/[2]
>
> What occasion is there for much talk? In every way the more the destructionist doctrine is examined for the existence of proof, the more it falls apart like a well in sand. We do not see any proof whatsoever. Hence the practical is established through the destructionist doctrines.

Śaṅkara's use of the term "*vaināśika*" is to be noted. It seems that he is caricaturing all the Buddhist schools as in some sense "annihilationist," for the term "*vaināśika*" is a derivative of the term "*vināśa,*" which means destruction. Śaṅkara then attacks the Buddha himself for contradictory statements in words that reveal his openly polemical intent.

> api ca bāhyārthavijñānaśūnyavādatrayamitaretaraviruddhamupadiśatā sugatena spaṣṭīkṛtamātmano'sambaddhapralāpitvaṃ, pradveṣo prajāsu—viruddhārthapratipattyā vimuhyeyurimāḥ prajā iti/[3]
>
> Moreover, by the Buddha (the Well-gone One, the *Sugata*) teaching the mutually contradictory triad—the doctrine of the

---

1. Radhakrishnan, Sarvepalli, *The Brahma Sūtra, Brahma-sūtra* II.2.32 p. 387
2. Balasubrahmanyam, T. K., *The Works of Śrī Śaṅkarāchārya,* Volume II, commentary to *Brahma-sūtra* II.2.32, p. 403.
3. Ibid., Volume II, commentary to *Brahma-sūtra* II.2.32, p. 403.

outer object-entity, the doctrine of consciousness, the doctrine of the Void—there is made evident in connection with himself the existence of the unconnected talk, or hatred for all people (with the intent that) these people should be confused by the assertion of contradictory significances.

2. Rāmānuja's Interpretation

This *sūtra*, "*sarvathānupapatteśca*," (*Brahma-sūtra* II.2.30) may be translated, in accordance with Rāmānuja's interpretation as follows: "And because of objection on all sides." In contrast to Śaṅkara, Rāmānuja devotes his entire commentary on this *sūtra* to an attempted refutation of the Mādhyamikas. Whereas Śaṅkara attempts to dismiss the Mādhyamikas in an off-handed manner, Rāmānuja attempts to present their position and refute it in a more elaborate manner. Rāmānuja even employs the term "Mādhyamikas" (adherents of the Middle Way) in connection with this school, whereas Śaṅkara employs the epithet "Śūnyavāda." Like Śaṅkara, however, Rāmānuja attempts to refute the Mādhyamika school on the basis of its supposed nihilism, as is evident in his use of the term "emptiness" (*tucchatva*) in his attempted refutation of the Mādhyamika's supposed position. Rāmānuja's presentation of the various Mādhyamika arguments for the non-arising of any entity from existence, non-existence, itself, or from another seems to be carried out in an impartial manner, except for his characterization of the Mādhyamika concept of liberation (*mokṣa*) as "entry into absence" (*abhāvāpatti*). Rāmānuja attributes to the Mādhyamikas the following position: it is not seen that a thing arises from existence, since its arising requires the destruction of something else, nor is it seen that it arises from non-existence for otherwise it would be composed of non-existence, nor does it arise from itself, for then anything could arise from anything.

> atra sarvaśūnyavādī mādhyamikaḥ pratyavatiṣṭhate/ śūnyavāda eva hi sugatamatakāṣṭhā/ śiṣyabuddhiyogyatānuguṇyenārthābhyupagamādinā kṣaṇikatvādaya uktāḥ/ 'vijñānaṃ bāhyārthāśca sarve na santi, śūnyameva tattvam; abhāvāpattireva ca mokṣaḥ' ityeva buddhasyābhiprāyaḥ/ tadeva hi yuktaṃ; śūnyasyāhetusādhyatayā svataḥ siddheḥ/ sata eva hi hetur-

anveṣaṇīyaḥ/ tacca sat bhāvādabhāvācca notpadyate/ bhāvāt tāvanna kasyacidutpattirdṛṣṭā; na hi ghaṭādiranupamṛdite piṇḍādike jāyate; nāpyabhāvādutpattiḥ sambhavati; naṣṭe piṇḍādike hyabhāvādutpadyamānaṃ ghaṭādikamabhāvātmakameva syāt/ tathā—svataḥ parataścotpattirna sambhavati. svataḥ svotpattāvātmāśraya (yādi) doṣaprasaṅgāt, prayojanābhāvācca/ parataḥ parotpattau paratvāviśeṣāt sarveṣāṃ sarvebhya utpattiprasaṅgaḥ/ janmābhāvādeva vināśasyāpyabhāvaḥ/ ataḥ śūnyameva tattvam[4]

Here, the Mādhyamika holding the position that all is void objects. The doctrine of the void is the paramount doctrine of the *Sugata*. By means of the principle of the object-entity suitable to the qualification of the intelligence of the disciples the doctrines of Momentariness etc. are declared."Consciousness and outer object-entities are not, Reality is the Void, the entering into absence is liberation—"such is the intention of the Buddha. It is enjoined as follows, because of self-provedness, by means of the non-feasibility of a cause in connection with the void, for the cause of an existing thing only is to be investigated. Therefore, an existing thing does not arise from an entity or the absence of it. The arising of anything whatsoever from an entity is not seen, for when a lump of clay is not demolished, a jar is not born. The arising from an absence is not possible, for when a lump of clay is destroyed the jar, etc. arising from absence would be composed from absence. Thereupon, arising from itself and from another is not possible because of the occurrence of defect in a basis consisting in its own arising from itself, and because of the absence of motive. Because of the non-speciality of the consequence in the case of the arising of one from the other, there would be the occurrence of the arising of everything from everything else. Because of the absence of birth there is the absence of destruction. Therefore, Reality is the Void.

Rāmānuja then attributes to the Mādhyamikas the position that birth, destruction, being and non-being are illusions, and

4. Viraraghavacharya, Sri Uttamur T., *Brahmasūtra-Śrībhāshya*, commentary to *Brahma-sūtra* II.2.30, p. 542.

that there can be illusion even when the substrate is not absolute.

ato janma-vināśa sadasadādayo bhrāntimātraṃ.

na niradhiṣṭhānabhramāsambhavād bhramādhiṣṭhānaṃ kiṃcit pāramārthikaṃ tattvamāśrayitavyaṃ; doṣadoṣāśrayatvajñatṛtvādyapāramārthye 'pi bhramopapattivad adhiṣṭhānāpāramārthye 'pi bhramopapatteḥ/ ataḥ śūnyameva tattvam/[5]

Hence, birth, destruction, being and non-being, etc. are only illusions.

Because of the impossibility of illusion without substrate no absolute reality whatsoever need be depended on as the substrate of illusion, and because of the possibility of illusion when the substratum is not absolute, like the arising of illusion when the fault and the knower are not absolute.
Hence, Reality is the Void.

In his attempted refutation of the Mādhyamikas, Rāmānuja equates their position with nihilism, even to the extent of accusing them of adhering to a doctrine of "emptiness" (*tucchatva*), which is not equivalent to the "void" (*śūnya*). Rāmānuja argues that existence and non-existence are both notions that can be applied to an existing given thing, and that to say, "Everything is void," is equivalent to saying, "Everything is existent," because it is differing states of existing things that are being discussed. Furthermore, Rāmānuja argues, if one has discovered voidness through some authority, he must acknowledge the truth of that authority; if there is no such authority, then again all is true. It is to be questioned, however, whether truth or the existent is the counterpart of voidness.

iti prāpte ucyate—sarvathā 'nupapatteśca—iti/sarvathānupapatteḥ sarvaśūnyatvaṃ ca bhavadabhipretaṃ na sambhavati/ kiṃ bhavān sarvaṃ saditi vā pratijānīte, asaditi vā, anyathā va; sarvathā tavābhipretaṃ tucchatvaṃ na sambhavati; loke bhāvābhāvaśabdayoḥ tatpratītyośca vidyamānasyaiva vastuno 'vasthāviśeṣagocaratvasya pratipāditatvāt/ ataḥ sarvaṃ śūnya-

5. Ibid., commentary to *Brahma-sūtra* II.2.30, p. 542.

miti pratyānatā, sarvaṃ saditi pratijānateva, sarvasya vidyamānasyāvasthāviśeṣayogitaiva pratijñātā bhavatīti bhavadabhimatā tucchatā na kutaścidapi siddhyati/kiṃca kutaścit pramāṇāt śūnyatvamupalabhya śūnyatvaṃ siṣādhayiṣatā tasya pramāṇasya satyatvamabhyupetyaṃ; tasyāsatyatve sarvaṃ satyaṃ syāt—iti sarvathā sarvaśūnyatvaṃ cānupapannam//[6]

When this is completed, it is said, "Because of objection on all sides." Because of objection on all sides, the voidness of everything intended by you is not possible. Do you recognize everything to be existent, non-existent, or otherwise ? On all sides the emptiness maintained by you is not possible, because it is set forth in connection with the words "entity" and absence and the acknowledgement of them that they are relating to different states of an existing given thing. Hence, by one acknowledging that all is void, as well as by one acknowledging that all is existent, it is declared that there is the capacity of different states in connection with everything existing; the emptiness intended by you is not established in any way whatsoever. By the wish to establish voidness after having perceived voidness by any authority whatsoever, the truth of that authority is affirmed; in the case of the non-existence of that (authority) everything would be true. In this way, on all sides the voidness of all is rejected.

Like Śaṅkara, therefore, Rāmānuja equates the Mādhyamika term voidness with a nihilism that asserts the non-existence of everything. Rāmānuja equates voidness with emptiness (*tucchatva*). Even Rāmānuja's argument that to say anything is non-existent is to say that it exists reveals that he considers voidness to be equivalent to non-existence.

Whether or not this argument is a valid way to attach existence to a given thing as its predicate, it is evident that Rāmānuja considers the existent to be the counterpart of the void. Therefore, Rāmānuja like Śaṅkara is liable to the charge of overpervasion by reason of presence and absence levelled at the Buddhist realists by Tsoṅ-kha pa, as discussed in the section of this work concerned with the Mādhyamikas. There Candrakīrti's

6. Ibid., commentary to *Brahma-sūtra* II.2.30, pp. 543-545.

explanation of Nāgārjuna's statement that what arises in dependence is not born is discussed. In effect, it is explained by Candrakīrti that to say that *dharmas* arise void of self-existence is not to say that they do not arise.

3. Madhva's Interpretation

This *sūtra*, "*sarvathānupapatteśca,*" (*Brahma-sūtra* II.2.32) may be translated as follows in accordance with Madhva's interpretation : "And because of objections on all sides." Madhva's commentary to this *sūtra* proceeds as follows :

> pramāṇābhāvātsarvaśrūtismṛtiyuktiviruddhatvācca naite paksā grāhyāḥ//[7]
>
> Because of the absence of authority, because of contradiction to the sayings of all the Śrutis and Smṛtis, these positions are not to be held.

In his interpretation of this *sūtra*, Madhva claims that these schools of Buddhism are to be rejected because they are opposed to the Śruti and Smṛti. It has also been observed that the advocates of the Madhva school not only attack the various schools of Buddhism in their interpretations of these *sūtras*, but also the systems of Śaṅkara and Rāmānuja.

---

7. Sharma, B.N.K., *The Brahmasūtras and Their Principal Commentaries*, Madhva's commentary to *Brahma-sūtra* II.2.32, p. 78, footnote 13.

CONCLUSION

In this work, an attempt has been made to compare the interpretations by Śaṅkara, Rāmānuja, and Madhva of those *sūtras* of the Vedāntic text, the *Brahma-sūtra*, devoted to a refutation of Buddhism. An attempt has also been made to compare the interpretation by each Vedāntic commentator of a particular Buddhist school's position with the actual Buddhist school's position as set forth in its own texts. It has been discovered that Buddhist positions were often distorted out of ignorance or deliberate intent, and that the Vedāntic commentators proceeded to build their refutations of Buddhism on the basis of incorrect assumptions. It may have been the case that other matters were of more pressing concern to the Vedāntic commentators than the refutation of Buddhism. It may have also been the case, especially for Rāmānuja and Madhva, that in appearing to refute Buddhist position, they were really attempting to refute other Vedāntic schools, like that of Śaṅkara. In any case, however, it may be concluded that Buddhist positions have not been portrayed correctly in the Vedāntic commentaries to the *Brahma-sūtra*.

In the section, "Śaṅkara's 'crypto'-Buddhism," the question of Śaṅkara's supposed "crypto-Buddhism has been explored. It has been discovered that there are parallels between Śaṅkara's Vedānta and Mahāyāna Buddhism, particularly in connection with the doctrine of nescience (*avidyā*) and the doctrine of the two truths, the absolute (*paramārtha*) and the practical (*vyavahāra*). It has been discovered that there is the possibility of a historical relationship between Śaṅkara's Vedānta and Buddhism through the teacher Gauḍapāda (or school by that name). It has been discovered that the notion of two truths provided Śaṅkara with a useful tool for setting forth his Advaita and for the "advaitinization" of the *Brahma-sūtra* tradition. A comparison between Śaṅkara's Vedānta and Mahāyāna Buddhism has also been made in connection with the concept of nescience (*avidyā*). It has also been discovered that for both traditions nescience is pre-eminent as that which is to be removed, and that for both traditions, nescience is two-fold in that it possesses a cognitional and a conational aspect. It has been ascertained that *avidyā* for Śaṅkara seems to possess a cognitional aspect in the epistemological realm as it does in Mahāyāna Buddhism. That is to say, just as nescience (*avidyā*) in the Mahāyāna context is a hindrance to the knowable (*jñeya-āvaraṇa*) in that through it one ascribes self-existence (*svabhāva*) to natures (*dharmas*) and which can be removed only through the insight (*prajñā*) that natures are selfless (*dharma-nairātmya*), so in Śaṅkara's thought, nescience is mistaken knowledge (*mithyā jñāna*) in that through it one superimposes a Self (Ātman) on that which is not-Self (*anātman*) and which can be removed by the discrimination (*viveka*) that is clear vision (*vidyā*). Śaṅkara, in his emphasis upon investigation and inquiry, has provided a "path," like Asaṅga, for the riddance of nescience in its cognitional aspect. According to Asaṅga, the path consists of the practices relating to insight (*prajñā*). According to Śaṅkara, the path consists of investigation into the Vedāntic texts, and the inquiry into Brahman.

It has also been found, through a study of Wayman's article, "A Study of the Vedāntic and Buddhist Theory of *Nāma-Rūpa*," that there is a certain basis to the charge of "crypto"-Buddhism levelled at Śaṅkara by the other Vedānta commentators. That is to say, Śaṅkara may have been accused of "crypto"-Buddhism for denying that there is a self in man to be identified with the Lord, for otherwise man would have created the mountains and rivers.

In Part II, an attempt has been made to compare the commentaries of Śaṅkara, Rāmānuja, and Madhva in connection with the *Brahma-sūtras* concerned with the refutation of the Buddhists, namely *Brahma-sūtra* II.2.18-32 in the case of Śaṅkara and Madhva, and *Brahma-sūtra* II.2.17-30 in the case of Rāmānuja. The similarities and differences among the three commentaries have been noted. Not only has the representation of Buddhism by the three Vedāntic figures been compared with positions actually set forth in Buddhist texts, but also the interpretations of three commentators have been compared with each other. It has been discovered, for instance, that Śaṅkara did not distinguish between the Sarvāstivāda and the Sautrāntika schools in his attempted refutation of these Buddhist schools which propound the teaching, "All exists" (*sarvam asti*). It has been discovered that the three commentaries to these *sūtras* reveal not only disagreements among the Vedāntic figures themselves but also differences in their perception of Buddhism. Buddhist concepts have been distorted by the Vedāntic figures, either out of ignorance or out of deliberate misinterpretation. Rāmānuja, Madhva, and the Madhva school while attempting to refute supposed Buddhist positions were also attempting to refute positions held by Śaṅkara and his school. In his commentary to the *sūtra* "*nābhava upalabdheḥ*" (*Brahma-sūtra* II.2.27), for example, Rāmānuja seems to attack Śaṅkara as a Buddhist hidden behind the cover of belief in the Veda because of the supposed position that the absolute is mere knowledge. It has been discovered that Rāmānuja, Madhva, and the Madhva school devote more attention to the work of the later Buddhist logicians Śāntarakṣita, Kamalaśīla, and Ratnakīrti, than does Śaṅkara.

It has been discovered that the Buddhist teaching of dependent origination was often misinterpreted by the Vedāntins, as is revealed in their critique of the absence of a conscious aggregating agent in Sarvāstivāda doctrine. Śaṅkara, for instance, in his interpretation of the *sūtra* "*ubhayahetuke 'pi tadaprāptiḥ*" (*Brahma-sūtra* II.2.18) criticizes the Sarvāstivāda notion of the atom on the basis of a conscious agent who could bring about the aggregation. He neglects, however, the Sarvāstivāda notion of depend origination, according to which a constructed thing is accomplished by means of conditions having assembled together. It has also been discovered that Madhva and his school misinterpret the Buddhist principle "*asmin sati, idam bhavati*" (when this is, that is), as is evidenced in their interpretation of the *sūtra* "*ubhayathā ca doṣāt*" (*Brahma-sūtra* II.2.23). Madhva and his school argue that this Buddhist principle signifies the simultaneity of cause and effect and that thereby an endless series of effects is created. The principle is set forth, however, as has been learned from the *Abhidharma-kośa*, in order to reveal the succession of birth and of members. Furthermore, a thing is declared in the *Abhidharma-kośa*, to proceed from its condition either immediately or gradually after an interval, but in no case simultaneously. It has been discovered that in his interpretation of the *sūtra* "*uttarotpāde ca pūrvanirodhāt*" (*Brahma-sūtra*

II.2.20), Śaṅkara attests his cognizance of the Buddhist doctrine, "When this is, that is," although in his interpretation of the previous *sūtra*, "*itaretara-pratyayatvād iti cen notpattimātranimittatvāt*" (*Brahma-sūtra* II.2.19), Śaṅkara seems to neglect this Buddhist doctrine when he attempts to refute the Sarvāstivādins for supposedly holding the position that causes (*nidāna*) involved dependent origination are the efficient cause (*nimitta*) of the aggregrates.

It has also been discovered that the Buddhist doctrine of Momentariness was misinterpreted by the Vedāntins. Śaṅkara, for instance, in his interpretation of the *sūtra* "*uttarotpāde ca pūrva-nirodhāt*" (*Brahma-sūtra* II.2.20), examines three alternatives supposedly held by the Sarvāstivādins for explaining the origination and cessation of a thing : that origination and cessation constitute a thing's own form (*svarūpa*), or another state of it (*avasthāntarā*), or an altogether different thing (*vastvantara*). It has been ascertained, however, that this presentation of the Buddhist position by Śaṅkara is not accurate, for the Sarvāstivādins regard birth (*jāti*), duration (*sthiti*), decay (*jarā*), and impermanence (*anityatā*) to be only characteristics (*lakṣaṇa*) of the *dharma* to be distinguished from the nature (*svabhāva*) of the *dharma*. This interpretation of Śaṅkara also ignores the position of the Sautrāntikas towards momentariness. The Sautrāntikas emphasized the notion of the series (*pravāha*) and denied the notion of a continuing entity (*dravya*); they interpreted the characteristics (*lakṣaṇa*) of *dharmas* (saṃskṛta in terms of the series. It has been discovered, however, that although Rāmānuja in his interpretation of the *sūtra* "*samudāya ubhayahetuke 'pi tadaprāptiḥ*" (*Brahma-sūtra* II.2.17) attests his cognizance of the Sautrāntika notion of the series, he misinterpreted this Sautrāntika doctrine. Rāmānuja argued that the series would be composed of parts, each of which is momentary or perishing; hence, according to Rāmānuja, the notion of the series like the notion of the aggregate is contradicted by the doctrine of Momentariness. Rāmānuja, however, ignores the Sautrāntika doctrine, as set forth in the *Abhidharma-kośa*, that the duration of the series is the series itself and that thus the series cannot easily be broken into parts. It has also been discovered that the Buddhist teachings of existence subsequent to non-existing (*abhūtvā bhāva*) and of absence subsequent to existing (*bhūtvā abhāva*) was misrepresented by the Vedāntins. Rāmānuja, for example, in his interpretation of the *sūtra* "*ubhayathā ca doṣāt*" (*Brahma-sūtra* II.2.22), attributed to the Buddhists the positions of origination from emptiness or passing into emptiness—positions not equivalent to the teachings of existence subsequent to non-existence and of absence subsequent to existing. Śaṅkara in his interpretation of the *sūtra* "*nāsato 'dṛṣṭatvāt*" (*Brahma-sūtra* II.2.26) also wrongly accuses the Buddhists of maintaining that entity springs from absence (*abhāvād-bhāva*).

It has been ascertained that both Śaṅkara and Rāmānuja misinterpret the Sarvāstivāda doctrine of the two cessations, the cessation-with-understanding (*pratisaṃkhyā-nirodha*) and the cessation-without-understanding (*apratisaṃkhyā-nirodha*). Although both Śaṅkara and Rāmānuja, in their interpretation of the *sūtra* "*pratisaṃkhyā'pratisaṃkhyānirodhāprāptiravicchedāt*" attribute to the Sarvāstivādins the position that that the cessations (*nirodha*) involve absolute destruction (*niranvaya vināśa*), it is not the case according to the *Abhidharmakośa* that either type of cessation signifies for the Sarvāstivādins the annihilation of *dharmas*. The cessation-with-understanding (*pratisaṃkhyā-nirodha*) refers to the non-attainment of contact with *dharmas* whose fluxes are increasing (*sāsrava-dharma*). The cessation-without-understanding refers to the obstruction of the origination of *dharmas* when they are not arising.

It has been discovered that the Sautrāntika teaching in connection with the basis (*āśraya*) seems to have been neglected by the Vedāntins. Śaṅkara argues in his interpretation of the *sūtra* "*itaretara-pratyayatvād iti cen notpattimātra-nimittatvāt*" that if aggregates are born from other aggregates in an endless series (*saṃtāna*), then in effect liberation would be desired by but attained by another. It has been ascertained, however, that the Sautrāntika position, as set forth in the *Sphuṭārtha* is that the basis subsists only as long as the defilement (*kleśa*) exists and then vanishes. It is not the case for the Sautrāntikas that "another" attains liberation; rather, it is the case that the basis vanishes. It has also been discovered that the Sautrāntika outlook toward the basis is different from Rāmānuja's treatment of the basis. Rāmānuja argues in his interpretation of the *sūtra* "*itaretara-pratyayatvād iti cen notpattimātra-nimittatvāt*" that the motivations (*saṃskāra*) require a basis for their continuance and that a basis which is momentary and perishing cannot support the motivations. It has been ascertained, however, that according to the *Abhidharmakośa*, the basis subsists only as long as the defilements subsist. When the defilements disappear by the capacity engendered through the path of the cultivation of vision, the basis too disappears.

It has been discovered that Śaṅkara misinterpreted the Sautrāntika doctrine of causeless destruction (*ākasmika vināśa*). In his interpretation of the *sūtra* "*ubhayathā ca doṣāt*," Śaṅkara attempts to refute the Sautrāntika notion of causeless destruction, or "*nirhetuka vināśa*" for Śaṅkara, by arguing that if the two kinds of cessation occur without cause, then the Buddhist path is useless, and that if the two kinds of cessation are the result of perfect knowledge, then the doctrine of Momentariness by which *dharmas* appear and disappear of themselves is abandoned. It has also been ascertained, however, that according to the Sautrāntika doctrine of causeless destruction (*ākasmika vināśa*), the destruction synonymous with momentariness is causeless because it is an absence and because only an entity can possess a cause. It has also been discovered that Rāmānuja also misinterpreted the Buddhist doctrine of the path. In his interpretation of the *sūtra* "*udāsīnānām api caivam siddhiḥ*," Rāmānuja attempts to refute the Buddhist concept of Momentariness by arguing that if there were momentary destruction (*kṣaṇapradhvaṃsa*), there would be production from a non-existent (*asadutpatti*) and hence nothing whatsoever would be achieved by effort; in other words, the Buddhist path would be useless. It has been ascertained, however, that according to the Sarvāstivādins, the cessation-with-understanding is an effect of the Path only through the medium of the *dharma* of reach (*prāpti*).

It has also been discovered that the Buddhist teachings in connection with space (*ākāśa*) were often misconstrued by the Vedāntins. In his interpretation of the *sūtra* "*ākāśe cāviśeṣāt*" (*Brahma-sūtra* II.2.24), Śaṅkara attributes to the Buddhist realists the position that space is the mere absence of hindrance (*āvaraṇābhāvamātra*). It has been ascertained that, according to the *Abhidharmakośa*, however, the Sautrāntikas define space as that having for its measure (*mātra*) the absence of the tangible (*spraṣṭavyābhāvamātramākāśam*), and the Sarvāstivādins define it as that which has the nature of non-hindrance (*anāvaraṇa-svabhāvamātramākāśam*). It has also been ascertained that Rāmānuja and Madhva misrepresent the Buddhist doctrine of space. In his interpretation of the *sūtra* "*ākāśe cāviśeṣāt*" (*Brahma-sūtra* II.2.23), Rāmānuja also mistakenly represents the Buddhist realists' conception of space as "mere absence." Madhva and his school in their interpretations of this *sūtra*, attempt to demonstrate that whatever is existent is non-momentary and that space is an example of their thesis. It has been ascertained, however, that for the Buddhists space is not existent (*sat*) in the same sense as a jar is existent. For both the Sautrāntikas and Sarvāstivādins, space is an unconstructed *dharma* to be distinguished from constructed *dharmas*.

It has also been discovered that although Śaṅkara and Rāmānuja, in their interpretations of the *sūtra* "*nābhāva upalabdheḥ*," attribute to the Vijñānavādins the position that the knowable (*jñeya*) is not different from knowledge (*jñāna*), the Vijñānavādins do not deny that there is an object external to the mind. For instance, Dignāga in the *Ālambana-parīkṣā* speaks of atoms as the cause of sensory representation although they do not appear therein. It has also been ascertained that although the Momentariness of the Yogācāra *vijñāna* is compared to the permanence of the Vedāntic *Ātman* by Vedāntins like Śaṅkara in his interpretation of the *sūtra* "*nābhāva upalabdheḥ*" (*Brahmasūtra* II.2.28), such a comparison only raises the question whether or not the Vijñānavādins are suggesting a different expression for the "Self," an expression which emphasizes its dynamic. changing nature.

It has also been discovered that the Vedāntins misinterpreted the position of the Vijñānvādins toward the waking and the dream states. According to the Vedāntins, the Vijñānavādins declare the waking state and the dream state to be similar in order to deny the external object. In his interpretation of the *sūtra* "*vaidharmyāc ca na svapnādivat*", (*Brahma-sūtra* II.2.29), Śaṅkara attributes to the Vijñānavādins the position that the waking state and the dream state are alike and that therefore the external object is to be denied. It has been ascertained, however, that perception, at least of the mental sort (*manovijñāna*), is being compared in the *Viṃśatikā* to the dream-state in that both occur at some remove from their objects, not because as Śaṅkara claims, the *Viṃśatikā* is denying that there is an object external to the mind. The analogy of the dream, it has been ascertained, is employed in the *Viṃśatikā* only to emphasize the temporal gap that exists between sensory perception and mental perception which is subsequent to the former as is remembrance. Furthermore, Rāmānuja in his interpretation of the same *sūtra*, attributes to the Vijñānavādins the position that since the waking-state and the dream-state are alike, all cognitions (*jñāna*) are void (*śūnya*). It has been ascertained, however, that according to the *Viṃśatikā*, the idea (*buddhi*) of direct perception (*pratyakṣa*) is compared to a dream because there is the defining activity of the mental perception (*manovijñāna*) and the cessation (*niruddhatva*) of the eye-perception, so that consequently the object-entity is not seen.

It has also been discovered that the Vedāntins misinterpreted the Vijñānāvāda doctrines of habit-energy (*vāsanā*) and ideation-store (*ālaya-vijñāna*). In his interpretation of the *sūtra* "*na bhāvo 'nupalabdheḥ*" (*Brahma-sūtra* II.2.30), Śaṅkara attributes to the Vijñānavādins the position that knowledge can be explained on the basis of habit-energies, without any reference to external object-entities. It has been ascertained, however, that according to the *Mahāyāna-saṃgraha* of Asaṅga, the notions of ideation-store and habit-energy are not intended by the Vijñānavādins to replace the external object, but are intended to explicate the processes of action and retribution. In his interpretation of the *sūtra* "*kṣaṇikatvācca*" (*Brahma-sūtra* II.2.31), Śaṅkara attempts to refute the Vijñānavāda notion of the ideation-store by arguing that if the ideation-store were momentary then it would be subject to the arguments he has earlier brought forth against momentariness, and if it were permanent (*sthira*) there would be abandonment of the principle of Momentariness. It has also been ascertained, however, that the coexistence of the two, the principle of voidness (*Śūnyatā*) and the principle of "the imagination of unreality" (*abhūtapari-*

kalpa) as revealed in the *Madhyānta-vibhaṅga*, attests that for the Vijñānavādins the principles of the eternal absolute and the changing phenomenal were not mutually exclusive.

It has also been discovered that the Vedāntins misconstrued the Logicians' position that the two authorities of perception and inference are separate. Madhva and his school, in their interpretations of the *sūtra* "*anusmṛteśca*" (*Brahma-sūtra* II. 2.25), attempt to refute the Buddhist's supposed assertion that recognition insofar as it affirms the oneness of things, as in the case of the flames of the burning lamp, is to be branded as illusory. It has been ascertained, however, that Dignāga in the *Pramāṇasamuccaya* has defined perception to be free of conceptualization (*pratyakṣaṃ kalpanāpoḍham*); in consequence, judgments concerning the oneness or non-oneness of the fire properly belong to the realm of inference (*anumāna*) in Dignāga's system.

It has also been discovered that whereas the phenomenon of memory (*smṛti*) and remembrance (*anusmṛti*) are adduced by Śaṅkara in his interpretation of the *sūtra* "*anusmṛteśca*" (*Brahma-sūtra* II.2.25) to be evidence of the perceiving subject (*upalabdhṛ*), they are for Dignāga and the Buddhist logicians evidence only for the existence of introspection (*svasaṃvedana*) and self-intuition (*svasaṃvitti*).

It has also been discovered that the association of the Buddhist concept of self-intuition (*sva-saṃvitti*) with the non-separation of the three factors—the subject (*grāhaka*), the object (*grāhya*), and self-intuition (*sva-saṃvitti*)—was misinterpreted by the Vedāntins. In his interpretation of the *sūtra* "*nābhāva upalabdheḥ*" (*Brahma-sūtra* II.2.28), Śaṅkara attempts to refute the Buddhist notion of self-intuition by characterizing it as the notion that perception experiences itself (*svayam anubhūyate*). Moreover, Jayatīrtha of Madhva's school, in his interpretation of the *sūtra* "*na bhāvo 'nupalabdheḥ*" (*Brahma-sūtra* II.2.30) in the *Tattva-prakāśikā*, argues that knowledge (*jñāna*) does not "shine forth" (*prakāśate*) in that knowledge cannot be an object to itself. It has been ascertained, however, that Jayatīrtha's and Śaṅkara's arguments falsely assume the separation of object, subject, and self-intuition in Buddhist thought. According to Dignāga in the *Pramāṇa-samuccaya*, only when the subject, the object, and self-intuition are seen as separate does the notion of self-intuition of perception become inconceivable.

It has also been discovered that the Vedāntins misinterpreted the position of the Vijñānavādins in connection with the causality of *saṃskāras*. Both Śaṅkara and Rāmānuja, in their interpretations of the *sūtra* "*uttarotpāde ca pūrvanirodhāt*," attribute to the Vijñānavādins the position that the existence of the antecedent moment constitutes the causality of the consequent moment. Śaṅkara argues that if the existence (*bhāva*) of the cause should be its activity (*vyāpāra*), then the effect would be imbued with the nature (*svabhāva*) of the cause. Consequently, Śaṅkara argues, the cause lasts for more than one moment and the principle of Momentariness is abandoned. It has been ascertained, however, that Śaṅkara does not take into account Asaṅga's position in the *Paramārtha-gāthā* that it is the origin which is the activity of the *saṃskāras* and that cause and effect are merely standpoints.

It has also been discovered that the issues involved in the concept of introspective perception (*svasaṃvedana-pratyakṣa*) were often misinterpreted by the Vedāntins. In his interpretation of the *sūtra* "*nāsato 'dṛṣṭatvāt*" (*Brahma-sūtra* II.2.15), Rāmānuja attributes to the Sautrāntikas the position that the imagery (*ākāra*) of an object-entity is imparted to the cognition, and rejects their supposed position by arguing that the attributes (*dharma*) of a factual base (*dharmin*) cannot be transferred to another object-entity. It has been ascertained, however, that in accordance with the teachings of Tsoṅ-kha-pa in the "Guided Tour," there can be no "passing over" (*kramaṇa*) of the features of the object-entity which is the factual base, because it is introspective perception which grasps the imagery as a reflection of an external feature without discursive thought.

It has also been discovered that the "middle view" of the Mādhyamikas (adherents of the middle view) was misconstrued by Śaṅkara, Rāmānuja, and Madhva as nihilism (Śūnyavāda in a derogatory sense); their doctrines were dismissed by Rāmānuja, for instance, as "*tucchatva*" (emptiness). It has been ascertained, however, that Mādhyamikas did not adopt the position of nihilism, as is amply affirmed by their texts. The term "Mādhyamika" itself indicates that the followers of this school were adherents of the middle view, which avoids the extremes of existence and non-existence. It has been ascertained that the nihilistic position for the Mādhyamikas represents an extreme that results from the assumption that entities either possess or do not possess self-existence (*svabhāva*), and from neglect of the middle view expressed in the saying, "What arises in depednence is not born." It has also been ascertained that despite Śaṅkara's assertion to the contrary in his interpretation of the *sūtra* "*kṣaṇikatvāc ca*". (*Brahma-sūtra* II.2.31), it need not be elaborated that the Mādhyamikas had discovered "another truth" (*anyattva*), as evident in Nāgārjuna's definition of "*tattva*" in the *Mūlamadhyamakakārikā* (XVIII.9).

Thus, in conclusion, it has been discovered that the three Vedāntic commentators have presented versions of Buddhist position—versions which they then proceeded to refute. In other words, their refutations were based on incorrect assumptions about Buddhist positions, although as has been discovered their criticisms of Buddhism provided merely a pretext for their criticism of other Vedāntic systems. In attacking the Vijñānavādins, for instance, both Rāmānuja and the school of Madhva availed themselves of the opportunity to attack the Vedāntins of Śaṅkara's school. In any case, however, the Vedāntins misinterpreted Buddhist teachings. Their critique of Buddhism, therefore, is for the most part misdirected.

BIBLIOGRAPHY

Aiyar, K. Narayanaswami. *The Thirty-Two Vidyas.* (Madras, India: Adyar Library and Research Centre, 1962, reprint).

Alston, A. J. *Śaṅkara on the Absolute.* Volume I of *A Śaṅkara-Source Book.* (London: Shanti Sadan, 1980).

Bākre, Mahādeva Śāstrī, editor. *The Brahmasūtra-Shānkarbhāshyam.* (Bombay: Nirnaya-Sagar Press, third edition, 1934).

Balasubrahmanyam, T.K., *The Works of Śrī Śaṅkarāchārya.* Volume I. "*Brahmasūtra Bhāshya.*" (Srirangam, India: Sri Vani Vilas Press).

Balasubrahmanyam, T. K. *The Works of Śrī Śaṅkarāchārya.* Volume II. "*Brahmasūtra Bhāshya.*" (Srirangam, India: Sri Vani Vilas Press).

Balasubrahmanyam, T. K. *The Works of Śrī Śaṅkarāchārya.* "*Brahmasūtra Bhāshya.*" (Srirangam, India: Sri Vani Vilas Press).

Balasubrahmanyam, T. K. *The Works of Śrī Śaṅkarāchārya.* Volume V. "*Māṇḍūkyopaniṣatkārikābhāṣyam.*" (Srirangam, India: Sri Vani Vilas Press).

Balasubrahmanyam, T. K. *The Works of Śrī Śaṅkarāchārya.* "*Vivekacūḍāmaṇiḥ and Upadeśasāhasrī.*" (Srirangam, India: Sri Vani Vilas Press).

Bhattacharya, Vidhushekhara. *The Āgamaśāstra, of Gauḍapāda.* Edited, translated, annotated. (Calcutta, India: University of Calcutta, 1943).

Bhikācārya Ainàpure and Anantācārya Aṣṭaputre. *Brahma-sūtras with Ānandatīrtha's Brahmasūtrabhāṣya and Jayatīrtha Muni's Tattvaprakāśikā.* MS. from, ff. 126, 101, 108, 46. (Bombay : Gaṇpat Kṛṣṇaji Press, 1883).

Conze, Edward. *Buddhist Thought in India.* (Michigan: University of Michigan Press, 1973, reprint).

Das Gupta, Surendranath. *History of Indian Philosophy*. Volume I. (Cambridge, England: University Press, 1963, reprint). Rept. Motilal Banarsidass, Delhi 1975.

Dutt, Nalinaksha. *Aspects of Mahāyāna Buddhism*. (London: Luzac and Company, 1930).

Dvivedin, Pandit Vindhyesvari Prasad. *Brahmasūtra With a Commentary by Bhāskarāchārya*. Chowkhamba Sanskrit Series, Numbers 70, 185, and 209. (Benaras: Vidya Vilas Press, 1915).

Gambhirananda, Swami. *Eight Upaniṣads*. Volume II. (Calcutta, India: Advaita Ashram, 1966, reprint).

Hamilton, Clarence H. *Wei Shih Er Shih Lun or the Treatise in Twenty Stanzas on Representation-Only*. Volume 13 of American Oriental Series. Translation from Chinese version of Hsuang Tsang. (New Haven, Connecticut: American Oriental Society, 1967).

Hattori, Masaaki. *Dignāga, on Perception*. Translation of *Pratyakṣa-pariccheda* of Dignāga's *Pramāṇasamuccaya* from the Sanskrit and Tibetan versions. Harvard Oriental Series, Volume 47. (Cambridge, Massachusetts: Harvard University Press, 1968).

Hiriyanna, Prof. M. "Bhartṛprapañca: An Old Vedāntin." *Indian Antiquary*. (April 1924)

Hixon, Alexander Paul. *Mahayana Buddhist Influence on the Gauḍa School of Advaya Vedānta: An Analysis of the Gauḍapāda-kārikā*. (Unpublished Ph.D. dissertation, Columbia University, 1976).

Inada, Kenneth. *Nāgārjuna*. (Tokyo: Hokuseido Press, 1970).

Ingalls, Daniel H. H. "The Study of Śaṃkarācārya." *Annals of the Bhandarkar Oriental Research Institute*. Volume XXXIII, (1952).

Ingalls, Daniel H. H. "Śaṃkara's Arguments Against the Buddhists." *Philosophy East and West*. Volume III, Number 4 (January 1954).

Joshi, Lalmani. *Studies in the Buddhistic Culture of India*. (Delhi, India: Motilal Banarsidass, 1967).

Kalupahana, David J. *Causality: The Central Philosophy of Buddhism*. (Honolulu, Hawaii: University Press of Hawaii, 1975).

Karunadasa, Y. *Buddhist Analysis of Matter*. (Colombo, Ceylon: Government Press, 1967).

Krishnamacharya, Embar. *Tattvasaṃgraha of Śāntarakṣita*. With commentary by Kamalaśīla. *Gaekwad's Oriental Series* 30. Volume I. (Baroda, India: Central Library. 1926).

Lamotte, Etienne. "*L'Ālayavijñāna* (Le Receptacle) dans le *Mahāyānasaṃgraha*" (Chapitre II). *Mélanges Chinoises et Bouddhiques*. Volume III 1934-1935. (Brussels: l'Institut Belge des Hautes Chinoises).

Lèvi, Sylvain. *Vijñaptimātratāsiddhi*. Bi bliothéque de L'Ecole des Hautes Etudes. 145th Fascicule. (Paris : Librairie Ancienne Honore Champion, 1925).

McDermott, A. C. Senape. *An Eleventh Century Logic of 'Exists'*. Translation of Ratnakīrti's *Kṣaṇabhaṅgasiddhiḥ Vyatirekātmikā*. (Dordrecht, Holland: D. Reidel Publishing Company, 1969).

Mayeda, Sengaku. "On the Author of the *Māṇḍūkyopaniṣad*—and the *Gauḍapādiya-bhāṣya*." *Dr. Raghavan Felicitation Volume*. (Madras, India: The Adyar Library and Research Centre, 1967-1968).

Mayeda, Sengaku. *A Thousand Teachings*. (Tokyo: Tokyo University Press, 1979).

Mahadevan, T. M. P. *Gauḍapāda*: *A Study in Early Advaita*. (Madras, India: University of Madras, 1952).

Murti, T. R. V. *The Central Philosophy of Buddhism*. (London: George Allen and Unwin, Ltd., 1960, reprint).

Nyaya-Tarkatirtha Ananta Kumar. "*Nirodha-Satya*." *Indian Historical Quarterly*. Volume XXXII, 1956.

Poussin, Louis de la Vallée. *L'Abhidharmakośa de Vasubandhu*. Tome I Volume XVI of Mélanges Chinoises et Bouddhiques. Translation with Notes. (Brussels: Institut Belge des hautes études Chinoises, 1971, reprint).

Poussin, Louis de la Vallée. *L'Abhidharmakośa de Vasubandhu*. Tome III, Volume XVI. *Mélanges Chinoises et Bouddhiques*. Translation with notes. (Brussels: Institut Belge des Hautes Études Chinoises, 1971).

Poussin, Louis de la Vallée. "*Note sur l'Ālayavijñāna*." Introduction to the translation of *Mahāyāna-saṃgraha* by Etienne Lamotte. Volume III, 1934-1935. *Mélanges Chinoises et*

Bouddhiques. (Brussels: l'Institut Belge des Hautes Études Chinoises).

Pradhan, Professor P. *Abhidharmakośabhāṣyam of Vasubandhu*. (Patna: K. P. Jayaswal Research Institute, 1975).

Radhakrishnan, Sarvepalli. *The Principal Upaniṣads* (London: George Allen and Unwin Ltd., 1969).

Rau, S. Subba. *The Vedānta Sūtras With the Commentary by Sri Madhvāchārya*. Translation. (Madras: Thompson and Company, 1904).

Sharma, B. N. K. *The Brahmasūtras and Their Principal Commentaries*. Volume II. (Bombay : Bharatiya Vidya Bhavan, 1974).

Shastri, Swami Dwarikadasa. *Abhidharmakośa*. With an auto-commentary of Vasubandhu and *Sphuṭārtha* (commentary of Yaśomitra). Bauddha Bharati Series-5, Part I (Varanasi: Baudha Bharati, 1970).

Sogen, Yamakami. *Systems of Buddhistic Thought*. (Calcutta: University of Calcutta, 1912).

Stcherbatsky, Th. *Buddhist Logic*. Volume I. (New York : Dover Publications, 1962, reprint).

Stcherbatsky, Th. *Central Conception of Buddhism*. (Delhi, India: Motilal Banarsidass 1970).

Thibaut, George. *The Vedānta Sūtras*. Part I, Volume XXXIV of *Sacred Books of the East*. Translation of Bādarāyaṇa's *Vedānta-sūtras* with Śaṅkara's commentary. Delhi, India: Motilal Banarsidass 1975.

Thibaut, George. *The Vedānta Sūtras of Bādarāyaṇa*. Part II, Volume XXXVIII of *The Sacred Books of the East*. Delhi, India Motilal Banarsidass 1975.

Tripathi, Chhote Lal. *The Problem of Knowledge in Yogācāra Buddhism*. (Varanasi : Bharat-Bharati, 1972)

Viraraghavacharya, Sri Uttamur T. *Brahmasūtra-Śrībhāshya*. Volumes I and II. (Madras : Sreevathsa Press, 1963).

Wayman, Alex. "A Study of the Vedāntic and Buddhist Theory of *Nāma-Rūpa*" *Volume in Honour of Professor J. W. de Jong on his Sixtieth Birthday*. (Canberra, Australia).

Wayman, Alex. "Dependent Origination—the Indo-Tibetan Tradition." *Journal of Chinese Philosophy*. Volume 7, Number 4, (December 1980). p. 276).

Wayman, Alex. "Reflections on the Study of Buddhist Logic," *Indologica Taurinensia*. Volume V (1977), Turin.

Wayman, Alex. "Yogācāra and the Buddhist Logicians." *The Journal of the International Association of Buddhist Studies*. Volume II, Number I, 1979.

Wayman, Alex. Review of *The Yogācāra Idealism* by A. K. Chatterjee. *Philosophy East and West*. Volume XV, Number I (January, 1965).

Wayman, Alex. "Analysis of the *Śrāvakabhūmi* Manuscript." *University of California Publications in Classical Philology*. Volume 17. (Berkeley: University of California Press, 1961).

Wayman, Alex. *Calming the Mind and Discerning the Real*. (A translation in part of Tsoṅ-kha-pa's Lam rim chen mo). (New York: Columbia University Press, 1979).

Whaling, Frank. "Śaṅkara and Buddhism." *Journal of Indian Philosophy*. 7 (1979).

INDEX

ābhāsa: apparent presentation, 136

abhāva: absence, non-existence, 33, 35, 44, 49, 60, 71, 164, 221-223, 237-238, 246, 248-250, 281-284, 289, 290, 291, 295, 303, 309, 326, 327, 364-368, 371, 375, 377.

Abhidharma: 17-18.

Abhidharmakośa: 17, 22-24, 26, 29, 34, 36, 37, 39, 41-42, 44, 171, 176, 190, 236, 240, 373-377.

abhūtaparikalpa: imagination of unreality, 56-57, 314, 318, 357, 378.

adhyāsa: superimposition, 136.

advaita: non-dualism, 99, 113, 117; nirviśeṣādvaita (unqualified dualism), 11-14, 161; viśiṣṭādvaita (qualified non-dualism), 11-14, 325.

ajāti: non-common origin, 99-102.

ākāra: imagery, 63-65, 286-287, 380.

ākāśa: space, 38, 44-45, 149, 155, 164, 221-231, 243-256, 376-377.

ākasmika vināśa: causeless destruction, 26-27, 376.

Ālambana-parīkṣā: 49, 52, 309, 377.

ālaya-vijñāna: ideation-store, 53-59, 64-65, 170, 342-343, 355-358, 360, 378.

aṇu: atom, 58, 75-78, 167, 185, 226-231, 306.

anumāna: inference, 50, 52, 58, 266, 289, 348, 379.

anuśaya: traces, 38, 297.

anusmṛti: remembrance, 58-60, 163, 175, 255, 257-278, 379.

anutpāda: without birth, 101; non-origination, 101-102.

apekṣābuddhi: interdependent cognition, 191-196.

apratisaṃkhyā-nirodha: cessation-without-understanding, 36-44, 63, 88, 169, 219-231, 235-236, 375.

artha: object-entity, 49, 52, 58, 173, 188, 286-288, 291, 305-323, 325, 331-335, 341-343, 343-345, 359-360.

arthakriyākāritva: efficiency, 78-81, 239-241, 251, 266-271.

Asaṅga: 54, 62, 63, 137-144, 201, 217, 230, 269, 319-320, 343, 378, 380.

asat: non-existent, 43, 64, 279, 288-289, 291, 298, 380.

āśraya: basis, 179, 188-190, 297, 355, 375.

ativyāpti: over-pervasion, 69-71.

ātman: 11-12, 88, 103, 116, 120, 129, 136, 278, 371; vijñānātman; cognizing self, 135, 140, 377.

avidyā: nescience, 12, 19, 23, 25, 97, 129-131, 132-144, 145-153, 184, 188, 371-372.

Bādarāyaṇa: 6.

Bhāmatī: 170, 313.

Bhāskara: 111, 117, 118-120.

Bhattacharya, Vidhushekhara: 99ff.

bhāva: entity, existence, 33, 35, 63, 71, 200, 237-238, 281-284, 289 290, 295, 375, 378, 380; consciousness, 345-351.

bhedābheda: difference and non-difference, 108, 127.

Brahma-sūtra: 5-8, 11, 12.

Brahman: 11, 123-131, 133, 144.

Buddha: 363.

Buddhaghosa: 19-20, 188.

Candrakīrti: 69-71, 75, 368.

Causation: 17, 19-27, 82-90, 171.

citta: thought, 51, 55, 103, 167, 355-356.

"crypto"-Buddhism: 95-155, 371-372.

darśana: vision, 236.
Das Gupta, Surendranath: 73, 78, 119, 121-122, 267.
dharma: 114-117.
dharma: nature, 18, 20, 22-23, 28, 30, 33, 54, 57, 62, 69-71, 86, 124, 136, 138-144, 163, 169, 188, 203, 223, 235, 262, 270, 290, 297, 357, 371, 374-376.
dharma, asaṃskṛta: unconstructed dharma, 17, 23, 36-45, 221, 223, 236, 247, 248, 254, 297.
dharma, saṃskṛta: constructed dharma, 28, 29, 45, 57, 172, 221-231.
Dharmakīrti: 50, 61, 64, 263, 308, 350, 356.
dharmin: factual base, 64, 247, 253, 286, 380.
Dignāga: 49-50, 52, 58, 59, 61, 64, 263, 265, 266, 275, 277-278, 287, 309, 345, 350, 356, 359, 377, 379.
dravya: continuing entity, 30, 33, 37, 76, 225, 311, 323, 374.
Dutt, Nalinaksha: 19-20.
dvaita: dualism, 11.

Gambhirananda, Swami, 115.
Gauḍapāda-kārikās: 99-117.
Govindānanda: 6.

Hattori, Masaaki: 49.
hetu: cause, 22, 41, 43, 54, 62, 83, 125, 165-179.
Hixon, Alexander Paul: 102-104.

Ingalls, Daniel: 107-111, 118-121, 262.
īśvara: 129-131, 145-153.

Jagannātha Tīrtha: 191-207.
Jaimini: 6.
Jayatīrtha: 58, 60, 63, 88, 162, 177-179, 208-209, 217, 226, 228, 239, 251, 274-278, 288-291, 298-301, 323-327, 335-337, 345-351, 359-360.
jīva: individual soul, 5, 13, 145-153.
jīvātman: 145-153.
jñāna: knowledge, 6, 11, 49-50, 51, 58, 60, 115, 122, 235, 241, 306-307, 320-323, 345-351, 360, 377, 379.
jñātṛ: knower, 264, 320.
jñeya-āvaraṇa: hindrance of the knowable, 132, 136, 138-141, 345-351, 371.
jñeya: knowable, 132, 136, 138-144, 345-351, 371.

Kamalaśīla: 62, 163-164, 173-179, 200, 210, 223-231, 241, 263-264, 270-271.
kāraṇa : cause, 191, 206-210, 215-217, 226-231, 238-241, 298.
karman: action, 12, 51, 53-54, 122, 136, 139-140, 170, 321, 343, 355.
kārya: effect, 62, 191, 206-210, 215 217, 226-231, 238-241.
Kāśakṛtsna: 6, 13.
kleśa: defilement, 39, 40, 57, 134-135, 375.
kleśa-āvaraṇa: hindrance of defilement, 132, 136-139.
kṣaṇa: moment, 33.
Kṣaṇa-bhaṅga-siddhi: 79-93.
kṣaṇika: mementary, 33, 253.
kṣaṇikatva: mementariness, 58, 296-297, 353-360, 378, 381.
Kumārila: 105.

Lévi, Sylvain : 76.

Madhva: 11, 13, 26, 45, 58, 60, 63, 69-71, 75, 82-83, 88, 161-381.
Madhyamaka-kārikā: 69-71, 99-104, 381.
Mādhyamikas: 67-71, 99, 288-291, 323-327, 358, 364-368, 380-381.
Madhyānta-vibhaṅga: 56, 57, 314, 357, 379.
Mahadevan, T.M.P.: 105, 111.
Mahāyāna: 102, 109, 132-144.
Mahāyāna-saṃgraha: 53-54, 55, 343, 378.
Māṇḍūkya-kārikā: 2
māyā: 103, 106, 148; magical display,

110-112, 124, 130; power of the Lord, 148-149.
māyāvādins: 118.
Mayeda, Sengaku: 7, 112-117, 133-135, 145, 153, 262-263.
mīmāṃsā: 5, 105-109, 311.
mithyājñāna: false knowledge, 128, 134-135, 136, 371.
mokṣa: liberation, 8, 12, 120, 186,364.
momentariness: 17, 28-35, 85-90, 164, 175, 186, 195, 200-206, 206-210, 210-217, 236-238, 250-256, 257-264, 281, 284-288, 295-297, 355-360.

Nāgārjuna: 75, 99-104, 381.
nāma-rūpa: name-and-formation, 97, 129-131, 145-153, 371.
nāma-rūpa, avyākṛta: unseparated name-and-formation, 102, 133-134, 145-153.
nāma-rūpa, vyākṛta: separated name-and-formation, 133-134, 145-153.
nidāna: cause, 19-22, 26, 181-187, 187-190, 205, 222, 374-375.
nimitta: efficient cause, 19, 24, 26, 374-375.
nirodha: cessation, 36-44, 61, 199-210, 375.

pañca-bheda: five-fold difference, 16.
paramārtha: absolute, 50, 59, 122, 127, 320, 324, 326, 371.
paramārtha-satya: absolute truth, 97, 123-131.
paramātman: Highest Self, 120.
parasparāpekṣā: interrelated consideration, 191.
paratantra: dependent, 124-125, 325.
parikalpita: imagined, 57-124.
Poussin, de La Vallée: 17, 26, 54, 343.
Prabhākara: 311.
pradhāna: 129, 146.
pradhvaṃsa: disruption, 85-90, 163.
prajña: insight, 38, 104, 136, 141, 144, 371.
pramāṇa: authority, 30, 52, 58, 61, 71, 142, 305, 311, 342-343.
Pramāṇa-samuccaya: 49, 59, 60, 379.
prāpti : reach, 40, 42, 43, 297, 376.
pratisaṃkhyā-nirodha: cessation with understanding, 36-44, 63, 88, 169, 219-231, 235-236, 241, 297, 375.
pratītya-samutpāda: dependent origination, 19-26, 155, 181-187, 199-206, 371-372.
pratyabhijñā: recognition, 90-93, 264, 271-278.
pratyakṣa: perception, 50, 51, 52, 58, 65, 266-267, 272-273, 332, 378-379.

Radhakrishnan, Sarvepalli: 6-7
Raghavendra: 193, 289-290.
Rāmānuja: 11, 12, 34-35, 36, 39, 43, 45, 49, 51, 61-63, 64, 69-71, 86-90, 117, 121-122, 161-381.
Ratnakīrti: 73-93, 163-164, 173-179, 216-217, 238, 267, 268.
Ratnaprabhā: 141, 169.
rūpa: formation, 30, 49, 52, 58, 164, 345.

sādṛśya: similarity, 90, 260-264, 265, 276.
sākśin: witness, 264, 316, 318-319, 356.
saṃskāra: motivations, 23, 24, 31, 61-63, 201, 342-343, 376, 380.
saṃskāra: 217, 230, 269.
saṃtāna: series, 88, 226-231, 355-356, 375.
samudāya: aggregates, 165-179, 226-231, 291, 374.
saṃvṛti: conventional, 125-126, 324, 350.
saṃvṛti-satya: conventional truth, 57, 123-131, 137, 350.
Śaṅkara: 7, 11, 12, 19, 21, 25-26, 35, 36, 39, 43-44, 49, 51, 53, 56, 60, 61-63, 69-71, 83-84, 90-93, 95-155, 161-381.
Sāṅkhya: 19, 20, 57, 147, 188, 314.
Śāntarakṣita: 62, 73-93, 163-164, 173-174, 200, 210, 217, 223-231, 241, 263-264, 270-271, 277-278.
Sarvāstivādins: 15, 17-45, 162, 165-179, 199-206, 210-217, 221-223, 235-236, 247-250, 253, 297.

sat: existent, 18, 45, 79, 237, 288.
Śatapatha Brāhmaṇa: 145-153.
sattā: being, 83.
sattva: existence, 78, 268, 325, 350-351.
Sautrāntikas: 15, 17-45, 64, 162, 171, 172-179, 187-189, 210-217, 235-236, 236-237, 245-248, 248-250, 253, 262, 277-278, 281, 284-288, 291, 297, 356-357.
Sharma, B.N.K.: 177-179, 190-196, 206-210, 215-217, 226-231, 238-241, 250-256, 271-278, 288-291, 297-301, 323-327, 335-337, 345-351, 359-360, 368.
skandhas: personal aggregates, 23, 24, 155, 165-179.
smṛti: memory, remembrance, 52, 59-60, 90-93, 263, 356.
Sogen, Yamakami: 171, 201.
Solomon, Esther: 132-144, 145.
Śrīharṣa: 162, 298.
śūnya: void, 51, 162, 167, 288-291, 324, 344, 364-368, 378.
śūnyatā: 314, 318, 357, 378.
śūnyatva: 56, 57, 344.
śūnyavāda, śūnyavādins: 69, 165-179, 288-291, 297-301, 323-327, 335-337, 380-381.
svabhāva: nature, 12, 18, 28-29, 44, 54, 63, 69-71, 79, 81, 136, 243-256, 290-371, 374, 380-381.
svarūpa: own-formation, 202, 374; nature, 129.
svasaṃvedana: introspection, 59, 60-61, 164, 263, 314, 379.
svasaṃvedana-pratyakṣa: introspective perception, 63-65, 287, 356, 280
svasaṃvitti: self-intuition, 59, 60-61, 263, 265, 271, 319, 350, 356, 379.

tādātmyā: identity, 13.
tattva: reality, 71, 118, 123, 181.
Tattva-saṃgraha: 73-93.
Trivikrama Paṇḍita: 206, 275-276, 336.
Tsoṅ-kha-pa: 63-64, 69-71, 137, 290, 367-368, 380.
tuccha: emptiness, 236-237, 248.
tucchatva: emptiness, 69, 241, 364, 366, 380.

Upadeśasāhasrī: 116, 133-135, 146, 262-263.
upādhi: limiting adjunct, 130.
upalabdhi: perception, 52, 141, 164, 303-327, 331, 341, 351, 377, 378-379.
Upaniṣad: 6, 11, 102-104, 107, 112, 114, 123, 128-129, 139-140, 145-153, 345.
upāsana: contemplation, 13; meditative exercise, 123, 131, 139-140.

Vādirāja: 88, 227.
Vaibhāṣika: 17, 83, 173-179, 187-190, 247, 262, 281, 285, 291, 357.
Vaiśeṣika: 177, 185-187.
vāsanā: habit-energy, 53-56, 103, 308-309, 322, 341-343, 350, 355-358, 360, 378.
vastu: given thing: 168-179, 203, 230, 270, 331.
Vasubandhu: 26, 52, 56, 320.
vedānta: 95-155, 161-381.
Vedāntins: 17, 21, 24, 35, 39, 44, 51, 58, 60, 63, 75, 82, 85, 70, 161-381.
Vedas: 102, 122, 145-153, 321.
vidyā: clear vision, 131, 136-137, 141, 372; science, 123; meditation, 190.
vijñāna: consciousness, 118, 129, 161, 305, 325, 344-345, 348, 350-351; ideation, 167; perception, 23, 24, 51, 61, 62, 307, 314, 320.
Vijñānavāda: 47-65, 102-104, 109-161, 201, 305-323, 314, 325, 331, 335, 341-351, 360.
Vijñānavādins: 47-65, 109, 122, 162, 165-179, 262, 263, 305-323, 331-335, 341-351, 377-379.
vijñapti: representation, 53, 333.
vijñapti-mātra: ideation-only, 57, 320.
Viṃśatikā: 51, 332, 333, 378.

vināśa: destruction, 26-27, 36, 43, 85-90, 163, 206-210, 226-231, 296, 363, 376.
vipāka: retribution, 54, 343.
viveka: discrimination, 136, 141, 371.
vyāpāra: activity, 63, 83, 200, 380.
vyāpti: pervasion, 78-79, 268, 290.
Vyāsatīrtha: 161, 178, 195, 209, 255, 277-278, 325, 345-35.1
vyavahāra: practical, 97, 121, 125-127, 321, 371.
Wayman, Alex: 49-50, 56, 57, 61, 63, 64, 69-71, 137-144, 145-153, 287-288, 314-318, 345, 357-358, 359, 371.
Whaling, Frank: 108.

yaugapadyam: simultaneity, 209, 211-217.
Yogācāra: 49, 56, 57, 65, 138, 286, 359-360.